ACCOUNTING INFORMATION SYSTEMS

A MANAGERIAL APPROACH

E.H.J. Vaassen

Professor of Accounting Information Systems
Maastricht University
The Netherlands

Deloitte & Touche
The Netherlands

JOHN WILEY & SONS LTD

Email (for orders and customer service enquiries): cs-books@wiley.co.uk
Visit our Home Page www.wileyeurope.com or www.wiley.com

Reprinted March 2005, November 2005

Other Wiley Editorial Offices

John Wiley & Sons Inc., 111 River Street, Hoboken, NJ 07030, USA

Jossey-Bass, 989 Market Street, San Francisco, CA 94103-1741, USA

Wiley-VCH Verlag GmbH, Boschstr. 12, D-69469 Weinheim, Germany

John Wiley & Sons Australia Ltd, 33 Park Road, Milton, Queensland 4064, Australia

John Wiley & Sons (Asia) Pte Ltd, 2 Clementi Loop #02-01, Jin Xing Distripark, Singapore 129809

John Wiley & Sons (Canada) Ltd, 22 Worcester Road, Etobicoke, Ontario M9W 1L1

Wiley also publishes its books in a variety of electronic formats. Some content that appears in print may not be available in electronic books.

Library of Congress Cataloging-in-Publication Data
A Library of Congress record has been applied for

British Library Cataloguing in Publication Data
A catalogue record for this book is available from the British Library

ISBN-10: 0–471–49928–5 (pbk)
ISBN-13: 978–0–471–49928–2 (pbk)

Project management by Originator, Gt. Yarmouth (typeset in 10/12pt Palatino)
Printed and bound in Great Britain by Biddles Ltd, King's Lynn, Norfolk
This book is printed on acid-free paper responsibly manufactured from sustainable forestry, in which at least two trees are planted for each one used for paper production.

CONTENTS

PREFACE ix

LIST OF ABBREVIATIONS xvii

Chapter 1: *An Overview of Accounting Information Systems* 1

AIS Untangled 2
Accounting and Administrative Organization, Internal Control, and Managerial Information Provision 5
The Roles of the Financial Auditor, the Controller, and the Information Manager 7
Positioning AIS 8
The Human Factor 10
International Developments 10
The Internal and External Role of Information 11
Toward a Theory of AIS 12
Introduction to the Following Chapters 14
Chapter Case 15

Chapter 2: *Cornerstones of Accounting Information Systems* 17

Introduction 19
Internal Control from an International Perspective 19
AIS Development Issues 24
The Governance Paradigm 25
The Management Cycle 27
The Uniform Basic Pattern of Information Provision 31
The Value Cycle 34
Basic Internal Control Terminology 42
Chapter Cases 50
Appendix: Representing Solutions to AIS problems 54
Frequently Made Errors 63

Chapter 3: *Organizations with a Dominant Flow of Goods* 65

Introduction 66
Trade Organizations 66
Production Organizations 76
Chapter Cases 85

Chapter 4:	*Organizations without a Dominant Flow of Goods*	89
	Introduction	90
	Organizations with a Limited Flow of Goods	91
	Organizations that Put Space and Time Capacity at Their Clients' Disposal	93
	Organizations that Put Knowledge and Skills at Their Clients' Disposal	97
	Government Institutions	100
	Chapter Cases	101
Chapter 5:	*Contingency Approaches to Accounting Information Systems*	105
	Introduction	106
	Alignment in a Complex Control Environment	107
	A Comprehensive Contingency Framework	113
	Control Concepts in the Comprehensive Contingency Framework	116
	Migrating toward the Essential Level of AIS Problems	119
	Chapter Case	123
Chapter 6:	*Information and Communication Technology and Related Administrative Concepts*	125
	Introduction	126
	Components of Information Systems	128
	Information System Development	137
	Contemporary ICT Applications	138
	ICT-enabled Innovations	145
	Chapter Case	150
Chapter 7:	*The Dynamics of Internal Control and ICT*	153
	Introduction	154
	ICT Infrastructure, ICT Control, and Internal Control	157
	Codes on Information Security	165
	ICT Infrastructure, Operations, and Internal Control	168
	Chapter Cases	174
Chapter 8:	*Bridging the Gap Between Internal Control and Management Control*	183
	Introduction	184
	Corporate Governance	184
	Quality of Decision Making, Information, and Information Systems	187
	Information Policy	191
	Information Requirement Analysis	192
	Management Control and Internal Control	194
	Synthesis	212
	Chaper Cases	216

Chapter 9: *The Integrative Role of the Accounting Information System in Managing Contemporary Organizations* 221

Introduction 222
The Accounting Information System as a Pivot in the Flexible Firm 225
Knowledge Valuation and Knowledge Management 228
Fraud 236
Assurance Services 238
Environmental Accounting 240
Just-in-time Production 241
ISO Certification 242
The Strategic Role of Information 243
Chapter Cases 246

Chapter 10: *Communications of Accounting Information Systems* 253

Introduction 254
The Purpose of a Control Description 254
Intended Audience 256
Conditions for an Efficient Control Description 258
Recording of the Control Description 265
Analysis of the Control Description's Efficiency 270
Toward an AIS Ontology 270
Chapter Case 272

APPENDIX: Further Case Studies 275

BIBLIOGRAPHY 313

GLOSSARY 321

INDEX 331

PREFACE

This book studies the discipline of accounting information systems from a managerial point of view. This view is eclectic, supportive of business administration, and holistic. It combines practice, education, and theory to provide multi-focus insights into the discipline. It also combines business-related issues with information and communication as well as information and communication technology-related (ICT) issues. Moreover, it bridges the gap between strategy formulation and strategy implementation. Following this holistic approach, educating students in AIS should not only help them develop more efficient practices, but also give them an enhanced motivation to study and try to see AIS problems in their broader context. Specifically, we sketch the context of AIS as depicted in Figure A. There are four main themes in this book: management, internal control, accounting, and information and communication technology. Each of these themes could have been discussed in more depth. However, given the specific viewpoint of the text, management, accounting, and information and communication technology are discussed superficially, whereas internal control is studied in greater detail.

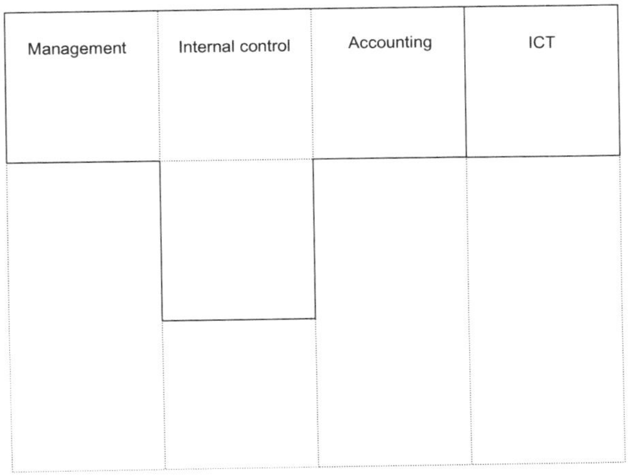

Figure A A managerial approach to AIS.

Within the context as sketched, our specific viewpoint on AIS has the following characteristics:

- It studies strategy implementation, not strategy formulation. However, strategy formulation is an important contingent factor and must therefore be discussed briefly.
- It studies ICT from a user's point of view, not from a system developer's. Like strategy formulation, ICT is an important contingent factor.
- It studies information relevance assurance by formalizing information systems development routines, formalizing information provision, and controlling the use of information, not by making more than superficial analyses of the content of data records, information requirements, and management reports.
- It considers managerial involvement at all hierarchical levels in operational activities as its guiding theme.

There are quite a lot of titles on AIS in the USA as well as in Europe. For Europe, we believe the main title is:

Gelinas, U.J., S.G. Sutton and A.E. Oram (1999). *Accounting Information Systems* (4th edn). South-Western College Publishing.

This title approaches AIS from an accountant's perspective. It focuses on the accountant's role as a systems auditor, and – to a lesser extent – as a systems designer. Because of this focus, internal control is the central theme of the book. For an in-depth discussion of internal control, the book could be used to complement our text. For the USA, we believe the main title is:

Romney, M.B. and P.J. Steinbart (2000). *Accounting Information Systems* (8th edn). Englewood Cliffs, NJ: Prentice-Hall.

This title also approaches AIS from an accountant's perspective. However, unlike Gelinas et al. it focuses on information and communication technology and its impact on the nature of accounting. Database design and data modeling are major topics in the book. As concerns the information and communication technology focus, this book could be used to complement our text as well. These and other current AIS titles are mainly US-oriented. Our book follows a continental European approach. Without having the pretension to know all about the difference between a US and a continental European approach, I believe there are some remarkable differences in appreciated styles of bookwriting. One of the most striking differences is that most US textbooks in the field use real-life examples in all their complexity to illustrate how specific concepts work in practice. In our approach, we use armchair cases that are heavily stylized to make them comprehensible in view of the concept under discussion. We only use real-life cases to indicate the importance of a specific concept, not to explain it. Also, the existing textbooks look at AIS from a monodisciplinary point of view whereas I follow a multidisciplinary approach. Consequently, *Accounting Information Systems: A Managerial Approach* can be an important complement to these books, and provide a valuable contribution to traditionally set-up AIS courses in that respect. Any AIS course using conventional AIS books may benefit from using this text to kickstart the course with a broad view on the discipline of AIS, or to wrap it up with a synthesis of AIS in relation to other disciplines. Independent of the place in the AIS curriculum, in both cases loose ends get connected.

During my teaching in several undergraduate, graduate and postgraduate programs at the University of Amsterdam and Maastricht University, I found that the fields of accounting and administrative organization and managerial information provision (local names used as alternatives to AIS), had not been innovative for a long time. In the last decade there has been a turnaround to incorporate more international elements in the study of business administration. This led, among other things, to the renaming and rethinking of disciplines taught in these programmes. Accounting and administrative organization and managerial information provision is now called AIS, to comply with international customs. Since international developments in information disciplines like AIS, management accounting, management control, information systems, and information management were – and still are – exceptionally pervasive and dynamic, there was momentum for renewal. Management science has traditionally been dealt with innovatively in the literature. Although the topics discussed in management science are mainly rooted in practice and sometimes in hype, we should not close our eyes to what happens in this discipline, since it provides the drivers for renewal. Hence, it influences every aspect of business administration, including, to a great extent, the information disciplines. So, starting off from management science, via other information disciplines we will be able to trigger innovative processes in AIS education.

I have several reasons for writing this book, but the main ones go back to the joy I share with my AIS colleagues and students in trying to find interrelationships between current developments in other information disciplines and management science, on the one hand, and AIS, on the other hand. The driver of these search processes is to find the value-added (apologies for the jargon) of AIS. Obviously, a managerial approach is the starting point of this quest. More concretely, arguments for writing a book that looks at AIS from a managerial viewpoint include:

- AISs increasingly provide the information for managerial decision making.

- An in-depth understanding of how AISs are developed is irrelevant to managers, so an accountant's or information system developer's approach – which are alternatives as can be observed in the AIS literature – only causes information overload. Auditors and accountants, in general, must think like managers to be able to add value and, hence, maintain their competitive advantage in an increasingly competitive market.

- Not only general managers but also information managers must understand their role toward AISs.
- Controllers must be able to bridge the gap between workforce and strategic management. Strategic management has the primary responsibility to gain and maintain competitive advantage, whereas the workforce is the primary source of data that enter into the AIS and that might be used by strategic management.
- Management is responsible for the internal control system, which is an inherent element of any AIS.
- Management plays a key part in corporate governance. They should know that, although they may be able to override any internal control system that is put in place, there are always corporate governance requirements that put limitations on their discretionary behaviour.

Although this text is my sole responsibility, I sometimes use the pronoun 'we', not to indicate that there are co-authors, but to create a feeling of guidance for the reader: together we are on a journey and there may be moments when we will get lost, but together we will find our way back and get on track again. This approach points out an important feature of this text, namely that it may discuss issues that have not yet been fully explored in the literature. By discussing these issues, I hope the reader's creativity will be triggered which should lead to new solutions, but also to more questions. I sincerely believe this is the true nature of high-level education.

The fact that there are no co-authors to this text does not mean that there is no need to thank the many people for all kinds of support they have given me during the writing of this book. So, thanks to:

- My friend Caren Schelleman, who is my collaborator on lots of projects.
- Jim Hunton, who inspires me and was a great host during my stay at the University of South Florida (Tampa) which greatly contributed to the peace of mind I needed to finish this text.
- My colleagues at the Universiteit van Amsterdam, Maastricht University, and University of South Florida.
- Participants at the annual European Conference on Accounting Information Systems, held since 1998.
- Bram Beek for his never-ending involvement in my professional and personal well-being. He seems to be able to keep up with the latest developments in our field. Moreover, he takes the time continuously to share his thoughts with me (and he doesn't even have an e-mail address).
- Chris Verdoner who gave some inspirational comments on the text at a very early stage of the project.

- Marcel Caubo and Maurice Franssen for their initial thinking on a managerial approach to AIS.
- Erwin Geeve for taking over a large part of my AIS-related administrative work at UvA and giving me the necessary relief to keep on thinking.
- Martin Hooft van Huysduynen for his hard work on AIS innovations at UvA. Some of the cases in this book are his creations.
- Inge, Bart, Niki, and Bob, what should I say?

Eddy Vaassen
Amsterdam, Maastricht, Tampa
October 2001

To Inkie

ABBREVIATIONS

AAO	Accounting and Administrative Organization
ATM	Asynchronous Transfer Mode
ASP	Application Service Provider
AI	Artificial Intelligence
ABACUS	Asea Brown Boveri Accounting and Communication System
AICPA	American Institute of Certified Public Accountants
BCCI	British & Commonwealth Bank or Bank of Credit and Commerce International
BIDE	Beginning, Increase, Decrease, End
BPR	Business Process Re-engineering
BI	Business Intelligence
BSC	Balanced Scorecard
COSO	Committee of Sponsoring Organizations of the Treadway Commission
CPA	Certified Public Accountant
CPU	Central Processing Unit
CRM	Customer Relationship Management
CSF	Critical success factor
DBMS	Database Management System
DDDS	Data Dictionary and Directory System
DML	Data Manipulation Language
DQL	Data Query Language
DBA	Database Administrator
DA	Data Administrator
DSS	Decision Support System
DMZ	Demilitarized Zone
DEMO	Dynamic Essential Modelling of Organizations
EDI	Electronic Data Interchange
EPROM	Erasable Programmable Read-only Memory
EFT	Electronic Funds Transfer
ERP	Enterprise Resource Planning
EIS	Executive Information System
ES	Expert System
FAR	Fixed Administrative Rate
GDSS	Group Decision Support System

HPCN	High-performance Computing and Networking
HTML	Hypertext Mark-up Language
HRM	Human Resource Management
IC	Internal Control
IS	Information System
ICT	Information and Communication Technology
IP	Internet Protocol
ISP	Internet Service Provider
IPsec	Internet Protocol Secure
ISO	International Organization for Standardization
JIT	Just in time
LAN	Local Area Network
MA	Management Accounting
MIP	Managerial Information Provision
MIS	Management Information Systems
MBTI	Myers–Briggs Type Indicator
MRP	Materials Requirements Planning
MRP II	Manufacturing Resource Planning
MC	Management Control
MP3	MPEG-I layer 3
MAC	Message Authentication Code
NIVRA	Nederlands Instituut van Registeraccountants
OLAP	Online Analytical Processing
PASD	Principles of Accounting System Design
PC	Personal Computer
POS	Point-of-sale
PIN	Personal Identification Number
PKI	Public Key Infrastructure
PGP	Pretty Good Privacy
P&L	Profit and Loss
RAD	Rapid Application Development
REA	Resources, events, agents
RCT	Reconciliations and control totals
ROM	Read-only Memory
RAM	Random Access Memory
SDLC	Systems Development Life Cycle
SFA	Sales Force Automation
SEM	Strategic Enterprise Management
SET	Secure Electronic Transaction
SSL	Secure Sockets Layer
STT	Secure Transaction Technology
S-HTTP	Systems Secure Hypertext Transfer Protocol
SBU	Strategic Business Unit
SIM	Subscriber Identity Module

TPM	Teleprocessing Monitor
Tempest	Telecommunications Electronics Material Protected from Emanating Spurious Transmissions
TQM	Total Quality Management
UPC	Universal Product Code
VAN	Value-added Network
VPN	Virtual Private Network
WAN	Wide Area Network
XML	Extended Mark-up Language
XBRL	Extended Business Reporting Language

AN OVERVIEW OF ACCOUNTING INFORMATION SYSTEMS 1

Information technology, globalization, and related developments have made business increasingly dependent on high-quality information for decision making. Business decision makers need assurance that they have relevant and reliable information available at the right time and at reasonable cost. Assurance can be obtained from the independent assurance professionals, whose job is to improve the quality of information for decision making, and from internal control designed to help management achieve its objectives.

Kinney (2000), p. ix

Control is a critical function of management. Control problems can lead to large losses and possibly even to organizational failure.

Merchant (1998), p. 1

After studying this chapter, the reader will have a sound grasp of what encompasses accounting information systems, and should be able to:

- Understand the difference between AIS as a system and AIS as a discipline.
- Explain what is an AIS.
- Define the following internal control-related disciplines:
  - principles of accounting systems design;
  - accounting organization;
  - accounting and administrative organization;
  - managerial information provision;
  - management accounting;
  - management control.
- Understand the relevance of AIS for managers, information managers, controllers and auditors.

- Sketch a brief history of AIS as a discipline.
- Position AIS as a discipline from an international perspective.
- Demarcate the boundaries of AIS as a discipline.
- Describe the relationship between AIS, on the one hand, and management, internal control, accounting, and ICT, on the other hand.
- Distinguish between technocratic and behavioural aspects of AIS.
- Explain the importance of an AIS theory.
- Explain the relationship between AIS and the theory of the firm.

Chapter Outline

This introductory chapter touches on a number of themes that are relevant in a managerial approach to AIS. The following chapters will elaborate on these themes. Before going deeper into this approach, a brief sketch of the evolution of AIS from an international perspective is given. The structure followed is based on the development of AIS from a toolset for designing a chart of accounts and the accompanying procedures, via AIS as an instrument for supporting the auditor in performing a more effective and efficient financial audit, to AIS as a control device. First, a number of the traditional concepts of AIS are discussed, representing the dominant evolution of AIS in continental Europe. Typical constructs like accounting and administrative organization, managerial information provision, and internal control are exemplified. Second, the relevance of AIS for the manager, the information manager, the controller, and the auditor is elaborated on. Third, from that broad perspective, AIS is then positioned on a two-dimensional scale where the supply and demand of information, and the behavioural and technocratic view form the two dimensions. Traditionally, AIS is involved with the supply and the demand of information, but is highly technocratic. Related disciplines like management accounting and management control are much more demand-oriented and behavioural, and information management is much more supply-oriented and behavioural. Thus, the human factor in AIS is introduced. A synthesis of these views leads us to a framework that will be used throughout the book, and that looks at AIS from four different angles: AIS in relation to internal control, AIS in relation to management, AIS in relation to accounting, and AIS in relation to ICT. The chapter concludes with some remarks on the relationship between AIS and the theory of the firm.

AIS Untangled

Accounting information systems (AIS) may be considered a discipline as well as a collection of systems. Usually, this distinction is made implicitly and does not lead to confusion because the definition and its context are self-explanatory. However, AIS – as a collection of systems as well as a discipline – has been subject to dramatic changes in the past century. As a result, it is not unambiguously defined in the literature and there is some confusion about the *raison d'être* of AIS as a specialized discipline and a collection of systems. In our view, this confusion is caused by the multitude of AIS-related concepts.

The definition of AIS that is maintained throughout this book is:

AIS studies the structuring and operation of planning and control processes which are aimed at:

- *Providing information for decision making and accountability to internal and external stakeholders that complies with specified quality criteria.*
- *Providing the right conditions for sound decision making.*
- *Ensuring that no assets illegitimately exit the organization.*

AIS relates to several more elementary disciplines of which accounting and administrative organization (AAO), internal control (IC), managerial information provision (MIP), and information systems (IS) are the main ones (see Figure 1.1).

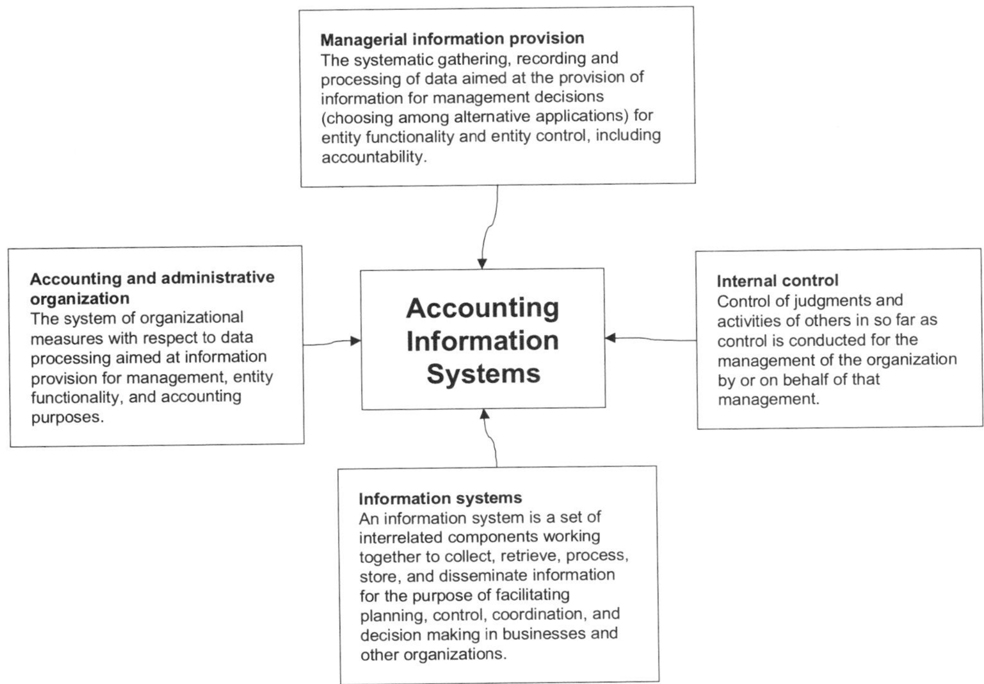

Figure 1.1 AIS and related disciplines.

These four disciplines do not necessarily reflect the historical developments which led to the emergence of AIS, but there certainly is some kind of time frame which may be overlaid onto it. An attempt to reconstruct the emergence of AIS reveals the following. At the end of the 19th century, the first writings on what was then called *principles of accounting system design* (PASD) were made in some European countries (e.g. the UK and the Netherlands). PASD studies the principles of the systematic recording of – sequential and interrelated – actions in a firm which culminate in accounts that reflect the conduct of business. The design of an effective and efficient chart of accounts was considered the main goal of this discipline. In order to employ such a chart of accounts, a set of procedures was developed simultaneously with the chart itself. There were procedures for the recording of transactions as well as for the checking of whether or not a transaction was correctly recorded. The latter feature was the first step toward a broad system of internal control. *Accounting and administrative organization* (AAO) originated from the need of the auditor for a toolkit that enabled him to realize his audit objectives in an efficient and effective manner. The auditing profession came into being in Europe at the end of the 19th century. This also led to the development of core discipline auditing. From the outset, the discipline of auditing had several comprehensive textbooks, which first provided general rules for an audit, before discussing specific control measures for certain types of company. In contrast, the discipline principles of accounting system design merely knew a literature that was strongly anecdotal, and which described the design of the bookkeeping systems of certain types of organization. A general textbook that laid down the foundations to describe each type of organization had not yet been written. The fact that an attempt to integrate codification of PASD took place in the second half of the 20th century does not mean that the discipline did not exist before that time. On the contrary, ever since there have been organizations, there must have been some form of accounting and administrative organization, since every organization needs to be governed to control the organization's transactions and values. This means that an auditing view of accounting and administrative organization is too narrow: accounting and administrative organization is primarily intended to control organizations, and the relevance for auditing is merely derived from that. This observation also indicates the relevance of AIS for managers, since managers attempt to adequately control organizations through the planning, governance, and continuous evaluation of activities.

Textbook Perils

At the beginning of the 20th century, a general textbook that laid down the principles of accounting systems design per type of organization had not yet been written. This led one of the leading Dutch authors in this field to state (Polak 1922): '. . . They [the students of principles of accounting system design] see the accounting system design but they lack the principles. . .'. This is why he undertook a first attempt at formulating such principles.

Although his principles were strongly grafted onto the design of the bookkeeping system, they can be regarded as the trigger to what later became called accounting and administrative organization. As the years went by, the discipline underwent a broadening evolution. In the 1960s the integral body of thought about accounting and administrative organization was recorded in a series of now standard textbooks: *Principles of Accounting and Administrative Organization: General Fundamentals* and *Principles of Accounting and Administrative Organization: Typology of Applications* by Starreveld, a Dutch professor.

Accounting and Administrative Organization, Internal Control, and Managerial Information Provision

There is a strong relationship between accounting and administrative organization, internal control, and managerial information provision. However, the nature of this relationship is a bit ambiguous. Starting with three examples from these disciplines, this section tries to clarify the three-cornered relationship. At this point, we can already state that there will probably always be some indistinctness in the demarcation of these disciplines.

Accounting and Administrative Organization

A recently appointed CEO of a production company holds the opinion that a good rapport with the shop floor is essential to manage a company properly. Soon after his appointment, he decides to have a look around the factory. The production manager gives him a short guided tour. The CEO notices that everybody apparently seems to know exactly what he or she is supposed to do and he decides to track a recently arrived forklift truck with components to gain more insight into the production process. The components are handed over to a production worker. Some papers are exchanged and the components are unloaded in a small storage area in the factory. After a couple of minutes another production worker arrives and removes the components from the storage area. The CEO observes that the employee in question does not record or input anything, and he seriously starts to worry about safeguarding the components, especially since he knows that they are valuable. According to plan, he tracks the employee and he sees that he starts to divide the components that he just picked up among several production workers who are assembling a final product. Each time a final product is finished, the production workers make a note on a list that is hanging nearby. The finished products are placed in a designated area in the production department, and every five minutes a warehouse clerk loads the goods onto a cart, fills in some papers and leaves the factory building with the products. By now, the CEO has realized that, apparently, an organizational structure has been set up such that the workforce knows exactly what they are supposed to do at every stage.

Internal Control

The CEO has seen enough of the factory and decides to study a number of procedures. He goes to the office and finds a number of files titled: 'Directives'. That was what he was looking for. He randomly opens one of the files and reads: 'Purchasing procedures'. According to this documentation, every buying order for raw materials needs to be authorized by the head of the purchasing department. A copy of that order is consecutively numbered and filed in a folder at the purchasing department and another copy is sent to the accounts payable department. On receipt of goods at the warehouse, the warehouseman has to fill in a receipt. This is sent to inventory records and a copy to the accounts payable department. A purchasing invoice that arrives is first numbered at the post room and then sent to the accounts payable department. Subsequently, the accounts payable department needs to perform the invoice check. This involves comparing the buying order, the warehouse receipt and the invoice with each other. When these match, a notice is sent to the procurement officer who signs the payment order. Apparently, both preventive (segregation of duties, procedures recorded in directives) and repressive (invoice check prior to authorization of payment) measures have been taken to steer the authorization of payment in the right direction.

Managerial Information Provision

The CEO wonders how the head of the purchasing department knew that he had to order components and how many, and when these components were needed in the factory. It seems that an inventory control system is in use that sends a signal, to order a fixed amount of components, to the purchasing department when the inventory in the perpetual inventory records reaches a minimum level and that delivery has to take place on a certain date to a certain department. At the end of each month, the finance department prepares a summary of the estimated purchase prices and the prices that were actually paid. This leads to a purchasing result that is explained by the head of the purchasing department, after which the CEO receives a performance report. With this information, he is able to gain a clear understanding of the effectiveness of the purchasing process and the way in which the values of the company (incoming goods and outgoing cash) are handled. With that understanding, he is able to get or keep a grip on the part of the organization that concerns purchasing. Thus, in reality he tests the actual course of the purchasing process and its outcomes against the conceived goals. Based on that test, he can make more or less dramatic adjustments such as instructing the head of the purchasing department to select other suppliers when purchasing was too expensive or the quality of the goods is not acceptable, adjusting the goals, redefining the performance measure 'purchasing result', or reorganizing the company and the information system to be able to react more alertly to market developments.

These examples show that by designing an accounting and administrative organization an adequate information provision can be realized which allows us to improve the quality of decision making and to get organizations under control. Hence, accounting and administrative organization, internal control, and managerial information provision are strongly intertwined.

The Roles of the Financial Auditor, the Controller, and the Information Manager

In their professional practice, financial auditors, controllers, and information managers continuously deal with modern developments in their core disciplines. For the auditors, this primarily concerns developments in accounting and administrative organization, financial accounting, and auditing; for the controller, accounting and administrative organization, financial accounting, and management accounting; and for the information manager, of course, information management. However, in their daily practice, the auditor, the controller and the information manager, from their own points of view, are engaged in controlling and advising regarding information provision.

The core task of the auditor is to audit financial statements and to provide reports on these statements based on his findings. The auditing process consists in part of judging the quality of the internal control system and in part of determining the reliability of the information as contained in the financial statements. Both assessments need to be seen as related: after all, as the quality of the internal control system improves, the auditor is more able to rely on this system and will in principal see less need for substantive tests which are controls aimed at directly establishing the reliability of the financial statements.

The controller is a generalist whose competence concerns the entire company, because he is the one pulling the financial strings. Incidentally, his influence can be more or less far-reaching, dependent on his position in the organization as either a line or a staff functionary. The controller is the intermediary between the shop floor and management and needs to make several translations as such. He is also the financial conscience of the company; for example, an investment decision is made based on, among other things, market expectations and the technical state of the existing production installation. The commercial manager may insist on optimal use of market opportunities, the technical director may insist on installation renewal. However, the controller will have to indicate whether certain wishes are feasible from a financial point of view.

The tasks of the information manager concern the managerial aspects of information provision within and by an organization. Information provision relies on the available information systems, which for their part predominantly rely on the available information and communication technology (ICT). The rise of the information manager took place in an era in which automation of information provision gradually obtained a regular place in management. Therefore, the information manager will be the expert *par excellence* in the field of ICT. Among other things, his job responsibilities will include:

- formulating the ICT policy;
- planning ICT;
- acquiring ICT resources (both software and hardware);
- exploitation and control of ICT;
- assessing the organizational consequences of the use of ICT;
- information systems development in the broad sense.

As experts in the field of accounting and administrative organization, the auditor and the controller will be knowledgeable about ICT as well, but this knowledge needs to be much less profound. The information manager will also be knowledgeable about accounting and administrative organization, but in turn this knowledge needs to be less profound. This means that the auditor and the controller, as experts *par excellence* in the field of accounting and administrative organization, and the information manager as an expert in the field of ICT play complementary roles in organizations.

General management – who are ultimately responsible for sound decision making on the basis of reliable and relevant information – plays a moderating role in co-ordinating and enabling cooperation between the financial auditor, the controller, and the information manager.

Positioning AIS

The discipline of accounting and administrative organization as described in this chapter, although fairly representative of the dominant continental European view, has not been disseminated in most Anglo-Saxon countries. We will therefore adhere to the internationally more accepted denomination of AIS, hence the title of the book. To position AIS *vis-à-vis* other related disciplines, we must develop a classification criterion. Contemplating that the link to contiguous disciplines can be made through the concept of information, a demand and a supply side can be distinguished, or, to put it differently, use of information, on the one hand, and production of information, on the other. The internationally established discipline of management accounting is concerned with the use of information for the purpose of making decisions and ultimately controlling organizations. In contrast, the also internationally established discipline of information management, traditionally also denoted *information systems*, deals with the production of information which nowadays always makes use of ICT. The interfaces between AIS and information management are, to a great extent, located in the area of information system development; for example, typical AIS topics that relate to information management include data modelling and the simultaneous development of internal controls and information systems.

The disciplines of management accounting (including management control) and information management partially overlap in a number of common elements. These common elements are found in management science. The interfaces focus on human behaviour within organizations. Management accounting and information management differ from AIS, especially with regard to this criterion. AIS traditionally has a more rigid, formal, procedural, clinical and therefore technocratic approach. This brings us to the second classification criterion (besides the production of information and the use of information): the behavioural versus the technocratic approach. Based on the two criteria, AIS can be positioned on the interface between management accounting and information management.

The position of AIS with respect to related disciplines, the related objects of study in a managerial approach to AIS, and the role of information functions within the organization is depicted schematically in Figure 1.2. Here, AIS is looked at from four different angles: AIS in relation to internal control, AIS in relation to management,

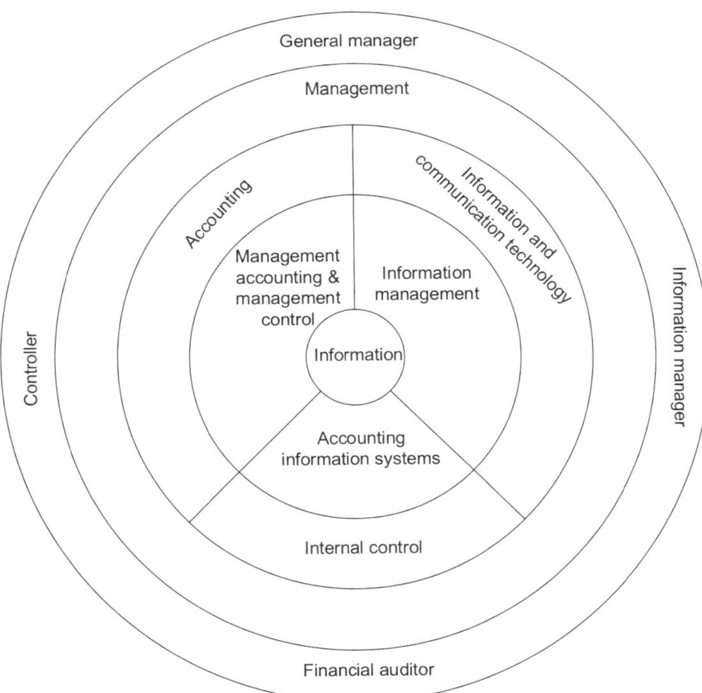

Figure 1.2 Information disciplines, related objects of study in a managerial approach to AIS, and the role of information functions within the organization.

AIS in relation to accounting, and AIS in relation to ICT. This framework will be used throughout the book, culminating in an analysis of the role of the accounting information system in managing contemporary organizations (Chapter 9).

The Human Factor

In prior sections, reference has been made to the importance of explicitly considering human behaviour as an object of study in information disciplines. Accounting and administrative organization is focused on governance and control of organizations and, therefore, on managing people. The applicable instruments are predominantly technocratic by nature. However, to get or keep a grip on organizations, a whole range of other control instruments may be applied that have their origins in management literature. Following authors such as Simons (1995b), Merchant (1998), and Ouchi (1979), nowadays the human factor is explicitly considered in discussions on control systems. Thus, a complete separate category of governance and control measures is introduced, generally denoted management control. Typical of this collection of control concepts is that, besides formal governance and control measures, ample attention is paid to formalizing informal measures; for example, motivating people by means of incentive schemes or creating a desirable organizational culture by means of setting the right tone at the top can become formal control procedures. In management science, several theories in this field have been developed; for example, creating a balance between salary and working conditions can contribute to a situation where people develop a certain loyalty to the organization and where they will mainly perform activities that contribute to attaining business goals. Obviously, in view of the rationalities and irrationalities of users of systems in organizations, an approach to AIS that does not consider the human factor is too narrow.

International Developments

Traditionally, internal control, accounting and administrative organization, and managerial information provision are disciplines that operate on the transaction level. After all, data are gathered with respect to transactions to arrive at adequate provision of information and safeguarding of the company's assets. As we have demonstrated, AIS is a discipline that integrates IC, AAO, MIP, and IS. Romney and Steinbart (2000) define an accounting information system as follows:

> *An accounting information system processes data and transactions to provide users with information they need to plan, control, and operate their businesses.*

However, Gelinas et al. (1999) define an accounting information system in a more limited fashion:

An accounting information system is a specialized subsystem of the management information system whose purpose is to collect, process, and report information related to financial transactions.

We believe some kind of evolution underlies this difference in viewpoint. In the 1950s, AISs were the first applications of computers to process transaction data. This concerned information systems that supported daily management by gathering and collecting data on financial facts. However, to meet managers' increasing information needs, traditional AISs did not seem sufficient anymore: information that is non-financial and not just focused on transactions (and therefore future-oriented or prospective) also became important for managers to get and keep a grip on organizations. This led to the rise of management information systems (MIS). Regarded in this way, a company's AIS would be part of its MIS. Nowadays, this is only partly true: AISs have obtained their own spot in the ABC – we can think of at least one type of information system for every letter of the alphabet – of information systems. Among accountants and controllers, there seems to be consensus on the role of AISs as the information systems of the future, since they are expected to deliver all information needed for business management, and in the desired format. However, the driver is still the transaction. Starting with information on transactions, information is further aggregated and combined with external data until it is useful for strategic management.

The Internal and External Role of Information

Many texts on information disciplines start with a discussion of the importance of information in our current society, which often is labelled an information society. Yet, a hundred years ago we also lived in an information society; for example, think of the hordes of writers and bookkeepers who had a full-time job recording all kinds of event within organizations on paper. Therefore, the term information society is not very newsworthy. But, sound provision of information within and between organizations is considered more important today than it was a century ago. The question is: Why? The answer is mainly related to developments in the fields of technology. After all, as a result of the technological developments in the fields of information and communication and transport, physical distance has become of minor importance in the world economy. The new economy has been introduced as the overall concept that incorporates all the developments that make traditional ways of doing business obsolete and dysfunctional. In the new economy, the number of potential competitors has increased dramatically. Buyers as well as suppliers are better informed, and therefore, have more bargaining power in relation to the company, and producers will recognize the opportunities of substitute products more quickly, resulting in faster and larger availability. Because of these competitive forces, the company will have to be able to react much more attentively to changing market conditions. Information is often designated as the fourth production factor, besides labour, raw materials, and capital. Thus, information could contribute importantly to the production of physical goods and services demanded by the market. This also indicates the role of information as a strategic instrument: by using information in the right way in the production process, competitive advantage can be gained.

Information plays a role in primary as well as secondary processes. In primary processes, information is the product that is sold. Examples of companies that consider information their core business are professional service organizations such as audit firms, management consultants, information brokers (e.g. gathering, processing, and providing world market real-estate prices or collecting airfare prices for certain arrangements and comparing them), but also banks who are increasingly taking on the role of information intermediary (among other things collecting, processing, and providing line of business data). In secondary processes, information supports primary processes; for example, to be able to determine in an industrial organization how many units need to be produced to meet demand, a manager may need information on his expected sales (competitive position, seasonal influences, the economic tide, the company's image, etc.), his current inventory level, his current production capacity and the required production time. In a broader context, he also needs to have an understanding of the capital requirements resulting from production, and the financial resources. In short, a seemingly simple decision could lead to a broad information requirement. Thus, the role of information can be twofold: output of a primary process and output of a secondary process. In both cases, information is used for governance purposes. In the first case, customers' governance processes are fed (external); in the second and last case, governance processes within the company, business unit, or division are fed (internal). Therefore, the relation between information and functional (primary and secondary) processes is always through the governance processes (Figure 1.3). Whether a company's core business is selling information or selling physical goods and services, information always plays a central part in meeting the customers' desires. For example, a hotel has rooms available on payment of the room rates. However, this is not just accommodating, it is hospitability. To fulfil this role successfully, such a system of information provision is required so that the guest does not notice the complexity of the hotel organization. In reality, this means that there are no queues at the reception desk, that the telephone is picked up after two rings, that a reservation that is made actually leads to an available room when the guest arrives, that the hotel bill contains exactly those amounts for which the guest has received something in return, and that the documentation in the hotel rooms about the available facilities and services is properly accessible.

Toward a Theory of AIS

AIS is a practice-oriented discipline. In spite of the tremendous developments in the fields of ICT, accounting, and management, a comprehensive AIS theory is still lacking. However, as already demonstrated in this chapter, AIS does have its

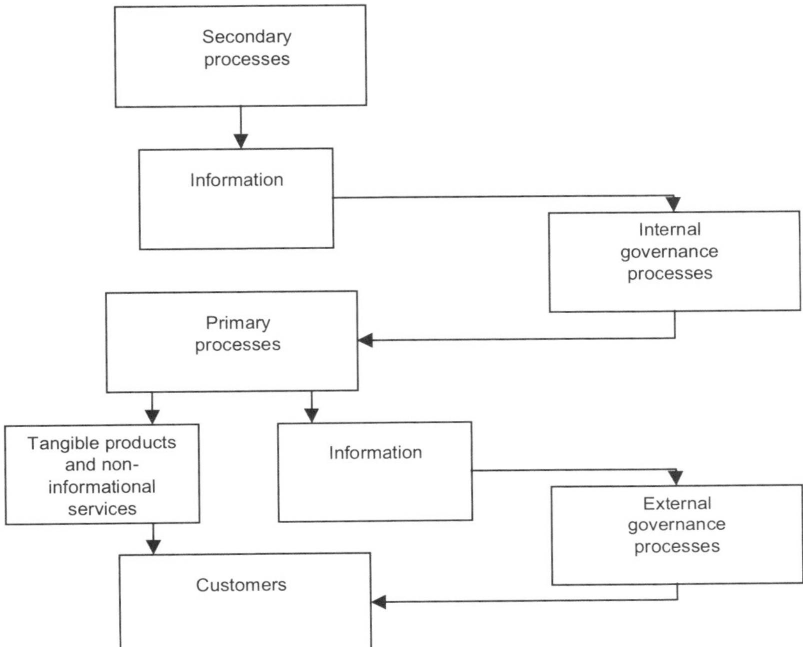

Figure 1.3 The internal and external roles of information.

specific themes and angles in the study of accounting in relation to systems. So, we encounter the remarkable phenomenon that, although AISs are studied at universities and other schools and are applied in practice, they lack a sound theoretical foundation. We try to build on findings from management accounting, management control, information management, and strategic management to contribute to the development of such a theory. Therefore, throughout the book we will discuss theoretical issues. At this point, we kick off our discussion of AIS theory with the simple premise that we will draw on the theory of the firm as the foundation of a theory of AIS.

The most influential streams within the theory of the firm are agency theory and transaction-cost theory. Both theories consider the firm as an institution that comes into existence when the market fails due to market imperfections. In particular, a lack of transparency is an important imperfection. As a result of market intransparency, some individuals may have more information at their disposal than others. They may exploit this information advantage and hence frustrate certain transactions and activities that would otherwise be realized. Firms can prevent productive, cooperative efforts from failing due to individuals exploiting their information advantage. They can do so by installing hierarchical relationships and entering all kinds of contract.

Transaction-cost theory and agency theory resemble each other because they both take a contractual view of the firm. An alternative view is embedded in the knowledge-based theory of the firm which is a subset of the resource-based theory. Whereas the contractual view provides explanations for the usage of instruments to limit the degree of freedom of individuals when doing transactions, the knowledge-based view provides explanations for the superior performance of firms as a result of the creation and integration of knowledge.

The theory of the firm tries to give explanations for observed phenomena. Yet, it has normative implications for business operations. The information disciplines especially, as discussed in this book, may benefit from findings about the theory of the firm; for example, a control system can be considered a bundle of mechanisms that replace the automatic coordination and the intrinsic motivation as provided by the price mechanism. Which instruments and processes will be efficient when establishing control depends on the causes of the market failures that underlie the existence of firms.

Introduction to the Following Chapters

This introductory chapter touched on the themes that we believe are important in a managerial approach to AISs. The next chapters study these themes in depth. We have chosen a structure in which a number of traditional concepts are discussed first. Therefore, Chapter 2 deals with the value cycle, the uniform base pattern of information provision, the governance paradigm, and the management cycle. Subsequently, Chapters 3–5 discuss contingency approaches to AIS. These chapters study the issue of alignment, which is important when developing AISs and embedded internal controls. The discussion of the alignment issue will go beyond the traditional approach in which gearing only takes place in the industry (typology) and in the specific company. Gearing to global, country, and personal characteristics will also be discussed. Chapter 6 deals with a number of developments in the field of ICT. These developments are discussed to introduce Chapter 7, which investigates the dynamic relationship between internal control and AIS. Subsequently, the main theme of the book is discussed in-depth in Chapter 8. Here, the relationship between internal control, which is traditionally considered an accounting and auditing concept, and management control, which is primarily considered a management concept, is investigated. Having arrived at Chapter 9, the path has been paved for a discussion of the role of the AIS in relation to managing contemporary organizations. Whereas Chapter 9 elaborates on the ascribed central role of the AIS, Chapter 10 presents a number of conditions that must be met to fulfil this role as well as some new directions for making the AIS more accepted. This chapter is about the communication of AIS-related issues within organizations to increase the AIS's efficiency.

Chapter Case

Case 1.1 Garage Business

A small garage business engages in the following activities:

- supplying and mounting of draw-hooks for caravans;
- supplying and mounting of fog-lamps;
- supplying and mounting of sunshine roofs;
- repairing of bodywork.

Besides the garage proprietor, there are five mechanics who can perform all tasks. The required parts are kept in stock.

In the last few years, profits have been declining. The garage proprietor thinks that this is mainly caused by some severe control problems within the firm. These problems include:

- When a customer brings in a car for a repair or a mounting job, an estimate is provided. Often, the actual price exceeds the estimate.
- When a customer brings in a car for a repair or a mounting job, an estimation of how long it will take is made. Often, this time is exceeded.
- Most clients pay by bank transfer. For that purpose, invoices should be sent to them a few days after the job has been finished. Often, the invoice is not raised or sent to the client.

Assignment

1. Give an explanation of the causes of the mentioned problems.
2. What measures would you take to solve these problems?
3. How would you apply a personal computer as a means to regain control over the business?

CORNERSTONES OF ACCOUNTING INFORMATION SYSTEMS

2

Assisting management in the control of a business organization is one of the primary objectives of an accounting information system

Romney and Steinbart (2000), p. 253

The cornerstones of internal control are:

- *Division of labor. This is aimed at (a) implementing segregation of duties, and (b) tracking the flows of values within an organization, specifically between the different elements of the value cycle.*
- *The mutual coherence between the various activities that arise from a specific transaction.*

Adapted from Nimwegen and Jans (1978), p. 26

After studying this chapter, the reader should be able to:

- Define control.
- Define internal control.
- Understand the relationship between AIS and internal control.
- Understand the meaning of the following concepts for internal control:
  - the governance paradigm;
  - the uniform basic pattern of information provision;
  - segregation of duties;
  - reconciliations and control totals;
  - analytical review;
  - typologies of organization;
  - checks and balances;
  - procedures;
  - supervision.

- Understand the interrelationships between these concepts.
- Describe a simple internal control system.
- Understand the relevance of distinguishing between a cycle approach and a typology approach to the development of an AIS and embedded internal controls.

Chapter Outline

Control in all its forms is the main managerial activity in organizations. Internal control is an important element of any AIS. Based on the concepts introduced in this chapter, the user is provided with the instruments to understand a simple AIS that embeds adequate internal controls. The adequacy of internal controls is dependent on a considerable number of contingency variables. One of the most important variables is the type of firm. This chapter introduces a typology of organizations based on the presence of a direct relationship between the flow of goods and flow of money. For every type of firm, there are a number of specific threats to achieving internal control goals. By determining the exposure to these threats, an internal control solution can be constructed. Within organizations, there are cycles of identical functional processes such as buying, selling, production, human resource management, and administering. The Anglo-Saxon approach to internal control problems is that threats, exposure, and solutions are not determined for types of organization, but for cycles within organizations. The underlying reasoning is that an organization is merely the combination of two or more cycles. However, it is the combination of cycles that makes the control problems in an organization unique. Therefore, the analysis of threats, exposure, and controls should take place on the organizational level and not on a cycle level. Obviously, there are more criteria than just the type of firm which play a role when setting the boundaries of classes of organization. However, the approach discussed in this chapter may be considered the dominant, traditional European continental approach.

Based on the typology of organizations, the concepts of value cycle, reconciliations and control totals, and segregation of duties are introduced. These concepts have proven to be of great value for achieving two major goals of internal control: assuring the quality of information and the safeguarding of assets. In order to put these goals in their proper context, a number of frameworks are outlined that may be helpful in understanding the path to the attainment of these goals. These frameworks are the governance paradigm, the management cycle, and the uniform basic pattern of information provision. Together with the typology of organizations, these may be considered the cornerstones of the dominant, traditional European continental approach to AIS.

Introduction

As discussed in Chapter 1, definitions of the constituent elements of the discipline of AIS have undeniable similarities and they provide definitions of phenomena which are clearly related to AIS. However, there are differences which make an unambiguous delineation of the discipline next to impossible. In order to reduce the confusion about terms, it is important to develop a list of key elements of the discipline of AIS. We will refer to this list as the *cornerstones of AIS*. Note that the idiosyncracy of the relationship between AIS as a collection of systems and AIS as a discipline culminates in a parallel list of key elements of an AIS as a collection of systems. In the remainder of the book, we will not elaborate further on the similarities and differences between AIS as a collection of systems and AIS as a discipline, and we will attempt to use wording such that the meaning is self-explanatory.

If a theory of AIS would be developed, we believe that the cornerstones as discussed in this chapter are the minimally required components of such a theory. The ideas that underlie AIS, and its related disciplines and concepts, have developed from the design of accounting systems, via auditing these systems, to control of businesses. Control has a wide variety of connotations; for example, the efficiency and effectiveness approach to control assumes that the designers of management information and control systems are concerned primarily with organizational performance, while the power and control approach focuses on the development of disciplinary practices in mental asylums, prisons, military barracks, schools, and other similar institutions which have aspects in common with factories and other organizations, and then the conflict approach tends to comprehend the world from a perspective which is suspicious of all motives, particularly those of managers of capitalist organizations. Since control as an integral part of all organizational activity, aimed at the attainment of organizational goals, is the key issue in our discussion of AIS, we will adhere to the efficiency and effectiveness approach to control. Hence control can be defined as:

> *All those activities aimed at having organization members cooperate to reach the organizational goals.*

Note that this notion of control includes positive as well as negative elements in that desirable events are pursued and undesirable events are avoided.

Internal Control from an International Perspective

Besides broadening the discipline of AIS to more *formalized* governance and control measures that used to be *informal* in nature, we can also observe a tendency towards a far-reaching international consensus on core concepts. Taking accounting and administrative organization as a point of departure, the following core concepts seem to aptly describe the discipline: the value cycle, segregation of duties, reconciliations and control totals (RCTs), typology of organizations, and internal control. Especially in the field of internal control, internationalization has led to the establishment of a common universal definition, and to the development of a standard against which organizations can assess their control systems and determine how to improve them. In 1992 the so-called COSO-report was published by the Committee of Sponsoring Organizations of the Treadway Commission. In essence, this report reflects a process of many years of growing awareness of the importance of internal control. Internal control, according to COSO, can be defined as:

> *a process, effected by an entity's board of directors, management and other personnel, designed to provide reasonable assurance regarding the achievement of objectives in the following categories:*
>
> - *Effectiveness and efficiency of operations.*
> - *Reliability of financial reporting.*
> - *Compliance with applicable laws and regulations.*

In 1994 the Committee added that the objective of *safeguarding of assets* forms a part of each of the other three objectives of internal control. The report discusses five mutually coherent components of internal control: control environment, risk assessment, control activities, information and communication, and monitoring.

Control Environment

The control environment is the foundation of all the other elements of internal control. It is about the norms and values of the organization with respect to control consciousness. We can think of the control environment as mainly consisting of aspects regarding organizational culture. However, it can also be interpreted much more broadly since it may include integrity and ethical values, commitment to competence, the task conception of the board of directors and the audit committee, management philosophy and operating style, the organizational structure, the assignment of authority and responsibility, and human resource policies and practices. The control environment has a pervasive influence on the way organizations are governed and controlled.

The Barings Case

The chain of events which led to the collapse of Barings, Britain's oldest merchant bank, is a demonstration of how not to manage a derivatives operation. The control and risk management lessons to be learnt from the collapse of this 200-year-old institution apply as much to cash positions as they do to derivative ones, but the pure leverage of derivatives makes it imperative that proper controls are in place. Since only a small amount of money (called a margin) is needed to establish a position, a firm could find it facing financial obligations way beyond its means. The leverage and liquidity offered by major futures contracts – such as the Nikkei 225, the S&P 500 or Eurodollars – means that these obligations, once in place, mount very quickly; thus bringing down an institution with lightning speed. This is in stark contrast to bad loans or cash investments whose ill effects takes years to ruin an institution, as demonstrated by the cases of British & Commonwealth Bank or Bank of Credit and Commerce International (BCCI).

BFS, a Singapore registered company and an indirect subsidiary of Barings Securities Limited, was originally formed to allow Barings to trade on the Singapore International Monetary Exchange. From late 1992 to the time of the collapse, BFS's General Manager and Head Trader was Nick Leeson. Prior to his move to Singapore in March 1992, Leeson worked for Barings in London in a back-office capacity for almost three years.

His senior managers assumed Leeson's positions were hedged. But, unlike outsiders who had to assume that these positions were hedged, Barings's management did not. They could have done something about it – they could have probed Leeson, they could have tried to obtain more information from their internal information systems, and most of all they could have heeded the warning signals available in late 1994 and throughout January and February of 1995.

But although Barings's fate was only sealed in the final weeks of February, the seeds of its destruction were sown when senior management entered new businesses without ensuring adequate support and control systems. The collapse of Britain's oldest merchant bank was an extreme example of operations risk (i.e. the risk that deficiencies in information systems or internal controls result in unexpected loss). Will it happen again? Certainly, if senior managers of firms continue to disregard rules and recommendations which have been drawn up to ensure prudent risk taking.

Adapted from International Finance and Commodities Institute (URL: http://risk.ifci.ch/).

Risk assessment

Risk asssessment is the identification and analysis of relevant risks to the achievement of objectives. It forms a basis for determining how the risks should be managed. A vital part of risk assessment is the formal or informal setting of objectives. These objectives fall within three broad internal control categories: operations objectives, financial reporting objectives, and compliance objectives. Operations objectives pertain to the enhancement of effectiveness and efficiency in moving an organization toward its goals. Financial reporting objectives relate to the preparation of reliable published financial statements. Compliance objectives relate to an organization's conduct of activities in accordance with applicable laws and regulations. After the objectives have been determined, a risk analysis can be performed. When conducting a risk analysis, some kind of model should be used. An example of such a model is depicted in Figure 2.1.

Every organization faces the risk of getting out of control; for example, the 200-year-old institution Barings, a British merchant bank, collapsed basically because it had inadequate controls in place. The first thing an organization can do is to try to

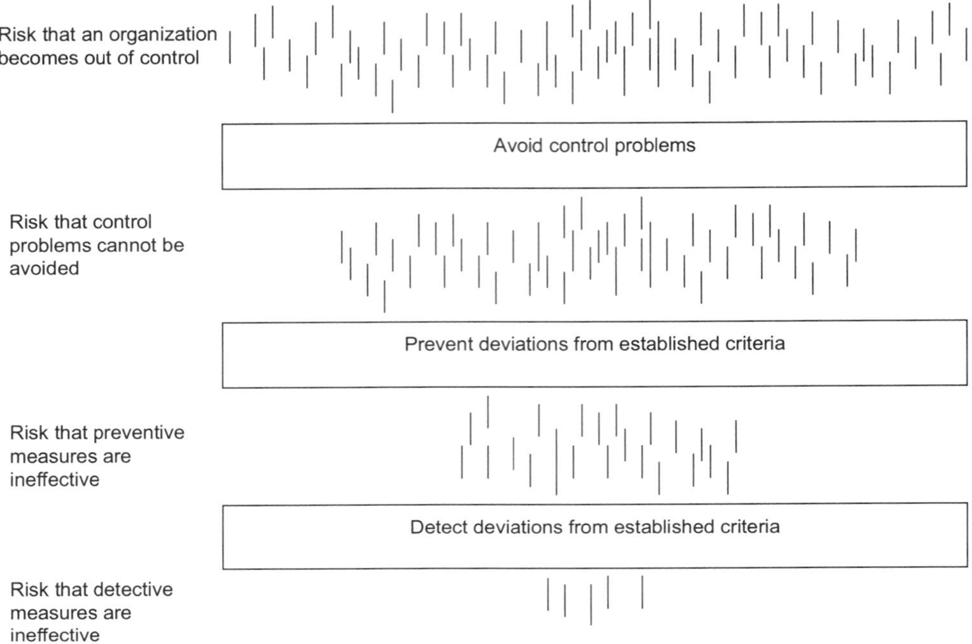

Figure 2.1 Risk assessment.

avoid risks by taking the right measures. Some risks can and some cannot be avoided. The risks that cannot be avoided must be dealt with by means of internal controls. Internal controls may be aimed at preventing deviations from established criteria from occurring or detecting deviations after they have occurred. The risk that remains after the internal control system has done its preventive and detective work can eventually be mitigated by an internal or external audit. However, complete assurance that deviations are non-existent can never be accomplished.

Deviations from Established Criteria

Established criteria that serve as norms in assessing deviations may originate from a variety of factors. Examples include (but are not limited to): laws and regulations, internal management guidelines, benchmarks, policy statements, control totals, or strategies. As can be seen from these examples, assessing deviations does not only consist of retrospective elements, but also of prospective elements (e.g. an established criterion may be that an early adopter strategy should be followed). If an organization does not respond in a timely fashion to innovations introduced by competitors, there is a deviation from an established criterion.

Control Activities

Control activities include segregation of duties, reconciliations and control totals, procedures for authorization, physical security of assets, analytical review, and supervision. They are aimed at ensuring that management directives are carried out and, hence, occur at all levels in the organization and in all functions. Of all components of internal control, the control activities are the most technocratic in nature. Control activities can be applied to operations, information provision, as well as ICT; for example, controls over information systems – which are the most widely known instances of ICT – include general controls like back-up and recovery procedures, disaster recovery plans, logon procedures, and encryption.

Information and Communication

Information and communication pertains to the recording of transactions, the matching of internal with external recordings, confirmations to third parties, communications of procedures and task assignments, accountability, and other management reports. Information and communication must meet certain quality requirements; for example, information must be reliable in order to enable people who need it to properly carry out their control tasks and other responsibilities.

Monitoring

Monitoring is a process that assesses the quality of an internal control system over time. It may take two different forms (or a combination of the two): monitoring as a continuous process and monitoring as separate evaluations. Internal control systems may change over time because the organization and its environment changes. As a result, once-effective internal control systems may become ineffective. In order to determine whether internal controls are still effective and to decide on the necessary adjustments, if the controls are no longer effective, monitoring activities will have to take place; for example, periodical physical stocktaking, comparing the results with the accounting records, and reporting on the differences are ongoing monitoring activities. This way an organization's management can gain insight into the effectiveness of the inventory security system.

Despite the report's influence within the international arena, the following critical comments can be made with respect to some of its views on internal control:

- Strictly speaking, the report extends internal control to management control, begging the question why the term internal control is used instead of management control. We will elaborate on this issue in Chapter 8.
- Internal control in the Anglo-Saxon tradition has a content that is less limited than internal control in a traditional, continental European sense, because the former implies a prospective element which is not present in the latter. The more limited

meaning of control is *checking against norms*, which contributes to organizational control in an *indirect* way only.

- The objective *reliability of financial reporting* applies to the quality of information provision within organizations and of organizations to their stakeholders. However, there are more aspects that apply to the quality of information than just the reliability aspect; for example, information should also be relevant.
- *Financial reporting* mainly pertains to external reporting and to financial quantities which can be collected from an organization's accounts. Internal reporting for decision making comprises more than just financial information.
- The listing of internal control elements is rather arbitrary. It is difficult to find an underlying dimension here. Nevertheless, the listing does cover the field of internal control fairly well, although there are some overlaps between categories. However, a classification is never a goal in itself, but a means to better understand certain phenomena. We believe that the COSO-report provides a classification that indeed contributes to a better understanding of internal control.

AIS Development Issues

The development of an AIS is aimed at contributing to the optimization of a firm's business processes in the achievement of its strategic goals. In this context, two remarks are to be made. First, when strategic business goals are at stake, upper management must play an important role. This implies that the AIS is the primary responsibility of business management. Second, optimality is not unambiguously determinable. The main rule is: if revenues of a specific AIS-related measure exceed the costs of it, then the measure contributes to the strategic business goals. However, the costs, and more importantly the revenues, of AIS-related measures cannot be quantified accurately despite the use of decision support systems, expert systems, and quantitative methods. This implies normal financial payback criteria cannot be used. It is necessary to keep this in mind when developing an AIS.

When developing an efficient AIS, a limited number of factors that determine the success of a business must be taken into consideration. Examples of these critical success factors include: corporate image, competitive edge, motivation of personnel, after-sales service, relation network, quality of production, and cost position. Critical success factors are influenced by all kinds of variable which must be measured in order to assess their impact on these factors. To create an environment in which the business can be optimally managed, information must be provided with regard to the values of these variables. Attention to these variables is one of the main themes when aligning strategy with AIS.

The Governance Paradigm

Governance and control are two strongly related concepts. To put it simply, by means of governing a business, management attempts to control it. From a rather traditional and narrow perspective, governance and control entails giving task assignments and holding workers accountable for fulfilment of their task. The heavily intertwined processes that take place here are those of *delegation* and *accountability*. Delegation involves a downward flow of information, whereas accountability involves an upward flow of information. Delegation always results in accountability. A concept that systematically represents the processes of delegation and accountability, as well as the role of information therein is the governance paradigm. According to this paradigm, a business consists of three interrelated subsystems:

- the control system;
- the controlled system;
- the information system.

In an open system, the system boundaries lie between the organization and the environment. Hence, the environment is also considered when schematically representing the governance paradigm (Figure 2.2). The governance paradigm is applicable to any type of system (e.g. a national economy, an industry, a business, a business unit, a department, or even a group or an individual working within a group or department). By means of the governance paradigms expression is given to the fact that (1) information and, more specifically, the information system is key to

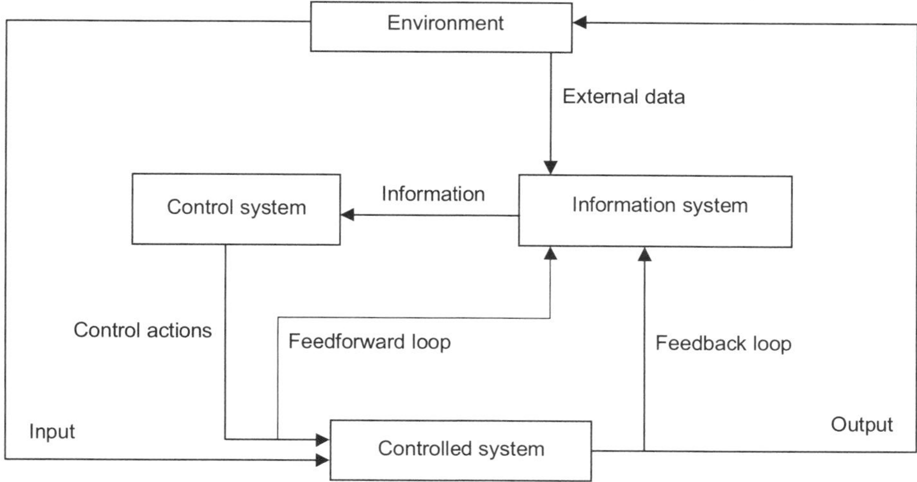

Figure 2.2 The governance paradigm.

governing a system; (2) there is a continuous interaction between the environment and the system; (3) the subjective choice of the system boundaries determines what information is considered internal or external, and (4) there is a manager (control system) who attempts to control the behaviour of a subordinate (controlled system) on the basis of often imperfect information; for example, a business may be considered a controlled system. This system is governed and controlled by the management of the business. Hence, management is the control system. Management needs information to govern the business. This information is acquired either from the information system or directly from the environment, or both. Management will give task assignments to workers within the business, who will account for their task fulfilment by means of the information system. In addition, the business will also account for its task fulfilment directly to the environment or, more specifically, to stakeholders (see Box: The Bus).

The Bus

The governance of a business may be compared with driving a bus. The driver is seated in front of the bus, behind the steering wheel. His task is to drive to bus to its destination. The windscreen and the rear-view mirrors provide him with the needed information. In addition, the passengers of the bus are a source of information. It is well known that driving a bus is a relatively easy task when compared with governing a business. Hence, the comparison between a business and a bus holds only partially. When the windscreen, which provides the driver – in this case, the manager – with a substantial part of the needed information, is blinded, the manager has only the rear-view mirrors and his passengers as sources of information. Here, two problems emerge. First, the rear-view mirror can only provide information about the past. Second, the passengers do not always provide the driver with reliable information. There is another complicating factor. The steering wheel that the driver – in this case, the manager – uses to steer the bus in the right direction is not directly connected to the wheels of the bus. Instead, the passengers – in this case, the manager's subordinates – each have a steering wheel of their own, which indeed is connected to the wheels of the bus. When the manager turns the steering wheel, he wants his subordinates to follow his example. From this viewpoint, governing a business (driving) in order to control it (reaching the destination) is merely a matter of collecting reliable and relevant information and trying to move the people within the business in the right direction.

There are two generic modes of reaction to control actions by control systems: feedforward mechanisms and feedback mechanisms. Basically, a feedforward mechanism tries to prevent undesirable events from occurring, whereas a feedback mechanism tries to transform undesirable outcomes of events into desirable outcomes (see Box: Brother and Sister). To make a well-grounded choice between feedforward and feedback mechanisms as control instruments, the consequences of each must be known in advance.

Brother and Sister

Those who have children know that little brothers and sisters fight a continuous battle, not to win, but just to fight. Parents are heavily occupied with these types of mini-war. What we are dealing with here is a rather complicated control problem. When little sister is playing with a doll, little brother also wants to play with that doll, which results in the doll being decapitated because little brother pulls the head and little sister pulls the legs. Parents have two options to control this awkward situation. The first is to watch the doll being demolished, father afterwards trying to repair it and mother plain speaking to the two warriors in order to prevent this undesirable process from occurring in the future. This is a feedback loop. The second is to take action before the doll is decapitated. During the battle, the two fighters are untangled and justice is done by the parents. This is a feedforward loop. Based on their experience and ability to raise children, the parents will make a trade-off between the consequences of watching the doll being demolished and untangling the fighters before decapitation takes place.

Feedforward and feedback mechanisms may be represented as loops in the schematical representation of the governance paradigm (Figure 2.2).

The Management Cycle

Governance and control are the most important processes that managers are occupied with. Whereas the governance paradigm presents a specific view on the understanding of management processes and the role of information therein, the management cycle indicates the steps involved in managerial activities. In the literature we can find several definitions of 'management'. However, an important common characteristic is that all managerial activities are aimed at steering organization members in the right direction. Ideally, there is a perfect congruence between organizational goals, as defined by management, and individual goals of the organization members. Generally, this congruence does not originate by itself. Managerial activities must be deployed to develop shared goals, to build such organizational structures that the necessary conditions are met to accomplish these goals, to provide incentives that workers think and act in accordance with these goals, to evaluate to what extent goals are met, and to take corrective measures if goal fulfilment is inadequate. Hence, the management cycle consists of the following stages:

1. Planning.
2. Structuring.
3. Execution.
4. Evaluation.
5. Adjusting.

At every stage, a backward jump to one of the earlier stages is always possible. The management cycle is an appealing tool for analysing managerial activities because of its simple, yet multi-purpose applicability. However, currently there is a tendency in business to have as little activities as possible follow predefined structures like the management cycle. By doing so, managers try to make organizations more flexible and innovative. In addition, when a long-term project is at stake, the specifications made at the start of the project are often subject to modifications. After having gone through the whole management cycle, the original specifications may have changed dramatically and the outcome of the project be obsolete even before the project has been finished. Examples are most profound in ICT projects. In this case, managers often prefer the so-called incremental system development methodologies instead of the linear system development methodologies which follow the structural approach of the management cycle. Examples of incremental (or non-linear) system development methodologies are rapid application development (RAD) and prototyping. It must be stressed that even organizations that do not wish to adhere to fixed plans or that follow incremental approaches apply certain variants of management cycles. These management cycles usually have the following characteristics: a short cycle time, a short planning horizon, a high level of detail, and a lower hierarchical level employing planning activities.

As stated earlier (see Figure 1.1), accounting and administrative organization, managerial information provision and internal control are often mentioned in one and the same breath and are also used interchangeably. On closer inspection, however, there are dissimilarities. These can be illustrated by means of the management cycle. The management cycle is a generic model of the organization's activities to guide the operations of people in these organizations. The management cycle is applicable to every level in an organization.

To realize strategic organizational goals, strategic management will display the following activities:

- formulating strategic organizational goals (planning);
- creating cross-functional collaboration between employees (structuring);
- allocating task assignments and providing resources to those employees (execution);
- testing the realization of the goals (evaluation);
- undertaking corrective or preventive measures if goals are not or insufficiently realized (adjusting).

At the tactical and operational level, similar activities will be developed. However, as the specification of these activities gets more detailed, differences will arise. Some of these differences are:

- The goals become more concrete; for example, the head of the purchasing department is responsible for keeping inventory above minimum level *X*.
- The number of degrees of freedom in creating cross-functional collaborations will be more limited; for example, if tactical management has developed an organizational structure that includes a separate warehouse and purchasing departments, then operational management cannot create a position in which warehousing and purchasing are combined.
- The task assignments will be more specific and will contain more detailed instructions; for example, supported by the information system, the head of the purchasing department will charge his subordinate to order *Y* units of product *A* from supplier *B* if the inventory records indicate that the minimum inventory level *X* has been reached.
- The norms for testing whether goals have been realized will be more specific; for example, to test whether the actual inventory is larger than the minimum level *X*.
- The measures taken to get out of a situation where goals are not realized are of a routine nature; for example, to test if the actual inventory level is found to be below the minimum level *X*, then the necessary amount is purchased.

Thus, it seems that the strategic business goals can be divided into more concrete goals which, in turn, can be further concretized as well. If an officer's job responsibilities are so extensive that, in fairness he cannot perform them on his own and if it is possible to divide the strategic business goals into subgoals, then division of labour can take place. That way, delegation of power and responsibilities takes place between the management levels to bring the process of realizing those goals under control.

If power and responsibilities are delegated, the need for control arises. After all, the higher level needs to establish that the goals that were set are indeed realized. To enable management to exercise control, the lower levels must account for the power and responsibilities delegated to them. The latter concerns managerial information provision. However, managerial information provision is much more than that. As part of governance and control of organizations, managerial information provision will take care of effective and efficient management, and that is exactly what managers are responsible for. All management positions have as a distinguishing feature that they prime other people's actions in an organization, monitor the progress of those actions, and adjust them when the manager deems this necessary for the sake of realizing formulated business goals. Essential concepts in managerial information provision are governance and control. Organizations are governed by making decisions (governance in the narrow sense), guiding the organization and its divisions (entity functionality), and giving account of the decisions that were made and the activities that were performed. Governance and control are related in the sense that by governing the organization we aim to control the organization or its divisions. Control is keeping the organization 'on track'. To govern (and therefore control) organizations, information is needed. Information can only be provided if certain data are gathered and recorded for that purpose. So, the domain of managerial information provision is concerned with gathering and recording data to provide information for governing organizations. Thus, managerial information provision is concerned with entity functionality. Accounting and administrative organization, on the other hand, is concerned with structuring of the governance processes within the organization. The relationship between managerial information provision and accounting and administrative organization can be aptly expressed as follows: accounting and administrative organization concerns the entire collection of organizational measures that directly or indirectly affects the adequate functioning of managerial information provision. Aspects concerning design as well as functioning need to be considered when developing an accounting and administrative organization.

It will be clear from the former that governance and control are key concepts in accounting and administrative organization, managerial information provision, and internal control. The relationship between AAO, IC, and MIP is depicted in Figure 2.3 by means of the stages of the management cycle.

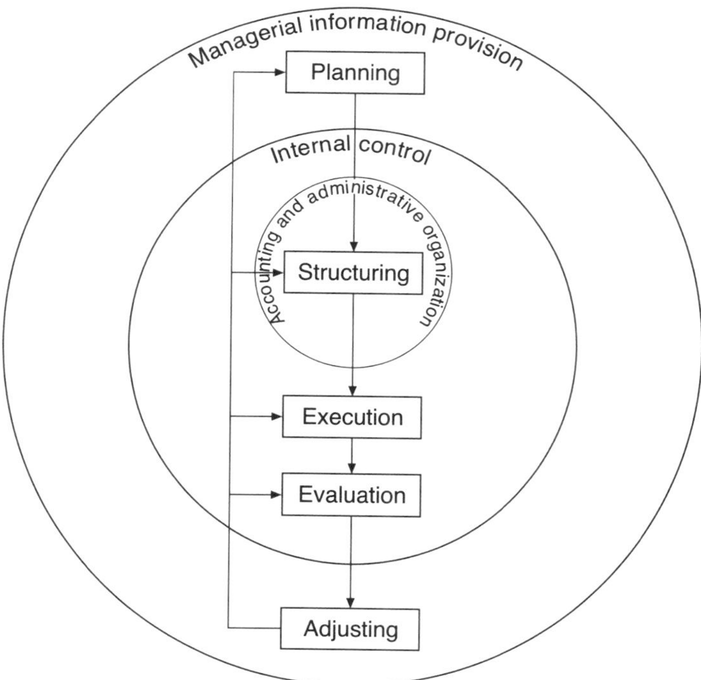

Figure 2.3 The relationship between AAO, IC, and MIP.

The Uniform Basic Pattern of Information Provision

Information plays a major role in the governance paradigm as well as the management cycle. From studying the information system, as incorporated in the governance paradigm, it appears that a further decomposition can be made. Information is meaningful data. An information system transforms data into information. It does so by applying certain procedures (mostly embedded in computer software) on input data in combination with data collections (mostly recorded in computer files). By means of this type of computer processing, the required output is generated. Every information provision process has the same uniform structure:

1. Input.
2. Processing, making use of procedures and data collections.
3. Output.

Together these elements constitute the uniform basic pattern of information provision. This uniform basic pattern is depicted in Figure 2.4. The uniform base pattern is valid for manual as well as computerized systems. After all, the only difference is in the media used; for example, input in a manual system may take place by means of postings to a ledger (sales, purchases, cash). Processing then takes place in accordance with a procedure prescribing that, once a week, the record in the ledger must be transferred to the general ledger. For this purpose, the general ledger accounts (cards) are manually lifted and updated. The information ultimately provided concerns the balance of that account at the end of the period. In a computerized system, input will take place by means of typing. A computer program – a list of instructions that must be executed by a computer in a prescribed sequence – will match the input with existing data in available computer files. Finally, the required information is printed out or displayed on the computer screen.

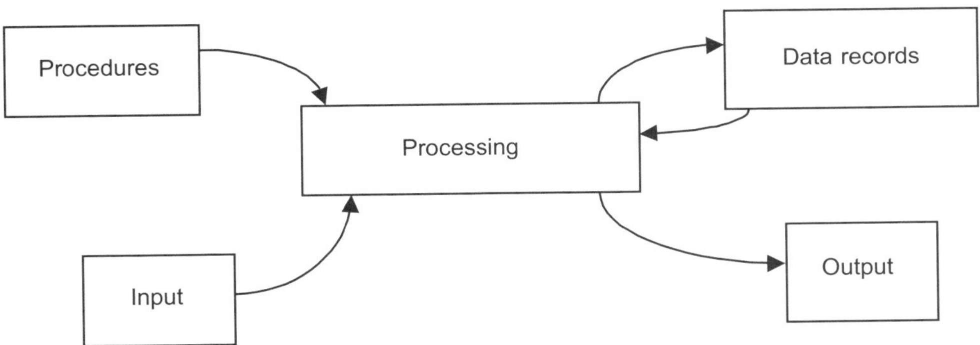

Figure 2.4 Uniform basic pattern of information provision.

Any information system can be modelled in accordance with the uniform basic pattern of information provision. Hence, in the schematical representation of the governance paradigm, the information system may be replaced by the uniform basic pattern of information provision.

Besides the insight the uniform basic pattern of information provision gives into processes of information provision and governance, it is a tool for analysing controls around and built into information systems. Especially with respect to complex automated systems, such as enterprise resource planning systems, this model can be helpful in reducing complexity; for example, a well-known classification of computer-related controls entails programmed controls, integrity controls, and user controls. This classification seamlessly reconciles with the uniform basic pattern of information provision. Programmed controls are involved with the processing of data, integrity controls are involved with computer programs and data files, and user controls are involved with the input of data and output of information.

In order to record data systematically, the technique of double-entry bookkeeping has been traditionally used in manual as well as computerized accounting systems. The meaning of the term 'double' is that mutations in a organization's equity are recorded in both magnitude and composition; for example, if an organization realizes a sales transaction and it gains a profit on that transaction (selling price exceeds cost price), then equity increases. Simply stated, the effect of this transaction can be observed in the balance sheet accounts 'cash' (which increases by an amount that equals the selling price) and 'inventory' (which decreases by an amount that equals the cost price). In the profit and loss account, the account 'sales' increases by an amount that equals the selling price, and the account 'costs of sales' increases by an amount that equals the cost price. Because the increase in cash exceeds the decrease in inventory, an increase in equity is realized (magnitude). Cash and inventory are, just like the other balance sheet accounts, statements of a certain position at a certain moment in time. The events that have led to an increase of equity are represented in the profit and loss account that comprises sales and costs of sales. If sales exceed costs of sales then a profit is realized. Just like the other profit and loss accounts, both accounts are statements of events because they represent the events that have happened between two moments in time, hence between states. The difference between equity before and after this transaction exactly equals profit calculated as the difference between sales and costs of sales (composition). As will become apparent in this book, internal controls frequently entail the concept of the value cycle. This concept is also based on the difference and the relationship between events and positions. Hence, it seems reasonable not to elaborate on the technique of double-entry bookkeeping here, but refer to it where considered relevant when discussing the value cycle. In addition, double-entry bookkeeping has been susceptible to some harsh criticism. New approaches include triple-entry bookkeeping, and REA accounting.

Triple-entry bookkeeping builds on the traditional notion of recording mutations in magnitude and composition of an organization's equity by including mutations in profit generating capacity. For that purpose, a new financial statement is developed that represents the increase or decrease in profit generating power. Here, each fact is still translated into currency units, but this does not only apply to financial facts; for example, in a triple-entry bookkeeping system when financial values are assigned to customer complaints, the bookkeeper – analyst would be a better denomination – must ask himself what the additional expenses are when a certain number of complaints of a certain nature are being lodged. Also, an entry into a triple-entry system may not even pertain to a transaction; for example, if the market interest rate drops, there is an effect on profit generating power. In a double-entry system, no record will be made of this fact. However, in a triple-entry system, the implications for the company's future profits, when refinancing takes place, are calculated. Just like double-entry bookkeeping, triple-entry bookkeeping suffers from some major shortcomings, including:

- Translating non-financial facts into financial facts is subjective, as is translating non-transactions into transactions.

- Each fact has to fit into a predefined chart of accounts. Reporting on facts that do not fit, or reporting information that is contained in the data entered into the system but aggregated to fit the chart of accounts, is impossible or only possible at additional expenses; for example, if a decision maker needs information on an individual debtor's contribution to a company's profit generating power, but the chart of accounts only allows one accounts receivable account to be used for all debtors, then a clerk – usually an assistant controller – must be hired to decompose the aggregate data.

To mitigate the shortcomings of traditional bookkeeping systems, including triple-entry bookkeeping, the basic idea behind the chart of accounts must be abandoned. Basically, the traditional debits and credits will have to be replaced by principles from data modelling. Since debits and credits are typical accounting concepts and data modelling is a typical information systems concept, we will be heading for a discipline at the crossroads. We believe AIS has all the features to be that discipline.

Data modelling is the process of defining a database in such a manner that it represents the most important parts of an organization and its environment.The goal of data modelling is to collect and record data on each business process. REA accounting distinguishes three types of object to model, namely: the acquired and used resources (R), the events in which the organization is involved (E), and the people, or agents, who are involved in these events (A). Using REA enables financial as well as non-financial record about business processes. Moreover, it allows financial statements to be produced at any time because each event is recorded in its most elementary form (e.g. a sales transaction may be on account, cash, or prepaid). Within REA accounting, each type of transaction is recorded in the same manner. However, specific payment characteristics are also recorded which greatly enhances the flexibility in information provision. Hence, REA accounting promises to meet the demands imposed by our current information society.

The Value Cycle

The value cycle is a model that enables visualization of segregation of duties, the clear description of the coherence between positions and events within organizations, the relationship between flows of goods and cash flows, and the classification of any firm in a typology of organizations.

The value cycle is a schematic representation of events in businesses that lead to changes in inventory, accounts receivable, accounts payable, and cash. In a way, it can be compared with the blood circulation of human beings. Typically, flows lead to an increase or decrease in observable states, from where new flows can originate. Figure 2.5 depicts the value cycle of a trade organization where there are no cash disbursements other than those in payment of vendor accounts payable and where there are no cash receipts other than those from customer accounts receivable. In this figure, ellipses represent events and rectangles represent outcomes from events. Events are processes that occur between two moments in time and are hence dynamic. Outcomes from events are positions that are measured at a certain moment in time and are hence static. Typically, the cash-flow statement or the profit and loss statement represent events, and the balance sheet represents

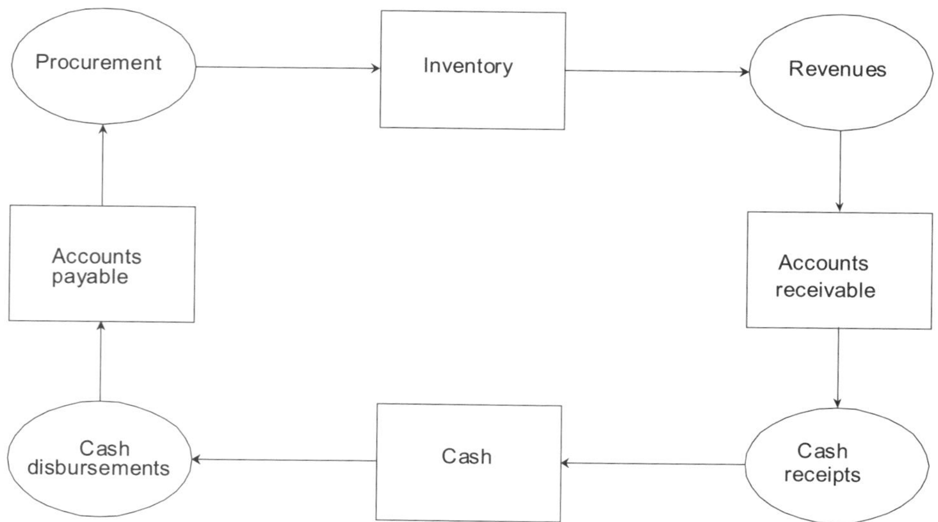

Figure 2.5 The value cycle in its most elementary form.

positions. As in every cycle, there is no natural starting or ending point. Hence, a discussion of this model starts with an arbitrairy choice. We will start with purchases.

When initiating purchase transactions, at least two positions will be directly influenced: inventories as well as accounts payable increase. If there are inventories, sales transactions can take place. Sales transactions lead to an increase in accounts receivable. If cash is received from customer accounts receivable, that money can be used to pay accounts payable, as a result of which accounts payable decrease.

Segregation of Duties

In organizations, several types of *division of labour* may occur. There is vertical division of labour taking place between hierarchical levels in organizations, based on the premises that there are managers and subordinates, and that managers have a maximum *span of control* forcing them to delegate authority to their subordinates. There is also horizontal division of labour taking place between peers, which is based on the premise that division of labour must be efficient, and hence tasks must be allocated to workers who have a comparative advantage in executing these assigned tasks because of their knowledge or skills compared with other workers. This type of division of labour usually puts functional processes at the heart of the organization. These functional processes take place within specialized departments like sales, purchasing, warehouse, human resource management, and production. Another type of division of labour is based on the premise that every form of division of labour must contribute to the accomplishment of internal control goals. Here, the functional processes themselves are not at the heart of the organization, but the *control* of these functional processes is. In the value cycle, as depicted in Figure 2.5, the following division of labour can be identified: procurement, inventory keeping, revenues (sales), maintaining accounts receivable, cash collection, custody of cash, cash disbursement, and maintaining accounts payable. Here we arrive at a division of labour that is based on an internal control criterion: segregation of duties. It is based on the creation of opposed interests between departments or employees. This seems contradictory with every form of organization, in that organizing implies striving for cooperation by creating shared goals in order to limit dysfunctional behaviour. However, both points of view (efficient division of labour and internal control) need not be conflicting, and, when they are, a cost–benefit analysis should resolve the conflict; for example, personnel expenses increase because the principle of segregation of duties induces creation of a function with very limited tasks. Such a function may have very limited direct value added with respect to the accomplishment of the formulated organizational goals. It may even be negative because the *out-of-pocket expenses* will increase. However, there may be an indirect effect because the *opportunity costs* resulting from segregation of duties may decrease. Consider an organization that has combined the buying and sales functions because buying requires a thorough knowledge of the sales market. The buyer/seller now has the opportunity to start a *shop within the shop*. The opportunity costs involved here are forgone revenues because the buyer/seller creates a separate flow of goods and money the profits of which flow in to his private account instead of the organization account. So, the opportunity costs and out-of-pocket expenses must be considered simultaneously when deciding whether or not to create segregation of duties. Eventually, this may lead to segregrated buying and selling functions, even if the resulting tasks are too limited for two separate full-time employees.

Segregation of duties

A wholesaler has combined its purchasing and quality-control functions because both require highly technical knowledge. From an efficiency point of view, this is acceptable. However, from an internal control point of view, two functions that should actually be separated are combined. When considering the task normally given to a purchasing department, it can easily be understood that an opposed interest is eliminated here because the purchasing department should buy goods at the lowest possible prices while taking the quality of the goods into consideration. If the purchasing function is not segregated from the quality-control function, there is a risk that this (combined) department buys at minimum prices without considering the quality of the goods received. If these functions were segregated, then the following would hold:

- the interest of the purchasing department is to buy at minimum prices;
- the interest of the quality control department is to detect defective or inferior goods;
- the purchasing department would consider the minimum quality level of the goods and would buy better quality at higher prices.

By creating opposed interests, a contribution is made to the validity and completeness of the records of the transfer of goods between business departments or between a business department and customers or other external parties; for example, the plant manager attempts to maximize production. Eventually, he may report a greater amount of goods being produced and transferred to the warehouse than the actual amount. On the other hand, the warehousing department will eventually attempt to report less goods received than actually took place. If there is a control function that retrospectively detects errors in the relationship between flows of goods and cash flow as represented by the value cycle (reconciling the production report with the receiving report), then both departments will probably be encouraged to report the actual amount. If, nevertheless, an error is detected by the control function, then information is required as to which of the two departments made a recording error. This information is readily available if accountability has been established on the goods transfer. *Establishing accountability* implies that the person who receives values puts his signature on a move ticket by means of which he indicates he has received the goods in the right quantity and quality.

Segregation of duties generally implies the creation of five functions:

- authorization;

- custody;
- recording;
- controlling;
- execution.

In the preceding examples, some functions were introduced. In terms of segregation of duties, the purchasing department and the sales department have an authorization function because they can commit the business to external parties. The warehouseman has a custody function because he is responsible for the safeguarding of inventories. The quality controller has a controlling function. The plant has an execution function because it is the site where production takes place. The recording function can be recognized in each of the functions; for example, the purchasing department records purchase orders, the sales department records sales orders, the storekeeper records the physical inventory, the quality controller records the number of products accepted or rejected, and the plant manager records the quantity and quality manufactured. The recording function can be physically found in financial administration (this is the bookkeeping department). Here, all decentralized recordings are gathered and processed. An important point when considering each function is that in every function there are elements of execution. It should be noted that only the primary tasks are of importance when determining which department or functionary has an execution function.

If a combination is made of the concepts of segregation of duties and the value cycle, it can easily be understood that each transition from event to position and from position to event ideally involves a segregated function. The recording function is not recognizable in the value cycle, yet, if all decentralized recordings are gathered in that function, it should be placed in the centre of the value cycle. Thus, a value cycle is created that explicitly considers segregation of duties and a separate recording function. This value cycle is represented in Figure 2.6. The organization structure could be overlaid on this figure. The recording function would then be performed by the financial administration. In this view, the financial administration is the pivot on which the whole organizational performance hinges. Hence, organizing the administrative processes could be a critical success factor for a business.

Reconciliations and Control Totals (RCTs)

The relationship between flows of goods and cash flow usually can be quasi-mathematically represented by means of so-called BIDE formulas: the value at the beginning of the period (B) + the increase during the period (I) $-/-$ the decrease during the period (D) = the value at the end of the period (E). However, the value cycle is more than just a set of independent relationships as they appear in the various BIDE formulas. Two individual BIDE formulas have at least one event or position in common; for example, the relationship between the inventory at the

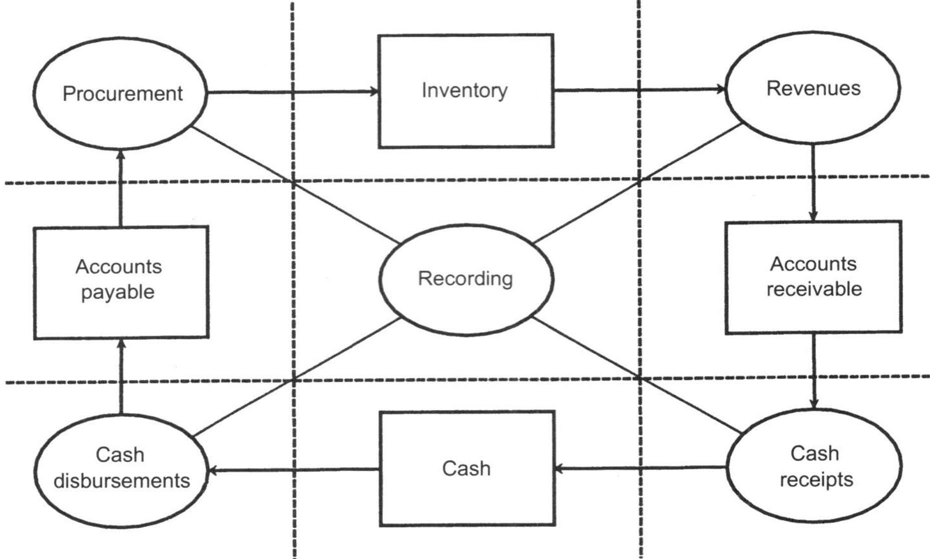

Figure 2.6 Value cycle with segregation of duties and recording function.

beginning and purchases, sales, and inventory at the end overlaps with the relationship between accounts receivable at the beginning and sales, cash receipts, and accounts receivable at the end because the event 'sales' is present in both relationships. Basically, there are four BIDE formulas which can be derived from the value cycle:

Opening balance inventory	+	Purchases	−/−	Revenues	=	Ending balance inventory
Opening balance cash	+	Cash receipts	−/−	Cash disbursements	=	Ending balance cash
Opening balance accounts payable	+	Purchases	−/−	Cash disbursements	=	Ending balance accounts payable
Opening balance accounts receivable	+	Revenues	−/−	Cash receipts	=	Ending balance accounts receivable

Because the control totals, as represented in these equations, are calculated in different departments or are under the responsibility of different employees, they are powerful instruments in any system of checks and balances. Since every event occurs in two equations, a so-called network of control totals can be constructed. In Figure 2.7, a network of control totals of a trade organization is depicted. Besides the control totals in this network, a wide variety of other control totals can be calculated for checking purposes; for example, subtracting the sum of the credits from the sum of the debits in a payroll clearing account, calculating the column totals in a trial balance, adding redundant data to an electronically input, stored, or processed amount, or calculating the total number of available man-hours billable to customers. Control totals are calculated for making reconciliations between the control total and some observed realization. Some examples of reconciliations are presented in the following boxes.

Payroll clearing account

The payroll clearing account is debited for the amount of gross pay, the cash account is credited for the amount of net pay, the amounts of the various deductions (e.g. taxes, social security premiums, and pension premiums) are credited to specific liability accounts. From the cost allocation process, labour costs are distributed to various labour expense categories (sales personnel, production personnel, accounting personnel, human-resource management personnel, etc.) by debiting the specific labour expense accounts and crediting the payroll clearing account. Typically, the journal entries would be:

Account	Debit	Credit
Payroll clearing account	*X*	
Cash		*A*
Income taxes to be paid		*B*
Social security premiums to be paid		*C*
Pension premiums to be paid		*D*
Costs of sales personnel	*P*	
Costs of production personnel	*Q*	
Costs of accounting personnel	*R*	
Costs of HRM personnel	*S*	
Payroll clearing account		*Y*

The reconciliation made here is that between the amount credited to the payroll clearing account and the amount debited to that account, so *Y* should equal *X*. This check is called a *zero balance check*.

Trial balance

A trial balance is the copy of all general ledger account balances into one list. It is called trial balance because it serves as an instrument that allows accounting personnel to check if the debits balance the credits. So, the reconciliation made here is that between the sum of the debited amounts and the sum of the credited amounts.

Redundant Data

When inputting sales orders, a clerk manually calculates the total amount ordered and inputs the total after he has input the separate orders. A programmed procedure calculates the same total amount ordered on the basis of the separate orders, as input by the clerk. Manually and automatically calculated totals are called *batch totals*. The reconciliation made here is that between the manually calculated batch total and the batch total as calculated by a programmed procedure.

Another example of redundant data is that extra data is added to a message sent by means of electronic data interchange (EDI). Suppose the number 123456 is electronically sent via the local area network of an organization. In order to verify that this message has not been damaged during data transportation, a seventh digit computed from the other six digits (following any agreed on algorithm) is added to the original number. This extra digit is called a *check digit*. A programmed procedure at the recipient's computer calculates the same check digit on the basis of the received number. The reconciliation made here is called a *check digit verification*.

Billable Man-hours

A public accounting firm sells man-hours. To do so, it hires qualified personnel like CPAs and accountants. An employee who has a full-time labour contract has to work 40 hours a week. This is the number of hours this employee should be present at work, denoted as shoptime. In a public accounting firm, being present at work may take the form of visiting a client or being present in one of the offices of the firm. The number of hours the employee spends on jobs for clients will normally be billed to these clients. This is called jobtime. The reconciliation made here is that between jobtime and shoptime, or, briefly, the *job/shoptime check*. Differences must be analysed and traced back to activities other than client-related jobs (indirect man-hours like those spent on continuing education, vacation, or illness).

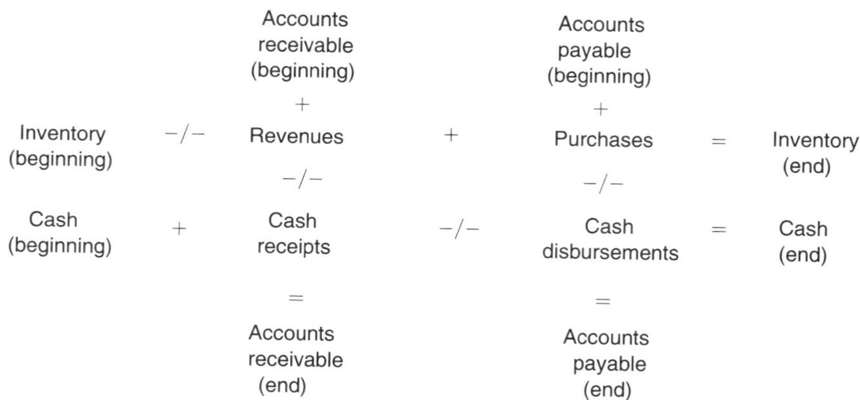

Figure 2.7 A network of control totals.

From synthesis of the value cycle and its related concepts, two basic laws emerge:

- The law of the relationship between offers and yields; for example, when raw materials, man-hours and machine hours are transformed into finished products, a normative amount of finished products can be calculated from the operations list in conjunction with the bill of materials. This normative yield can be used to perform analytical review procedures on the performance report of the production department by comparing realized production with normative production.
- The law of the relationship between positions and events; for example, the cash position changes as a result of cash receipts, which is an event.

These laws form the basis of every system of reconciliations and control totals.

Internationally, the value cycle and embedded control totals have not yet received much attention. As a matter of fact, Anglo-Saxon literature makes no mention of the term at all. However, McCarthy – the godfather of REA accounting – developed a model that resembles the value cycle to a great extent. Whereas the value cycle is still based on the double-entry bookkeeping model, McCarthy's model goes one step further by rejecting the idea of having accruals and deferrals built into the accounting system. Whereas the practical relevance of the value cycle may be questionable, we believe that it is an important didactical model that provides great insight into some basic AIS concepts. Furthermore, international literature and AIS practices accept the relevance of the concept of segregation of duties, which makes a discussion of the value cycle even more relevant because it underlies segregation of duties.

Typology of Organizations

An organization can be considered a unique collection of cycles. Determining threats, the exposure of each threat, and the potential controls for each threat per cycle is the common approach to risk analysis in AIS problems. Although this may seem an adequate approach, it has one major flaw because the idiosyncrasy of the collection of cycles within one organization results in different threats, exposures, and controls than the sum of individual threats, exposures, and controls per cycle. Therefore, a *typology of organizations* must be developed on the basis of internal control criteria. Similar to the cycle approach, threats, exposure, and controls are determined. However, in the typology approach, they are not determined per cycle but for each type of firm.

The basic idea behind a typology of organizations is to develop a framework for classifying organizations or parts of organizations in such a way that for each type a set of standard internal control measures can be derived. Hence, by determining the category to which an organization belongs, a basis is created for an internal control description. Such an approach gives space to a focus at organization-specific (i.e. not category-specific) threats, exposures, and controls.

We can think of many different typologies of organization. However, considering the importance of the value cycle and its related concepts for internal control, a classification based on the relationship between the flow of goods and cash flow is most suitable. The main classification criterion, then, is the coherence between the various elements of the value cycle. The stronger this coherence, the higher a specific organization is positioned within the typology of organizations. Because every organization has a flow of money, but not every organization has a flow of goods, the two main categories distinguished in the typology of organizations are organizations with a dominant flow of goods and organizations without a dominant flow of goods. The typology presented here has many similarities to some well-known industry classifications. However, the main difference is that industry classifications are based on some kind of natural distinction between organizations without an unambiguous choice for any criterion, whereas our classification is based on just such a criterion. The typology of organizations that will be used throughout the book is depicted in Table 2.1.

It should be stressed that most organizations fall into more than one category. The recommended approach is first to identify the revenue categories, and subsequently to determine the type of firm for each revenue category; for example, a governmental institution that issues passports and hence collects legal charges bears features of organizations with massive data processing. When this governmental institution hires a contractor to build a library in order to exploit it, it bears features of a organization that puts non-specific space and time capacity at its clients' disposal.

The next two chapters will discuss the main threats, the exposures, and the internal control measures for each of the two main categories of organization: organizations with a dominant flow of goods and organizations without a dominant flow of goods. Since internal control jargon is pervasive throughout these chapters and the remainder of the book, and mainly to avoid confusion about semantic matters, we will conclude this chapter with a brief discussion of some basic internal control terminology. In addition, we present a framework for representing solutions to AIS problems in the Appendix to this chapter.

Basic Internal Control Terminology

Parties involved in AIS must understand each other's language. So, there must be agreement on the terminology used and its meaning. As a matter of fact, the academic literature on AIS more and more recognizes the need for an ontology to serve as the directory and dictionary of the discipline. This section tries to resolve some of the terminological issues without pretending to develop an AIS ontology. The following control instruments are discussed:

- detailed versus total checks;
- direct versus indirect checks;

Table 2.1 Typology of organizations (adapted from Starreveld *et al.* 1998)

Organizations with a dominant flow of goods	Trade organizations	Organizations that mainly sell to other organizations	E.g. wholesalers in groceries, wholesalers in electrotechnical equipment for the contracting industry
		Organizations that mainly sell to final consumers	E.g. supermarkets, department stores, drugstores
	Production organizations	Mass-production organizations (including agrarian and extractive organizations)	E.g. brickyards, oil organizations, consumer electronics manufacturers, breweries, car manufacturers, and – in the agrarian and extractive area – forestry, mining organizations, fishing industry, agriculture
		Piece-production organizations	E.g. house-building contractors, airplane builders, shipyards, utility industry
Organizations without a dominant flow of goods	Organizations with a limited flow of goods	Organizations with a limited flow of own goods	E.g. restaurants, bars, publishers of newspapers
		Organizations with a limited flow of goods owned by third parties	Auctioneers, garage businesses, bicycle repair stores
	Organizations that put space and time capacity at their clients' disposal	Organizations that put specific space and time capacity at their clients' disposal	E.g. hospitals, hotels, mains, transportation firms, oil pipeline companies, airlines
		Organizations that put non-specific space and time capacity at their clients' disposal	E.g. swimming pools, cinemas, railroad organizations, libraries
	Organizations that put knowledge and skills at their clients' disposal	Organizations that sell man-hours	E.g. public accounting firms, law firms, cleaning organizations
		Organizations with massive data processing	E.g. telephone providers, Internet providers, application service providers, pension funds, banks, insurance organizations
	Governmental institutions		

- negative versus positive checks;
- formal versus material checks;
- policy control;
- expectations control;
- standards control;
- compatibility control;
- execution control;
- efficiency control;
- progress control;
- custody control;
- self-checking.

As can be observed from this listing, the terms 'control' and 'checks' are both used to refer to control instruments. What actually happens when controlling or checking activities are employed is that an actual, realized position or event is compared with a standard. As we have seen, the terms that are typically used here are the German *ist* (what is) and *soll* (what should be); for example, posting to the individual customer account within the accounts receivable subsidiary ledger (*ist*) is compared with the individual contract in the contract register (*soll*), or realized period-to-date figures are compared with preceding years' period-to-date figures. Every control instrument is based on comparing *ist* and *soll*. In spite of the fact that these terms seem odd, they are appealing because they reduce the basic problem in controlling and checking to its most elementary form, namely comparing *ist* and *soll* and, if necessary, taking subsequent corrective action.

Period-to-date Figures

Sales or costs of sales may follow a seasonal pattern; for example, a producer of soft drinks will sell more during the summer than during the winter. Analytical review procedures that compare realized monthly sales (*ist*) with normative monthly sales (*soll*) as derived from one or more preceding periods will not be effective if the seasonal pattern is not considered. As a result, decision making may be flawed. Take the following case (× €1,000):

	Sales	*Cumulative*	*Costs of sales*	*Cumulative*	*Gross profit*	*Cumulative*
2000						
Spring	27,000	27,000	20,500	20,500	6,500	6,500
Summer	55,000	82,000	43,250	63,750	11,750	18,250
Fall	25,000	107,000	18,750	82,500	6,250	24,500
Winter	10,000	117,000	7,000	89,500	3,000	27,500

	Sales	*Cumulative*	*Costs of sales*	*Cumulative*	*Gross profit*	*Cumulative*
2001						
Spring	30,000	30,000	22,500	22,500	7,500	7,500
Summer	60,000	90,000	50,000	72,500	10,000	17,500
Fall	30,000	120,000	25,000	97,500	5,000	22,500
Winter	15,000	135,000	11,000	108,500	4,000	26,500

Comparing the 2001 fall sales with the 2001 summer sales would reveal that sales have gone down by 50%. However, since there is a seasonal pattern, it would be better to compare the 2001 cumulative fall sales with the 2000 cumulative fall sales. Performing this analytical review procedure reveals that sales have gone up by 12%. These cumulative figures are called year-to-date figures. This type of accumulation can be done for any period of time, leading to month-to-date or quarter-to-date figures.

Detailed versus Total Checks

Detailed checks may take place integrally or on a sample basis; for example, the population of customer accounts receivable may be checked by investigating each customer account separately (integral), or by investigating a sample of customer accounts. Total checks generally are more efficient than detailed checks because only totals of a population are investigated; for example, the population of customer accounts receivable is checked by investigating the coherence between the opening balance of the accounts receivable general ledger, revenues, cash receipts, and the ending balance of the accounts receivable general ledger. Figure 2.8 illustrates the difference between detailed and total checks.

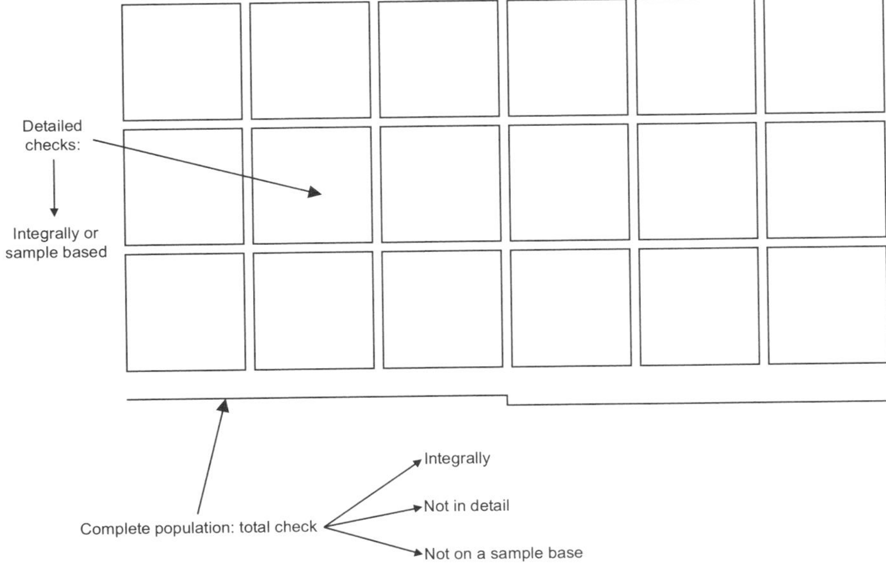

Figure 2.8 Detailed and total checks.

Direct versus Indirect Checks

Direct checks are applied on processes, whereas indirect checks are applied on outcomes of processes. This distinction is relevant because there is a pronounced relationship between the applicability of these checks and management level. Since direct checks are applied on processes, assignments, and procedures, and lower hierarchical levels are mainly controlled by specifying the tasks to be performed, these checks are especially applicable at the operational level. Indirect checks, as they are applied on outcomes of processes, are more oriented towards higher hierarchical levels because, here, specific task assignments are less prevalent. The higher the management level, the more degrees of freedom that exist when performing a task. Hence, indirect checks are especially applicable at the tactical and strategic management level; for example, performing a stocktaking or watching to see if a cleaning team work efficiently are direct checks, whereas reconciling the inventory listing with the goods receipt listing, and the picking list, or checking whether a reportedly cleaned office has been efficiently cleaned are indirect checks. Figure 2.9 illustrates the difference between direct and indirect checks.

Negative versus Positive Checks

A negative check is aimed at the completeness of a registration whereas a positive check is aimed at the validity of a registration. The terms 'negative' and 'positive' refer to the starting point of the tests. In a negative check, the starting point is not the registration itself but a complementary registration (e.g. an independently prepared cash receipts journal). In a positive check, the starting point is the registration itself (e.g. the balance due customers accounts receivable list). Figure 2.10 illustrates the difference between negative and positive checks.

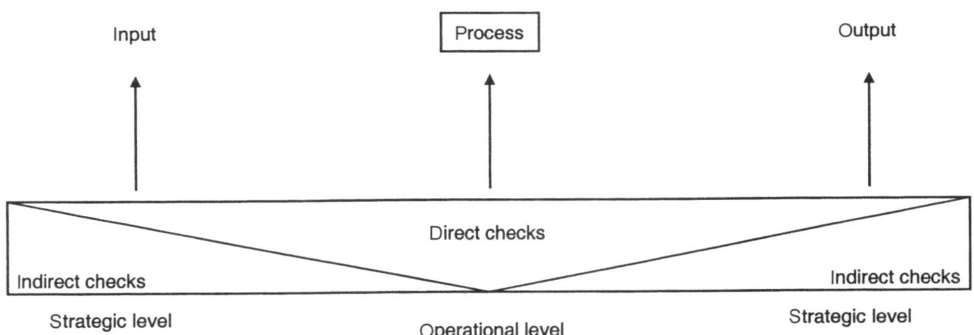

Figure 2.9 Direct and indirect checks.

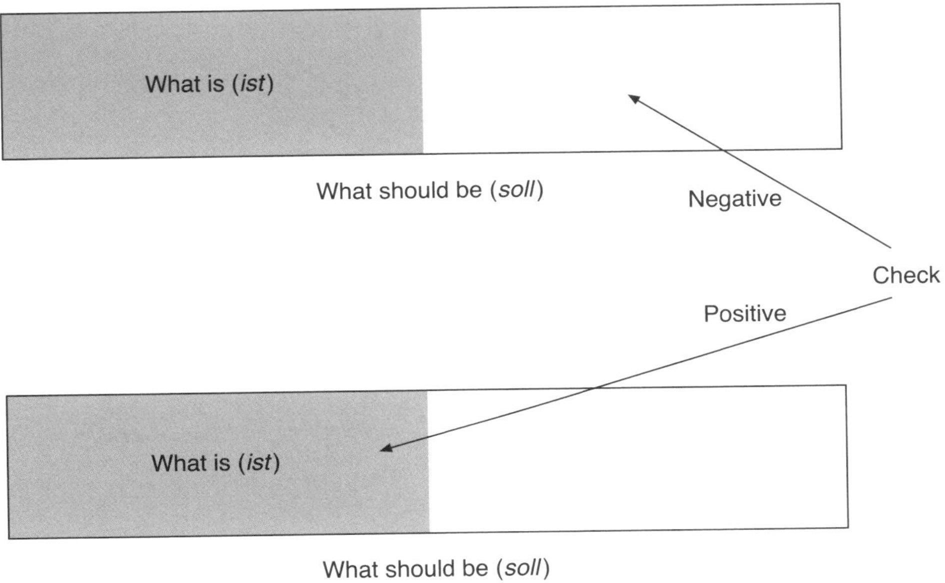

Figure 2.10 Negative and positive checks.

Formal versus Material Checks

A formal check is aimed at testing the agreement between procedures and a registration or provided information. Here, the *soll* position is made up of procedures which are issued by means of directives. A material check is aimed at testing the agreement between actual positions or events and a registration or provided information. Here the *soll* position is made up of actual positions or events. In both formal and material checks, the *ist* position is created by the registration or provided information; for example, a formal check would be to test whether the warehouseman's signature is on a receiving report, whereas a related material check would be to test whether or not the recorded inventory opening balance equals the inventory according to the physical count. Figure 2.11 illustrates the difference between formal and material checks.

Policy Control

Policy control is aimed at assessing whether or not the starting points for established policies are acceptable. Note that this does not mean that a check is done if the one and only correct policy has been chosen. Rather, it is a marginal test. Since policy generally is made at higher hierarchical levels within organizations, policy control deals with decision making at the strategic and tactical level; for example, a municipality has formulated the policy that city grounds will be privatized within the next

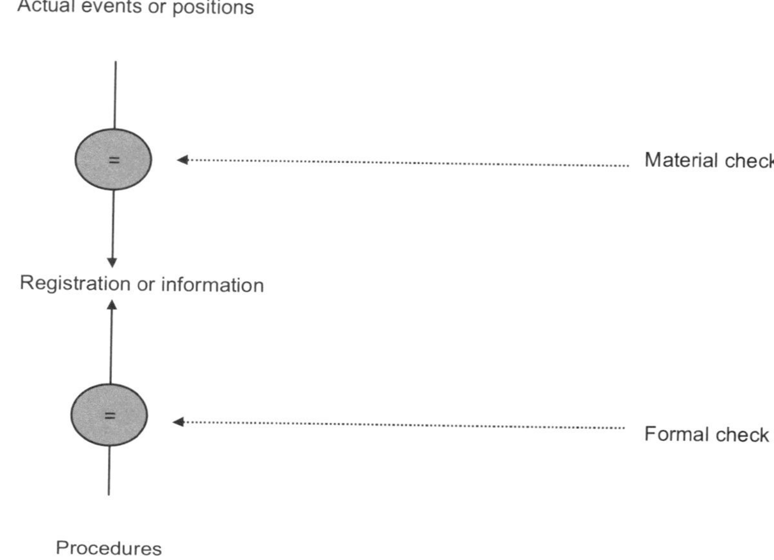

Figure 2.11 Formal and material checks.

25 years. Policy control will include a check on the desirability of such a privatization by citizens. After 25 years, when, indeed, the city grounds have been privatized, it may appear that this policy was good or not. However, this is not an issue in policy control.

Expectations Control

Expectations control is aimed at assessing the fairness of expectations and calculations on the basis of which policy has been formulated; for example, in warfare a government may expect the enemy to deploy biological weapons. Hence, the policy decided on is to mobilize all its citizens to purchase gas masks. Expectations control assesses whether this expectation is realistic by using intelligence to investigate the enemy's ability to produce and deploy biological weapons on a large scale.

Standards Control

Standards control is aimed at assessing the acceptability of standards. Before a standard (or any other norm) is used as a *soll* position in a control activity, the acceptability of this standard must be assessed. Such an assessment typically checks whether calculations are mathematically correct, whether all the variables to be included indeed have been included, and whether the assumptions made are acceptable; for example, a purchasing budget is formulated in order to control procurement activities by the buying department. Before such a budget is approved by management and the other parties involved, it is checked to see whether this budget is based on the right algorithm considering the budget methodology to be employed (fixed or variable budgeting), whether all the buying activities are quantified in the budget, and whether the buying prices used are realistic.

Competency Control

Competency control is aimed at assessing whether decision making is done by authorized functionaries within the organization. This type of control is often straightforward since it mainly involves determining who made a decision, and checking that her name is on an official list of authorized persons. Such a list usually contains signatures and initials and, hence, is denoted a signature list; for example, when a person signs off for a payment to be effectuated, the financial administration department (by comparing the signature on the payment order with the signature list) check to see if this person is authorized to sign off for this payment in relation to the budget involved.

Execution Control

Execution control is aimed at assessing the quality of the execution of the assigned tasks performed by subordinates on different hierarchical levels; for example, a foreman in a production department closely supervises his workers in order to increase production efficiency, whereas the production planning department periodically compares the production plans with actual production. Both are controls on the efficiency of workers in the production department.

Efficiency Control

Efficiency control is aimed at assessing the degree to which operations have been optimized in order to maximize operational economy and effectiveness; for example, a business performance report is prepared that indicates actual raw material usage, man-hour usage, and machine hours usage in relation to applicable standards. Applicable standards may be developed as follows. Starting off from the actual production quantity, the normative usage of raw materials, man-hours, and machine hours can be calculated and presented along with actual usage. Because this method calculates the applicable standards from actual production, and hence works backward, it is called the *retrograde method* for standard determination.

Progress Control

Progress control is aimed at the continuity of processes with respect to efficiency; for example, when a manager delegates authority to a subordinate, she may want to perform progress control on the task fulfilment by the subordinate in order to check whether he undertakes the necessary actions and does so to the best of his capabilities.

Custody Control

Custody control is aimed at safeguarding assets; for example, a typical internal control activity that serves as a custody control is stocktaking performed by the warehouseman in cooperation with an independent control functionary such as an administrative clerk or someone with a designated internal control role.

Self-checking

The checking done by a person on his own work, under his own responsibility, is denoted as self-checking; for example, a person makes a manual calculation and recalculates it following exactly the same procedure for checking purposes, or a person enters data into the information system and compares the overview of these data, as shown on the screen, with his source documents. Some authors consider self-checking the opposite of internal control. However, we believe that, within the broad notion of internal control as brought forward by the COSO report, self-checking is an intrinsic element thereof; for example, self-checking will be enhanced if the control environment improves, but it can also be found in procedures which support control activities.

Chapter Cases

Case 2.1 Liability Position Three Organizations (adapted from NIVRA)

Provide a description (in just a few sentences) of the differences with respect to the administrative organization between the following businesses. Also indicate the causes of these differences.

Wholesaler
A wholesaler sells many articles. These articles are purchased from many vendors. Payment of these vendors must be made within 30 days after receipt of the goods. If payment is made within eight days then a discount of 2% is granted. If payment is made after 30 days then interest of 1% per month is charged. About 25% of the vendors provide a bonus on the basis of annual sales to the wholesaler. This bonus increases progressively with sales. Goods received are stored in a warehouse.

Fruit and Vegetables Auction House
A fruit and vegetables auction house processes 1,000 to 2,500 parcels per day (depending on the season) from about 5,000 farmers and growers. The goods are supplied in uniform boxes, which are owned by the auction house and for which a deposit must be made by the vendors. The farmers and growers receive 90% of the auction revenues and the full deposit that they made for the boxes. Billing takes place one day after the auction. Payment must be made at the eight days after the auction.

Employment Agency
An employment agency has about 1,000 employees who are hired by its clients. These temporary employees (temps) are paid weekly. Payments for assignments that end before a week is completed are made 1 day after. Payments consist of the wages, taxes, social security premiums, and, for about half of the temps, pension premiums to various pension funds. The taxes and social security premiums are paid at the end of each quarter. The pension premiums are paid quarterly in advance on the basis of the estimated sum of wages. At the end of the quarter, a postcalculation is made. Payment deficits are penalized by 15% of the deficit. Payment surpluses are paid back without interest.

Case 2.2 Flow of Goods (adapted from NIVRA)

Provide a description (in just a few sentences) of the differences with respect to internal controls between the following businesses. Indicate the causes of these differences, the type of firm (typology of organizations), the differences in measurements points, and the differences in procedures.

Importer of Cars
An importer of cars sells one make in about 40 different models. Clients are consumers as well as businesses. A warranty is given per car. Only standard models are held in stock. Other models can be delivered within one month. The importer has negotiated a credit term of two months with the manufacturer. Consumer accounts receivable are paid on a cash basis and business accounts receivable on account (payment within 14 days after receipt of the invoice).

Wholesaler in Groceries
A wholesaler in groceries sells thousands of different articles. Its buyers are retailers who all have a creditplate issued by the wholesaler. That creditplate is used to record all sales to these retailers. Payments are made at a cash register that can read the creditplate and that produces an invoice for each sales transaction.

Packing Activities of a Big Beer Brewery
A brewery delivers its beer to bars and restaurants in barrels. These barrels remain at the buyer's premises between about one week and one month. The deposit to be made by the buyer for each barrel is €250.

Case 2.3 Electro Inc.

Electro Inc. is an installer of all kinds of electrotechnical supplies in the house- and utility-building contractors industry. Most of the contracts are based on fixed fees, in combination with clauses about additional and subtractive work. However, contracts may be based on actual costs.

When the production capacity of the company is insufficient, subcontractors are hired. The contracts with subcontractors are based on actual costs. The amounts due are settled at the moment of work completion by the subcontractor.

The company employs about 100 people. The management team consists of a sales manager and a technical manager. The internal organization is as follows:

- administration and automation;
- works;
- order department;
- production planning department;
- billing department;
- procurement and warehousing.

Order Acceptance

The order department receives enquiries from potential customers. For every enquiry, a detailed budget calculation is made.

Planning

When a customer has decided to place an order with the company, the production planning department develops a global capacity usage plan and a production scheme. Furthermore, this department issues production orders which demarcate the start of the execution stage of a project.

Execution

Every project is staffed by mounters and general foremen. The general foremen are in charge on small works. On big works, the general foremen are accountable to project managers because of the complex control problems that may arise here. The general foremen are responsible for the functioning of a system of jobtime tickets and move tickets. Materials are stored in the general warehouse, which is safeguarded by the warehouse manager. He may only move goods from the warehouse when an official materials requisition is made. There are 20 vans. Each of these has a fixed amount of high-value equipment and materials on board.

Procurement

Purchasing is based on fixed contracts in order to minimize inventory levels. The general foremen and project managers are authorized to place orders at will with a limited number of wholesalers in electronics equipment.

Billing

Billing of fixed-fee amounts takes place in four terms. At the moment the contract is agreed 10%, after completion of chasing work (making holes and grooves in walls) 40%, at the moment of initial completion 45%, and at the moment of final completion (after the responsible authorities have approved the installation) the remaining 5%. Additional work is billed separately after final completion. Subtractive work is made payable after final completion by means of credit memos. If a customer has unsettled accounts, clearing takes place. If a customer does not have any unsettled accounts, Electro Ltd does not undertake any action but waits for a signal from that customer.

Billing of actual-cost contracts takes place in three terms. At the moment the contract is agreed 10% (of the budgeted costs), at the moment of initial completion 40% (of the budgeted costs), and at the moment of final completion the remaining amount on the basis of actual costs.

Administration and Automation

The IT environment may be labelled computer significant (i.e. moderately dependent on the continuity of the information system).

Assignment

Provide a general normative description of the internal controls.

Appendix: Representing Solutions to AIS problems

Introduction

When solving AIS problems, a distinction must be made between contemporary or traditional approaches to representing solutions. This appendix describes both approaches and explains the links between them.

Contemporary Approaches

In contemporary approaches to representing solutions to AIS problems, the following stepwise approach can be adhered to:

1 Identification of threats.
2 Assessment of the exposure of these threats.
3 Determination of the position in a framework.
4 Determination of applicable control concepts.
5 Determination of applicable control instruments.

Threats

Threats may stem from an internal or an external source. External threats concern those factors that cannot directly be influenced by the organization or that are difficult to predict. They may be caused by bottlenecks as well as forgone opportunities. Internal threats concern weaknesses within the internal organization. Since internal control is part of the internal organization, internal control weaknesses are internal threats. A bottleneck is a negative event or state that cannot be directly influenced by the organization. The only way to deal with bottlenecks is to try to be as informed as possible and react adequately if such a negative event or state emerges. Examples of bottlenecks are when there is a seasonal pattern that causes erratic movements of the market; a business has a cost–leadership strategy whereas the costs are partly uncontrollable because of currency fluctuations; a local government issues a protectionist law; or a country gets involved in war. A forgone opportunity is a positive event or state that cannot be influenced directly by the organization. Here, strategic uncertainties that may be favorable to the organization are at stake. If the organization does not react properly to an emerging opportunity, competitors may gain competitive advantage. The monetary losses caused by foregone opportunities are *opportunity costs*; for example, a business fails to enter the e-business market and hence loses market share; a producer of consumer electronics develops an innovative product but fails to market it properly; or a competitor of a firm continuously succeeds in being one step ahead of this firm in designing new products. Internal weaknesses are negative events or states that can be influenced directly by the organization. Weaknesses in internal controls may stem from a great variety of sources, such as unsatisfactory pairings of duties, insufficient control

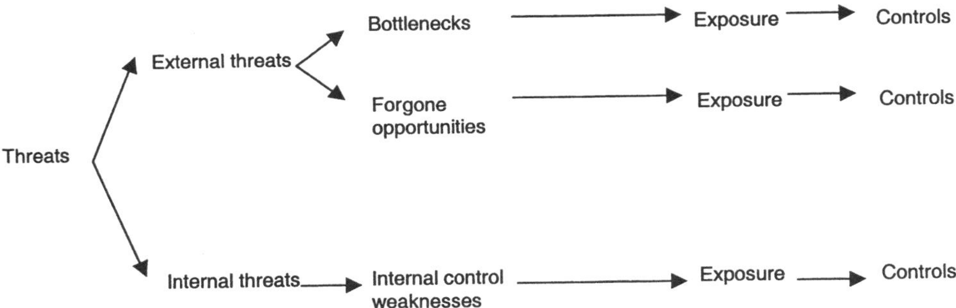

Figure 2.12 The relationship between threats, exposure, and control instruments.

procedures, badly motivated personnel, lack of goal congruence, or faulty information systems.

Exposure

Exposure to a threat is the potential adverse effect should that threat become a reality; for example, if a business fails to react to changing market conditions, its market share may decrease. Ultimately, the firm may go bankrupt. So, the exposure may be somewhere on the continuum between losing market share and going bankrupt. Quantification of the exposure is generally preferable to making a trade-off between control effectiveness and economy. However, from a practical point of view, this is often not possible; for example, management often does not know how much the market share will go down, and it often does not know the exact relationship between bankruptcy and declining market share.

Figure 2.12 depicts the relationship between threats, exposures, and control instruments.

Position

The position of threats in a coherent framework enables a structured discussion of the exposures and controls related to this threat. Hence, there is an increased likelihood that identified threats are complete and well thought out. Chapter 5 introduces a framework that may serve this role.

Concepts

A conceptual approach to AIS problems paves the way for efficient solutions. Here, efficiency, especially, applies to making use of existing control frameworks (see Chapter 8), and enabling a concentrical approach towards solutions where rationalizations are made on the basis of a top–down – generic to specific and global to detailed – approach. Following this approach, the essence of AIS problems can be pinpointed more accurately.

Control Instruments

The choice of applicable control instruments is the most complex part of the approach to solving AIS problems from an integrative control perspective, as outlined in this section. The instruments may be management controls, internal controls, or information controls. Management controls pertain to operations, information provision, and ICT infrastructure. To define applicable management controls, and be as accurate and complete as possible in doing so, some kind of framework must be used. The objects-of-control framework as developed by Merchant (1982, 1998) is appealing because of its simplicity and its practical applicability. This framework is discussed in Chapter 8. Besides management controls, the – from an AIS viewpoint – more traditional internal controls and information controls are discussed throughout the book.

There are different types of AIS problem. The basic tenet of a managerial approach to AIS is that strategic issues, ICT issues, and AIS core concepts are considered simultaneously. The next section discusses a more traditional and, hence, technocratic approach to the identification and solution of AIS problems. We will refer to this approach as an isolated accounting and administrative organizational viewpoint on AIS problems.

Traditional Approaches

Each type of AIS problem requires a certain type of solution (Figure 2.13). In addition, AIS problems may also give rise to a discussion of theoretical issues that, in one way or another, are related to the case in hand. The types of questions related to these issues are not addressed in this section because they can be very diverse and, therefore, cannot efficiently be captured in a general framework.

Information Requirements of Management

There are two different types of AIS problem within this category:

- a listing of information needs;
- an analysis of information needs.

A *listing* is less comprehensive than an *analysis*. The person who is solving the case must try to put himself in the place of the management and, thus, try to think of what information is needed for decision making and accountability. There is no need to give arguments about why certain information elements are relevant or to make a distinction between different hierarchical levels (unless explicitly formulated as the problem to be solved). On *analysing* issues regarding the information needs of management, it is important to make a distinction between strategic, tactical, and operational management levels. These information needs must be analysed separately at each management level and for each department or function. Also, for each information element, whether it is in a listing or in an analysis, the *soll* and *ist*

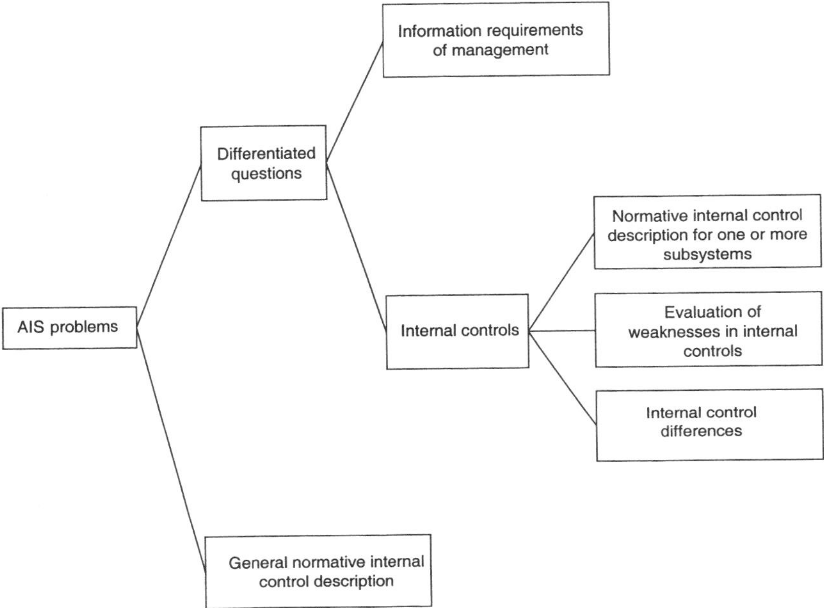

Figure 2.13 A decomposition of types of traditional AIS problem.

positions must be described. It is usually helpful to use some kind of standard framing; for example, 'The following information is needed for comparison with budgets, preceding periods' figures and *year-to-date figures*: . . .'.

Before starting any description of information needs, the information analyst must ask himself the following questions:

1 At which level is information required?
2 What information is needed for the user to make the right decisions?
3 What tests may be performed by the user in order to assess the reliability of the information?
4 Who is able to provide the required information?
5 What is the required frequency of information provision?

A general analysis of information requirements should at least consist of information about the following issues:

- Planning and budgeting;
- finance (e.g. debt/equity or liquidity ratios);
- order position;
- purchasing;

- inventory;
- production;
- selling;
- Return on investments.

From the contingency factors discussed in this chapter, the type of organization and the industry in which it operates are specific focal points in this analysis.

Sometimes the information requirements of specific functions or departments are required; for example, CEO, CFO, head of the production department, head of the production planning department, head of the buying department, etc. Be as specific as possible in describing the information needs of these persons.

Questions about Internal Controls

When addressing issues regarding internal controls, three types of case are encountered:

- an internal control system that must be developed for a certain cycle or aspect of business (normative internal control description);
- an existing internal control system that contains some weaknesses (evaluation of weaknesses in internal controls);
- a comparison of internal control systems in different types of organization or in different organizational settings (internal control differences).

Normative Internal Control Description

Questions about normative internal control descriptions may be of the format: 'Provide a normative description of the internal control system for the transaction cycle ...'. Here, it is recommended that the proposed solution focuses on the following internal controls:

- specific segregation of duties;
- comprehensive coherence tests and other reconciliations;
- analytical review;
- procedures in headlines.

It is not necessary to describe the administrative and organizational conditions (see 'Governance Paradigm'). As a matter of fact, it is highly recommended not to describe these conditions when another question about a general normative internal control description is asked (again, see 'Governance Paradigm'). The above type of question may be supplemented by an indication of the assertion that is made; for example, 'Provide a normative description of the internal control system for the completeness of revenues' or '... for the validity of costs'. Clearly, these questions are more focused and hence may go into more detail.

Evaluation of Weaknesses in Internal Controls

Questions about the evaluation of internal control weaknesses may be along the lines of: 'Identify the internal control weaknesses in the current operation of the business for the transaction cycle ...'. In addition: 'for each control, offer possible solutions to the weaknesses'.

Internal Control Differences

In a changing environment, organizations have to adapt. Hence, it often happens that internal control systems must change; for example, the organization may go through a business process re-engineering programme as a result of which a functional orientation is traded for a process orientation. Obviously, the possibilities for typical internal control measures like segregation of duties and comprehensive coherence tests become less. The type of case that focuses on these changes may consist of two questions on the basis of the before and after images. Typically, a description of the current organization is first given by asking: 'Can you provide a normative internal control description?' Subsequently, a description of the transformed organization is given, and the same question is asked again.

A General Normative Internal Control Description

Often, traditional AIS problems contain only one question: 'Can you provide a general normative internal control description'. This question must be interpreted very broadly. The following must be distinguished:

1 the type of organization as derived from the typology of organizations;
2 threats;
3 administrative and organizational conditions;
4 description of internal controls;
5 managerial information.

Subsections 1, 2, and 3 are introductions to the actual solution that is provided in subsection 4. The underlying reason for ending an AIS case with a subsection on managerial information (Subsection 5) is that a thorough knowledge of the firm is needed before we can determine what information is required at each management level. When a full description of all controls is made, as is the case in a description of internal controls, then that knowledge is considered to be present. Furthermore, such a description mainly discusses measures at the transaction level. Therefore, an extension of analyses to management levels (strategic, tactical, and operational) must be presented at the end of the description to make a link to the managerial aspects of controlling businesses.

1 Type of Organization

The typology of organizations must be used when assessing internal controls because it gives an indication of the standard set of internal control measures that are generally in place in each type of organization. Determining the type of organization is especially important when making a description of the administrative organization that is tailored to the specific business in the case. Normally, a comprehensive description must be made within three hours, filling 10–15 pages of text. Therefore, it is impossible to tackle all aspects of a business within such a short time frame and thereby not exceed that number of pages of text. Indicating the type of firm implies that the set of internal controls that is inherent to that type of firm need not to be described. As a result, a (necessary) focus on specific internal control measures is possible. The *inherent* matters of attention must be mentioned (if explicitly mentioned at all) in this subsection and not in the section regarding threats. In many cases, there are more revenue categories. Each revenue category may be considered a different type of firm. Hence, for each revenue category, the type of firm must be determined.

2 Threats

In this subsection, the points for consideration that are specific for the business at hand must be mentioned. In a traditional AIS view, threats may only refer to internal control weaknesses, and not to bottlenecks or forgone opportunities. Most cases contain from five to nine points that must be addressed in the AIS description. It is important to present a brief list of matters for attention before making references to solutions. Remember, we are talking about AIS problems; therefore, any point for consideration mentioned must have an AIS solution.

3 Administrative and Organizational Conditions

Administrative and organizational conditions serve as disciplines for internal controls that will be described in subsection 4 (i.e. the actual solution). Here, attention must be paid to:

- Segregation of duties. To be mentioned are: the name of the function or department, tasks, and type of segregation (authorizing, custody, recording, controlling, and executing).
- Measures relating to automation (e.g. there are back-up and recovery procedures and there is a data processing hot site).
- Management guidelines (e.g. a voucher package, consisting of the purchase order,

the invoice and the bill of receipts is assembled together with the disbursement voucher).

- Budgets, price calculations, and standard unit costs (e.g. the standard unit costs are calculated on the basis of cost budgets).

Segregation of Duties

First, it is important to recognize the difference between a function and a task: a function may contain more than one task. Hence, when discussing segregation of duties for certain functions or departments, each function must be decomposed into tasks before mentioning any segregation of duties. In this general introductory section, three elements may be described:

- unsatisfactory pairings of duties that are present in the business (also mention them as a threat, provide a brief motivation and direction towards the solution here);
- segregation of duties that cannot be described under one of the functional headings in the actual solution to the problem;
- a general indication of functions that are to be segregated at a minimal level and functions that are essential to the business.

To avoid confusion among the readers of the AIS description, this part of the report should be concluded with the phrase: 'The specific segregation of duties will be described in Subsection 4'.

Measures Relating to Automation

There are four areas for consideration:

- physical security;
- preventing unauthorized alteration or use of records and programs;
- data integrity;
- Back-up and recovery.

It is highly recommended that these general 'umbrella' measures are addressed at this point in the analysis and not separately for each transaction cycle in the actual solution, because these measures are applicable for any transaction cycle. Examples of measures that can be mentioned here are: access controls via passwords and access control matrices, before and after totals or images, checking input reports, file back-ups on the basis of the grandfather–father–son principle, dataprocessing of hot sites, etc.

Management Guidelines

Generally, it is better to consider management guidelines as part of the actual solution for each transaction cycle. Only when very specific guidelines are required, which have an overall influence on the business process, should these guidelines be addressed in this section. Conclude with the phrase: 'The remaining management guidelines will be described in the Subsection 4.

Budgets, price calculations, and standard unit costs
Attention must be paid to the annual master budget and its composition. Standard unit costs are calculated on the basis of the annual cost budget and production norms. These standard unit costs form the basis for the cost price. When a specific cost allocation system is used, this must be addressed in this subsection together with its consequences for the administrative organization. Some relevant budgets are:

- sales budget;
- cost budget per department;
- cash budget;
- purchase budget;
- production budget.

We should always consider that management must approve budgets and standards and that administration often reports to management on any differences between the budgets and the actual results (business performance report).

4 Description of the Internal Controls

The description of internal controls contains the actual solution to the problem; therefore, it is important to follow a structure that matches the problem. A description may take place per department or per transaction cycle; for example, a logical transaction cycle-based order of presentation in a production firm is:

- purchasing;
- production;
- inventory;
- sales;
- human-resource management;
- financial management.

The former three can be in reverse order. A department-based order of presentation would be:

- buying department;
- production department and production planning department;

- warehousing;
- sales department;
- personnel department;
- administration and automation department.

Never introduce departments that are not mentioned in the case assignment. It often seems logical to create a separate internal control department. However, unless it is explicitly requested in the case assignment, do not create such a department. Within each section (department or transaction cycle), the description is very similar to the normative internal control description. The following elements should be discussed:

- Specific segregation of duties. Always mention the department, the tasks, and the type of segregation.
- Control totals and reconciliations. Be as complete as possible. Always mention the sources of data that are used in these control activities.
- Analytical review. Generally, the head of administration performs the analytical review tasks within the internal control system.
- Procedures in headlines. A procedure indicates how the activities within a process must be performed. Note that a process is a series of sequentially organized activities of input, processing, and output, which is aimed at a general or a specific organizational goal, an activity is a task within a specific process.

In addition, a listing of computer files and their records must be provided. For purposes of avoiding inconsistencies, it is recommended that this list is kept on a separate page as an appendix to the proposed internal control solution when making the AIS description.

5 Managerial Information

Managerial information may be described in a manner that is similar to the listing as mentioned in Subsection 3. Stereotypes should be avoided, implying that information needs described here must be tailored to the case at hand. The listing of information needs must be in a logical order.

Frequently Made Errors

Some factors may lead to flawed AIS descriptions and hence have a negative impact on AIS communications. They include:

- Plain theory is communicated instead of a specific solution to the case in hand. This can be referred to as the *theory-dominance* effect.
- Redundancy (e.g. segregation of duties in Subsection 3 is similar to segregation of duties in the description of the internal controls). This can be referred to as the *redundancy* effect.
- Repetition of the case without adding information regarding the solution. This can be referred to as the *case-repetition* effect.
- Wrong place in the report (e.g. solutions are contained in Subsections 1 and 2. This can be referred to as the *misclassification* effect.
- A practical observation is given instead of a normative optimum. This can be referred to as the *practice* effect.
- The solution does not match the identified threats. This can be referred to as the *inconsistency* effect.
- The solution is too expensive or unrealistic. This can be referred to as the *inefficiency* effect.
- The description of reconciliations and control totals and other key internal controls is incomplete. This can be referred to as the *incompleteness* effect.
- There are inconsistencies between computer files. This can be referred to as the *cross-reference* effect.
- Assumptions are made with respect to incomplete information about the organization's primary processes. This can be referred to as the *assumption* effect.
- Absence of a solution to the problem and, at the same time, presenting a solution to another problem. This can be referred to as the *epiphenomenality* effect.

ORGANIZATIONS WITH A DOMINANT FLOW OF GOODS

3

Confirmation of receivables and observation of inventories are generally accepted auditing procedures. The independent auditor who issues an opinion when he has not employed them must bear in mind that he has the burden of justifying the opinion expressed.

SAS No.1, section 331

After studying this chapter, the reader should be able to:

- Identify the threats and exposure to them that are inherent in trade organizations and production organizations.
- Develop a normative internal control system for trade organizations and production organizations (including agricultural and extractive organizations).
- Explain the role of a normative internal control system for each type of organization that is distinguished.
- Describe the information needs for primary processes within distinguished organizations.
- Explain how information flows must be controlled in each type of organization so as to provide information that is reliable and relevant for their functioning.
- Describe the tasks of the accounting department, the controller, and designated internal control roles with respect to the provision of reliable and relevant information.

Chapter Outline:

This chapter distinguishes trade organizations from production organizations (including agricultural organizations and extractive organizations). These organizations can all be characterized by the presence of a dominant flow of goods. The value cycle in these organizations is relatively tight when compared with organizations without a dominant flow of goods. As a result, reconciliations and control totals can be applied as control instruments. For each type of organization, the threats from an internal control point of view are identified. To determine what control measures need to be taken, the exposure of each threat is discussed.

Based on the threats and the associated exposure, a set of internal control measures is defined.

Introduction

This chapter discusses various types of organization, threats specific to these organizations, and the consequences of these threats for the internal controls that are to be put in place. The typology of organization is a useful tool for distinguishing the threats to various types of organization, as well as the necessary internal controls. Following the structure of the typology of organizations (see Table 2.1), this chapter discusses trade organizations and production organizations. Together, these organizations constitute the main category of organizations with a dominant flow of goods.

Trade Organizations

Trade organization activities involve purchasing goods, selling goods, and keeping goods in stock for some time without processing them. However, this does not mean that no value adding takes place. A further distinction can be made between trade organizations that predominantly sell to other organizations, on the one hand (wholesalers), and trade organizations that predominantly sell to final consumers on the other (retailers, such as supermarkets). An overview of identifiable threats for trade organizations is provided in Table 3.1. When a threat is specific to retail or wholesale, this is explicitly indicated; if it is of a more generic nature for trade organizations, then no further indication is given. Because we do not intend to provide an exhaustive discussion of controls in trade organizations, we will not elaborate on all the threats that can be identified, but will merely discuss some of the main issues that crop up.

For trade organizations, controlling the completeness of revenues relies heavily on the value cycle discussed in Chapter 2 and the relationships that can be distinguished in this cycle. The tailpiece of internal control in trade organizations is stocktaking. Stocktaking is necessary to determine whether the stock, as indicated by the perpetual inventory records, actually present in the warehouses. Therefore, proper stocktaking procedures are important controls to mitigate the threats of ready-to-sell products, unreliable inventory records, billing errors, and all the other threats that have an impact on the completeness of revenues; for example, during stocktaking, receipt or distribution of goods may not take place, since existing stock needs to be determined as accurately as possible. In addition, the stocktaker needs to be independent from the custody function. However, in his custody function, the warehouseman needs to be present during stocktaking as he is responsible for the inventory, and he needs to observe possible differences between the actual inventory and the inventory according to the perpetual inventory records.

Table 3.1 Threats to the achievement of internal control goals, their exposure, and main internal control solutions in trade organizations

Threats	*Exposure*	*Main internal controls*
'Ready to sell' products (retail)	Theft of products by employees	Supervision Periodical stocktaking
Shop within the shop (retail)	Loss of revenues	Segregation of duties between sales and purchasing Clear communication of purchasing and sales procedures to vendors and customers
Shifting of stocks between branches	Incompleteness of revenues is concealed	Simultaneous stocktaking
Many customers (retail)	Difficult to obtain detailed customer information	Adequate controls over the customer master files
Tight margins	Low fault tolerance	Tight controls over the inventory and accounts receivable Daily analytical review on margins at the product level
Creditworthiness of customers (wholesale)	Invalid sales and hence loss of revenues	Procedures for checking creditworthiness at customer acceptance
Shipping errors (wholesale)	Customer complaints Loss of revenues	Well-designed picking and packing lists Segregation of duties between warehouse and logistics department (sales department provides information to both) Adequate customer complaints procedures Reconciliation of sales orders, picking tickets, and invoice
Goods received are not in agreement with purchase orders	Unsaleable goods High costs of sales	Quality and quantity checks on receipt of goods Establish accountability by warehouse on receipt of goods Segregation of duties between warehouse and purchasing Reconciliation of purchase orders and receiving reports
Vendor invoices are not in accordance with goods received	High costs of sales	Quality and quantity checks on receipt of goods Establish accountability by warehouse on receipt of goods Segregation of duties between warehouse and accounts receivable function Reconciliation vendor invoices and receiving reports

Continued

Table 3.1(*cont.*)

Threats	*Exposure*	*Main internal controls*
Billing errors (wholesale)	Loss of revenues	Pre-billing Reconciling purchases with sales
Lapping (retail)	Loss of interest revenues and, eventually, potential complete loss of cash	Segregation of duties between recording, custody, and authorization with respect to cash Surprise cash counts Procedures with respect to rotating cash custody function Independently preparing follow-up letters to debtors (when lapping scheme applies to accounts receivable)
Capital intensive inventories (wholesale)	Continuity of business	Reliable and timely information about ordered and received goods, sold and delivered goods, and market expectations
Cash (retail)	Theft of cash	Segregation of duties between recording, custody, and authorization with respect to cash Surprise cash counts
Accuracy of sales prices	Loss of revenues	Integrity controls over price files Segregation of duties between recording and sales authorization Sample-based checks on billed prices
Shifting of sales transactions between periods	Loss of revenues	Integrity controls over price files Segregation of duties between recording and sales authorization Sample-based checks on billed prices
Accuracy of purchase prices	High costs of sales	Integrity controls over vendor files containing price information Segregation of duties between recording and purchase authorization Sample-based checks on purchase prices in relation to agreed prices with vendors
Shifting of purchase transactions between periods	High costs of sales	Integrity controls over vendor files containing price information Segregation of duties between recording and purchase authorization Sample-based checks on purchase prices in relation to agreed prices with vendors, purchase requisitions, orders, receipt of goods, and vendor invoices Appropriate purchase requisition procedures

Threats	*Exposure*	*Main internal controls*
Inventories on display (retail)	Theft of inventories	Physical access controls to the shop
Relatively unpredictable product demands	Decision about what and when to buy is critical to the continuity of the business	Market research
Relatively simple sales transactions (retail)	Sales order, shipping order, bill of lading, picking and packing lists, invoices, and other documents are generally not prepared	Use of a cash register Secondary segregation of duties between cash register operators and head cashier
Important to obtain detailed vendor information	Opportunity costs as a result of wrong vendor choice	Adequate vendor information system
Sales on account (wholesale)	Loss of revenues	Segregation of duties between recording, custody, and authorization with respect to accounts receivable Periodic aging of accounts receivable
High accounts receivable	High working capital financing costs	Follow-up procedures Periodic aging of accounts receivable and analytical review Integrity controls on accounts receivable files
Relatively complex sales transactions (wholesale)	Sales order, shipping order, bill of lading, picking and packing lists, invoices, and other documents are generally prepared	Segregation of duties between sales department, accounts receivable administration, warehouse, and logistics Secondary segregation of duties between cash register operators and head cashier
Unreliable accounts payable records	Inadequate accounts receivable management, resulting problems with creditors, and loss of reputation	Primary recording of vendor invoices immediately at receipt Checking accounts for goods to receive and invoices to receive
Unreliable inventory records	Suboptimal ordering moments, high costs of inventory, keeping out of stocks, resulting loss of clients, and forgone revenues	Periodical stocktaking Analytical review on inventory recordings Adequate procedures for back orders
Discounts	Forgone revenues	Management guidelines for allowing discounts (discount tables) Sample-based detailed checks on allowed discounts according to sales invoices

Moreover, with his knowledge, he can advise the stocktaker on technical issues. The type of stocktaking method is among other things dependent on the way in which inventory records are kept. One type of stocktaking is integral stocktaking, where the entire stock is taken at the same time. If inventory records contain a specification (e.g. by article type), stocktaking can be done separately for each article, at a time when regular business is the least disrupted or when stock is at a minimum level (e.g. after a sales promotion action). This stocktaking method is called cycle counting. The stock is taken in such a way that, over a certain period, all articles are counted at least once. If there are multiple locations where similar stocks are kept, stocktaking must be done at one and the same time, to prevent shifting of stock. This is called simultaneous stocktaking; for example, when an organization has multiple branches, a deficit at location *A* may temporarily be replenished from the inventory of location *B*. If stocktaking at location *B* is done subsequently to stocktaking at location *A*, the inventory shifted from location *B* to location *A* may be moved back to location *B* in order to prevent the stocktakers detecting the shifting of stock. Simultaneous stocktaking will counteract the threat of shifting of stock.

When purchase prices strongly fluctuate, the times at which purchases are made must be recorded by a role independent of the role who has custody over cash. A threat that may crop up here is the shifting of transactions through time; for example, by administratively shifting purchases made in a period with low market prices to a period with high prices, the differential money amount can be withdrawn from the organization. In this case, proper segregation of duties between recording, cash custody, and purchase authorization is an essential preventive measure. In addition, the purchase requisition procedures need to be sharpened such that purchase requisitions are followed up within a limited period of time. Furthermore, the line of documents from purchase requisition to vendor invoice must be investigated on a sample basis. When purchase prices are more stable, fixed administrative rates can be used for recording. In that case, scrutinizing the differences between actual purchase prices and fixed administrative rates in combination with sample-based detailed checks on individual transactions are important control measures to be performed by the head of administration, the controller, or someone with a designated internal control role.

For a trade organization, the revenues' *soll* position can be determined by making control totals and reconciliations according to a BIDE formula. The components of this formula are then filled in as follows:

- The value of the inventory at the beginning of the period (*B*) and its value at the end of the period (*E*) are determined by means of stocktaking.
- The increase during the period (*I*) (i.e. the purchases) is retrieved from the purchases journal.
- The decrease during the period (D) (i.e. the sales) is the *soll* position to be compared with sales according to the sales journal.

The controller is responsible for performing this check. She analyses differences, if any, and prepares a management report.

Since trade organizations do not transform raw materials into finished goods, the number of measurement points within the value cycle is relatively small. This entails the threat of having a shop within the shop: some transactions from purchasing to selling may not be accounted for in the organization's records. Unfortunately, the application of the aforementioned BIDE formula will not eliminate this threat since *soll* and *ist* reconcile. A sound internal control system calls for a mix of control measures. It is of great importance that a satisfactory segregation of duties is made between sales authorization, purchases authorization, and custody of ready-to-sell products, as too many tasks or a limited number of hands should be avoided. With respect to authorizing purchase and sales transactions, additional control measures include among other things, implementing procedures by means of management guidelines. As far as possible other organizational roles should be involved, and redundant recordings must be made for checking purposes (e.g. the use of contract registers as *soll* positions).

Shop within the Shop

The importance of clear-cut management guidelines for a purchasing department is repeatedly shown, not just for purchasing clerks, but also for vendors, so that they know exactly how to order, deliver, and pay. Unfortunately for the purchasing department under consideration, these guidelines did not exist for the suppliers, due to which the purchasing clerk placed orders with various suppliers who immediately resold them to acquaintances and friends. Obviously, revenues were pocketed by the purchasing clerk, while the purchases were allocated to a number of his employer's cost centres. A number of suppliers had had to wait a long time for their money. Since the purchasing clerk was their contact person, he was able to stall them with all kinds of excuse. Amazingly, not only did the patient suppliers continue with new deliveries, but they also delivered goods that did not belong to the ordinary set of goods of our client. Even more so, a number of shipments were delivered directly to the purchasing clerk's home address. In a final discussion, the purchasing clerk admitted to having his own shop within the shop. All goods he had ordered this way he had always resold. Our client is now looking for a new purchasing clerk. The new purchasing clerk definitely needs to operate differently from his predecessor. The organization's suppliers will receive written guidelines, explaining how orders are to be placed, who will be authorized to do so and at what addresses deliveries are to be made. In addition, these guidelines will also contain instructions for dealing with arrears or departures from the established ordering methods. Obviously, the last two issues need to be reported to management, not to the purchasing department.

(Source: Hoffmann (1997). *Detective Tips for Business*. 117 (May) [*Recherchetips voor het bedrijfsleven*].)

The price policy applied to sales is determined by the organization itself. An important threat is caused by a complex discount policy. From an internal control viewpoint, fixed sales prices without allowing discounts is ideal since in that case reconciliations and control totals will be unambiguously applicable. However, commercial policy should, in general, not be dictated by internal control limitations; for example, if there are fixed discount percentages per client category, additional attention needs to be paid to measures for preventing shifting sales records from a client with a lower discount percentage to a client with a higher discount percentage. The more specific the discounts per customer, the more difficult reconciliations and control totals can be as internal control measures. In that case, compensating controls must be put in place, such as the separate recording and disclosure of discounts per customer and performance of analytical review – for which the controller is responsible – including a comparison of actual discounts for preceding periods' amounts, period-to-date figures, budgets, and other customers' discounts. This anaysis can be made per individual client or client category, per vendor, per sales representative, per geographical area, or any other meaningful accounting unit.

Period matching is an important issue when sales prices frequently have to be modified; for example, a supermarket chain with 30 or so branches decreases its prices for a number of products. Measures need to be taken to mitigate the threat that branch managers could account for sales of these products, which occurred prior to the price decrease, as sales occurring after the decrease.

Within a trade organization, managerial information on the gross profit margins per product group, inventory levels, obsolete stocks, and various ratios such as a turnover ratio per product group, sales per square metre shop surface area and per employee, and the percentage of revenue loss owing to breakage and theft, are clearly important for managerial decision making. For management to be able to identify trends and unusual patterns, comparisons with budgeted numbers and variance analyses must be prepared by the controller or the assistant controller. In addition, in many cases, external benchmarking (within the industry or even with other organizations having best practices) or internal benchmarking (with other branches, business units, or divisions within the organization) can provide an idea of the organization's performance. The AIS must be organized in such a way that it can generate this information.

When an order received by the sales department is feasible because the potential customer is considered creditworthy and the required goods are in stock, this will result in an instruction to deliver the good sold. The invoice for the client is prepared as well. The way in which the delivery order is produced depends on the billing system used by the organization. A distinction can be made between pre-billing, post-billing, and intermediate billing. Management's choice for any one of these systems is determined, among other things, by the organization's commercial policy. For example, the required speed of delivery, customer expectations, competitive position, and industry customs determine the effort the organization can put into internal controls aimed at meeting an organization's commercial policy. In addition, it is important that all data necessary for billing is known by the order department before the warehouse is notified. Various billing systems differ with respect to the document that forms the basis of the invoice.

As for pre-billing, invoices are prepared using authorized orders. A copy of the sales invoice is subsequently printed in the warehouse, serving as a picking ticket for the warehouseman. Be aware of the fact that pre-billing does not imply that the invoice is sent to the client prior to the delivery of goods. An advantage of pre-billing is that reasonable assurance is given that no goods are shipped for which no invoice has been made. After all, the rapport between the sales invoice to be sent and the warehouse picking instruction is built into this billing system. However, pre-billing is only possible when the feasibility of the sales order is known before packing has been done. All products carried by the organization need to be in stock, and the measurement unit for warehouse distribution needs to equal the measurement unit for billing; for example, a cheese wholesaler uses kilograms as its measurement unit for billing whereas the measurement unit for warehouse distribution is the number of cheeses. Pre-billing cannot be applied in this case, since the amount of kilograms of cheese to be shipped cannot be determined in advance.

When the warehouse ships the goods ordered by means of copies of the authorized orders, and the invoice is prepared on the basis of the packing ticket, this is called post-billing. Billing takes place after the order is reconciled with the packing ticket as entered into the system or approved by the warehouseman after having packed the goods. Among other things, post-billing is used when incomplete information for the goods to be distributed is available in advance. The cheese wholesaler mentioned above is an example, as is the situation in which a specific article number needs to be stated on the invoice because of warranty obligations. It would be most efficient to have these numbers reported in the warehouse, but, for reasons of segregation of duties, the warehouse should receive only the minimum required amount of information.

A billing system that combines pre-billing and post-billing is intermediate billing. In the case of intermediate billing, invoices are prepared on the basis of the customer order. At the same time, the goods ordered by the customer are picked by the warehouse based on a copy of the customer order. By means of a copy of the sales invoice, the shipping department checks whether all shipped goods have been billed by matching the picking ticket with the invoices. Because of the availability of automated integrated information systems, intermediate billing is hardly ever encountered in practice.

The controller is responsible for the validity and completeness of billing. An important check to perform here is the reconciliation between the shipped goods according to the perpetual inventory records and the total of the amounts billed according to the accounts receivable administration. In addition, samples of sales transactions are examined for use of correct prices, discounts, and delivery conditions.

Sales of goods on account result in accounts receivable records being kept by the organization that sells these goods. Custody and safeguarding of accounts receivable takes place by keeping debtor records. For corporate finance purposes, management needs information on the size and composition of the company's equity, debts, and cash flow. Accounts receivable are especially important for trade organizations, implying a need for information about customer account balances. In addition, information, on a more detailed level, is needed such as the sales per expiration date for each debtor. This way, insight can be gained into the composition of account balances in terms of the relative importance of each debtor in the accounts receivable total, the average term of credit allowed, and possibilities for ageing. Also, timely payment by debtors is monitored. As part of accounts receivable control, periodically those debtors are identified whose term of credit has expired without receipt of payment by the organization. Measures need to be taken to collect these potentially bad debts. In general, the accounts receivable department will take care of the follow-up towards the debtors involved. However, they will not do this until after the sales department has been consulted for advice on the potential causes, potential sensitivities among the debtors involved, and the importance of maintaining these specific customer relationships; for example, a client may want to discuss possible quality or quantity deviations among the delivered goods or mis-statements in the invoices. Follow-up to bad debts can be done via various collection methods including writing follow-up letters, by telephone, by e-mail, by visiting the debtor, and by handing over the outstanding receivables to a debt-collection agency. By keeping records of the methods used and the effectiveness of each of these methods, statistics are obtained on the most effective way of following up bad debts.

The form of accounts receivable recording depends on the information needs of the organization. The nature of the sales relationship is important as well. For payments by instalment's registration per debtor in the general ledger or a subledger is necessary. This form of recording accounts receivable is also applicable when there are regular sales transactions between a customer and the organization. In that case, the sales information system also needs to provide information on terms of payment, outstanding receivables, and payment record. In contrast, when sales transactions are non-recurrent, sporadic, or of minor financial importance, recording receivables at the level of individual debtors is less efficient and chronological recording per invoice number or date, or a ledgerless accounts receivable administration on the basis of sales invoices, might be a better option. However, ICT has enabled recording per individual debtor in such situations as well.

The accounts receivable administration with registration per debtor in the general ledger or a subledger is the basis for rating debtors' creditworthiness by the sales department when making offers or when accepting orders for credit sales. This rating compares information about credit limits and the applicable payment conditions with the actual customer account balances. Determining the credit limit per client is a complex task because many variables may be of importance. These credit limits, along with the credit policy, must be set by a credit manager. She produces management guidelines – preferably embedded in applicable software – that provides a benchmark for the sales department to approve or reject a sales transaction with a certain customer. Low credit limits result in enhanced credit control, but may result in sales transactions being rejected and, hence, forgone revenues. Generous credit limits stimulate sales, but also increase the likelihood of bad debts. Since sales clerks' performances are often evaluated on the basis of generated turnover and rewarded by means of promotion prospects or additional pay, and should they be authorized to set credit limits, they will be in a position to boost sales by just heightening credit limits. Therefore, sales clerks should never determine credit limits. However, because of the threat of damaging customer relationships, sales clerks must have some discretion in applying the credit policies as set by the credit manager. A secondary segregation of duties within the sales department between the department head and the sales clerks and representatives usually provides a solution to this dilemma.

Organizations must try to meet customer demands in the best way they can. Customer-oriented trading requires an account management system that provides detailed information about customer characteristics including buying behaviour, key decision makers, and all kinds of seemingly trivial issues; for example, the fact that a key decisionmaker has just started to recover from an illness may not seem relevant from an entirely rational point of view. However, from a customer relationship viewpoint, paying attention to this in communications with that person may be crucial in maintaining a good relationship with that customer. Customer complaints are certainly a non-trivial issue. Systematic registration and analysis of clients' complaints is highly advisable. From an internal control viewpoint, complaints need to be recorded by a department independent of sales to give reasonable assurance on the reliability of the data recorded. In addition, customer orientation necessitates regular examination and evaluation of customer demands and wishes. Other indicators for the extent of an organization's customer orientation are the occurrence of returns (percentage of all deliveries), the number of service or warranty claims, turnaround times with respect to service and repairs, and the level of warranty costs per month.

The importance of cash transactions is decreasing since credit cards, chipcards, and virtual money replace cash more and more. Some visionaries expect a completely cashless society in the near future. However, especially in trade organizations, there is still a lot of cash traffic going on and, hence, the internal controls regarding the function of the cashier are still important. The cashier has custody over money and is responsible for the presence of cash. Control of receipts and expenditures is possible as a cashier should only perform transactions for which he is authorized by another role within the organization. This is evident for cash expenditures, but note that it also applies to cash receipts. The cashier records cash transactions in a cash book. All cash transactions are also recorded in financial administration by the administration department. The controller is responsible for periodically reconciling financial administration with the cash book, using reconciliations and control totals; for example, the opening cash balance of a certain day plus the cash receipts minus the cash expenditures during that day must be present in the cash register, which is checked by means of a cash count.

A threat involved in cash transactions is lapping. If there is an unsatisfactory pairing of duties between cash custody and cash recording, then the cashier will have the opportunity to record cash receipts later than they actually took place, or record cash disbursements before they actually take place; for example, customer *A* pays €100 to the cashier as payment for invoice *X*. The cashier temporarily steals this money and, in order to conceal the theft, he does not record the cash receipt in the cash journal voucher. When customer *B*, later on, pays €150 in payment of invoice *Y*, the cashier does not record this cash receipt as a payment of customer *B* on invoice *Y*, but as the payment of customer *A* on invoice *X*. Later, when customer *C* want to pay invoice *Z*, this is recorded as the payment of customer *B* on invoice *Y*. When this process continues, the cashier continually enjoys illegitimate credit from his employer. This scheme is called *lapping*.

Lapping

As regular as clockwork, we examine unexpected cash deficits. Often, these deficits turn out to be caused by an employee suddenly dipping into the cash box (an employee, by the way, who does not need to be involved in cash transactions within the company). In other cases, the money just seems to have suddenly disappeared. Closer examination reveals that, in reality, there was an increasing deficit, caused by employee 'loans'. This occurs when there is unsatisfactory control over daily turnover, or the cash receipts and deposits with the bank. The employee will only deposit part of the cash with the bank and record his loan' as change that needs to be present in the cash box for the next working day. Should the loan get out of hand, then there is a sudden large cash deficit.

(Source: Hoffmann (1996). *Detective Tips for Business* 113 (September) [*Recherchetips voor het bedrijfsleven*].)

Production Organizations

To a large extent, production organizations are comparable with trade organizations. After all, both types of organization have a dominant flow of goods and a related flow of money. In principle, the threats involved in the control of purchasing and sales, storage processes, and financial processes do not differ. A typical difference between production and trade organizations is that the former have a technical transformation process creating value-added. From a control point of view, this has three important implications:

- There is a disruption in the flow of goods. It is not easy to directly relate the amounts of raw and auxiliary materials used to the amounts of finished goods obtained, among other things because of waste and dropout.
- Occupation of production capacity is important. Therefore, use of man- and machine hours needs to be recorded and checked for acceptability.

- Often, production organizations produce multiple types of product. Thus, cost control and cost price calculation are more important and more complex here than they are in trade organizations.

The typology of organizations distinguishes several types of production organizations to account for the variety of transformation processes that exists. Obviously, these different types of production organization have different needs for information and internal controls.

Within the category of production organizations, a main distinction can be made between mass-production organizations and piece-production organizations. This distinction is based on a customer specificity criterion. Piece production concerns individual, specific customer wishes whereas mass production concerns an impersonal market with generally applicable wishes. In addition, agrarian and extractive organizations are also considered production organizations. Although they have much in common with mass production, they have some distinct features that should be taken into account when assessing the necessary internal controls. In general, the technical transformation process is much more uncertain here with respect to the relationship between inputs and outputs than in other production organizations.

An overview of the potential threats involved in production organizations is presented in Table 3.2. When a threat is specific to piece-production, mass-production, or agrarian and extractive organizations, this is explicitly indicated; if it is of a more generic nature for production organizations, no further indication is given. Because we do not intend to provide an exhaustive discussion of controls in production organizations, we will not elaborate on all the threats that can be identified, but will merely discuss some of the main issues that crop up. In addition, since production organizations also engage in purchasing, selling, and storage activities, some of the threats applicable to trade organizations obviously also apply here. We will not repeat them.

In principle, mass production thrives on standard conditions. This implies that standard amounts are produced as stock, standard procedures are followed, demand is estimated, and planning, job preparation, production, and production progress control are relatively simple. Since piece production, planning and job preparation are more complex, production does not proceed following standard procedures, and production progress control gets more complex.

Production organizations are usually capital-intensive. Therefore, investment in production facilities requires special attention, resulting in investment plans. In such plans, investment selection criteria, capacity usage, depreciation, financing, and the organization's employment of working capital are mapped to avoid over-investment or underinvestment.

Table 3.2 Threats to the achievement of internal control goals, exposure to them, and main internal control solutions in production organizations

Threats	*Exposure*	*Main internal controls*
Insufficiently reliable production standards (piece production)	Deficient products, flawed decision making with respect to production targets, and demotivated personnel	Technical and financial post-calculation, matching with standards, business performance reporting, analytical review on these reports, and standards control by means of reconciliations and control totals with respect to flows of raw materials, man-hours, machine hours, and finished products Develop tight standards for activities as in activity based costing (ABC)
Unit pricing differences	Loss of revenue	Analytical review on units accounted for in relation to used packaging materials
Investments in production facilities	Overinvestment and/or underinvestment	Investment planning
Insufficient product quality	Customer complaints, loss of reputation, long-term survival at stake	Quality control client satisfaction measurement
Complex flow of goods	Loss of inventories	Controls within the value cycle (RCTs)
Shifting of revenues and costs between projects or production runs	Unreliable production records, forgone revenues, and unreliable input for new pre-calculations	Segregation of duties for independent recording of costs Analytical review on the revenues and costs of projects Allocation of projects to project managers on a sequential basis, not on a simultaneous basis
No natural triggers that demarcate the start and end of the primary process (mass production)	Accounting is aimed at cost price determination instead of performance evaluation and control of the primary process	Department-based pre- and post-calculation
Insufficient alignment between production and demand (mass production)	Dissatisfied customers and loss of revenues, and increasing stocks, which may lead to obsoleteness, increasing investment in inventory working capital, and increased inventory costs	Production planning system Market research to get an insight into customers' needs
Shipping errors	Customer complaints, and loss of revenue	Well-designed picking and packing lists Segregation of duties between warehouse and logistics department (sales department provides information to both)

Threats	*Exposure*	*Main internal controls*
Work in progress (piece production)	Valuation of work in progress Enhanced risk of erroneous business performance reporting	Segregation of duties between accounting department, production planning department, and production department Production progress controls and reporting Procedures for cost price calculation
Product design	Incurring costs for products where there is no demand	Market research
Misalignment between product design and production capacity (piece production)	Inability to deliver the ordered goods and resulting loss of reputation and future sales	Bill of materials and recipes Design procedures Segregation of duties between the production planning department, the production department, and a control role for coordination purposes
Standard cost setting	Over or undervaluation of work in progress, financial losses as a result of incorrect price setting of finished products	Management guidelines for cost allocation and officially approved rates Procedures for standard cost setting as an integral part of the budgeting process Periodical alignment between actual and expected rates
Excessive processing time (piece production)	Goods not finished on time, customer complaints, loss of reputation, and financial losses	Production planning system Progress checks by production planning department Analytical review on production reports
Potentially complex projects (piece production)	Incorrect billing and incorrect valuation	Management guidelines for partial billing in accordance with project progress and valuation of work in progress Sample-based checking on agreement between data of billing and actual project progress Analytical review on valuation
Uncertainty about yields (agrarian and extractive organizations)	Erroneous financial reporting	Analytical review on business outcomes in relation to industry ratios published by third parties
Environmental pollution	Loss of reputation	Procedures for compliance with environmental regulations Sample-based checks on compliance with environmental regulations

Continued

Table 3.2 (*cont.*)

Threats	*Exposure*	*Main internal controls*
Seasonal patterns (agrarian and extractive organizations)	Continuity of operations	Guidelines with respect to outsourcing, limits on investment in machinery, and limits on hiring people Cash-flow planning
Small- or medium-sized (agrarian and extractive organizations)	Inadequate information provision and safeguarding of assets	Analytical review RCTs on complementary services
Orders are the natural triggers that demarcate the start and end of the primary process (piece production)	Accounting is aimed at performance evaluation and control of the primary process	Order-based pre- and post-calculation (order results reporting)

Production organizations use production standards in their technical transformation processes. Based on these standards, the number of raw and auxiliary materials and manpower and machine power capacity used for a certain number of finished goods can be determined, using the retrograde method. This standard use is compared with actual use, and the controller analyses possible differences and reports thereon to management. Due to the repetitive character of mass-production processes, production standards can be tighter than in piece-production processes. Because of the tightness of the standards, the relationship between offers and yields is easy to recognize, as it is for trade organizations. However, a difference is that the one-to-one relationship in trade organizations is usually replaced by an *n*-to-one relationship where one product is made out of various raw and auxiliary materials (e.g. the production of a car), or a one-to-*n* relationship (e.g. a wrecker's yard). Due to the unique character of production processes, piece-production processes have standards that are less tight and, therefore, less clear relationships can be identified. However, subdividing the piece-production project into activities instead of products may well increase the tightness of the standards; for example, a contractor building a house may develop standards for bricklaying, carpentry, or even, on a more detailed level, for connecting a tap or a pipe. On the other hand, the ever shortening of product life cycles in mass production makes it more difficult to arrive at crystallized standards, necessitating the same activity-based approach as with piece production.

The most important differences between mass and piece production concern production planning and pre- and post-calculation (including budgeting and variance analysis). These subjects are briefly discussed below. Subsequently, mass production and piece production are described in more detail.

Production Planning

Based on an organization's strategic plan and annual planning, production is specified in a production plan. This planning encompasses capacity planning (the amount of production capacity is necessary for the sales expected according to annual planning), occupation planning (linking [expected] orders to available capacity, which may result in over or understaffing, necessitating additional measures such as using temporary workers in case of understaffing or temporary periods of overtime), and detailed planning (allocating activities to people and machinery).

Production planning must be assigned to the production planning department, or simply the production office, which is independent of the production department. Production office tasks include job preparation, production order issuance, progress control, and technical post-calculation. Production orders are detailed descriptions of what and in what quantity must be produced in the next production run. A production order also contains the required authorizations for providing specified quantities of the raw materials and equipment to use, an indication of who should be working on what order, start and end time of the production run, as well as task descriptions for production personnel if the activities to be performed are non-routine. Raw materials and equipment may be supplied by a closed or an open warehouse, depending on the value of the goods and constraints in the production process; for example, if the production process is delayed because of unavailability of a specific item, as a result of a waiting line at the warehouse desk, this may cost more than the enhanced internal controls will yield. In this case, the constraint is the warehouse ordering process. If there is another process constituting the constraint, a certain warehouse waiting time is allowed up to the time the warehouse ordering process becomes the constraint.

Pre- and Post-calculation, Budgets, and Variance Analysis

Within production organizations, post-calculation must be compared with pre-calculation to evaluate production efficiency in terms of economy and effectiveness. A satisfactory segregation of duties needs to be in place regarding pre-calculation, usually done by the production planning department, production execution, and post-calculation. Technical post-calculation can conveniently be done by the production planning department, whereas financial post-calculation is the controller's task. For mass production, pre- and post-calculation are performed per department, called process costing. For piece production, pre- and post-calculation are performed per order, called job-order costing. The source of a threat is the validity and completeness of production data. Therefore, before the controller can perform the post-calculation, controls must be put in place to provide reasonable assurance that the production data as well as the used standards are valid and complete; for example, production software must have been tested thoroughly before implementing, the standards as recorded in the standards file must be periodically reviewed for reasonableness, and offers and yields must be reconciled using the retrograde method.

Differences identified by variance analyses are not just caused by inefficiencies but also by using less tight standards in pre-calculation. These differences are called budget variances. Initially, the head of the production department is held responsible for efficiency variances, whereas the production planning department is held responsible for budget variances. Price variances, which are caused by difference between the standard prices of raw materials, man-hours, and machine hours, and the actual prices according to vendor invoices, are the primary responsibility of the purchasing department.

For certain production companies, the sales price may strongly depend on the packaging that is used; for example, economy packs with six pieces or units instead of one, or litre bottles versus half-litre bottles. A threat is that sales for more expensive packaging are accounted for as sales of less expensive packaging. To prevent this threat resulting from differences in unit pricing, the number of products manufactured needs to be related to the usage of packaging material. In this case, proper revenue control is based on analytical reviews comparing flow of goods with complementary flow of goods; in this case, the flow of packaging material.

An important aspect of cost price calculation is the allocation of indirect costs to products, since it implies an assessment of the value of overhead costs, and the determination of internal prices. Since the method of charging a price for overheads is comparable with vendors billing the organization for delivered products and services, a sort of internal market is created within the organization. The creation of internal markets is mainly aimed at increasing efficiency and effectiveness of operations (see our discussion of the objectives of internal control according to the COSO report, p. 20) and can hence be considered a control instrument (see also our discussion of market control in Chapter 8). However, there are also theoretical objections against allocating indirect costs to products as this allocation will inevitably be somewhat arbitrary. Cost allocation charges burden production managers with costs they themselves cannot control, which may put pressure on the objective of cost control to enhance efficiency by enhancing planning and control processes.

Measuring the effectiveness of costs other than direct production costs causes a threat to cost control; for example, a €200,000 marketing budget may not have been exceeded, but that does not give any information about the effectiveness of marketing efforts undertaken with this budget. To adequately control overheads, additional and mostly non-financial business performance measures must be defined (e.g. measuring sales after a specific advertising campaign).

Another threat for management is the danger of shifting costs between projects. For simultaneous execution of multiple projects, the costs pertaining to a certain project may be accounted for as the costs of another project, perhaps because the project leader wants to conceal unsatisfactory results for that certain project. Especially for piece production, this is an important threat, as there are many possibilities for results to deviate from standards. These possible shifts complicate a realistic view of the state of the project. For cost-plus projects, where actual costs should be billed, billing may in that case be incomplete as a result of costs being shifted toward contract price projects where a fixed fee is billed along with explicitly approved additional and subtractive work. In addition, another result of shifting costs between projects leads to corrupt databases of cost standards being used in making offers for new projects.

Mass Production

As indicated, by and large mass production (except for agrarian and extractive organizations) is characterized by tight standards to be used in standard calculations for all products manufactured by the organization. After the manufactured quantities of each product have been determined, the allowed usage of raw and auxiliary materials and man- and machine hours can be calculated. If there are several production departments, this is done for each department. Periodically, actual costs are compared with the allowed costs per department by the head of administration, the controller, or someone with a designated internal control role.

Each production department reports on the results of the production process by means of a production report. This report contains:

- Raw and auxiliary materials received from the warehouse and used in the production process.
- Man- and machine hours used in the production process.
- Amount of produced finished goods.
- Amount of waste and dropout obtained.

The controller compares these actual results with the standards from pre-calculation and prepares a performance report for the organization's management. Other data on the progress of the production process are obtained from the warehouse, the technical department, and the quality control department. Validity and completeness of production data is established by reconciliations and control totals. Examples include:

- Raw and auxiliary materials received by the production department should equal the delivery of these materials by the warehouse.
- The number of man-hours reported in production reports (the jobtime) should equal the hours workers were present on the shop floor according to the payroll records (shoptime).

- The number of machine hours reported are compared with statements from the technical department on the number of available machine hours.
- The amount of finished products according to the production report should equal the amount of received products by the finished products warehouse, shipping documents, or reports from the quality control department.

Agrarian and extractive organizations are largely comparable with mass-production organizations. However, they have some distinct features that may entail specific threats. Since products are influenced by natural circumstances that are often not controllable or only so in a limited way, these types of organization have less tight relationships between offers and yields than do trade organizations and, to a lesser extent, other production organizations; for example, weather conditions, long process times causing more uncertainty about output, or the processing of biological materials that may follow unpredictable transformation patterns. Special attention must be paid to environmental issues; for example, agrarian organizations may cause harm to the environment through the use of pesticides; extractive companies may do so by mining for disproportionate amounts of minerals.

Piece Production

Due to softer standards, the planning of piece-production processes is more global than mass production. Global annual planning results in flexible production planning and in a production budget with larger tolerances. Man- and machine hour rates are determined using the production budget and the expected capacity utilization of production departments and machinery. Compared with the tight rates for mass production, these piece production rates will need to be adjusted more often.

In piece production, order acquisition is important because orders trigger the production process. Orders received by the sales department are communicated to the production planning department. The production planning department prepares a detailed pre-calculation, incorporates every order in short-term planning and thus prepares execution of the orders. This implies having designs made of the product and product parts, preparing bills of materials and recipes, ordering raw and auxiliary materials that are not part of the organization's regular stock, preparing short-term planning based on available man- and machine hours, reserving stock, material and personnel, and calculating the ultimate date by which operational activities need to begin with reference to the delivery date that is set. Based on this detailed calculation, the capacity that was tentatively reserved can be definitively allocated to the particular order.

To keep a grip on the production process, large works are technically subdivided into sequential stages. This is done as early as the pre-calculation. During execution, the controller prepares the post-calculation and provides a variance analysis per stage. The subdivision into sequential stages may also be practical for determining the valuation of work in progress and the moment of revenue recognition; for example, work in progress may be valued as follows: value at the beginning of the period + direct costs −/− billed instalments. Billing of instalments takes place on the basis of pre-defined stages at the end of which a certain percentage of the work is announced finished. Revenues are recognized simultaneously at the completion of each stage.

Determination of a product's or a project's cost price is important for the planning and control of production processes. By comparing the pre- and post-calculations of these cost prices, efficiency of the production processes, reliability of standards in use, and fairness of prices can be assessed. Specifying a cost price is also important for determining the sales price and the margin to be realized on each of the products carried by the organization. This may influence the composition of the organization's range of products.

Chapter Cases

Case 3.1 Sales and Accounts Receivable (adapted from NIVRA)

1. Indicate the essential functions of the accounts receivable administration and its related tasks.
2. Indicate those internal control measures that are necessary to guarantee a satisfactory execution of these tasks.
3. Describe four ways in which accounts receivable can be recorded.
4. Provide a normative internal control description with respect to the accounts receivable administration for the two organizations described below. Besides the position of accounts receivable, the creation and settlement of receivables deserve specific attention.

Finance Company
A finance company grants credits with various terms, partly on security and partly blank. Second or third mortgages are accepted as security. Collateral in the form of cars, boats and the like are accepted as well. Credits may be granted at a fixed interest percentage during the entire credit term, or at percentages which are adapted monthly to market developments. Monthly instalments are either fixed amounts or annuity determined (a fixed sum of instalments and interest).

Furniture Store
A furniture store sells against cash payment and on account. Sale on account is offered only to clients with a valid machine-readable charge card (badge). The store uses two systems for billing sales on account: monthly invoices or (separate)

invoices for each transaction. Monthly invoices are due within one month of the billing date. The other invoices concern larger purchases and are payable in three monthly installments. The store uses a microcomputer for periodic billing and the accounts receivable administration.

Case 3.2 A Business in the Precision Engineering Industry (adapted from NIVRA)

A business in the precision engineering industry is engaged in production and sale of various types of wire and filaments for the electrical and electronics industry. The business produces for stock, rather than to order. It employs 200 people. The management department supervises the following subordinate departments (among others):

- Production, including the following departments: Operations Office, Wire-drawing Department, and Filaments Department;
- Warehouse;
- Purchasing;
- Sales;
- Administration;
- Automation.

The business produces the following products:

- Wire – The Wire-drawing Department produces wire made both from pure metals (copper and nickel) and alloys. The wire the firm produces is used in the manufacturing of filaments or is sold to other users.
- Filaments – In the filament department, wire is cut into short lengths, of 5 to 10 cm, and pieces of various sorts of wire are then fused together. Filaments are used by lighting manufacturers for production of light bulbs.

Metals which are used as raw materials in production are purchased from both domestic and foreign metal producers. The purchase prices of these materials vary with the state of the market. The production of wire and filaments generates fairly valuable metallic wastes.

Wire and filaments are sold by length to the electrical and electronics industry, either via written orders or orders by telephone.

The selling price of the finished products depends on the quality of the order and are also regularly adjusted in accordance with market shifts. The scrap metal from production is periodically sold to metal dealers at the going market price.

The business has a computer of sufficient capacity, with terminals in several departments. Considerable use is made of the computer for the various activities of the business.

Assignment

Provide a general normative internal control description.

Case 3.3 Brickyard (adapted from NIVRA)

Introduction

A public limited company produces bricks for exterior walls. The bricks are available in one size and one colour, in several different qualities.

Sale

The company sells its products to builders merchants. In general, the General Manager enters into sales contracts, which are blanket order contracts with a duration of several months. The prices that are agreed per sales transaction do not include carriage, are per 1,000 bricks and strongly depend on colour quality and demand. Bricks with a bad colour quality do not command much of a price.

Clay Extraction and Clay Storage

The company has entered into a long-term contract for clay extraction. The company pays an agreed price per cubic meter of clay extracted. The clay is dug out by means of excavators and transported to the factory by trucks. After grinding, the supplied clay is taken and stored in the clay depository by means of a conveyor belt. Fluctuations in the clay supply have not been overcome and compel the company to keep a large buffer stock.

Pressing and Drying

To obtain the desired colour for the bricks, the clay from the depository is mixed with limestone in a marl–limestone dosing installation. The mixing proportion depends on the colour of the clay, which is not constant. An automatic pressing installation is connected to the dosing machinery. The pressing installation puts a fixed number of bricks on a 'brick board'. These brick boards are manually put on a truck. Trucks always holds 10 brick boards. The bricks are dried by placing a fixed number of trucks in the drying installation. Bricks are pressed and dried only during daytime.

Baking

The dried bricks are moved from the trucks to large fire-resistant kiln ('oven') wagons. In this process, rejected bricks are removed and reground to clay. Bricks are baked on a continuous basis (also at night). The kiln wagons are transported through the kiln at a constant speed. There are always 50 wagons in the kiln.

Sorting and Storage

Based on colour quality, the baked bricks are sorted into three categories:

- satisfactory;

- less satisfactory;
- unsatisfactory.

Breakage occurs in this process. The bricks are stored at the outdoor warehouse in packs having a fixed number of bricks, which are all placed, in one go, on the trucks that pick up the bricks. Since the direct demand for bricks and the amounts sold due to blanket order contracts fluctuate greatly, sometimes large – partly unsold – stocks are present at the outdoor warehouse.

Payroll
There is a fixed shift of personnel for each production phase and for internal transport between the two phases, with fixed hourly wages plus a bonus that depends on the amounts processed.

Maintenance
Maintenance of durable means of production is assigned to third parties. The associated expenses are important.

Assignment

Provide a general normative internal control description.

ORGANIZATIONS WITHOUT A DOMINANT FLOW OF GOODS

4

It is now widely recognised that the effective management of knowledge assets is a key requirement for securing competitive advantage in the emerging information economy. Yet the physical and institutional differences between tangible assets and knowledge assets remains poorly understood.

Boisot (1998), cover copy

After studying this chapter, the reader should be able to:

- Identify the threats and exposure to them that are inherent in service organizations.
- Develop a normative internal control system for service organizations.
- Explain the role of a normative internal control system for each type of organization that is distinguished.
- Describe the information needs for primary processes within the distinguished organizations.
- Explain how information flows must be controlled in each type of organization so as to provide information that is reliable and relevant for their functioning.
- Describe the tasks of the accounting department, the controller, and people with designated internal control roles with respect to the provision of reliable and relevant information.

Chapter Outline

This chapter discusses service organizations in a wide variety of forms. These organizations can all be characterized by the absence of a dominant flow of goods. The value cycle in these organizations is relatively loose when compared with organizations having a dominant flow of goods. As a result, reconciliations and control totals are less applicable as control instruments. Instead, more reliance must be placed on internal organization. Just as in the preceding chapter, for each type of organization, the threats from an internal control point of view are defined. To determine what control measures to take, the exposure of each threat is discussed. Based on threats and associated exposures, a set of internal control measures is defined.

Introduction

Organizations without a dominant flow of goods appear in a wide variety of forms. However, these organizations have in common that their main source of revenues are intangible goods such as services. Hence, we will refer to these organizations as service organizations. Compared with organizations having a dominant flow of goods, service organizations are characterized by a limited flow of physical goods or none at all. In general, service organizations provide resources other than physical goods as the main revenue generating activity (e.g., restaurants, garages, public accounting firms, banks, or insurance companies). Often, in these organizations, available capacity and utilization of that capacity are important starting points for controlling the completeness of revenues. Hence, the primary recording of capacity and a system of checks and balances to check capacity usage must be focused on. Here, the capacity offered mainly consists of space and time in combination with personnel. However, this approach is not in all cases the most efficient. If service organizations have a limited flow of goods, controlling the completeness of revenues must be based on the relationships between purchasing, storage, production, and sales processes. Here, the generally less tight relationship between usage of goods and cash inflow complicates the determination of the revenues' *soll*-position. This necessitates application of additional control measures, such as an analytical review of the relationship between the provided services and the physical goods that accompany these services.

As services cannot be kept in stock, control of investments (including investment planning) in service capacity is an important issue, as is control of the occupation of available service capacity. With respect to optimal occupation, control activities are short-term-oriented. In addition, dependent on the specific type of service organization, capacity usage does not necessarily result in revenues; for example, whether or not a swimming pool or a greyhound bus is completely occupied or completely empty makes no difference to the necessary availability and the capacity costs to be made. So, there is only a remote relation between capacity usage and costs, on the one hand, and revenues, on the other hand. Therefore, control systems should not focus solely on financial information, as this might induce management to concentrate only on cost savings without considering other objectives that may be strategically important. Non-financial measures that management could use for measuring performance include:

- measures of client satisfaction after the service has been delivered (e.g. interviews and customer complaints systems);
- direct measures of the service process (e.g. test buyers and personal inspections);

- proxies of client satisfaction (e.g. measuring waiting time as an approximation of client satisfaction).

Dependent on the nature of activities, several types of service can be distinguished within the category of service organizations. The typology of organizations as presented in Chapter 2 (Figure 2.8) forms the basis for our discussion of organizations without a dominant flow of goods. Hence, we will discuss the following service organizations:

- organizations with a limited flow of goods;
- organizations that put space and time capacity at their clients' disposal;
- organizations that put knowledge and skills at their clients' disposal.

In addition, we will briefly discuss some issues related to governmental institutions, which often have many similarities with service organizations.

Table 4.1 summarizes the threats that are inherent in service organizations. Just like our discussion of threats, exposures, and controls in trade and production organizations, we limit our discussion to the main issues evolving from these threats.

Organizations with a Limited Flow of Goods

Service organizations with a flow of goods are, to some extent, comparable with trade and production organizations. The flow of goods is the starting point for controlling a major part of the information flow within these service organizations. These organizations are usually characterized by some kind of transformation process (e.g. in a restaurant meals are produced using all kinds of ingredient). Similarities can be found in the standard calculations of production organizations. However, there are some significant differences. The most important differences concern capacity employment and the relationship between usage of goods and related revenues. In service organizations, the capacity is directly put at the clients' disposal, whereas, in production firms, it is only indirectly employed to satisfy clients' needs by using it for technical transformation processes. Moreover, the relationship between capacity usage and related revenues is usually less tight in service organizations. Because capacity plays an important role in controlling this type of service organization, additional attention should be paid to the planning of activities that contributes to an optimization of capacity usage, on the one hand, and to an enhanced alignment between capacity and revenues, on the other (e.g. reservations in a restaurant).

The typology distinguishes organizations that have a limited flow of their own goods and organizations where these goods belong to third parties. This difference only has an impact on the threats, exposures, and controls stemming from the absense of a cash outflow in payment of vendor invoices. However, in both cases,

Table 4.1 Threats to the achievement of internal control goals, exposure to them, and main internal control solutions in service organizations

Threats	*Exposure*	*Main internal controls*
Valuation of human capital	High market-to-book value	Personnel information system Personnel and cultural controls
Personnel accountability	Validity of personnel costs	Job/shoptime control
Investments or disinvestments in capacity	Completeness of revenues	Segregation of duties between authorization to make investments or disinvestments in capacity and recording of investments or disinvestments Procedures for investments and disinvestments
Unauthorized capacity expansions without having to make significant investments	Completeness of revenues	Segregation of duties between the custody of devices that allow capacity expansions and the authorization of additional services to be provided from these capacity expansions Reconciliation of sales and expenses from complementary activities
Substitutes for the physical flow of goods	Near-money (quasi-goods) movement	Physical custody controls over near-money Segregation of duties between custody of near-money, production of near-money (externally; by a reliable printing firm), receiving of near-money, and use of near-money for the intended goal (access controls) RCTs with respect to the near-money movement (quasi-goods) Pre-numbered quasi-goods
Unreliable information provision	Wrong decisions	–
Regular periodical amounts to be received	Completeness of revenues from fixed regular periodical cash collections	Theoretical cash collection register (standing register) Automated bill generation
Mis-specification of contracts	Completeness of revenues	Contract register as a *soll* position to compare with the sales records

the primary recording of the service request is crucially important for the completeness of revenues. The primary recordings are compared with data obtained from other departments or officials within the organization; for example, in a restaurant, the primary registration of the order made by the waiter can subsequently be compared with the registrations of the kitchen (including buying), the reception, and payment to the waiter or the cashier. In general, the control system in organizations with a limited flow of goods must be designed such that personnel charged with executing duties (e.g. the kitchen in so far as meals are prepared) and authorization (the reception or the cashier in a restaurant) cannot influence the primary registration (e.g. the waiter in a restaurant). If such a segregation of duties is not possible, alternatively such control measures can be taken that completeness of revenues is establlished by using sequentially numbered tickets (e.g. jobtime tickets or move tickets). When exposure to a threat with respect to the completeness of revenues is substantial, both measures may be put in place simultaneously.

Organizations that Put Space and Time Capacity at Their Clients' Disposal

For organizations that put space and time capacity at their client's disposal, a distinction can be made between specific and non-specific capacity. This difference is crucially important for the applicable control measures.

Organizations that put *specific* space and time capacity at their client's disposal strive for optimal usage of their maximum capacity. In terms of internal control, capacity and usage (maximum capacity minus vacancy) and the registration of the primary request, such as a reservation, deserve special attention. For control of revenue completeness, the following reconciliations and control totals are generally applicable:

$$\text{Available capacity} -/- \text{Vacancy} = \text{occupation}$$

$$\text{Occupation} \times \text{Rate per capacity unit} = \text{Revenues (}soll\text{-position)}$$

The determination of available capacity causes a threat to the completeness of revenues since maximum revenues are determined by expansion or reduction of that capacity. Therefore, investment and disinvestment procedures, as well as segregation of duties between authorization of investment and disinvestment, and recording of cash flow are applicable controls. There is an additional threat when maximum capacity can be expanded without making significant investments (e.g. a hotel that charges a rate per bed or adds beds to a room). Measures need to be taken to prevent unauthorized capacity expansion. To mitigate this threat, segregation of duties between the custody of devices (e.g. beds) that allow capacity expansion and the authorization of additional services to be provided from this capacity expansion must be realized along with reconciliation of the recorded sales with related expenses; for example, in a hotel, accounts of the complementary service of housekeeping are used, showing which rooms are occupied and which are not. The head of administration relates these reports to the occupation report from the reception, which serves as the basis for billing.

Vacancy also needs to be considered because occupation is calculated as the difference between vacancy and maximum capacity. An employee independent of the reception or reservation department should be charged with vacancy control; for example, in a hotel, an employee working in the administrative department should check whether rooms that should not be occupied according to the capacity usage schedule are indeed empty.

A special case is the category of organizations that provide transportation services for physical goods or virtually physical goods using pipelines and wires. Although it can be argued that organizations that provide transportation of intangible goods, using cables, satelites, or any other devices for electronic communication, do also put space and time capacity at their clients' disposal, we will discuss these organizations along with organizations that put knowledge and skills at their clients' disposal (specifically, organizations with massive data processing) because the relationship between available capacity and revenues is often very ambiguous here.

In the case of physical goods or virtually physical goods, the service mainly consists of being connected to a network of pipelines or wires; for example, gas, water, and oil are brought to customers by means of pipelines and electricity is brought to customers by means of wires. The price charged for this service is mostly included in the product price and largely depends on the use made of the pipelines or wires. The completeness of revenues is controlled by installing meters. If fees are partially variable, the meters need to be read periodically. Preferably, this reading is done by functionaries independent of collecting and accounting for the revenues. To prevent collusion, meter readers need to rotate between districts. A complication is that it often is impossible to read all the meters at the same time, necessitating use of estimates. Usage is calculated by subtracting from the current reading that of the prior meter reading. To establish that meters are read for all connections, the head of administration reconciles the readings and the connections file. In addition, if meters have to be bought or leased to be able to get connected to the service, completeness of revenues can be substantiated by reconciling the number of meters sold or rented and the revenue statement. Drafting a value cycle for these organizations is usually not easy due to leakage, temperature changes (gas), inaccuracies in the meter recordings and readings, and the inherent uncontrollability due to the large areas covered.

For organizations that put non-specific space and time capacity at their clients' disposal, vacancy control is not practically possible. This is due to a high change frequency, or a specific space area that is hard to mark out (e.g. a swimming pool or a pop festival).

In contrast to reservation of specific space and time capacity, no registration of reservation is kept. Service use is made dependent on goods that serve as proof of cash receipts in payment of services. Hence, these goods are not goods in the sense that they intrinsically have value, but merely that they have an underlying nominal value. For that reason, they are also denoted quasi-goods or, because of their resemblance to money, near-money. The absence of a flow of physical goods is handled by introducing a flow of quasi-goods and trying to control that flow instead. Near-money forms the starting point for controlling the completeness of revenues. Near-money can be defined as goods, typically of low intrinsic but high nominal value, that serve as proof of cash receipts in payment of services; for example, a token for a coffee machine, entitling the owner to services provided by or on behalf of the organization that has put them into circulation. For purposes of controlling the completeness of revenues, the purchasing, storage, and sales processes of quasi-goods are related by means of the following reconciliation, to be made frequently (preferably daily):

Beginning inventory of quasi goods + Inventory increase
−/− Ending inventory of quasi-goods = *Soll* position of the number of quasi-goods sold

The head of administration distinguishes as many revenue categories as there are different nominal values of quasi-goods, and calculates the *soll* position of the number of quasi-goods sold for each of these categories. He then relates the sum of these *soll* positions to cash receipts according to the following reconciliation:

Cash at the end of the day −/− Cash at the beginning of the day
+ Cash payments = Cash receipts

The presence of a considerable flow of cash is another inherent threat in these types of organization. We have elaborated on this threat in our discussion of trade organizations in Chapter 3. The legitimacy and validity of the rate is usually checked by means of a physical access control at the entrance to the space where the service is provided. To prevent more use being made of the quasi-good than intended, the quasi-goods must be invalidated during ticket inspection (e.g. the ticket inspector tears off a part of the ticket on entrance to the cinema). There must be segregation of duties between the person who invalidates the quasi-goods and the person who authorizes sales; for example, the ticket inspector in the cinema should not be involved in the sale of tickets at the ticket counter.

The presence of near-money imposes a number of internal control requirements on the organization including:

- the creation of near-money has to be decided on by an authorization function;
- the quasi-goods must be ordered from a reliable printing firm;
- the delivery of quasi-goods involves a separate dispatch advice sent to an employee other than the one who receives the quasi-goods and, hence, keeps them in custody;
- there must be instructions naming the employees who are allowed to receive the quasi-goods;
- current stocks of quasi-goods must be kept as small as possible to limit exposure to misappropriation;

- inventory counts are frequently made by persons independent of the custody (receipt of quasi-goods), authorization (value creation), and recording (general ledger and control registers) personnel.

Near-money

People are admitted to the Dutch theme park Efteling if they have a one-time-only ticket or a season ticket. The one-time-only tickets are available at different rates, as distinctions are made between individual admission, group admission, a train–theme park combination arrangement, and consignatory tickets sold by, among others, the Tourist Office. Furthermore, children younger than four years of age can visit Efteling for free, there are reduced rates for senior citizens and handicapped visitors, and there is an opportunity to buy a two-day ticket.

There is a primary segregation of duties between the receipt of newly printed tickets, the sale and distribution of tickets, and ticket inspection at the gate. All tickets received and distributed, as well as cash receipts at the ticket counter are recorded in the organization's information system. These records provide the basis for setting up, by someone with a control role, of the flow of quasi-goods and related cash flow. The cash flow is further analysed for checking purposes. In addition, management assesses revenues by using weekly business performance reports.

After analytical review of the flow of quasi-goods and the related cash flow, the revenue *soll* position can be determined. This *soll* position is reconciled with the general ledger and records made by the cashier. Because of the large amounts of cash, cash counts are done on a daily basis, and cash is deposited with the central cash register. Every day, the bank picks up the cash in the central cash register by means of security vans.

Revenues show a clear seasonal pattern. For checking purposes, revenues per period are analysed in view of the budget, the comparable period of last year, the number of visitors, expenditure in the park, and labour costs. Historical and statistical data are important here. The prognosis is adjusted daily, depending on the weather forecast.

(Efteling: Accounting and auditing aspects of the account of revenues and project administration. Adapted from *De Accountant*, (July/August) [De Efteling: de accounting- en auditing-aspecten van de opbrengstverantwoording en projectenadministratie].)

Instead of ordering near-money from third parties, it is increasingly produced within the service organization itself using an automated system; for example, when buying a train ticket, there are two alternatives: buy one at the ticket counter, giving details of the trip to a front-office clerk who inputs the data into the computer, or buy one at an automated ticket machine, typing in the details of the trip yourself. In both cases, the ticket is printed after the customer has indicated her exact travel plan, creating the quasi-goods at the same time. Control of information provision with respect to near-money changes as a consequence. Control of completeness of revenues can no longer be established using reconciliations and control totals as mentioned. Since near-money is created at the moment of the sale itself, there is no beginning or ending inventory of quasi-goods, nor is there a purchase of these quasi-goods. In this modified situation, value creation must be reliably recorded in the automated system. Therefore, security measures need to be taken with respect to the automated system, such as computer access control matrices, control of sale price tables, and the automated construction of reconciliations and control totals for the *soll*-position of sales. A threat is the possible misappropriation of the paper used for printing near-money. Therefore, use of special paper (watermarked, bar-coded, difficult to forge, etc.) and special attention to controlling the flow of paper by means of tight inventory controls is called for.

Organizations that Put Knowledge and Skills at Their Clients' Disposal

The last type of service organization concerns organizations that put knowledge and skills at their clients' disposal. The following two types are distinguished within this category: organizations that sell man-hours and organizations with massive data processing.

Within organizations that sell man-hours, the starting point for the assessment of completeness of revenues is accountability of hours worked by the professionals who deliver the services, related to the applicable rate in case of cost-plus projects, or fixed fees agreed in the case of contract-price projects. Control of information flows in these service organizations is, to some extent, comparable with that of service organizations that put specific space and time capacity at their clients' disposal, as reconciliations and control totals are very important in this respect:

$$\text{Shoptime} - / - \text{Indirect hours} = \text{Jobtime}$$
$$\text{Jobtime} \times \text{Rate} = \textit{Soll} \text{ position of revenues}$$

When an organization only has cost-plus projects, these reconciliations and control totals are essential in determining the completeness of revenues. This is less so when an organization has contract-price projects. In that case, jobtime and the number of hours charged to specific projects in the project administration must be reconciled. Furthermore, for contract-price projects the pre-calculation on which the contract price for a project is based must be compared with the actual hours spent on that project.

Because organizations that sell man-hours often define projects as their revenue drivers, there are many similarities with piece-production organizations; for example, the treatment of work in progress and the shifting danger when there are contract-price projects as well as cost-plus projects.

Analytical review is an important control instrument for these service organizations; for example, the ratios between chargeable and non-chargeable hours per employee in a public accounting firm, and comparison of these numbers with the budget, prior periods, comparable employees, and, if possible, other offices of the firm.

In contrast to trade organizations, production organizations, organizations with a limited flow of goods, organizations that put space and time capacity at their clients' disposal, and organizations that sell man-hours, a flow of physical or virtually physical goods is lacking in organizations with massive data processing; for example, financial institutions like banks or insurance companies, Internet service providers, and telephone providers only have flows of money. Therefore, the value cycle's usability for controlling information provision is very limited. As a consequence, for these organizations there is an increased threat that their information provision is not reliable. The importance of preventive measures increases when detective measures such as reconciliations and control totals, and analytical review are not possible. Internal control measures for organizations with massive data processing, therefore, include segregation of duties, and directives and procedures. In addition, since ICT is predominant in these organizations due to the massive-character of data flows, high demands on automated processing of data and information provision must be made.

Insurance Companies

Insurance organizations sell certainty by taking over individual clients' risks and spreading these risks over other clients. Hence, an insurance organization mediates in having its clients share their risks with others. Obviously, insuring is the primal function of an insurance organization. Because insurance organizations receive large amounts of money from premium payments for potential future payments like damage claims or life insurance payments, they have excess cash which should be invested in accordance with the organization's treasury policy. Hence, investment is a secondary function of insurance organizations. These activities, concerned with efficient management of an organization's cash flow are generally referred to as treasury management.

Threats include:

- estimating too low risks for new business;
- validity of claims;
- completeness of premiums;
- valuation of premium reserves.

Controls include:

- segregation of duties between accepting new business, calculating premiums versus expected risks, authorizing premium rates, premium collection, financial administration, and testing compliance with procedures and directives;
- management guidelines with respect to policies for acceptance of clients;

- computer security controls;
- reconciliations and control totals based on theoretical cash collection registers.

Telebanking

Electronic banking can be used for making an authorized cash outflow payable. Usually, the software is put at the clients' disposal and is then used by the bank to provide information to their clients via electronic communication (e.g. exchange rate information) and can be used by clients to send payment orders and other transactions to their banks. Data from financial administration and the electronic banking system are thus integrated; for example, a salary payment run from financial administration is automatically sent to the bank for processing immediately after authorization by the general manager.

Using electronic banking requires a number of security measures to guarantee reliable information exchange between the bank and its clients. Authorizing payments in an electronic payment setting needs careful control of digital signatures in order to ensure logical access security, if possible combined with a smart card. The payment authorizing functionary must be able to check the legitimacy of the amount to be paid (e.g. by means of control totals for payment orders, which can be sent to the bank with the payment batch). Other important control measures mainly concern physical access security and guaranteeing reliable application of the software. This involves entering into a contract with the bank for mutual liability and an extensive test of the controllability of the software package.

Banks

Banks offer all kinds of financial services including intermediary services between demand for and supply of money (interest revenues), security and currency trading (provision revenues). An important acitivty within banks is treasury management. This involves governing, optimizing, and monitoring financial positions, financial flows, and the risks associated with these positions and flows. Thus, treasury management is involved in attracting financial resources to the organization, cash-flow management, controlling currency and interest risks, and asset–liability management.

Information provision mainly concerns the position taken by the organization to have insight into the financial risks that the organization faces. Thus, this position needs to be valued at current value, as historical information on derivatives is meaningless. This also implies that information from third parties, external information, is necessary. Internal information is necessary to assess the current position and take action where needed based on this assessment. The current position needs to be assessed in terms of interest, currency, and the like. Frequency of reporting needs to be based on the intensity of trading and the size of the position taken.

Threats include:

- the emergence of derivatives causing high exposure in relation to the amount of money involved;

- uncertain environment;
- no flow of goods;
- complex ICT deployment.

Controls include:

- Segregation of duties between front office and back office. The front office (traders, authorizing) deals with potential lenders and issuing loans. The back office (administration, recording) is charged with the recording of transactions initiated by the front office (recording and confirming of transactions engaged in, and keeping track of the positions taken through these transactions).
- Setting boundaries to security traders' activities by imposing monetary and quantitative limits per period, transaction types, allowed counter parties, and establish rapport.
- Procedures for front office and back office to operate and report independently from one another, confirmation procedures requiring confirmation of every transaction with the counter party, to be initiated by the back office so transactions that are possibly not recorded can still be discovered.
- Programmed controls, such as existence checks, reasonableness checks, check on mathematical accuracy on data entered into the system for processing.

Government Institutions

Government institutions are not, or only to a limited extent, influenced by market forces. Examples of the first category are police and defence; examples of the latter are education, public transport, and hospitals. Government interference substantially influences the functioning of those markets. Government institutions usually involve services aimed at the benefit of society, which is hard to translate into financial terms. Important control measures for these organizations are budgets and directives and regulation. In these types of organization, budgets have an authorizing and task-setting function used for controlling the organization. For each budget component, a careful definition of its objectives and the amount to be spent on that objective is provided. It is often stated that government institutions are activity-oriented (i.e. financial resources as a means of achieving activity goals), and that organizations that are influenced by market forces are primarily oriented towards financial results with activities being the means of realizing financial goals to guarantee continuity. Agreement on goals is important for controlling government institutions. Due to the activity orientation of government institutions, results for these organizations are not measured so much in financial terms, even though some financial limits cannot be exceeded, but in non-financial terms such as reaction time of the police to a call, and availability of education or health care. Defining non-financial performance criteria such that they become measurable must consider the performance levels per policy objective in relation to the quality criteria of the various information users.

In contrast to budgets of organizations influenced by market forces, government institutions focus less on the planning function of these budgets and allow less discretion to enter into the budgeting process. In addition, government institutions traditionally attribute only little meaning to what customers think of them. Therefore, legitimacy of expenditure has always had a special meaning here. Legitimacy implies that the amount spent on a certain goal does not exceed the budget set for that goal, and that the expenditure has indeed been made to meet that particular goal.

Within the scope set by the institution's annual budget, which is based on the long-range budget, budgets are allocated to middle management (e.g. department heads in hospitals). Within these budgets, middle management can operate largely independently. The allocation of these budgets is tied to financial and other quantitative conditions. The performance or products to be delivered and the associated costs, and if possible the quality level desired, are recorded, as are the measurement points to assess the realization of goals. This takes the form of a management contract between general management and middle management. Subsequently, progress is checked during the contract period with a frequency agreed by both parties.

Chapter Cases

Case 4.1 Hopperwood

In 1997, a former fraternity decided to organize a dance festival. It appeared to be a resounding success, and it grew into a great event. This year, there are 15 sites with just as many DJs. The number of visitors has been growing progressively since the first festival. Starting with almost 5,000 visitors in 1997, last year peaked at more than 100,000 visitors. That year, the festival was for the first time held in a rural area near the city of Hopperwood because not a single urban location was able to manage the enormous crowds of people flocking in.

Revenues

The entrance fee is €50 per person. For that amount visitors will get access to all the acts. It is forbidden for visitors to take their own food and drink with them. Food and drink are sold against tickets that cost €1 each. Catering is completely outsourced to one company. Food and drink tickets are available at a limited number of ticket counters at the festival grounds. There are no other revenue categories. After the festival, the caterer hands in the received tickets and receives 90% of the sales price.

Expenses
The main expense category is the money spent on DJ acts. Contracts have been closed with all the DJs. Other expenses include the costs of the festival grounds, energy, first aid, security, and marketing. Transportation to and from the festival grounds is outsourced to a limited number of bus companies. Visitors can make free use of these buses. Furthermore, it is agreed with the city that extra police and firefighter deployment will be reimbursed by the festival organization. Repair of damage to city properties will also be at the organization's expense.

Contingency Planning
The organization seriously takes into account that unwanted events will occur during the festival. In their planning, a distinction has been made for three contingencies. First, violations of laws and regulations. This comprises the dealing of narcotics, sound pollution, and, in general, disruption of public order. Second, calamities like the outbreak of riots, flocking in of large numbers of visitors without valid entrance tickets, extremely bad weather conditions, or the flows of people to, from, and at the festival grounds getting out of control. Third, technical malfunctions like the breakdown of sound and light installations, bus connections, and the collapse of stands and stages.

Future Events
Last year, several things went wrong. Many buses never arrived at the festival grounds as a result of a traffic jam at the festival access roads. Unfortunately, during the festival there was a major thunderstorm, leading many people to panic. Lots of people were trampled and got injured as a result. The city has made it clear that the organization will have to be more professional in order to be granted a permit for the next year.

Assignment

1. What threats may occur within this organization? Make a distinction between internal and external threats, and give an indication of the exposure to each threat.
2. What segregation of duties is necessary in this organization to improve the quality of operations and information provision, and enhance compliance with pollution acts and other laws and regulations?
3. Describe the relevance of internal control for the contingency planning within this organization.
4. What information does the city of Hopperwood need in order to decide whether or not to grant a permit for next year's festival?

Case 4.2 Avalon Estates

The real-estate company Avalon Estates owns and rents a large number of houses and some office buildings. Under the leadership of its general manager, the following departments are in place:

- building bureau;
- leasing office;
- estate management and inspection;
- maintenance;
- administration and automation;
- secretariat.

Houses and offices are developed on the company's own account and built by third parties, or bought. In both cases the building bureau is involved. Financing of assets is done via private loans with pension funds and insurance companies.

Rents of houses and offices are paid monthly, quarterly, biannually, and annually. Payment must be done in advance. House rents are normally raised by a fixed percentage once a year. Office rents may be raised once a year too, but here there are also some specific arrangements including ten year fixed rent, ten year fixed rent with a right to buy at a fixed price, and annual raises by different percentages. The lease contracts for offices and some lease contracts for houses contain clauses for service costs. These service costs include security costs, costs of cleaning stairways and halls, and costs of garden maintenance. Payment of these costs is done annually on the basis of a post-calculation. For that purpose a monthly advance payment is charged. Renters are allowed to pay in one of the following ways:

- via bank payment forms provided by Avalon Estates;
- via periodical payments;
- via automated cash collection.

Payments must have been received before the start of the new leasing term. Default is very common.

Assignment

1. How can Avalon Estates be classified in the typology of organizations?
2. What threats are inherent to this type of organization?
3. What threats are specific for Avalon Estates?

4. Provide a normative description, in headlines, of the internal controls aimed at the completeness and timeliness of rental and service revenues.
5. What data must be recorded in the contracts with renters of houses and what internal controls must be put in place to ensure the integrity and continuity of these data?

CONTINGENCY APPROACHES TO ACCOUNTING INFORMATION SYSTEMS

5

Because each entity has its own set of objectives and implementation strategies, there will be differences in objectives structure and related control activities. Even if two entities had identical objectives and structures, their control activities would be different. Each entity would be managed by different people who use individual judgments in effecting internal control. Moreover, controls reflect the environment and industry in which an entity operates, as well as the complexity of its organization, its history and its culture.

COSO (1994), p. 55

After studying this chapter, the reader should be able to:

- Determine the main contingency variables to AISs and embedded internal control systems.
- Understand exposure to these threats.
- Indicate the relationship between contingency factors and controls.
- Understand the distinction between the business domain, the information and communication domain, and the ICT domain.
- Understand the distinction between strategy formulation and strategy implementation.

Chapter Outline

Customizing an internal control system to specific contingent factors may improve efficiency. This chapter introduces two contingency approaches to AIS and embedded internal control systems. In the first approach, the most important contingency factors are national characteristics (such as culture and degree of regulation), industry characteristics (such as the presence of a dominant flow of goods and the industry culture), business characteristics (such as the organizational culture and the contracts the business is involved in), and personal characteristics of the people of the firm (such as risk aversion, experience, cognitive style, education, and ability). In the second approach, two common contingency factors put forward by the management accounting literature – strategy and ICT – are integrated into a more generic comprehensive contingency framework. This framework is used throughout the book to analyse AIS problems, to position contiguous disciplines, and to demarcate professional occupations.

Introduction

An important question to be raised when building an AIS is: Why do internal control systems differ between firms? All kinds of factor may explain these differences. In the management control literature, a wide variety of so-called contingent factors are discussed. However, in the internal control literature, the contingency approach seems to be somewhat underdeveloped, even though customizing an internal control system to specific contingent factors may improve efficiency.

The efficiency-improving feature of a contingency approach can easily be demonstrated by means of customization of an internal control system to a specific firm versus customization of the system to the industry of that firm. The minimum required intensity of internal control may differ between individual organizations, as a result of which firm specificity may lead to a higher required intensity of internal control for one organization and a lower required quality for another organization. Should a less specific contingent factor, such as the industry, be chosen as the main factor to gear an internal control system up to, the worst performing internal control systems within the industry would constitute the bottleneck and, hence, lead to an unnecessary high quality of internal control for the industry as a whole (Figure 5.1).

Gearing up to industry or individual organizations is only one example of the alignment of internal controls to contingencies. A contingency is a situational factor that, individually and collectively, affects the efficiency of an organizational design parameter. Since internal control is an organizational design parameter, a contingency approach could also apply to internal control. In organization and management control research, contingency approaches have been investigated for decades. However, as has already been indicated in Chapter 1, internal control does not have such a long international research tradition. As a result, contingency approaches to internal control have not yet been systematically investigated. However, customization of internal controls to the type of firm, as discussed in the preceding chapters, may be considered a contingency approach to internal control *avant la lettre*.

A typical feature of the contingency studies that have been conducted is that the choice of contingent factors seems to be random. Merchant (1998, p. 729) gives a brief overview of contingent factors in management control systems. Based on the management control systems literature, he classifies factors into three main categories:

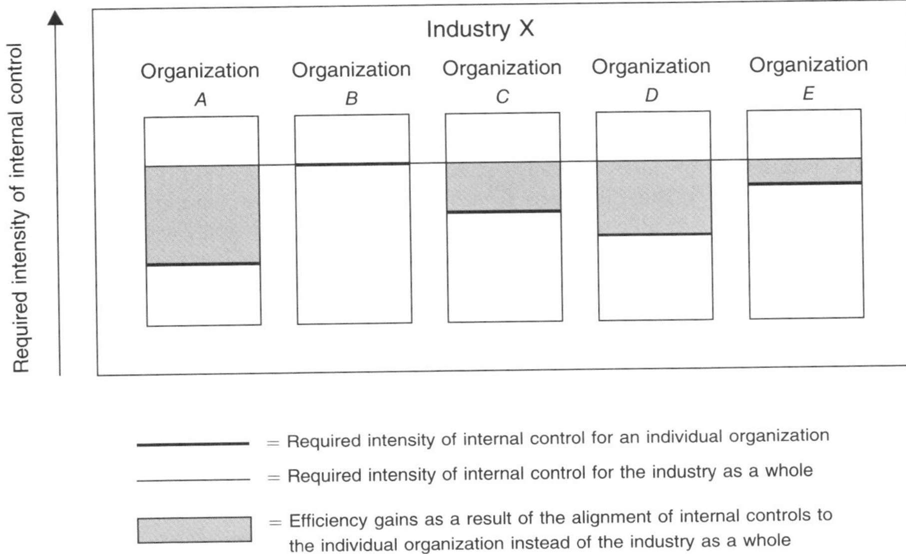

Figure 5.1 The efficiency of industry and individual organizations as contingent factors for internal controls.

organization and people factors, mission and strategy factors, and environmental and technology factors. Within each category a wide diversity of more or less interrelated factors exist. Also, within each factor, multiple variables may be defined. A meta-conclusion from the contingency research is that this approach, albeit appealing, is complex and, therefore, extremely difficult to apply. To make it more applicable, an arbitrary selection of a coherent set of variables must be made. In this chapter, we will present two frameworks that may be used when aligning controls with contingent factors.

Alignment in a Complex Control Environment

Our increasingly global environment with an ever-increasing variety of types of organization, ICT that both enables and causes types of information provision and communication which were considered utopian for centuries, and extreme worldwide competition constitute a complex control environment for most organizations. In order to reduce environmental complexity, we introduce a contingency framework that consists of five interrelated layers (Figure 5.2).

Twinning Programmes in Eastern Europe

Since the fall of the communist regimes in Eastern Europe, these countries have been going through major societal and economical change processes. Western European countries try to support these developments and offer help in a wide variety of areas.

On the inititiative of international institutions such as the World Bank (http://www.worldbank.com/), the European Commission (http://europa.eu.int/comm/), and the European Bank for Reconstruction and Development (http://www.ebrd.com/), several support programmes have been developed to improve business activities in these countries such that they will be able to compete in the world market in the near future. Some of these programmes are conducted as technical assistance projects, others as so-called twinning programmes. Twinning stands for the combination of technology and winning. Twinning projects are aimed at establishing more prolonged relationships than technical assistance programmes do.

In practice, many of the twinning programmes do not reach their goals satisfactorily. Some of the causes are beyond the reach of project management (e.g. the lagging macro-economic development as well as the – according to Western measures – often extinct, illogical, and too restrictive governmental regulations in some Eastern European countries). However, part of the cause is within reach of project management; for example, project management sometimes fails to recognize the differences between Eastern and Western cultures, which leads to miscommunication, vain attempts to carbon-copy Western governance and control philosophies in Eastern companies, and even complete project runaways.

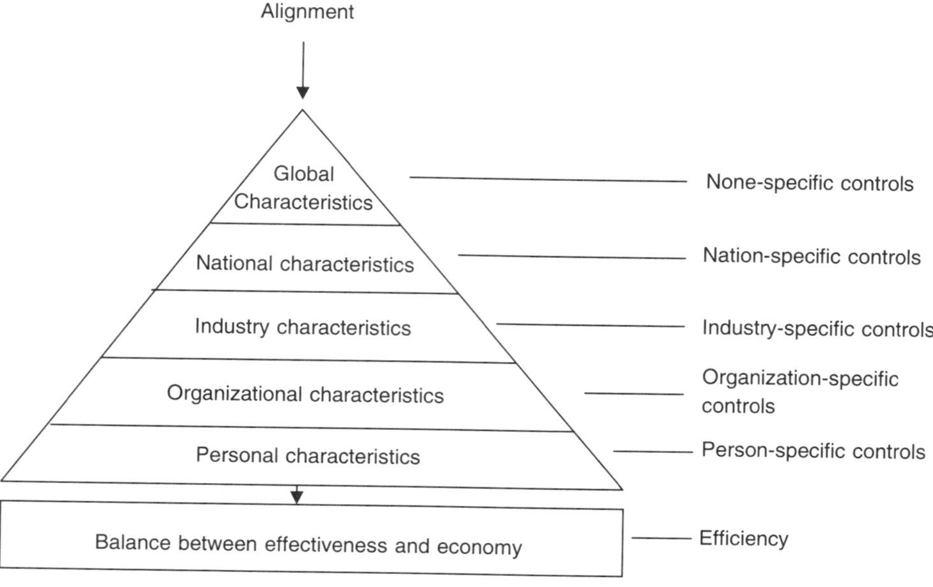

Figure 5.2 A five-layer contingency framework.

Layer 1: Alignment with Global Characteristics

This layer focuses on controls involving all human beings. The emphasis here is on the alignment of controls and policies which are beneficial to the long-term survival of the planet. The issue at stake here is sustainability: our current economic activities should be undertaken in such a way that future generations will not suffer from the negative consequences thereof. Basically, sustainability consists of three elements: an economic dimension, a societal dimension, and an environmental dimension. For each of these dimensions, a set of specific goals can be defined. For example, within the economic dimension, a company may want to pursue a certain increase in shareholder value. Within the societal dimension, that very same company may want to pursue good relationships with local government by offering more than the necessary employment. Within the environmental dimension, this company may want to invest in 'green' electricity utilities. These goals may be conflicting, and it is a challenge for management to balance them. Accounting plays a role in this balancing act in that a so-called triple bottom line, consisting of an organization's economic, societal, and environmental performance, is reported. The scope of alignment to global characteristics is very wide. This implies that, ideally, every organization on our planet should comply with norms and values associated with sustainability. Hence, in an ideal world, the controls applied here are autonomous (i.e. independent of any contingent factor). Unfortunately, our world is not ideal. For example, consider the great differences between developed countries in their environmental policies (tolerable CO_2 emission in the USA is higher than in most European countries), and their conceptions of human rights (the death penalty, common in some American states, is considered inhumane in most European countries, mercy killing is not acceptable in the USA and a lot of European countries, whereas it is legal – under strict conditions – in the Netherlands).

Layer 2: Alignment with National Characteristics

In this layer, nation or society-specific controls are developed. Alignment takes place with the specific characteristics of the country where the organization resides, and where transactions are completed. Important elements in this alignment are national culture, the judicial system, and the economic environment. To make an effective alignment with any of these contingencies, they must be measured; for example, aligning with national culture implies that national culture must be operationalized (see Box). When the well-known cultural dimensions as developed by Hofstede (1980) are applied to control systems, some interesting relationships may be derived. A culture high on power distance is expected to rely heavily on centralization as a means to avoid control problems. An individualistic culture may benefit from group-based rewards as incentives for cooperation, whereas a collectivistic culture may not want to apply any form of performance-based rewards. A masculine culture could rely on control systems that define targets and measure the progress toward those targets, whereas a feminine culture may want to rely on shared values and beliefs as part of their control systems. Finally, a culture high on uncertainty avoidance may have a strong preference for fixed procedures as codified in a control handbook describing the accounting and administrative organization.

Operationalizing National Culture

Hofstede (1980) distinguished four cultural dimensions: power distance, individualism, masculinity, and uncertainty avoidance. His research has been much cited and his classification is dominant in international research and business. *Power distance* may be high or low. High power refers to the extent that members of a certain society accept that institutional or organizational power is unequally distributed. *Individualism* is opposed to *collectivism*. This dimension refers to whether or not individuals see themselves as an individual or as part of a group. In an individualistic society, people tend to put their self-interest before the group's interest. In a collectivistic society, people are motivated by group interests. *Masculinity* is opposed to *femininity*. Masculinity puts an emphasis on achievement, assertiveness, and material success. Femininity puts an emphasis on relationships, modesty, and the quality of life. *Uncertainty avoidance* can be strong or weak. People strong on uncertainty avoidance feel uncomfortable when the future is unknown and ambiguous.

Layer 3: Alignment with Industry Characteristics

In this layer, industry or firm-specific controls are developed. The typology of organizations and the subsequent discussion of organizations with a dominant flow of goods and organizations without a dominant flow of goods in the preceding chapters is illustrative of this approach. Here, internal controls are geared towards the presence or absence of a dominant flow of goods. However, there are other industry-specific contingencies. Typical examples of such factors are industry culture, and industry-specific governmental regulations; for example, aligning controls with specific governmental regulations implies that these regulations must be well understood by the members of the industry. Furthermore, if they understand the regulations, they must be willing to comply with them, and they must have the right instruments and people to do so.

Layer 4: Alignment with Organization Characteristics

In this layer, organization-specific controls are developed. As has been common when designing industry-specific controls, this type of alignment has also been performed for decades in the development of internal control systems. Traditionally, the more visible organizational characteristics have been used to align controls; for example, a company gives discounts to customers on the basis of their cumulative orders. Controls include a discount table authorized by an official management guideline, application of the discount table by the sales department and sample-based checking of the correct application of this table by the administration, and reconciling gross revenues, discounts, and net revenues by the administration at the end of the reporting period. However, there are other, often less visible, organization-specific contingencies. Typical examples are organizational culture, organizational strategy, organizational structure, information systems, leadership styles, and specific competencies; for example, aligning with organizational culture implies that organizational culture must be operationalized (see Box).

> ***Operationalizing Organizational Culture***
>
> Organizational culture is the collection of shared values and norms that exist in an organization and that are formally or informally taught to incoming employees. Organizational culture is influenced by various factors including: the beliefs and values of the organization's founder; the national culture of an organization's native or host country; the industry culture; problems of external adaptation and survival that pose challenges to be met via the creation of a coherent culture; and management deliberately effectuating cultural controls. From these factors, a set of proxies for organizational culture can be derived (e.g. Vecchio, 1991). First, the measures and controls managers apply. Note that a lack of performance measures is also an indicator of a certain organizational culture. Second, the manner in which managers react to critical incidents; for example, the presence or absence of willingness to take advantage of crises. Third, the types of deliberate role modelling offered by managers; for example, the design of the organizational structure as chosen by management on the basis of technical considerations influences the pattern of formal and informal relations. Fourth, the criteria managers use for distributing rewards and punishments.

Layer 5: Alignment with Personal Characteristics

In this layer, person-specific controls are developed. Every person may be considered unique. Customization of control systems to every specific member of an organization would cause some practical problems. If an employee leaves the organization and is replaced by another person, this would imply a change in control system. In an age of employability without lifelong commitment to one firm, this is highly dysfunctional. Also, control systems would become extremely complex. For example, imagine an organization employing 100,000 people. This organization would have to create 100,000 different control systems. A feasible approach to customizing control systems to personal characteristics is to distinguish a limited number of types of person. Such a classification could be based on personality traits, cognitive style, or risk aversion, but also on more overt human characteristics like the propensity to commit fraud; for example, persons who are likely to perpetrate fraud will always necessitate tight controls whereas those less likely to perpetrate fraud will only need soft controls.

There is a lack of theory in the field of customization of control systems to personal characteristics. Questions that need still to be answered are: What personal characteristics determine the nature of controls? How do these personal characteristics interact with these controls? Is alignment to personal characteristics necessary? Is such an alignment possible? What are the benefits of this alignment? Our knowledge of this field is highly anecdotal and based on common sense. However, if we broaden our vision on control systems to personnel selection and placement, then the measurement of people's cognitive styles gains relevance. Potential employees may be hired on the basis of a selection process that makes use of the relationship between professional occupation, personality, and the types of person the organization desires.

Strongly related to the alignment of controls with personal characteristics is the alignment of information provision with personal characteristics. Unlike the alignment of controls, there is a well-established literature on information provision and decision making in relation to personal characteristics. Again, a classification of personality types must be used to make customization of information to personal characteristics practically feasible. To determine the information requirements of a decision maker, two approaches may be followed: the value and the events approaches. The value approach is based on the premise that the provider of information or the designer of the information system knows which decision models are used by a decision maker and, thus also knows what information in which format is relevant for this decision maker. The events approach is based on the premise that the provider of information or the designer of the information system does not know what decision models are used by a decision maker and, thus, cannot determine what information in which format is relevant for the decision maker. Decision models are mental processes which are applied to stimuli (information) to make decisions. The nature of these decision models is mainly dependent on the subjective manner in which decision makers deal with provided stimuli, and this partially depends on their personal characteristics. Here, we enter the field of research into behavioural aspects of information processing, called *human information processing* research. This research reveals that decision making is strongly dependent on the subjective characteristics of decision makers. The cognitive style, especially, is a factor of great importance; for example, it appears that people with an analytic cognitive style perform better when provided with aggregated data and those with a non-analytic cognitive style perform better when provided with non-aggregated, more elementary data. This example supports the view that the conflict between the value approach and the events approach may be resolved by classifying an individual in a certain cognitive-style category, making use of prior knowledge regarding the relationship between a certain cognitive style and information needs, and, subsequently, reasoning toward the expected information needs of that individual.

Operationalizing Personal Characteristics

An example of a personal characteristic is a person's cognitive style. Cognitive style can be defined as the characteristic, consistent mode of functioning individuals exhibit during perceptual and intellectual activities. A wide variety of tests have been developed to measure cognitive style. For example, the Myers–Briggs Type Indicator (MBTI) measures a person's mode of information gathering, mode of information processing, whether she is introverted or extroverted, and whether she has a preference for perceiving or judging. The MBTI is a paper-and-pencil test consisting of about 100 items. With respect to the operationalization of cognitive styles in relation to information provision, the dimensions information gathering and information processing, especially, have some interesting features. Information gathering may be intuitive or sensing. Intuitive types prefer to deal with possibilities, dislike routine activities, and don't need complete information before entering into decision processes. Sensing types prefer to deal with hard facts, use their senses in collecting information, like structured settings, and, as a consequence, they strive for information as complete as possible before entering into a decision process. Information processing may be feeling-oriented of thinking-oriented. Feeling types use subjective values when making decisions, thereby discriminating between valued and not-valued. Thinking types follow a logical decision process, thereby discriminating between true and false.

The Balance between Effectiveness and Economy

Effectiveness and economy must always be balanced when designing control systems (and any system in general). Effectiveness of control systems refers to the degree to which the goals of operating such systems are attained. Here, the question at stake is if organizations, and more specifically the people within organizations, act in accordance with management's intentions. Economy of control systems pertains to the degree to which minimization of costs of controls is strived for. For example, from an effectiveness point of view a minimum number of functions (and hence employees) of five is necessary for enabling segregation of duties between authorization, custody, recording, controlling, and execution. From an economy point of view, the number of employees is minimized at such a level that the necessary primary activities can reasonably be performed. This number could be as low as one person. Balancing effectiveness and economy might imply that the number of employees is reduced to three people. It is important to note that the number of employees must be such that effective controls are accomplished while making use of a minimum of resources. In our view, this dual goal can be called efficiency.

A Comprehensive Contingency Framework

This section develops a comprehensive contingency framework that can be used to describe, analyse, and solve those AIS problems that may arise in contemporary businesses. The framework is adapted from Maes (1998) and the strategic alignment model is from Henderson and Venkatraman (1993). It should be stressed that the framework is not solely aimed at AIS problems, but is generic in nature. The framework is two-dimensional. The first dimension is strategy formulation versus strategy implementation, or the external domain versus the internal domain. The second dimension is the business domain, the information and communication domain, and the ICT domain.

Within the first dimension, in the external domain, the business is positioned toward its competitors. The main managerial task is to formulate strategy in such a way that competitive advantage can be accomplished. In the internal domain, the business tries to structure itself and put itself to work in such a manner that the intended strategy can be realized. The AIS is important in helping an organization to adopt a sustainable strategic position, since it provides the necessary information to align business activities and to connect the business with the outside world. Hence, the AIS can bridge the gap between the external and the internal domain.

As illustrated in Chapter 1, one of the features of the discipline of AIS is that it studies the ways in which data are collected, recorded, and processed in order to provide relevant and reliable information for decision making and accountability. Thus, information can be studied from at least two angles. First, information is provided to support or enable decision making (i.e. the decision relevance paradigm). Second, information is provided on a wide variety of performance indicators for accountability purposes (i.e. the accountability paradigm). In both instances, there is an underlying reality – the business – which is the object of information provision. Ideally, there is a one-to-one relationship between information and the business. In practice, this relationship is one-to-one only seldomly because information often cannot provide a perfect representation of the underlying reality, or can only do so at unreasonably high costs. The efficiency of data collection, recording and processing, and information provision is strongly influenced by the media – imagine them as transportation vehicles – used to inform and communicate. The collection of these media is generally referred to as information and communication technology (ICT). Obviously, the current state of information and communication technology determines the efficiency of data collection, recording and processing, and information provision to a large extent. So, there is a strong interrelationship between information (and communication), the business, and ICT. These domains and their interrelationships constitute the second dimension for classification of AIS instruments.

Before continuing our discussion of the comprehensive contingency framework, we must resolve an issue which has only implicitly been tackled in the preceding chapters. AIS is about information and communication, as are the contiguous disciplines of management accounting and information management. COSO considers information and communication one of the five components of internal control, and indeed managers use information for decision making and accountability. An unambiguous definition of information and the related concept of communication can now be given on the basis of what has been discussed in the previous chapters. In addition, the main source of information (namely data) should also be carefully defined in order not to end up in a Babel-like confusion about semantic issues. So, here it is. Information can be defined as all the processed data that contribute to the

	Business	Information communication	ICT communication
Strategy formulation	Organization strategy	Information strategy	ICT strategy
Strategy implementation	Operations	Information provision	ICT infrastructure

Figure 5.3 Comprehensive contingency framework based on the dimensions for classification of AIS problems.

recipient's understanding of applicable parts of reality. Data are the most elementary representations of applicable parts of reality, which do not have meaning until they are processed. Communication is the process of sending and receiving data or information.

There is a continuous alignment and balance-seeking interaction between the elements of the two dimensions of the comprehensive contingency framework. As we have already indicated, the framework may be used for the description, analysis, and solution of any business problem. We choose to apply this generic framework and tailor it to classify AIS problems. Figure 5.3 depicts the comprehensive contingency framework.

To make this framework more specific to AIS, a further refinement must be made. The concept of control is strongly related to AIS. Control can be looked at from several viewpoints. From a business perspective, control is aimed at the continuous attainment of a company's goals. This is generally referred to as the effectiveness and efficiency approach (Baker 1998). Within this notion of control, decision making and accountability are enablers of control. A number of control concepts can be distinguished. The comprehensive contingency framework comprises a cascaded control framework, in the sense that these control concepts can be overlaid on it. The control concepts that are directly linked to the cells in the framework include, but are not limited to, internal control, information control, ICT control, strategic control, and management control. These control concepts can be overlaid on the comprehensive contingency framework (Figure 5.4).

	Business	Information communication	ICT communication
Strategy formulation	Strategic control	Strategic control	Strategic control
Strategy implementation	Management control Internal control	Management control Internal control Information control	Management control Internal control Information control ICT control

Figure 5.4 Control concepts overlaid on the comprehensive contingency framework.

Control Concepts in the Comprehensive Contingency Framework

Obviously, internal control, as defined by the Committee of Sponsoring Organizations of the Treadway Commission (COSO 1994), provides instruments for strategy implementation. Effectiveness and efficiency of operations and safeguarding of assets primarily pertain to operations in the business domain. Reliability of financial reporting primarily pertains to the information provision in the information and communication domain, as well as to the ICT infrastructure in the ICT domain. Compliance with laws and regulations pertains to all three domains. Internal control is not aimed at strategy formulation. However, strategy formulation is *indirectly* influenced by internal control; for example, when management wants to formulate the organizational strategy, then they need effective internal and external information as input for their decision-making process. The internal control system creates such conditions for data collection so that effective information can indeed be provided. The issue of strategy formulation is at stake in strategic control, which is not part of the internal control system. Hence, internal control is limited to the strategy implementation level.

Information control can be defined as all those activities employed by or on behalf of an organization's management to ensure the reliability and relevance of information provision for internal or external use and the proper functioning of underlying information systems. Since strategy formulation does not *directly* influence information reliability or information relevance, information control is limited to strategy implementation. Anglo-Saxon literature usually refers to the concept of information control as internal accounting control or just accounting control, as opposed to administrative or operational control. This implies that information control pertains to the information and communication domain as well as to the ICT domain on the strategy implementation level.

Internal Accounting and Operational Controls

Internal accounting controls are aimed at providing information in accordance with defined quality requirements. Operational controls (or administrative controls) are aimed at the effectiveness and efficiency of business operations. The definition of internal control, as presented in the COSO report, considers both aspects by identifying effectiveness and efficiency of operations (operational controls) and reliability of financial reporting (internal accounting controls) as objectives. In the COSO definition, the evolution of the concept of internal control, from an instrument to help auditors determine the most efficient method of planning a financial audit to a central principle of good management, is made visible. The distinction between internal accounting controls and operational control can also be illustrated by means of the comprehensive contingency framework. Operational controls mainly fit into the business domain, whereas accounting controls mainly fit into the information and communication domain and the ICT domain.

Preventive and Detective Controls

Preventive controls are mainly aimed at creating conditions for reliable information and efficient and effective business operations, and making detective controls possible. They are designed to deter unavoidable control problems before they arise. Detective controls are aimed at checking outcomes from business processes in order to assess the reliability of information and the efficiency and effectiveness of the underlying business operations. They are designed to discover control problems soon after they arise. A third category of controls, which could fit into this classification, are corrective controls. Corrective controls are designed to remedy problems discovered through detective controls. Corrective controls may be considered a part of detective controls.

Overlaps between Classifications of Control Instruments

When comparing classifications of internal controls between internal accounting controls versus operational controls and preventive controls versus detective controls, there is a partial overlap. The distinction between internal accounting controls and operational controls seems more in accordance with recent developments in the fields of auditing (including assurance services and operational auditing), controlling, information management, and management in general. The scope of the distinction between preventive and detective controls seems somewhat narrower. The following matrix presents some examples of overlapping controls and the preventive and detective controls classification:

	Accounting controls	**Operational controls**
Preventive controls	Segregation of duties, hiring qualified accounting and data processing personnel, effectively controlling physical access to facilities, utilizing well-designed documents, establishing suitable procedure for authorizing transactions.	Establish effective procedures for budgeting and standard setting, issuing instructions and directives, effectively screening executives before they are hired.
Detective controls	Duplicate checking of calculations, preparing bank reconciliations, verifying the proper use of all pre-numbered documents, preparing monthly	Preparing periodic performance reports that highlight variances between actual and standard costs and revenues, policy control, standards control reporting

ICT control is a somewhat ambiguous concept, because it has not been accurately defined in the literature. One instance was developed in practice, because there was a need for ICT-related cost control. ICT costs can be distinguished into costs that are directly related to investments in hardware, software, and people, and costs caused by projects that underperform (delays, cost increases, limited functionality, etc.). Like

ICT benefits, the latter category of ICT costs is extremely difficult to measure. This justifies a specialized discipline like ICT control. Another instance of ICT control can best be clarified by means of defining it as all those activities employed by or on behalf of an organization's management to ensure the proper functioning of an organization's information systems. Since information system development is critical to its proper functioning, this notion of ICT control includes controls in the information system development process. It must be recognized that the gap between both notions of ICT control is not as big as it seems, because the probability of a well-developed and proper functioning information system being cost-effective as well is high. We therefore adhere to the latter definition of ICT control. ICT control pertains to the ICT domain on the strategy implementation level.

Strategic control is aimed at formulating the right strategy, given the specific circumstances of an organization. Logically, this control concept pertains to the strategy formulation domain. Strategy formulation may concern the business domain, the information and communication domain, and the ICT domain.

Management control can be defined as all those activities management employs to have its people think and act in accordance with the business's goals. Hence, management control provides the instruments to implement strategy. An important element in management control is the efficient use of a company's resources. Here, reference is made to capital, material, and human resources. This indicates the broad scope of management control. Just like internal control, management control pertains to the business domain, the information and communication domain, and the ICT domain.

From the framework in Figure 5.4, we can see that management control and internal control are similar in nature. Yet, some authors argue that there are differences (e.g. Romney and Steinbart 2000). These differences cannot be accounted for by the framework. For that reason, we either need an additional dimension or we must find proof that differences are fictitious. Management control, unlike internal control, has a strong focus on behavioural aspects of organizational performance. However, an even larger difference between management control and internal control is that management control has evolved from the idea that businesses need instruments to implement their strategies, whereas internal control has evolved from the idea that business transactions must be organized and executed properly. Following the COSO definition of internal control, there is hardly any difference – at least in theory – between management control and internal control. However, since the COSO definition represents a significant move away from an internal control definition, that is confined to internal accounting controls, to a definition that also addresses objectives in the business domain, we must go back to the roots of internal control in order to determine the core of AIS problems. The issue of the similarities and differences between management control and internal control will be further discussed in Chapter 8. The primary objective of internal control used to be the reliability of information. Internal control as we conceive it today, being much broader, is an evolutionary form of internal accounting control. So, the core of internal control and, hence, the core of AIS problems is formed by information provision. This core can be found in the information and communication domain at the strategy implementation level (Figure 5.3).

Migrating toward the Essential Level of AIS Problems

As demonstrated throughout this book, AIS – as a discipline – is primarily involved with the quality of information for decision making and accountability. Hence, the core element of AIS problems is information provision, and the main control concepts are management control, internal control, and information control. Since information control is a subset of internal control, the solution to any AIS problem must be found within information control and management control in so far as it concerns the information and communication domain. Control over ICT infrastructure, strategy formulation, and business operations are all supportive of control of information provision. Hence, we will refer to strategy implementation in the information and communication domain as the essential level of AIS problems.

We can now instantiate the third and fourth steps in the approach to solving AIS problems as introduced in the Appendix to Chapter 2:

1. Identification of threats.
2. Assessment of the exposure of these threats.
3. *Determination of position in the comprehensive contingency framework.*
4. *Determination of applicable control concepts.*
5. Determination of applicable control instruments.

Position in the Framework

The framework consists of six cells, which can be referred to as shown in Figure 5.3. Strategy is a unifying theme that gives coherence and direction to the actions and decisions of an individual or organization (e.g. Grant 1998). Based on the vast literature on and the wide variety of definitions of strategy, we believe there is consensus on the meaning of strategy for gaining competitive advantage. *Organizational strategy*, as the main notion of strategy, is about how an organization can continuously defeat its competitors by doing the right things. It is about outperforming competitors. However, strategy also acts as a vehicle for information and communication within organizations. Here, the notion of *information strategy* comes into play. As we have demonstrated in Chapter 1, information plays a key role in our information society, be it as a marketable product or as an instrument to facilitate managerial decision making. Information strategy serves two goals. First, it can support organization strategy and, hence, influence the organization's competitive position *indirectly*. Second, it can influence the organization's competitive position *directly*. In both instances, information strategy provides guidance to desirable organizational behaviour and is part of organizational strategy. ICT strategy is part of information strategy and, hence, is also part of organizational strategy. Just like information strategy, ICT strategy can influence the organization's competitive position in a direct as well as an indirect fashion.

Organizational Strategy, Information Strategy, and ICT Strategy

In contemporary organizations, there is a continuous alignment between organizational strategy, information strategy, and ICT strategy. The Internet offers unique possibilities for gaining competitive advantage. Potential clients that normally would not be interested in doing business with a certain company because of geographical constraints now come within reach. Here, we see that ICT may play the role of an enabler of changing organizational strategies. The question is: What comes first, organization strategy or ICT strategy, or perhaps information strategy? The truth is there is no answer to this question. Let us look at the following fictitious but nevertheless realistic scenario. The CEO of a wholesaler proposes to his board members that the firm gets involved in e-business. He motivates his proposal by means of the following arguments: (1) ICT allows us to build flexible information systems for gaining access to potential customers at relatively low costs; (2) we must lower our costs to remain competitive; (3) our current clients require faster delivery times following order placement; (4) our current clients require exact information about delivery times; and (5) there is a market of new economy firms that require their vendors to engage in interorganizational information systems to enable fast and seamless communication.

The board members are convinced that e-business cannot be overlooked any longer. However, they feel that they have to reformulate their organization strategy if they want to enter e-business. Recently, the board has received some criticism because they did not seem to be able to formulate a proper organizational strategy. Finally, they were able to convice the market that they have formulated such a strategy. Changing the strategy again, now, would have a negative impact on the company's reputation. The CEO agrees, but explains that it is not the organizational strategy that is at stake, but rather information strategy and ICT strategy. He believes all his arguments pertain to either information strategy or ICT strategy. First, striving for a full exploitation of the possibilities of ICT is a matter of ICT strategy. Second, striving for decreasing costs by means of ICT deployment is also a matter of ICT strategy. Third, striving for faster delivery times is a matter of information strategy because faster delivery will automatically occur when information flows become faster. Fourth, more exact information about delivery times is a matter of information strategy. Fifth, engaging in interorganizational information systems is a matter of ICT strategy. The board is not convinced since organizational strategy is about outperforming competitors; however, by means of the proposed measures, there is indeed a great chance that competitors will be outperformed. The CEO argues that a focus on gaining competitive advantage is at stake here by either exploiting or mitigating information imperfections. Hence, it is strategy, but limited to information and ICT.

Control Concepts

The six cells discerned in the framework refer to the control concepts indicated in Figure 5.4. If internal control and management control are to converge in what might be called organizational control, an integration of the constituent control instruments of both control concepts must be made. This issue is discussed in depth in Chapter 8. For now, it is important to realize that the core of AIS problems is information provision, which is in the lower middle cell of the comprehensive contingency framework. Hence, the applicable control instruments can be found among management controls, internal controls, and information controls. Any control problem that stems from one of the other cells in the framework must be rerouted toward the information provision cell. When a threat is identified, and its exposure and position within the framework are determined, the following situations may be encountered within the context of Figure 5.3:

- The threat is in the organizational strategy domain. The questions to be raised are: (1) What are the consequences of this threat – if becoming a reality – for information strategy? (2) What are the consequences of this threat – if becoming a reality – for operations? (3) What are the consequences of the changes in the information strategy domain for information provision? (4) What are the consequences of the changes in the operations domain for information provision?
- The threat is in the ICT strategy domain. The questions to be raised are: (1) What are the consequences of this threat – if becoming a reality – for information strategy? (2) What are the consequences of this threat – if becoming a reality – for ICT infrastructure? (3) What are the consequences of changes in the information strategy domain for information provision? (4) What are the consequences of the changes in the ICT infrastructure domain for information provision?
- The threat is in the information strategy domain. The question to be raised is: What are the consequences of this threat – if becoming a reality – for information provision?
- The threat is in the operations domain. The question to be raised is: What are the consequences of this threat – if becoming a reality – for information provision?
- The threat is in the ICT infrastructure domain. The question to be raised is: What are the consequences of this threat – if becoming a reality – for information provision?

A Threat in the Organizational Strategy Domain

An organization aims to promote human environmental awareness. Its strategy is focused on developing as broad a range of activities as possible and, thus, realizing its idealistic goal on the broadest scope. Besides a limited set of routine activities, all kinds of other activities that its staff members consider important contributions to the attainment of the organization's goal may be undertaken. In the past, some more and less successful initiatives have been developed, such as sponsoring scientific research, organizing symposia, disseminating idealistic advertisements using various media (radio, television, the Internet, billboards, and the like), contributing to the extra costs of environment-friendly production processes, carrying out environment-friendly production processes, nature-improvement programmes (such as tree planting days), soil cleaning activities, and helping to dismantle and remove environment-harming production installations. The organization emphasizes that it does not want to employ an aggressive approach in performing these activities.

A threat within the organizational strategy domain is that the organization displays undesirable activities. Undesirable activities are defined by the organization as those that involve an aggressive approach.

Question 1	What are the consequences of this threat – if becoming a reality – for information strategy?
Possible Answer 1	The information strategy should put internal information about operations at the heart of the organization.
Question 2	What are the consequences of this threat – if becoming a reality – for operations?
Possible Answer 2	Operations should focus on controlling its people in such a way that they do not become involved in aggressive activities.
Question 3	What are the consequences of the changes in the information strategy domain for Information provision?
Possible Answer 3	Information provision should be aimed at maximizing information collection on deviations from the rule that no aggressive approach should be followed in pursuing the organization's objectives.
Question 4	What are the consequences of the changes in the operations domain for information provision?
Possible answer 4	Information provision should focus on the measurement of the number of times the organization's people were involved in aggressive activities.

In our approach to AIS, we search for the informational aspects of business administration and ICT employment. This leads to the stepwise approach, as described here. In addition, we must realize that the discerned control instruments can be applied in detail only to information provision. In accordance with the approach taken in this book, AIS is studied from a managerial perspective. However, this does not imply that AIS broadens its scope to the other information disciplines – management accounting and information management. Nevertheless, it provides instruments to diagnose threats that can be solved by making use of instruments from these related disciplines. In conclusion, AIS provides instruments to find *solutions* to threats in the information provision cell, and it provides instruments to *diagnose* threats in the operations, the strategy, and the ICT infrastructure cells.

As can be seen by relating the comprehensive contingency framework to Figure 2.12 (Appendix to Chapter 2), it can also be used to analyse the relationship between threats, exposures, and control instruments. The external threats can be positioned in the upper rows of the framework, the internal threats in the lower rows. Again, it is important to note that a detailed discussion of traditional internal controls and information controls is only suitable when a threat is encountered in the information provision cell. All other threats cannot lead to more than a diagnosis and a superficial discussion of controls.

Chapter Case

Case 5.1 Moscow Bank

The Dutch consulting firm 'Consult FI' is involved in a twinning programme together with the Russian bank 'Moscow Bank'. The project is financially supported by the European Commission and a local Dutch bank. It is aimed at informing and training management and employees of the bank on issues related to doing business in a market-oriented economy. Part of the programme involves the application of contemporary accounting and control philosophies.

The project is not proceeding well. Although the advice given by the Dutch consultants is considered helpful, concrete action has not been undertaken yet. Employees of Moscow Bank attribute this to their busy agendas; the day-to-day work still must be done. The consultants sense that Moscow Bank's management subscribe to this explanation. Although management keep on promising to do their utmost to make a turn for the better, significant action is not visible. The supporting organizations are starting to lose confidence in this project and consider withdrawing from it.

Assignment

1. Make an analysis of the most probable factors that cause this project to fail and the factors that obstruct the successful future functioning of the bank on the basis of Western accounting and control philosophies. Focus on cultural differences between the Netherlands and Russia.
2 Write a report for the European Commission that contains an initial solution to the problems encountered.

Tip: you can find a lot of information on the cultural characteristics of the Netherlands and Russia on the Internet.

INFORMATION AND COMMUNICATION TECHNOLOGY AND RELATED ADMINISTRATIVE CONCEPTS

6

As you probably know, information technology is changing the way we do just about everything.

Moscove *et al.* (2001), p. 4

After studying this chapter, the reader should be able to:

- Understand the relationship between information and communication technology, business administration, and information systems.
- Describe the components of information systems.
- Distinguish the main approaches to information system development.
- Understand the features of some widely used contemporary information systems.
- Understand the need for ICT professionals and managers to develop a common language.
- Understand the main characteristics of some ICT-enabled innovations such as e-business, business process re-engineering, customer relationship management, business intelligence, and strategic enterprise management.

Ultimately, the reader will have the necessary basic knowledge of information and communication technology to efficiently study the subsequent chapters.

Chapter Outline

This chapter introduces different instances of information and communication technology (ICT). Without having the intention to be exhaustive, some important ICT issues are put forward. For the purpose of this chapter, ICT is discussed in isolation from the other three main themes of the book (i.e. accounting, internal control, and management). In order to give a clear indication of ICT for contemporary business administration, the role of ICT professionals in ICT environments as opposed to user environments is described. First, ICT is defined. The starting point is the functioning of computers and their constituent elements. Here, input and output devices, processing devices, storage devices, as well as communication devices are discussed. Information systems are the most overt manifestations of ICT which justifies a brief discussion of information system development issues as well as a somewhat more elaborate discussion of the components of information systems. Furthermore, some specific examples of contemporary ICT applications are discussed because of their impact on modern organizations, including enterprise resource planning, databases and data warehouses, decision support systems, expert systems and neural networks, groupware, and executive information systems. Finally, some ICT-enabled innovations are discussed including e-business, business process re-engineering, customer relationship management, business intelligence, and strategic enterprise management.

Introduction

Information and communication technology comprises all the electronic media used to transport information between senders and receivers and to support or enable communication. As we indicated in Chapter 5, information can be defined as all the processed data that contributes to the recipient's understanding of applicable parts of reality. Communication, on the other hand, is the process of sending and receiving data or information. This is, in a nutshell, what ICT is all about. With non-electronic media, the term ICT should not be used. Instead, the more abstract notion of documentary media would more accurately describe all the media, electronic as well as non-electronic, used to transport information. In this sense, a piece of paper is a documentary medium, but not an ICT application. Following the same line of reasoning, e-mail is an ICT application as well as a documentary medium.

As we have already demonstrated, ICT is an integral part of managing contemporary organizations. We believe a basic ICT knowledge is important to managers for several reasons:

- Managers are ICT users since they send and receive information, and, by doing so, continuously communicate with other members of the organization and third parties.
- Decisions and evaluations are made on the basis of information and communication. ICT is employed to make information and communication more efficient.
- ICT is an enabler of organizational change. Within change processes, managers play a major role in collaboration with change agents and ICT specialists. In order to adequately fulfil this role, managers must be able to communicate with the

change agents and the ICT specialists. This implies that a common language must be spoken. In our current environment, ICT is the enabler of most organizational change processes. Hence, ICT terminology is most likely to serve as that common language.

- Management is responsible for internal control. Internal control is heavily influenced by ICT developments (see Chapter 7). So, management is indirectly responsible for ICT and, especially, for integrating ICT with the information processes and the business processes within an organization and between organizations.

Information systems are the most overt manifestations of information and communication technology. If we define a system as an organized way of undertaking actions in order to attain certain goals, then an information system is an organized way of inputting data, processing data, and providing information aimed at the attainment of organizational goals. The term information system did not blossom until data input and processing, and information provision became automated. So, seen in the light of our definition of ICT, when talking about information systems this implies talking about ICT. An information system consists of five main components. In order to efficiently discuss these components, we will follow the framework as depicted in Figure 6.1.

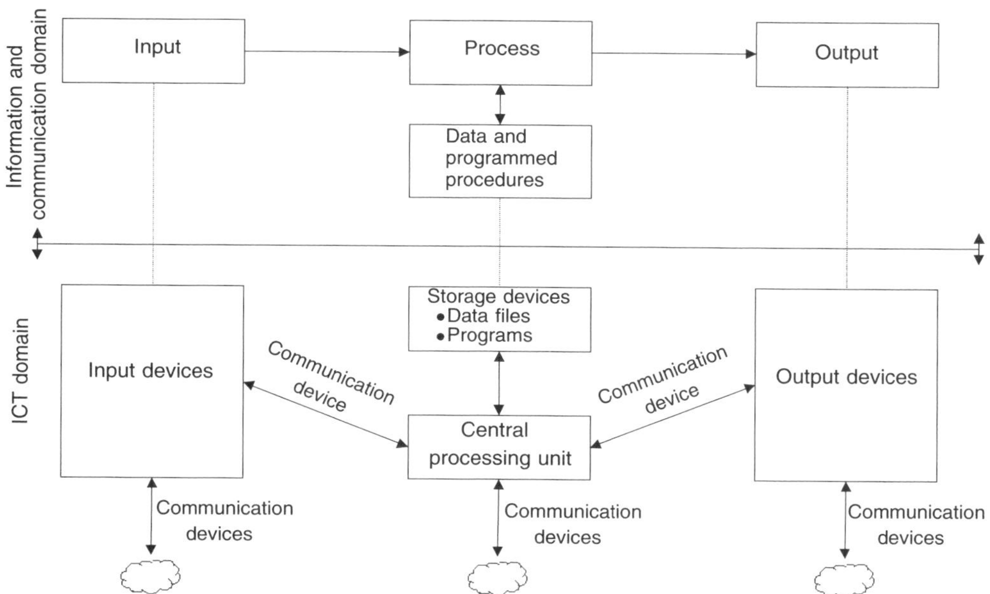

Figure 6.1 A framework for discussing the components of information systems.

In the comprehensive contingency framework as developed in Chapter 5, information and communication is discerned from ICT. In Figure 6.1 the same distinction can be recognized. Input, processing, data and programmed procedures, and output pertain to data and information content as referred to in the information and communication domain. Note that this part of the framework is in accordance with the uniform basic pattern of information provision as discussed in Chapter 2. Input devices, storage devices, central processing unit (CPU), output devices, and communication devices pertain to ICT. In the next section we will adhere to this classification.

Components of Information Systems

The heart of any information system is the computer. We could have a deep philosophical discussion about the term 'computer' (e.g. nowadays it obviously has much more functionality than just computing) but we will just stick to the internationally accepted denomination. There are several types of computer with varying degrees of complexity. The more complex a computer, the easier its constituent components can be identified. The personal computer (PC) – also microcomputer – is the most well known and least complex member of the family. The supercomputer is the most complex device. It performs so-called high-performance computing and networking (HPCN) tasks and is used for applications in technological scientific research, meteorology, environmental research, climate modelling, industrial design, and fast data processing in financial institutions. Supercomputers earn their name because they are faster than any other class of computer. Examples of supercomputers are the SGI Origin 3000, which uses the technique of parallel processing (having more than one processor working at one time on the same task), the CRAY Origin 2000, which is also a parallel system, as is the IBM RS/6000 SP, and the SGI Onyx2 RealityMonster, which is a graphical system. Within the range between the PC and the supercomputer, the mainframe and the minicomputer can be positioned. The primary differences between mainframes and minicomputers are that mainframes require highly specialized programmers, operators, and analysts, and must be housed in controlled rooms such as the data processing centre, automation department, computing department, or ICT department. Probably the most well-known minicomputer is the IBM AS/400.

Input Devices

Input devices, as do output devices, impose speed constraints on information systems since they are the slowest components of any information system. Input can be done by humans, which we will refer to as manual input, but it can also be done by means of computer applications, which we will refer to as automated input. In general, automated input increases data processing speed.

Data may be input online or batch. In both cases, data may or may not first be captured on paper as a separate recording before keying it into the computer. However, considering the speed increase that can be accomplished by inputting data online, when compared with batch input, it seems highly inefficient to first capture data on paper in an online system. Conversely, in batch-oriented systems, data must be captured somehow – on paper as a separate recording, or otherwise, like a pile of bills, sales orders, or cash receipts – before keying it into the computer. Records used to capture data are generally denoted as source documents. The most commonly used manual input device is the keyboard. In their quest for more user-friendly computers, computer and software builders have invented devices such as the mouse (or derived devices such as pointing pens, touchpads, and trackballs), touchscreen technology, and voice recognition software which, indeed, caused a revolution in user interface development. All of these devices have in common that the aim is to make the action to input data more user-friendly by means of technological solutions. An alternative approach is to aim for higher quality of source documents. A typical example of this approach is the turnaround document. A turnaround document is produced by the information system of the organization that wants to initiate a certain transaction. For example, a utility company produces bills with a payment slip attached to it. This payment slip contains all the data needed by the accounts receivable department to process the cash receipt, whereas this information would not always have been available when a customer-made form had been used as the source document. Turnaround documents can even be designed such that they can be processed automatically.

When use is being made of automated input devices, this is generally referred to as source data automation. Examples are machine-readable turnaround documents, and any other document that makes use of some kind of standard format to represent data in machine-readable form. The technology used here may be magnetic ink character recognition, or optical character recognition. The old-fashioned punchcard made use of a coding system that translated characters into holes in a card that could only be inserted into the punchcard reader if each card in a pile was properly stacked in accordance with the stacking system (e.g. the upper right corner of the punchcard is cut away so that any improperly stacked card will be identified immediately). A by now also traditional, but unlike the punchcard, still viable approach to source data automation is the bar code, which consists of a number of lines that together form a unique code that can be scanned with infrared scanning equipment. The coding systems used here may vary, but for product identification, there is the universal product code (UPC) standard that has been adopted worldwide. An important application of the UPC can be found in point-of-sale (POS) systems. POS systems make use of an optical scanner for reading the bar code that contains product data which refer to a certain inventory item and trigger further processing in the inventory files and the cash or accounts receivable files. Nowadays, frequent use is made of coding systems that make use of magnetic stripes or chips. Most debit or creditcards have a magnetic stripe which may contain a wide variety of information about the cardholder, but which may only contain a unique reference to the cardholder's files. ATM cards, bank cards, or PIN cards also make use of magnetic stripes for user identification. The cardholder uses it for making payments via countertop terminals and for withdrawing cash from her bank account. By having the magnetic stripe read by the terminal, the owner identifies herself, and, by inputting her PIN, the owner proves that she is the person she claims to be (i.e. she authorizes her transaction request). The smart card makes use of chip technology. It contains a chip, which is a microprocessor combined with a memory chip. The electronic wallet concept (with sometimes fancy names such as the CHIPKNIP or the CHIPPER) makes use of smart card technology. Such an electronic wallet can be charged by the cardholder by going to a charging device comparable with an automated teller machine, using the card as an identifier, authorizing by means of a PIN, and inputting the amount to charge to the card. From that moment on, the card contains the amount of money that was charged to it. Payments can be done by having it read by a countertop terminal operated by the vendor and connected to the bank of the cardholder or a clearing institute. When doing payments like this, no authorization is needed after identification is successful. It is easy to understand why such a card is called an electronic wallet. Once it is stolen, the thief can use it without needing any authorization. A modern approach to source data automation is the use of radio frequency tags. Such a tag is attached to a product or any other object so that it can be tracked in one way or another. The tag sends and receives radio signals that are used to track the object.

Storage Devices

There are two types of storage devices: primary and secondary memory. Primary memory is used for internally storing and retrieving data and program instructions. It may be read-only. Read-only memory (ROM) is usually used for storing parts or all of the operating system. Primary memory may also be temporarily writable. Here, erasable programmable read-only memory (EPROM) is used for a very limited number of writing actions and an almost unlimited number of retrieving actions. Also, for temporarily writable memory capacity, random access memory (RAM) is used. RAM loses its contents as soon as the power is shut off. A modern primary memory device is flash memory which, rather than the complicated writing process of the EPROM, may easily be rewritten several times. Once it is written, it does not lose its contents even if the power is shut off. Secondary memory is used for permanently or semi-permanently storing data and program instructions on external devices like hard disks, floppy disks, magnetic tape, or optical disks (CD-ROM or CD rewritable).

In order to store data, some kind of file storage system must be used. For a clear understanding of the way data are recorded, we will describe the logical – as opposed to physical – file organization. This implies that the decision whether or not to use a database is not as yet taken into consideration. A file consists of records about a certain entity. A record is a collection of data values that describe specific attributes of an entity. A file description typically contains a primary key and the other attributes belonging to that primary key. Among the attributes, there may also be references to primary keys of other files. These references are called foreign keys. A primary key is a unique identifier of a record. A secondary key need not be unique because it may refer to a group of records; for example, an article code may be the primary key in an inventory file whereas the physical location code of the inventory item, as recorded in that very same file, may be the secondary key that can be used for sorting the inventory items for picking purposes.

A distinction can be made between master files and transaction files. A master file contains data that do not change frequently or that may only change as a result of transactions recorded in a transaction file that has a reference to the primary key in the master file; for example, the inventory master file has the following record layout (note the underlining to indicate that this is the primary key to this file):

article code, article description, quantity in hand, sales price, location in warehouse.

This master file will only be updated when:

- either one of the records – article description, location in the warehouse, or sales price – changes; or
- the sales or purchases transaction file indicates that, during a specific time period, inventory items have been dispatched or received.

The sales transaction file may have the following record layout:

sales transaction code, customer code, article code, quantity dispatched.

The purchases transaction file may have the following record layout:

purchase transaction code, vendor code, article code, quantity received.

An analogy can be made between master files and ledgers which both contain the results of transactions, and between transaction files and journal vouchers which both contain transactional data.

Central Processing Unit

The term 'central processing unit' (CPU) stems from the time when mainframes and minicomputers were the most common computer systems used. With the emergence of the PC, the term CPU seems somewhat overdone, because what is referred to here is simply the microprocessor that is the heart of every PC. The microprocessor is a silicon chip that is no bigger than a thumbnail and does all the computations the computer is supposed to do. It is merely an integrated circuit that consists of millions of switches that can be switched on or off. Imagine a microprocessor or any CPU to work as follows. When a switch on the integrated circuit is switched on, it has power, and it can be read as having the code 1. If it is switched off, it does not have power, and it can be read as having the code 0. Such a code is called a binary digit or, briefly, a bit. By grouping eight bits together, a byte is formed. A byte represents one character like a digit in our decimal system or a letter of the alphabet. When storing data, the meaning of these terms become most clear. A floppy disk generally can contain 1.44 megabyte (MB) of data. Since 1 MB is 2^{20}, this means that it can store $1.44 \times 1{,}048{,}576 = 1{,}509{,}949$ characters. Hard disks in PCs can nowadays store more than 100 gigabyte (GB). Since 1 GB is 2^{30}, this means that they have storage capacity for more than $100 \times 1{,}073{,}741{,}824 = 100{,}073{,}741{,}824$ characters. In commercial communications of storage capacity, the notion of 1 MB is often used to implicitly refer to 1,000,000 bytes, and 1 GB to implicitly refer to 1,000,000,000 bytes; for example, Iomega's 250 MB zip-disk is advertised as having a capacity of 250 MB, whereas it contains 'only' $250 \times 1{,}000{,}000 = 250{,}000{,}000$ bytes and not $250 \times 1{,}048{,}576 = 262{,}144{,}000$ bytes.

The speed of a computer is mainly determined by five factors:

- The frequency of the processor's electronic clock. Frequency is measured as cycles per second; for example, a processor speed of 1,000 megahertz, which is very common for PCs nowadays, indicates that 1,000 million cycles per second can be done.

- The number of bits that can be processed in one cycle. Older PCs could process 4 bits per cycle whereas the latest PCs can process more than 128 bits per cycle.

- The number of bits transmitted at one time from one part of the computer to another. This is called the data bus size.

- The number of parallel processors. The more processors that simultaneously work on one job, the higher the processing speed. This principle is successfully applied in supercomputers. Also, making use of the Internet, using the right software allows PC users to make their processor available for heavy processing tasks such as searching an extremely large database or – and this actually happens – trying to find new solar systems.

- The nature of the processor. Processors can be graphics-oriented, arithmetic-oriented, or more general in nature. Intel's Pentium is of a more general nature. A compatible arithmetic co-processor could increase computer speed up to 200 times.

When inputting data, a distinction can be made between batch input and online input. A similar distinction can be made when processing data: batch processing and real-time processing. Hence, a matrix can be developed that summarizes the combinations of input and processing modes (Figure 6.2).

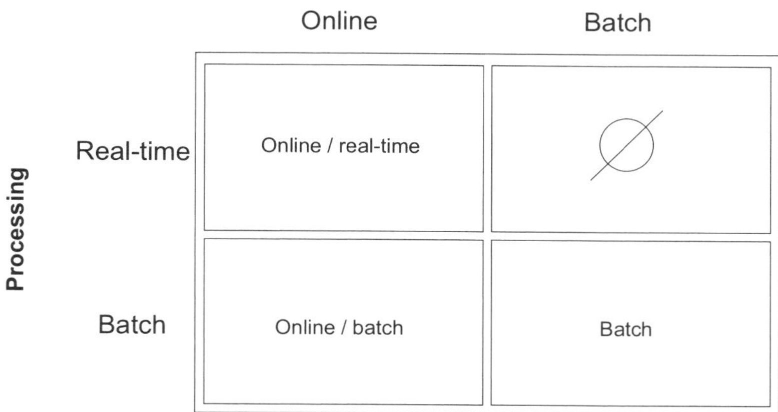

Figure 6.2 Combinations of input and processing modes.

Output Devices

Output of one information system may well serve as input of another information system. Hence, like input devices, output devices may be paper-based or electronic. The main output devices are printers. A wide range of printers can be distinguished, but the most frequently used are – in climbing degree of output quality – the matrix printer, the inkjet printer, and the laser printer. Electronic output may be presented on a computer screen or a data projector, but also in a less directly readable form such as floppy disk, hard disk, CD-ROM, or by using data transmission lines like telephone lines, television cables, or specialized network infrastructures like value-added networks (VANs).

Communication Devices

Communication devices are used throughout every part of any information system. As can be seen in Figure 6.1, there may be communication: between input devices and the outside world such as other information systems within or outside of the organization; between the CPU and storage devices, input devices, output devices and the outside world; and between output devices and the outside world.

Electronic communication generally takes place via a network. There are several types of network. A network that does not go beyond a certain geographical location is called a local area network (LAN). A LAN can be configured in three basic ways (see Figure 6.3):

- Ring configuration (e.g. a token ring network). In this type of network, each device is directly connected to two other devices. This implies that there are

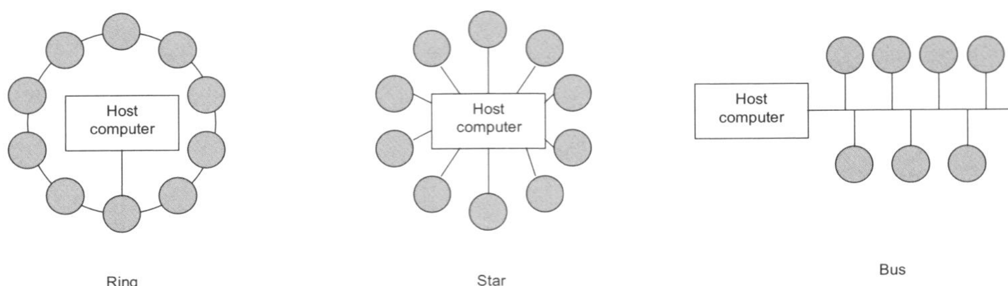

Figure 6.3 Alternative LAN configurations.

only two directions a message can go. If one of these two directions cannot be followed, then the other one is the only alternative. Because of this, the ring network is relatively sensitive to breakdowns.

- Star configuration. This configuration has a central host computer which maintains one-to-one communication lines with each device in the network. Because of this set-up, it is a solution that requires much wiring and, therefore, is comparably expensive. The trade-off is that this type of configuration is less sensitive to breakdowns because if one node goes down, the other nodes will not be affected and will continue to work.
- Bus configuration (e.g. an Ethernet network). In this configuration, each device is connected to a central bus channel. So, if one connection breaks down, then this has no implications for the remaining connections. However, if usage (i.e. the number of devices connected to the bus) becomes more intensive, then this type of network progressively becomes slower. The bus configuration is a relatively simple and safe structure, and it stands midway between the advantages and disadvantages of the star and the ring configuration. Perhaps this explains why Ethernet more or less has become the standard in most LANs.

If a LAN is transferred to a wider area, geographically crossing organization boundaries, then it is called a wide area network (WAN). Hence, WANs are used within organizations that have more than one office, branch, outlet, or production facility and that need to be able to efficiently communicate via electronic channels with each other. Whereas communication via a LAN usually makes use of company-owned equipment to operate the network, communication via a WAN usually makes use of hired long-distance data communication channels like the Internet or a value-added network (VAN) which is operated by an independent company who provides all the hardware, software, and service to make the communication channel work. A WAN may be configured in either of two ways: decentralized or centralized. In a decentralized system, each entity (business unit, department, or any other departmental unit) connected to the WAN has its own computer and possibly its own LAN. A decentralized system usually is better equipped to meet individual entity needs than is a centralized system. In a centralized system, all devices are connected to a central computer which, on the one hand, makes it more controllable but, on the other hand, makes it less sensitive to changes in individual entity needs.

Decentralization and Centralization in an Organizational Context

In view of the meaning generally assigned to the terms 'decentralization' and 'centralization' – referring to decision-making power and not to some kind of physical allocation – an analogy can be made between the role of the computer in a WAN and organizational decision making. Managers may centralize decision-making power. When doing so, they want to avoid control problems by making all the important decisions themselves, instead of having them made by their subordinates (see Chapter 8). However, they may also decentralize decision making by handing over the authority to make decisions to their subordinates. Thus, they want to make responses to market changes more direct and appropriate. Analogously, in a centralized WAN, the central computer does all the processing, whereas, in a decentralized WAN, processing is done at local computers.

Large automation departments usually have heavily centralized systems. The users are responsible for inputting the right data, and the automation department is responsible for appropriately processing and storing these data. Output may be generated locally or centrally. With the emergence of so-called client/server configurations in the 1980s, a new dimension was added to the decentralization/centralization debate. As a result of the increased potential of ICT for decentralized processing, the role of the automation department, with large mainframes doing all the computing jobs, has become more and more superfluous in most small and medium-sized companies, and even in many big companies. The technology applied here is the use of desktop computers – or in more general terms: intelligent terminals – as clients of a server system. The client sends requests for data processing to the server which performs some preparatory processing of the data and sends only the requested subset of a larger database to the client for local processing. Client/server configurations are now very common in LAN and WAN applications. Clients may be fat or thin. A fat client has enough memory and processing capacity to run applications locally. A thin client does not have enough memory and processing capacity to do this. Instead, applications run on a specific server and make use of fast communication lines to enable this. The net PC is an example of such a thin client. In the early days of mainframe computing, this type of computer would have been called a dumb terminal. The major advantage of the net PC over traditional client/server configurations is that data processing is concentrated at one physical location, which greatly enhances controllability.

Communication by means of a WAN became within reach of even the smallest companies through the advent of the Internet. The Internet makes use of the Internet protocol (IP) for transferring messages between senders and receivers. In order to be able to make use of the Internet, a user enters a contract with an Internet service provider (ISP) who has the infrastructure in place to provide individuals and organizations with a connection to the Internet. The Internet is intended for communication between organizations or persons that do not form legal entities. New developments regarding the Internet include intranets, where the IP is used for communication within organizations via a LAN or a WAN, and extranets for applications where limited access to internal data and information is allowed to third parties. Virtual private networks (VPN) are examples of relatively secure communication infrastructures within an extranet. In the early days (1970s) of electronically transferring data between organizations, a more rigid format was used for the layout of electronic messages. This format usually was industry-dependent and could only be used when two parties agreed to use that specific format. Additionally, the technical infrastructure for this type of communication required joining an existing proprietary third-party network. The overall term for this concept was electronic data interchange (EDI). Because EDI basically performs the same functions as the Internet, the term could be used for all types of electronic data communication, including the Internet. However, from a semantical viewpoint, this might be confusing. We therefore reserve the term EDI for the standardized business-to-business transferral of electronic messages.

Web pages may or may not be connected to a database. The most simple form of web page may only consist of data in word processor format (e.g. in MS Word). However, there are languages specifically designed to create web pages and links between web pages and which eliminate the need for software to translate documents that are in different formats into one uniform format. In essence, a mark-up language consist of codes – also denoted tags – that can be attached to data elements; for example, the data element 'net income' receives the tag 'NI'. Hypertext mark-up language (HTML) is the most simple example of such a language. When HTML gets less efficient and data structures become more complex and more flexibility is needed with respect to expandability and platform choice, extended mark-up language (XML) comes into play. XML is platform-independent (e.g. Windows, UNIX, mainframe, or Linux), expandable (e.g. it lets you create your own tags), and self-describing, meaning that it describes data elements in terms of their name as well as their content (e.g. <date>September 11, 2001/<date>). Also, compared with EDI, XML is much more flexible. Advantages of XML include: it is in a readable data format, it is vendor-neutral, all major software products are becoming XML-enabled, and XML will be the de facto standard for electronic communication. At the moment, there are over 400 XML-based specifications and protocols, some of which already have well-developed taxonomies containing the tags used and their meaning. Extended business reporting language (XBRL) is an example of such an protocol. It is XML-based and aimed at financial accounting in a standardized format. XBRL is especially relevant for accountants because it promises to standardize financial reporting via the Internet so that companies' financial statements become more comparable.

With the increasing speed of computers and communcation lines, a new type of service firm is emerging: the application service provider (ASP). An ASP is a company that offers a website containing software that can be used from a distant location which does not need to be downloaded in order to use it; for example, SAP (in collaboration with Hewlett-Packard and Qwest) makes its ERP package available to smaller companies that don't have the budget to install it on their own computer. Making use of ASPs is a form of outsourcing.

Related to EDI is the effectuation of electronic payments, denoted as electronic funds transfer (EFT). EFT is commonplace is countries where checks are only seldomly used. Most European countries nowadays have abandoned traditional checks and, instead, put great effort in improving international standardization in making electronic payments. When EFT is applied, a so-called clearing house which collects and processes all payments between banks must be in place. As an alternative to EFT, credit-card payments may be used. In that case, the buyer authorizes the vendor to withdraw a certain amount of money from his credit card.

Information System Development

Information system development traditionally takes place following a life cycle approach, the systems development life cycle (SDLC). This approach is strictly linear, which means that a number of stages must be gone through in a prescribed sequence. However, it should be noted that it is always possible to return to a prior phase in the SDLC. The stages may vary per SDLC, but in many instances the management cycle can be recognized by paying close attention to the planning phase; for example, systems analysis (planning), conceptual design (planning), physical design (planning), implementation and conversion (structuring), operations (execution) and maintenance (evaluation and adjusting) are typical stages in an SDLC. Because this approach resembles the flow of water coming down from a waterfall, it is expressly called the waterfall approach. There are several reasons for following such a stepwise approach, including:

- it leads to a systematic development of the application;
- it provides several measurement points or milestones which enable measurement of project progress;
- it facilitates communication between ICT experts and users;
- it leads to a check that all the defined hardware, data and software requirements have been included;
- it causes each application to be developed in accordance with agreed basic principles;
- it may lead to efficiency improvements.

In contemporary information system development projects, linear approaches are only seldom effective. The main cause of this is that many modern information systems must be organization-wide and fully integrated, as a result of which these systems become extremely complex. Often, specifications that were made at the start of the project may as well be completely discarded because they have become obsolete with the end of the project in sight. As a result of the strictly planwise, phased, and linear approach of the SDLC, the system is often found to be not meeting newly defined specifications. In order to avoid this, system development may take place making use of a so-called incremental method. In such a method, the strictly stepwise approach is abandoned in favour of a heuristic approach that makes small steps one at a time and that favours trial and error. An example of an incremental approach is prototyping.

Prototyping

Prototyping is an approach to systems development in which a simplified working model of an information system or a part of an information system is developed in order to enable user testing. Typically, prototyping involves the following activities:

- identification of basic system requirements by meeting with the user to agree on the size and scope of the system and to decide what the system should include and exclude;
- development of an initial prototype that meets agreed requirements;
- identification of changes needed by users, making adjustments by developers, evaluation or experimentation by users, and liaising with users until the desired level satisfies them;
- build the production system.

Prototyping is especially useful when it is difficult to identify a usable set of requirements; for example, users may be unable to verbalize their information needs, a prototype then may consist of a number of menus and screens which trigger users into specifying what part of the prototype they approve and disapprove of, and what other specifications they would like to be included in the system. The system developer will continue to get back to the users until they agree on the system specifications and are satisfied with the system. When applying a prototyping approach, it is important to recognize that users have a central role in systems development. As a matter of fact, the emergence of prototyping was fuelled by the rise of end-user computing where data processing was heavily decentralized and managers were able to extract the information they needed by using powerful, high-level end-user computing languages. Moreover, managers were highly dissatisfied with the irresponsiveness of ICT specialists and were looking for ways to improve data processing and, simultaneously, avoid control problems within the organization's information and communication processes.

Contemporary ICT Applications

In this section, some specific examples of contemporary ICT applications are discussed because of their impact on modern organizations, including enterprise resource planning, databases and data warehouses, decision support systems, expert systems and neural networks, groupware, and executive information systems.

Enterprise Resource Planning

Enterprise resource planning (ERP) is a concept which originated from logistical concepts such as materials requirements planning (MRP) and manufacturing resource planning (MRP II). Instead of using several systems to manage a company's business, ERP is a means for a company to streamline traditionally separate operations into one system. Information, shared through a common ERP system, flows from operation to operation. It thereby creates more efficient processes, higher quality reporting, and simpler company-wide communication. Hence, ERP is an integrated, process-oriented, organization-wide ICT solution designed to facilitate the achievement of an organization's goals and objectives. So, ERP is aimed at integrating a company's operational information systems in such a way that work processes are supported. ERP systems encompass many business applications, such as general ledger, payroll, supply chain management, manufacturing and business intelligence. Although very costly to implement, ERP systems have been adopted by many companies in recent years due to the potential for lowering operating costs, shorter cycle times, and higher customer satisfaction. Successful adoptions of ERP systems have also been linked to business process re-engineering efforts and implementation of best practices as in benchmarking.

Advantages and Disadvantages of ERP Systems

Advantages:

- Implementation forces the firm to critically examine existing business processes.
- ERP systems increase an organization's efficiency as a result of improved adjustment.
- Within a given range, ERP applications are configurable to suit the firm's business processes.
- Users are empowered due to increased information sharing across the enterprise.
- Information for decision making gains relevance because it can combine internal with external data and information.

Disadvantages:

- High costs associated with software licence, computer hardware, implementation, and ongoing maintenance.
- While ERPs are somewhat flexible when first purchased, they ultimately become relatively inflexible as the business rules are defined in the system.

- In the long run, inflexiblity of ERP applications can inhibit a firm's adaptability and responsiveness to changing customer demands and competitive pressures.
- Due to the complexity of implementations, most firms end up changing their business processes to fit the ERP software.
- ERP systems are internally focused, which can be a handicap given the rapidly evolving e-business model.

Organizations that implement an ERP system will find out that its impact on the way they conduct business is tremendous. We anticipate, in the near future, that there will be three major extensions of ERP systems. The first is the extension of ERP systems from information systems to knowledge systems. The accompanying ICT on top of the ERP system is groupware, data warehouses, and intranets to facilitate knowledge creation and integration. Here, the information system must enable the organization to get a sound grasp of its own true abilities and how it can improve them. The second is the application of ERP systems as interorganizational information systems. The accompanying ICT is EDI, Internet, and point-of-sale applications. Here, the information system must enable the organization to understand the needs of its suppliers and customers. The underlying assumption is that if an organization gets a better understanding of its supplier and customer needs, it will be more successful. The third extension is the use of an organization's ERP system for learning about its suppliers' and vendors' true abilities and what they need to know in order to be successful. The underlying assumption is that trading with successful suppliers and customers will make an organization itself successful as well. The accompanying ICT applications are extranets and supplier and customer self-service applications whereby suppliers and customers are allowed to retrieve information from an organization's information system; for example, a vendor is allowed to check an organization's inventory files in order to be able to determine if that organization needs a stock replenishment.

Databases and Data Warehouses

A database is a set of interrelated data that has two important features. First, it is aimed at avoiding data redundancy. This implies that every data element is only recorded once. Second, it is application-independent. This implies that a multiple logical view of data is strived for. Multiple means that more than one viewpoint to access the data can be chosen. Logical means that we are not talking about the physical appearance of the database, but about how it appears to users (i.e. as one big bag of data). Data in this big bag can be retrieved or updated, subject to approval by the assigned authorities. There are several types of database. However, the type most commonly used in modern database environments is the relational database. The relational database model represents each data element in the database in the form of tables that contain cross-references – via primary and foreign keys – to other tables. In order to operate a database – as is the case in almost every ICT solution – a combination of hardware, software, and people is needed. Since databases intend to cover the data storage needs of complete organizations, ample physical storage and processing capacity is needed. Software requirements include a number of modules that, together, must take care of an efficient operation of the data base. The database management system (DBMS) is the main software used to operate a database. It is a specialized computer program that handles all the data traffic to and from the database. In daily speech, the terms 'database', 'database management system', and 'database system' are often incorrectly used interchangeably. The database system is the combination of the database and the software used to operate the database, including the application programs. For example, the module 'accounts receivable', which retrieves customer payment data from the database to construct an accounts receivable ageing report, is part of the database system although it does not belong to the DBMS nor the database itself. The DBMS consists of several sub-modules. The data dictionary involves all the information about the data elements contained in the database. It is a meta-representation of the database, meaning that it provides the semantics needed to understand what is meant by every data element in the database. For example, the data dictionary contains the following meta-data about the inventory item name in the inventory records:

- description – complete verbal description of the inventory item;
- record(s) in which it is contained – inventory record;
- source(s) – initial purchase order, warehouse man;
- field length – 25 characters;
- field type – alphanumeric;
- module(s) in which it is used – inventory module, sales module, purchase module;
- output(s) in which it is contained – inventory status report, picking ticket, packing ticket, purchase orders, sales orders;
- authorized users – no restrictions.

Another element of the DBMS is the data directory which can best be compared with the contents or index of a book. It contains all the meta-data needed to locate a certain data element in the database. Usually, the data dictionary and data directory are mentioned in the same breath: data dictionary and directory system (DDDS). A third module in the DBMS is the teleprocessing monitor (TPM). Since a database is shared by multiple users at various geographical locations, there may be access conflicts and violation attempts. In order to control access, the TPM makes use of assigned priorities to users, and allows access to a certain data record only if the user–module–data combination is contained in the access control matrix. In Chapter 7, we will elaborate on the information security issues involved here. The languages used to manipulate the database are also part of the database system. Here, a distinction can be made between data oriented languages and information-oriented languages. The class of data oriented languages is generally referred to as data manipulation languages (DMLs). A DML is used for maintaining the database which includes such operations as: altering, adding, and deleting portions of the database. The class of information-oriented languages is generally referred to as data query languages (DQLs). A DQL is used to retrieve data from the database for further processing such as sorting, categorizing, summarizing, calculating, and presenting that information in a format that is understandable to the end-user.

There are two important organizational roles that support the functioning of databases: the database administrator (DBA) and the data administrator (DA). The DBA must have technical skills to handle the detailed database design work and to tune it for efficient use. The DA, on the other hand, must have administrative skills to handle managerial and policy issues, and to interact efficiently with database users. Theoretically, these roles could be combined in one function, but only a few people have both sets or skills. Moreover, the need for a specialized technical database role has increased dramatically with the emergence of electronic communication. As a result, the workload of the DBA has increased as well, necessitating a split between the DBA and the DA.

As databases developed, the highly idealistic goal was to capture all organizational data – and even beyond – in one large collection of records. Because ICT did not allow this goal to be realized efficiently, smaller databases were developed which were still substantial improvements on the old situation, when there were lots of different master files containing redundant and often inconsistent data, and which did not allow access to applications other than the ones for which they were developed. Nowadays, ICT has reached such a level that these large databases can indeed be successfully realized. The generic term used for the concept of having large databases covering all the data needed for decision making and accountability is data warehousing. However, a data warehouse is more than just a big database. Bill Inmon, one of the first advocates of data warehousing, gives the following features of a data warehouse (Inmon, 1996):

- It is subject-oriented. Data recorded in data warehouses is centred around subjects such as products, markets, customers, locations, etc. Because of this approach, a data warehouse fits well with process orientations to organizations. The main issue is that every informational activity must add value to the organization. This is best accomplished by making the value driver the subject of information provision.
- It is integrated. Data are only recorded once for the whole organization. Many company-wide information systems, like ERP systems, now provide a data warehousing module.
- It is time variant. The moment in time at which, or the time span over which information is needed, is completely irrelevant. Information can be retrieved at

any moment in time, over any period. The traditional annual or quarterly closings in AISs are no longer necessary if this feature of a data warehouse is met.

- It is non-volatile. A data warehouse manager is responsible for ensuring the integrity of all the data in the data warehouse. Modification may only be made via him. This implies that operational systems like accounts receivable, accounts payable, inventory, logistics, marketing, human resource management, etc. are not allowed to make modifications to data in the data warehouse.

The reasons for developing data warehouses may be diverse. First, a focus of the information provision on clients and potential clients is necessary in a highly competitive environment. Second, because of shorter life cycles and time to market, information must be available as fast and flexibly as possible. Third, in order to ensure data integrity, there must be segregation of duties between the warehouse manager and the provider of the data. Data warehouses have the potential to meet the resulting requirements.

Decision Support Systems, Expert Systems, and Neural Networks

Decision support systems (DSS) are computerized information systems aimed at improvement of human decision making. As the word indicates, these systems support decision making, they don't replace it. Also, DSSs contain facts and not subjective human knowledge. The basic form of a DSS is a spreadsheet used for what-if analyses, goal seeking (e.g. determining the necessary gross salary to arrive at a certain net salary, or determining the internal rate of return of an investment project), or what-if analyses (e.g. constructing a business performance report comparing this year's figures with budgeted figures and reporting exceptions). Specialized DSS software may be used for computer simulation in cases where analytical tools are not appropriate, because of incomplete information or too many variables involved. For example, a production facility has problems in determining the minimum required inventory level because vendor delivery times and sales follow an unpredictable pattern, inventory costs are only known within a certain bandwidth, and out-of-stock opportunity costs are completely unknown. Obviously, in order not to waste valuable company resources, inventory should be minimized. This problem can be solved by simulating the buying, inventory keeping, and sales processes, making use of probability theory. The outcome of such a simulation, then, could be that there is an $x\%$ probability that the company loses a certain amount of money because of too high or too low inventory levels. The decision maker can use this information to motivate his actual decision about what, when, and where to purchase.

Expert systems, on the other hand, do replace human decision making by presenting proposed decisions to their users. For that purpose, subjective expert knowledge is recorded in these systems' knowledge bases which is used to simulate the experts' decision making. When using the term 'expert system', it usually implies that it consists of so-called production rules or, in other words, if-then-else statements. Expert systems do not have learning abilities. So, every piece of knowledge has to be put in by the developer on the basis of knowledge acquisition among one or more experts. Neural networks go one step further in that they contain learning mechanisms that enable them to fine-tune their embedded knowledge, just like humans do when encountering new cases. The overall category of software that covers neural networks and expert systems is called artificial intelligence (AI).

A car diagnosis expert system

A car mechanic encounters a problem in a car in which its engine stops running when it takes a turn to the right. He may make the diagnosis that there must be a short circuit in the car's electronics caused by a wire touching the car's bodywork. If this decision were modelled in an expert system, some applicable production systems could be:

If Engine malfunctions AND The car makes a turn AND The car drives faster than 50 miles an hour

Then There is a loose contact – probability = 50% OR There is a malfunctioning gas pump – probability 20% OR There is a problem with the ignition – probability = 35% OR there is a problem with the brakes – probability = 10%

If There is a problem when the car makes a turn in one specific direction

Then There is a loose contact – probability = 80%

From this example, we can see that only probabilities are given as outcomes of the expert system, and that inferences cannot be made with absolute certainty. Of course, this is similar to how the real expert would work. Dependent on his number of years of task-specific experience, his education as a mechanic, and his talent for diagnosing car trouble, the expert will be able to increase the probability of a certain diagnosis being correct. Note that in other decision-making tasks, probabilities may take a binary form, thus only having values at the scale ends of 0% or 100%.

Groupware

Groupware is the generic name of software that enables more efficient communication within and between organizations, or, more specifically, within any group that works towards a certain deliverable. The type of communication that is enabled by groupware is often not tied to any fixed format. Typical applications of groupware are Lotus notes, ICQ (appropriately pronounced as: 'I seek you'), MS Messenger, MS Netmeeting, but also the sharing of documents and messages via e-mail or other electronic data communication channels. Basically, groupware combines the power of computer networks with the directness and personal touch of face-to-face contact. It can be used for brainstorming sessions and also for fast information exchange for the support of business processes. In addition, it lets users hold computer conferences, schedule meetings, maintain a personal or departmental calendar, manage projects, or jointly design complex products. An instance of groupware aimed at the support of decision making in groups of people is the group decision support system (GDSS). Like DSSs, GDSSs support decision making without substituting the human decision maker involved.

Executive Information Systems

An executive information system (EIS) allows end-users, at the tactical and strategic managerial level, to produce the information they find necessary themselves. This category of information systems is highly diverse as to its appearance. At one end of the scale, an EIS may necessitate a query language to extract data from a database, while, at the other end of the scale, the EIS may be completely pre-programmed to provide the information the executive specified during the early stages of system development. Data warehouses enable EIS to provide superior information for executive decision making. Especially when these data warehouses are built on top of a company's ERP system, they may be able to combine internal company data, financial as well as non-financial and quantitative as well as non-quantitative, with external data about vendors, competitors, and customers, and, within the product markets, the labour markets, and the capital markets.

In Chapter 9, the information and communication components of non-financial performance evaluation are discussed. Here, we want to make a final remark about the ICT-supporting non-financial performance evaluation. Executives need quick access to all the information available at the moment of decision making. Imagine a board of directors trying to formulate a company's strategy. A so-called management cockpit room would then benefit the strategy formulation process tremendously because all the information in whatever format (narratives, graphs, or in figures) can be presented on surrounding electronic panels in the boardroom. Such a room is not fiction. One of the major advantages of such an advanced ICT application is that information overload can be regulated. Of course, this might also be a major disadvantage since management must be skilled in operating this high-tech EIS. If they fail to get the right skills, the information appearing on the surrounding screens will become useless because it loses its meaning and causes information overload. A less profound, but highly pragmatic ICT solution to the information relevance problem is to use software that makes non-financial information better understandable by having executives choose their preferred formats. Software that supports multidimensional performance evaluation concepts like the balanced scorecard (see Chapter 9) performs this role.

ICT-enabled Innovations

ICT-enabled innovations constitute a rather heterogenous group of products, philosophies, and concepts. We will briefly discuss the following instances of ICT-enabled innovations:

- e-business (including Internet portals);
- business process re-engineering;
- customer relationship management;
- business intelligence;
- strategic enterprise management.

E-business

Electronic commerce was among the first e-business applications. It refers to all sales-related activities that make use of electronic communication by means of the Internet. The principle is as follows: the customer determines what he wants to order via the website of the vendor, or a portal that compares different vendors, and, after having chosen the product and – if applicable – the vendor, he places an order via the website of the vendor, via a portal, or via a traditional method such as telephone, fax, written order, or just by visiting the store. So, e-commerce may be as simple as having a website for displaying the products that are for sale, which is a non-interactive application. However, it may also be more complex, offering customers the possibility to order products via the website, which is an interactive application. Interactive applications enable a fully-fledged use of the potentials of the Internet for e-commerce activities. A more advanced application is integration of an organization's website with the information systems – usually ERP systems – of that organization. When e-activities extend beyond a website for marketing and sales applications, then the term e-business is most commonly used to indicate those business processes that are one way or another influenced by the chosen electronic communication philosophy.

Internet Portals

E-business activities often make use of so-called Internet portals. An Internet portal is a website that is a major starting point for users when they want to find information or conclude a transaction on the Internet. An Internet portal can be compared with a physical portal that you can enter in order to make a choice among the several doors that can be opened from that portal. A distinction can be made between general Internet portals and specialized Internet portals. Some major general portals are Startpagina.nl, Excite.com, Altavista.com, Netscape.com, Lycos.com, CNET.com, MSN.com, and AOL.com. Examples of specialized portals include Techtarget.com (for ICT professionals), Happytravel.nl (for travellers), Accountingweb.nl (for accountants), and Fool.com (for investors). Companies with Internet portals have attracted much investor interest because portals are looked upon as being able to command large audiences and, hence, large numbers of advertising viewers. Typical services offered by portals are a directory of Internet sites, facilities to search for other sites, news and weather sites, stock quotes, address information, discussion forums, and product comparison sites.

In an e-business environment, a process orientation as opposed to a functional orientation seems more appropriate because it enables the organization to be in closer and more direct contact with the market, increasing operational efficiency, and achieving internal as well as external integration goals more effectively. As a result, any organization can only reap the full benefits of e-business when a horizontal structure is chosen, as is the case in a process orientation. Business process re-engineering is the vehicle to arrive at such a process orientation.

Business Process Re-engineering

A modern flow in the literature at the crossroad of management, accounting, and ICT is *business process re-engineering* (BPR). BPR is aimed at designing business processes in such a way that optimal use is made of the opportunities offered by ICT. It is the thorough analysis and complete redesign of business processes and information systems that achieves dramatic performance improvements. Management will focus more on the processes than on existing departments and hierarchies. This means that the organization is canted from vertical (command and control) to horizontal where certain customer(group)s, product(group)s, or markets are central; for example, the process of settling a claim by an insurer can be performed more efficiently – and in a more customer-friendly manner – when as little data traffic as possible takes place between departments and joint responsibility is put in the hands of the various employees involved in the relevant process.

The following seven basic principles underlie BPR:

1 Organize around outcomes, not tasks. This implies that one person is held responsible for the entire process and that the work of each person in the process is aimed at the final product or outcome of that process.
2 Have output users perform the process. This implies that workers should have more autonomy than they used to have in the functionally oriented organization; for example, those who need a certain product must also do the ordering directly with the vendor. This is usually feasible with insignificant stocks.
3 Have those who produce information process it; for example, orders are input into the information system for processing by the same person who places the orders and, hence, produces information.
4 Centralize and disperse data by means of ICT. To achieve economies of scale, businesses will centralize operations, but, to be more responsive to changing circumstances and customer needs, businesses will decentralize operations. Corporate-wide databases combine the advantages of both centralization and decentralization.
5 Integrate parallel activities. Parallel activities that contribute to the same product or service must be aligned at an early stage of the process in order to reduce additional work after the activities have been completed; for example, while building a house, the holes and the channels for the power outlets and the electric

wires are already made by the bricklayers by omitting bricks at the designated places.

6 Empower workers, use built-in controls, and flatten the organizational chart. Those who do the job have decision-making power for that job. As a result, managers can shift their attention from supervision and control to support and facilitation. ICT plays an important role here; for example, workers are supported by expert systems, DSSs, or groupware to enable sound decision making.
7 Capture data only once, at its source. The keystone of integrated systems is to have single input combined with multiple use.

BPR and enterprise resource planning are often undertaken for the same reasons. Organizations that implement an ERP system will have to transform from a functional to a process orientation. BPR actually performs such a transformation. So, ERP is the catalyst for process change. In addition, a good aid in determining the norms that should be strived for in re-engineering business processes is benchmarking. Benchmarking is the process of identification, familiarizing and adopting superior practices as observed in our own or other organizations, aimed at improving our own performance. ERP systems may play an important part in providing the necessary information for benchmarking purposes. Table 6.1 relates the basic principles of BPR to ERP.

In the last few decades, BPR has gained popularity as a concept that could lead to the enhanced efficiency and effectiveness of organizations. However, due to many BPR projects that failed or did not live up to their full potential, we believe it is over the hill. In more recent literature, a tendency for more flexible firms from the outset can be observed. The postmodern organization, or simply the flexible firm, is the new hype in this area. This concept is especially aimed at the creation and integration of knowledge in organizations in order to continuously innovate and gain competitive advantage as a result. We will elaborate on issues related to knowledge management in Chapter 9.

Customer Relationship Management

Organizations need to attempt to meet their clients' wishes in the best way they can. Customer-oriented trading demands account management or customer relationship management (CRM). Besides the general organizational information recorded in a regular accounts receivable administration, an account management system also needs to contain information on, for example, the relevant employees and key decision makers of the various organizations. This concept can best be illustrated by means of an example. Take a small grocery store that provides the people in the neighbourhood with the necessary food and other products needed to keep their households running. The storekeeper runs the store with his wife. They have had a long-term relationship with each customer and, as a result, know exactly what special treats must be employed to make each individual customer happy with the

Table 6.1 The relationship between the seven basic principles of BPR and ERP

BPR	*ERP*
Organize around outcomes, not tasks.	ERP follows a process orientation of organizations.
Have output users perform the process.	ERP accomplishes that data are input from within the work processes in order to initiate these work processes.
Have those who produce information process it.	ERP accomplishes that data are input from within the work processes in order to track the progress of these work processes.
Centralize and disperse data by means of ICT.	ERP plays an important part in workflow management, and hence in distributing data and information.
Integrate parallel activities.	ERP follows a process orientation where multidisciplinary teams are the most important entities.
Empower workers, use built-in controls, and flatten the organizational chart.	ERP enables the enforced use of specific program modules by means of soft parameter settings.
Capture data only once, at its source.	The explicit goal of ERP is to record data only once for all applications.

service and products of the grocery store. This knowledge is not codified, rather it is in the heads of the storekeeper and his wife. When the small grocery store grows bigger, partly as a result of extremely satisfied customers, the storekeeper will find out that he is no longer able to collect all the necessary customer information, to memorize it, and to use it when needed when a customer arrives. The workers that now do the sales may have some specific knowledge about some customer, but this is highly dispersed, anecdotal, and hence difficult to apply. ICT may provide the tools to collect, store, and retrieve the needed customer information when a specific customer arrives. The process of collecting, recording, and retrieving customer-specific knowledge is referred to as customer relationship management. The small grocery store that grew and started employing ICT is an example of sales force automation (SFA). SFA was among the earliest CRM applications, starting in the last decade of the 20th century. A more recent development is the emergence of analytical CRM products, which have evolved from data warehousing and online analytical processing (OLAP), which enable a user to easily and selectively extract and view data from different points of view. For example, an OLAP tool enables the user to create a report that contains the sales of product *X* during the last month, the sales of product X in the same month last year, and the sales of other products during these time periods. An OLAP database is generally much smaller than a data warehouse because it only contains the data needed for the required analysis. A typical representation of potential data that may be used for OLAP is a data cube (a three-dimensional viewpoint). OLAP is an efficient approach to get an insight into available data when the decision problem is known. A concept related to OLAP is data mining, which is an efficient approach when the decision problem is not known, but there is a large data set that might be of interest. Data mining may be helpful in arriving at a manageable database for OLAP purposes.

Business Intelligence

Whereas ERP originates from the need to control flows of goods and money at the operational level, business intellligence (BI) is primarily aimed at opening up the information contained in ERP databases for managerial information provision. BI consists of a broad category of applications for collecting, storing, analysing, and providing access to data to facilitate decision making by managers. BI applications include DSS, OLAP, and data mining.

Strategic Enterprise Management

Strategic enterprise management (SEM) promises to enable managers to link strategy formulation to strategy implementation, drive product and customer profitability, and increase shareholder value. Whereas BI is aimed at supporting decision making at the tactical level in organizations, SEM aims to facilitate information provision for strategic decision making. Typical applications of SEM are executive information systems. For example, Oracle SEM is a package that provides an organization with the ability to carry out strategic planning, taking into account that organization environments are subject to constant change. It operates via the Oracle Enterprise Data Warehouse which can store and retrieve data from multiple sources, Oracle as well as non-Oracle applications. The package can be built on top of any ERP system.

Chapter Case

Case 6.1 BUZZ

BUZZ is a medium-sized company that specializes in advice and mediation with respect to information problems. The organization consists of the following departments:

- management;
- secretariat;

- administration and automation;
- sales and marketing;
- human resource management;
- product groups.

The range of products includes:

- knowledge management – advising on the control of information provision in organizations where the primary processes require much expertise, but where workers are uninformed about available knowledge within and outside the organization, the organization continually loses its knowledge, and responses to customer problems are too slow;
- information mediation – searching for relevant information on a multitude of topics on behalf of customers;
- business process re-engineering – ICT-enabled redesign of organizations that puts the customer at the heart of the analysis;
- information requirements analysis – assessment of information needs of management for decision making and accountability.

Operating Procedures
The company has three branches throughout Sweden. Every advisor has one of these locations as his operating base, but may also use flexible office space at the other two locations. Advisory services are performed by means of face-to-face contact with clients, written communication, and electronic communication.

Billing
The actual number of hours spent on a client are billed along with the expenses made by the advisors. Expenses include: travel and lodging, purchase of specific information products, and software licenses or purchases. Incidentally, fixed prices may also be agreed. The head of each product group is authorized to mark down a bill if deemed necessary. However, before doing so, he must discuss this with the head of the sales and marketing department.

Personnel
There are five function categories, numbered 1 through 5. The accounting and secretarial employees are in category 1, and management is in category 5. The advisors, HRM employees, and sales employees are in categories 2 through 4, and can be moved up on the basis of seniority, education, and performance. Management believes in continuous education and conducts a thorough educational policy.

Automation
Because of the nature of advisory projects, there is a dominant automation environment. ICT is pervasive throughout all business processes of BUZZ. Management wants to be a pioneer in the field of ICT deployment, but often has to deal with the inadequate ICT infrastructures of clients. Although this may be considered a promising advisory area, it also hinders the efficient and effective execution of

BUZZ's core activities. BUZZ's stategy is expressly not aimed at system development and the only feasible solution seems to engage in strategic alliances with system houses.

Operations
As a result of the tremendous growth of the organization, it is no longer fully equipped to optimally meet customer demands. Management senses that market opportunities are not exploited and that existing clients do not get the quality they expect. In addition, the administration does not have the processing capacity to adequately deal with the wide variety of transactions.

Assignment

How can ICT improve the quality of operations within this company? Discuss the possibilities for ICT and give a brief indication of the benefits to the organization.

7 The Dynamics of Internal Control and ICT

Because computers play such a large part in assisting us to process data and to make decisions, it is important that their use be controlled.

Weber (1999), p. 6

Internet security has a way to go before it can be considered secure. As a company introduces a new security program, a hacker often finds a way to compromise it.

Romney and Steinbart (2000), p. 305

After studying this chapter, the reader should be able to:

- Understand the alignment processes that take place between internal control and ICT.
- Understand the relationship between ERP, business process re-engineering, and internal control.
- Explain the role of ICT in controlling organizations.
- Describe the strategic importance of information and ICT.
- Distinguish between new-age segregation of duties and traditional segregation of duties.
- Distinguish between internal control, information control, and information security.
- Understand the importance of codes of conduct for information security.
- Make a diagnosis of threats that stem from electronic communication.
- Define the appropriate measures of information security in relation to distinguished threats.
- Understand the evolution of organizations in relation to ICT developments.

Chapter Outline

Since the book takes a managerial approach to AIS, a holistic view of businesses is taken. A core discipline that comes into play here is information management since it studies the alignment between the business, information, and the ICT environment. Again, we make use of the comprehensive contingency framework as introduced in Chapter 5. This framework will serve as the main framework for investigating this alignment. Central to the first part of the chapter is the alignment between ICT infrastructure, ICT control, and internal control. In Chapter 6, an isolated approach to ICT was taken. As electronic communication becomes more and more pervasive, information control as a specialism becomes more mature. Information security is the technical component of information control. In this age of e-business and Internet proliferation, information security is a topic that should be an integral element of AIS as a discipline and any AIS. After a short 'intermezzo' on codes on information security, which makes the transition between the first and the second part of the chapter, the alignment between ICT infrastructure, operations, and internal control is discussed.

Introduction

In Chapter 6, we discussed some basic ICT issues. Here, we discuss the dynamic relationship between ICT and internal control. The relationship is dynamic because there is a mutual influence between internal control systems and ICT. Internal controls being influenced by the application of ICT can, among other things, be observed when controls migrate from the execution stage to the system development stage, when information provision gets automated, when programmed procedures are employed instead of manual controls, or when information security measures are taken to mitigate threats evolving from electronic communication. Here, a distinction can be made between positive and negative effects of ICT proliferation on internal control. A positive influence may be anticipated when control problems are avoided by having a programmed procedure in place that enforces information system users to follow a fixed sequence of steps in order to fulfil a specific task assignment. A negative influence may be anticipated when measurement points like the transferral of documents, physical goods, or common money from one person to another are integrated in the information system and, hence, are not visible any more. ICT application being influenced by internal controls can be observed when controls are built in information systems and, hence, the applied ICT is influenced by the need for internal control. As a result of these intertwined relationships, any existing balance between internal control and ICT is subject to continuous change and, hence, is dynamic by nature.

There are three ages of economic evolution that can be distinguished in developed countries (see e.g. Toffler 1990):

- the agrarian age;
- the industrial age;
- the information age.

These ages partially overlap and cannot be exactly positioned on a timescale because there are differences between countries' paces of development. To give a general indication, the agrarian age lasted until the second half of the 18th century, the industrial age started during the second half of the 18th century and has not yet come to an end, and the information age started a few decades ago. Currently, we are in some kind of transitional stage between the industrial and the information age. The agrarian age could be characterized by the power of the guilds that were governed on the basis of unambiguous agreements between members. As a result, competition was virtually non-existent. The industrial era could be characterized by the severe concentration of power in increasingly bigger corporations which were mainly involved in production activities, and the important role of competition. The information era, or the third wave, can be characterized by the emergence of new organizational forms that go beyond industry boundaries, national borders, and markets. The third wave economy is dominated by service organizations (including trade and the financial sector) where information and knowledge are the most important competitive instruments. Production activities that used to be core competences of many organizations are frequently outsourced to often under-developed countries with low wage levels, whereas the development of new products is done in the developed economies. Moreover, the service industry more and more dictates the conditions under which contracts are settled between product developers and manufacturers.

Specialist knowledge of products, local markets, and the necessity to combine a variety of production technologies and information and communication technologies have led to organizations forming alliances, partnerships, and joint ventures. In this setting, outsourcing and the so-called economical networks will be the new forms of cooperation. Economical networks require high-quality information provision between the affiliated partners, and between the economical network and third parties. The information provision within an economical network is denoted internal information provision, and the information provision between economical networks is denoted external information provision. The so-called virtual organization is an instance of the economical network. In a virtual organization, the activity range is dominated by electronic transactions, conveniently denoted as e-activities (e.g. e-business, e-commerce, e-procurement). This type of organization is highly dependent on high-quality information provision because the flows of physical goods and money are of secondary importance compared with information about the location and state of the physical goods and money. For example, an organization that engages in e-business may not have its own inventories. Instead, it knows what vendors can supply the goods its clients have ordered, or what warehouses have stored these goods. Hence, this type of organization requires information that meets the highest possible standards in order to function properly. In this arena, information control – as a subset of internal control – has received considerable attention in practice, education, and theory. However, we believe that a broadening of this discipline towards the field of information security is necessary. Moreover, we believe that AIS must be the discipline that conveys this broadening because of its strong relationship with internal control, and the central role of the accounting information system in any organization.

E-activities play an unequivocal part in our current economic environment. Trade via the World Wide Web (WWW) is growing and the so-called new economy, where the old rules of the game are no longer valid, has begun its rise. The new economy is an artefact who's *raison d'être* has not yet been proved. On the contrary, we encounter more and more evidence that the so-called new rules lead to the bankruptcy of typical new economy organizations; for example, of the many Internet businesses that started up in the last five years, only a very small percentage are still in the market. The estimated value of these companies appeared to be far too optimistic, as a result of which the lack of positive cash flow could not longer be offset by positive future expectations. Notwithstanding the criticism about the new economy concept, we will use this term because it is by now commonplace to do so. Moreover, on a macro-level, the new economy, as opposed to the old economy, can be used in the same fashion as the economical network, as opposed to the traditional organizational form, on a micro-level. Organizations from the old economy that make the switch to e-activities often do not realize that creating a website is just the beginning of an extensive change process. Especially, adjustments to or complete redesign of the internal organization are often underestimated; for example, reconciliations and control totals which used to be major internal control tools, are replaced by other tools like cultural controls that are often less manifest.

The comprehensive contingency framework, as introduced in Chapter 5, can be used to clarify the relationship between internal control and ICT. ICT control is part of the broader concept of internal control, and can be defined as all those activities employed by or on behalf of an organization's management to ensure the proper functioning of an organization's information systems. As has already been indicated, the main cells of interest to the discipline of AIS are those in the strategy implementation part of the comprehensive contingency framework. Starting from the ICT infrastructure (see Figure 5.3), there are two paths that can be followed. First, there is the path that goes from the ICT infrastructure cell, via the ICT control cell in the overlaid control framework (see Figure 5.4), to the internal control cell. This path involves, among other things, measures for information security, programmed procedures, and general controls. Second, there is the path that goes from the ICT infrastructure cell in the comprehensive contingency framework, via the operations cell, to the internal control cell in the overlaid control framework. This path involves all kinds of

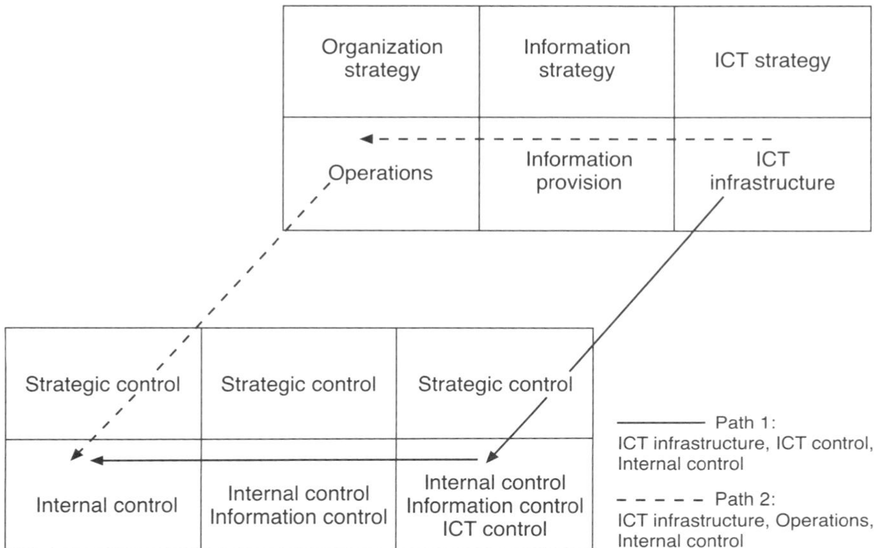

Figure 7.1 The alternative paths covering the relationship between internal control and ICT.

ICT-enabled innovation in the business domain such as enterprise resource planning, business process re-engineering, and e-business that should lead to operational excellence. In Figure 7.1, alternative paths covering the relationship between internal control and ICT are depicted.

ICT Infrastructure, ICT Control, and Internal Control

This section discusses the main threats that come from ICT proliferation, and electronic communication specifically, and presents some potential ICT controls to be employed to mitigate these threats. There are four categories of threat to information quality that come from ICT proliferation:

- confidentiality;
- integrity;
- availability;
- authenticity.

This section elaborates on these threats. Note that each of these threats involves humans who are purposely trying to make this threat become a reality. The activity of purposely trying to make one or more of these threats become a reality is generally called hacking, and the perpetrators are called hackers. Although hacking is mostly considered illegal, there are differences in individual countries' legislation. In addition, as a result of the speed of ICT proliferation, legislation has problems keeping up with modern developments in this area.

Confidentiality means that only authorized persons are allowed to have access to specific parts of information. Confidential information should not become available to people who want to use it for their own advantage or for the disadvantage of the entity the information is about. Instances of threats in this category are unauthorized logical or physically data access, traffic analysis, deduction and aggregation of information, and unauthorized reproduction of software. Unauthorized data access may take place by physically gaining access to the system, or gaining logical access via the lines used for data communication. Also, less sophisticated techniques are used such as searching trash cans for hardcopies of confidential information. For example, a hospital was accused of having harmed their patients' privacy because it had thrown away, without shredding, misprinted patient files, parts of which were readily readable. The files were found in the hospital's trash container, just outside the building. Traffic analysis means that messages are intercepted by people other than the intended receivers and further analysed. This usually takes place by making use of electronic eavesdropping, which is the interception of radio signals transmitted by electronic communication devices or output devices like computer monitors. Deduction and aggregation of information means that different data sources, which individually do not have meaning to a non-informed person, are combined such that the result is meaningful data, hence information; for example, a student code and a grade behind that code is meaningless except for those who know what name is behind each student code. Lately, there has been a lot of attention to privacy law enforcement aimed at prohibiting files from different sources to be combined. Finally, unauthorized reproduction of software is practiced by many people without thinking about its illegal nature. The term generally used here is software piracy. The software contained on floppy disks and CD-ROMs, or downloadable from websites may or may not be free. If it is not free, then making a copy of it should always result in a payment.

Integrity is often used interchangeably with reliability. Often, the term 'integrity' is used to specifically refer to information in automated systems, whereas the term 'reliability' is of a more generic nature. We will use the terms in this fashion. Information is said to be reliable if it is valid and complete (see Chapter 8) and, hence, integrity means that information that is electronically communicated is valid and complete. Instances of threats in this category are unauthorized destruction or modification of data, unauthorized modification of programs, replay, and invalid message sequencing. Unauthorized destruction or modification of data means that people who are not allowed to delete or modify data as stored in the system, transported over communicaton lines, or in progress within the system, find a way to do so. Unauthorized modification of programs means that people who are not allowed to modify programs find a way to do so. Replay means that a message is eavesdropped on, recorded, and sent again at the discretion of the perpetrator; for example, when an authorized person types his password to gain access to the system, this is recorded by a hacker who can use it later to gain access to the system himself. Finally, invalid message sequencing means that a series of messages is eavesdropped on, recorded, and sent again at the discretion of the perpetrator, but in a different sequence; for example, different versions of a contract to be agreed are presented in reverse order, as a result of a hacker trying to obstruct the negotiations.

Availability means that information must be at the intended user's disposal, on time, and at the right place. Instances of threats in this category are denial of service as a result of defects, denial of service as a result of system overload, and unauthorized use of hardware. Denial of service as a result of defects means that a system breaks down because there are technical problems. Denial of service as a result of system overload means that a system may break down when its required capacity is not sufficient to fulfil the data processing needs of its users. On system development, necessary capacity can be calculated. However, there may be unforeseen circumstances such as a sudden increase in the activities of the organization, or hackers trying to attack the system in order to make it break down; for example, a well-coordinated attack by means of so-called e-mail bombs, where hackers worldwide cooperate to send e-mails to one and the same server address at the same time, may overload the receiver's system. Finally, use of hardware by unauthorized persons may lead to the system being unavailable for the intended users.

Authenticity means that the sender and receiver of a message are who they claim to be. In electronic communication, where face-to-face contact is absent, this aspect of information control becomes more and more important. Instances of threats in this category are masquerading and repudiation. Masquerading means that a person appears in an electronic communication session and identifies himself as someone else. If that 'someone else' is an authorized person, then the sender may send messages to the wrong person, or the receiver may receive messages from the wrong person. Repudiation means that the sender denies that he has sent a message, or that the receiver denies that he has received a message.

The instances of threats, as mentioned here, may pertain to more than one category of threats; for example, unauthorized modification of data (integrity) may lead to a system breakdown and resulting denial of service (availability) or a logfile containing incorrect information about the sender of specific messages (authenticity).

In order to mitigate these threats, several methods for information security are available. In Table 7.1, the aforementioned threats are combined with applicable methods for information security.

Encryption

Encryption is the transformation of information by means of a specific algorithm into a format that is not understandable by those who receive it unless they know the

Table 7.1 Threats evolving from electronic communication and applicable methods for information security

Method for information security	*Threats evolving from electronic communication*													
	Confidentiality					*Integrity*				*Availability*			*Authenticity*	
	Unauthorized logical access to data	*Unauthorized physical access to data*	*Traffic analysis*	*Deduction and aggregation of information*	*Unauthorized reproduction of software*	*Destruction or unauthorized modification of data*	*Destruction or unauthorized modification of programs*	*Replay*	*Invalid message sequencing*	*Denial of service as a result of defects*	*Denial of service as a result of system overload*	*Unauthorized use of hardware*	*Masquerading*	*Repudiation*
Encryption	✓		✓	✓	✓	✓	✓						✓	✓
Event logging	✓		✓	✓	✓	✓	✓	✓	✓			✓		✓
Access control	✓		✓	✓	✓	✓	✓					✓		
Routing control	✓		✓	✓	✓					✓	✓			
Physical security		✓		✓	✓	✓	✓			✓		✓		
Fall back systems						✓	✓			✓	✓			
Data recovery						✓	✓							
Date and time stamps								✓	✓					
Confirmations								✓					✓	✓
Priority and pre-emption											✓			
Authentication													✓	✓
Digital signature													✓	✓
Message authentication codes													✓	

algorithm to transform it back to the original format. There are several encryption methods. A public key infrastructure (PKI) enables users to securely and privately exchange data through the use of a public and private key pair that is obtained and shared through a trusted third party. Whereas a PKI makes use of a private as well as a public key, a private key infrastructure makes use of one key only: a private key that is only known to the sender and receiver of an encrypted message. Applying a PKI should make breaking the code more difficult. Pretty good privacy (PGP) is software for encrypting and decrypting e-mails, files, and digital signatures that are sent over the Internet. PGP makes use of a PKI. If PGP is used for the encryption of a digital signature, then the receiver can verify the sender's identity and know that the message was not changed during transmission. PGP is the most widely used encryption software, used by individuals as well as corporations. It has become the standard for e-mail security. A secure variant of the Internet protocol (IP) is Internet protocol secure (IPsec). IPsec is employed to make Internet connections as secure as private networks and, hence, IPsec is frequently used to create virtual private networks (VPNs). Secure electronic transaction (SET) is a system for ensuring the security of payment information on the Internet. It was supported initially by credit-card companies and Internet software companies. With SET, a user receives a digital certificate which can best be compared with an electronic credit card containing information that should uniquely identify and authenticate its possessor. SET makes use of secure sockets layer (SSL by Netscape), secure transaction technology (STT by Microsoft), and system's secure hypertext transfer protocol (S-HTTP by Terisa). Just like PGP, SET uses a PKI. SET is especially applicable in transmitting payment information over the Internet.

Event Logging

Event logging means that a logfile is kept in order to record critical security incidents. After finding out that security has been broken, the logfile can be scrutinized along with its data so as to take corrective measures. A special occurrence of event logging is intrusion detection. Intrusion detection uses specialized software to trace hackers by detecting atypical patterns in the usage of an infrastructure.

Access Control

The term 'access control' refers to measures aimed at preventing logical access to the system. An access control matrix should be in place to prevent unauthorized persons from gaining access to the system.

Routing Control

By means of routing control, a message can be transported over a route the sender or the receiver prefers. Since Internet traffic cannot be controlled like this, additional routing control measures must be taken to avoid messages following unsafe or too crowded routes. An important device for routing control is the firewall. It is aimed at concentrating all the electronic communication between an internal network (usually within one organization) and the outside world (the networks of other organizations) at one point. All communication with the outside world then runs via the firewall which serves as the gatekeeper for incoming and outgoing electronic communication. By concentrating the traffic at one point, security measures can be focused there, as a result of which they will be easier to apply and be more effective. This techique can be compared with a building having only one entrance. Everybody who wants to enter the building has to go through this entrance. By guarding this entrance, undesirable persons can be locked out, and people leaving the building can be monitored to see whether they have stolen any of the organization's assets. A firewall consists of a combination of hardware and software. The stronger the preventive nature of a firewall, the more severe the built-in controls will be, and consequently, the speed of electronic communication with the outside world. This is a trade-off that always has to be made when putting a firewall in place. Firewalls can be bypassed if surrounding organizational measures are inadequate; for example, if a firewall is in use to protect a LAN from unwanted incoming and outgoing messages, but a user installs a modem and hooks his computer up to a regular telephone line, then the firewall is no longer effective. There are two basic configurations for installing a firewall when there are separate servers for communication via the Internet and the organization's information systems. The first option is to put the firewall between the outside world and the web server. The advantage is that penetrating the website will normally be frustrated, the disadvantage is that when someone succeeds in penetrating the website, then the whole information system of the organization lies open for potential hostile and harmful attacks. The second option is to put the firewall between the web server and the organization's information systems. The main advantage of this set-up is that electronic communication with the outside world is not slowed down by the firewall. However, the disadvantage is that the website may come under attack and be modified by unauthorized persons. For example, a mail-order company in the Netherlands, which engages in e-commerce activities via a website exhibiting a selection of its product range, discovered that hackers had found an easy way to modify the texts and photos on the website. Fortunately, the hackers did not find a way to get through the firewall behind the web server aimed at protecting the company's underlying information systems. As a result, the only damage done was that the website looked messy. No underlying files were damaged. Usually, a combination is made of two firewalls, one before the website and another before the organization's information systems. The zone in-between the two firewalls sometimes – and with a slight sense of drama – is called a demilitarized zone (DMZ) to indicate that it is an area where there are no weapons and, hence, no battles between aggressors and defenders.

Physical Security

Physical security is aimed at prohibiting access to hardware, data, and programs for unauthorized persons by means of physical measures. This category of measures includes, among others, putting locks on the doors to the computer rooms, safe storage of back-up files, using fire-resistant walls and doors for the computer room, and employing sprinkler systems. A special physical security measure is to place computer screens only in so-called anti-tempest rooms in order to avoid unwanted electronic eavesdropping on the electromagnetic radiation normally transmitted by computer screens. Tempest is a term that originates from military jargon. It is an acronym for telecommunications electronics material protected from emanating spurious transmissions.

Fallback Systems

Fallback systems include the employment of data processing hot sites and data processing cold sites. These sites can be used if the primary systems break down. A data processing hot site is completely identical to the primary system, and hence can also be referred to as a redundant system. It usually can be made available for operation at very short notice, varying from a few minutes to a few hours. Organizations that are heavily dependent on their information systems usually have a data processing hot site at their disposal. Examples of these types of organization are banks, insurance companies, pension funds, and investment funds. In order to make efficient use of data processing hot sites, these systems are often used for educational purposes and off-line software development. A data processing cold site is not readily available for operation but contains the necessary infrastructure to build a copy of the primary system within a relatively short period of time. Since the hardware still has to be installed, it may take a few days or even a few weeks to make the system fully operational. Often, fallback systems are not owned by the organization itself but outsourced. Here, a commercial service organization provides the hardware required for data processing should the system of a client break down.

Data Recovery

Data recovery is the activity of restoring data that were erroneously destroy or modified. The recovery of data, especially, that have been lost during electronic communication sessions creates is an important issue. If such a data set is completely lost at the receiver's site, then recovery can only take place by resending it. However, a receiver of data may not know whether or not data has been lost. For that purpose, confirmation of receipt has to be used. If data have only partially been lost, then recovery may take place by putting the message in its context and deriving the missing data elements from that context. Computerized systems are generally well equipped to apply programmed procedures for automatically filling the missing data elements. The principle behind these techniques is that every electronically communicated message contains redundant data that is used to determine whether the message has been received properly and to repair occurring errors. Data recovery is often mentioned in the same breath as back-up files. Back-up files are periodically made carbon copies of the original files and are used for data recovery purposes if data in the original files have been lost. The general procedure followed here is based on the grandfather–father–son principle. Periodically, the files are copied. The copy is then called the son, whereas the original is called the father. When a copy is made of the son, a new son is born and the original father becomes the grandfather. By following this procedure there is always a back-up file, of the back-up file, which creates the additional security that data can be recovered at a reasonable expense. It is important to have a plan in place that contains the procedures to be followed and the individual responsibilities of the persons involved. One such plan is a disaster recovery plan which is aimed at having the information system work properly as soon as possible after a disaster has taken place. Disasters may be of a general nature like fires, earthquakes, floods, high winds, wars, and terrorist attacks, but also of a very specific nature like virus attacks, e-mail bombs, hackers gaining unauthorized access to a company's information system, software bugs, human errors in inputting data or handling files, and computer fraud. A disaster recovery plan should include, among other things, written instructions on how to act in case of an emergency, a training scheme for those involved, assigned authorities to leading actors of the plan, and periodical and unannounced practice sessions.

Date and Time Stamps

By adding a date and a time stamp to a message, the receiver acquires a certain level of assurance that the message has not been delayed, that it isn't a message that has been sent earlier (mitigating the replay threat), and that it has been sent in the right order relative to other received messages (mitigating the invalid message sequencing threat). Instead of or in addition to date or time stamps, messages may be sequentially pre-numbered so that each message is uniquely identifiable.

Confirmations

By using receipt confirmations, the sender acquires additional assurance that the intended receiver of a message has indeed received the message. By using delivery confirmations, the receiver acquires additional assurance that the sender has indeed sent the message. These confirmations are often automatically produced by the electronic communication system and sent to the sender or the receiver.

Priority and Pre-emption

Priority refers to processing the prioritized messages first when the electronic communication network gets overloaded. Pre-emption goes one step further by not just postponing the non-prioritized messages, but by deleting them.

Authentication

On authentication, a user in a communication session assesses that another user in that communication session is the person he claims to be. There are several authentication methods. Examples are passwords (also PIN codes), physical possession of specific objects (e.g. chipcards), and biometric keys like iris recognition and finger prints. In addition, in order to be sure that the right receiver is contacted, a callback system can be put in place. In such a system, the sender contacts the intended recipient of a message, disconnects, and has the intended recipient ring a pre-specified telephone number, e-mail, or IP-number.

Digital Signature

A digital signature may be compared with a real signature. By putting his signature to a document, a person establishes accountability for the receipt of cash, goods, services, or information, or he declares that he is the sender. A digital signature specifically refers to the sending or receipt of information. A digital signature is employed to prevent unauthorized modification of data, and to substantiate the identity of the person placing the signature.

Message Authentication Codes

A message authentication code is an extra data element that is attached to a message as a check on the correct transferral of that message. For example, a control total is calculated on the basis of the number of characters in a message and added as an additional character to that message. On receipt of this message, the recipient's software uses the same algorithm for calculation of the control total and compares this control total with the control total as added to the original message. If both control totals are equal, then the recipient has acquired additional assurance that the message has been transferred correctly.

Codes on Information Security

Codes on information security are aimed at the development of a system of generally accepted practices for dealing with information security issues from both an organizational and a technical point of view. These codes serve as management standards that should operationalize abstract terms such as confidentiality, integrity, availability, and authenticity, in order to make them understandable for consumers and business partners and, hence, increase their trust in electronic communication as applied in, among other things, Internet commerce. Formal ratification of the structuring of a system of generally accepted practices within a specific organization is an instance of certification. Just like preparing for an ISO certificate (see Chapter 9), organizations can prepare for certification of conformity with a code on information security. Among the organizations that are currently preparing for such a certificate are representatives of the old economy (traditional production and trade firms) as well as the new economy (application service providers, Internet service providers, information intermediaries, and other Internet start-ups). Paradoxically, codes on information security, which are typical products of the old economy, are expected to play a major part in the further establishment of the new economy.

The initial attempt to develop a code on information security was made in the UK and took the form of a bundle of best practices in the field. This code was the result of the cooperative efforts of a great number of corporations and, hence, was broadly based. The next stage in the developmental process was involved internationalization, where professionals from different European countries (*inter alia*, the UK, Germany, Norway, and the Netherlands) started to cooperate. Each participating country chose its own means of creating a broad basis for the code; for example, in the Netherlands, the Dutch Normalization Institute (Nederlands Normalisatie Instituut) supervised the realization of the code, and the Ministry of Economic Affairs, the Ministry of Transport and Communications, the Dutch Banking Institute (Nederlandse Vereniging van Banken), the Electronic Commerce Platform, FENIT, and the major employers' associations expressed their explicit desire to stimulate application of the code. Currently, the code is more and more used by private and public organizations as the basis of their information security activities.

The code embraces more than a hundred security measures, divided over ten categories. Table 7.2 summarizes these measures.

Codes on information security are aimed at bringing information security within organizations up to a minimum acceptable level in order to increase mutual trust between organizations or parts of organizations. These codes are baselines, implying that their elements are considered by their developers to be the minimal required to meet due-dilligence principles. For environments where increased information security risks are anticipated, a risk analysis may give cause for additional security measures.

Codes for information security are more and more used as bases for certification of information security within organizations. Certification is based on an accredited scheme and has two cornerstones: a compliance statement of the organization's management, and the results of an ICT audit as performed by an independent auditor. The desired certificate should be issued by an accredited organization. The main advantage of having acquired an information security certificate is that trade partners have evidence that the information security measures of the certified organization meet certain quality requirements. In addition, the certificate can be used as an internal incentive to strive for even better information security measures, and to visualize the results of the information security efforts. By formulation of a code and certification on the basis of such a code, only some of the control problems that arise from ICT employment are covered. In addition, there is a need for controls of a technological nature related to ICT and, more specifically, electronic communication.

Table 7.2 Information security measures contained in the code on information security

Security categories	*Key measures*
Security policy	Policy statement with the goals of information security. Description of the organization's interests in having adequate information security. Approval of the information security policy by the organization's management and setting the right tone at the top.
Organization of security	Designing information security functions (assigning tasks and responsibilities), coordinating information security efforts, and holding people accountable for their actions regarding information and ICT. Explicit agreements with third parties on cooperation in the field of information exchange and the information security measures to be taken.
Classification and management of companies' assets	Gaining insight into the company's assets and their owners. Using classification schemes for information and information systems that enable an integrative view on business issues, information issues, and ICT issues in relation to information security.
Personnel	Education and training aimed at enhanced security awareness. Selection and placement of personnel. Paying attention to information security issues in formal personnel evaluations.
Physical security and environment	Putting physical access controls in place in the user environment and the automation department. Establishing a clear desk policy. Having wiring and computer equipment well organized. Issuing guidelines for the use of peripherals like organizers, mobile telephones, personal modems, floppy disks, zip drives, and tapes.
Computer and network management	Organizing ICT management. Recording authorized ICT management guidelines. Exploiting technical security measures. Giving follow-up to security incidents. Putting information security controls in place.
Access control	Designing a formal authorization procedure for the access to information and ICT resources (password management, user registration, and individual traceability). Managing resources for authentication and authorization.
Development and maintenance of systems	Paying attention to security issues during system development. Implementing sound change management practices.
Continuity management	Having contingency plans and controls in place (disaster recovery planning, back-up procedures, fallback procedures and systems, and periodical training sessions for disaster management).

Continued

Table 7.2 (*cont.*)

Security categories	*Key measures*
Monitoring and oversight	Periodically performing audits and other oversight acitivities aimed at information security policy compliance and compliance with legal and contractual obligations in the area of information security. Performing ICT audits with a focus on information security.

ICT Infrastructure, Operations, and Internal Control

This part of the chapter discusses some ICT-enabled innovations and their relationship with internal control. Hence, we study the effects of ICT in the business domain of the comprehensive contingency framework. These effects follow a path that goes from the ICT infrastructure cell in the comprehensive contingency framework, via the operations cell, to the internal control cell in the overlaid control framework.

E-business and Internal Control

Old-economy organizations may make use of traditional internal control concepts, as discussed in our chapter on the cornerstones of AIS (see Chapter 2). When engagement in e-activities increases and organizations migrate toward forms that enable them to compete in the new economy, these cornerstones gradually become less important. One of the main problems is that flows of goods and money, as well as tangible data and information, cease to exist as visible objects within reach of the organization. All the data and information enter and leave the organization in an electronic way, and flows of goods and money often bypass the organization that buys or sells them via electronic communication. In the case of bitable goods such as music, software, and texts that are electronically transmitted, there is no physical flow of goods at all. This eliminates an important stepping stone for the internal control system. A related problem is that this invisibility of flows of goods, information, and money is perceived by vendors and customers as an additional risk. As we will see throughout this chapter, this is completely justified. However, e-activities have many advantages. To mention a few: work processes are upgraded and labour satisfaction increases, physical stores are no longer necessary which reduces costs, congestion of roads reduces because the number of people travelling back and forth to their work decreases, trade is done on the world market which most likely leads to a better relation between prices and quality, and customers can be approached more directly which especially enables tuning service characteristics to the individual customer's desires. To make full use of these advantages, vendors and customers must be convinced that engaging in e-activities is safe in many respects. A sound internal control system that has kept up with the latest developments in the new economy should contribute to enhanced trust in e-activities.

The main threat to e-activities that needs to be mitigated, by means of organizational controls, is insider misuse. Note that insider misuse may be intentional or not, and that intentional misuse is much more difficult to trace than unintentional misuse. Fortunately, unintentional misuse occurs much more frequently than intentional misuse. Because of the absence of physical and, therefore, visible measurement points, misuse will in general be more difficult to prevent or detect in electronic environments. When engaging in e-activities, the value cycle, as introduced in Chapter 2, cannot satisfactorily provide measurement points any more. Value cycle-based control totals and reconciliations as well as segregation of duties, which are traditionally considered powerful control tools, then become inapplicable. Importantly, the database manager, who plays a major part in maintaining the integrity of the database that underlies e-activities, will be able to manipulate all organizational data and, hence, pre-eminently embodies unsatisfactory pairing of duties. In order to mitigate the threats that come from e-activities, additional preventive and detective controls have to be put in place.

Let's take the value cycle of a trade company as a starting point for our analysis. As we demonstrated in Chapter 2 (see Figure 2.6), there is a recording function that captures all the events pertaining to procurement and cash disbursements, and revenues and cash receipts. In general, the recording function is embodied as a database. Making a transformation to e-activities leads to the following adjustments in the value cycle:

- Inventory is not under the authority of the organization. As a result, there is a direct link between procurement and revenues. Since the inventory role is bypassed, there may be flows of goods that are completely invisible to the organization.
- In addition to the recording – primary – database, there is a second database for checking purposes, called the checking database.

The value cycle for a trade firm engaging in e-activities is depicted in Figure 7.2.

By employing web-based technology, an organization may simplify many of its processes. For example, vendor selection, on the basis of inviting offers, becomes much easier by making use of the search engines and portals available on the Internet for product and vendor comparisons, receipt of offers from potential vendors can take place via e-mail, orders can be placed online at the vendor's website, receipt of customer orders can take place via the website, billing can take place via the Internet, and delivery can take place directly from the vendor to the customer, bypassing the organization. However, in spite of the simplification of these primary processes, internal control measures will need some adjustments or even complete redesign when an organization engages in electronic communication.

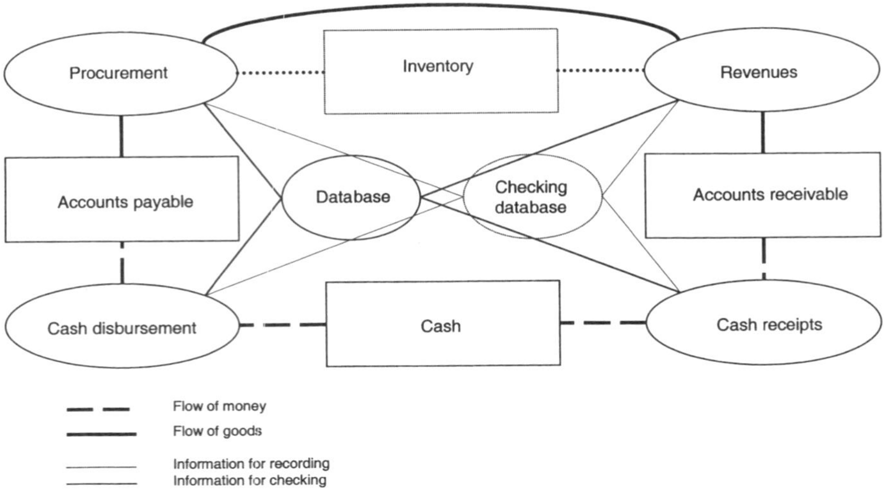

Figure 7.2 Value cycle for a trade firm engaging in e-activities.

Internal Control Adjustments Induced by Engaging in Electronic Communication – Some Examples

- Parties must agree on the conditions that support electronic transactions. Of course, this is no different from non-electronic transactions, but there may be some specific caveats; for example, non-electronic transactions are commonplace and are often supported by standard industry-wide terms of delivery whereas electronic transactions may require additional arrangements, such as privacy protection and validity of electronic signatures.
- When EDI orders are being placed, there must be programmed procedures in place to check whether order specifications are within predefined bandwidths. Should an upper or lower boundary be exceeded, then a further investigation is required by an authorized person within the organization. For example, if an order is placed for 100 pieces of article *A*, and the predefined bandwidth for acceptance is plus or minus 10%, then a shipment containing 89 pieces is not accepted automatically but left to the discretion of the head of the buying department. These kinds of requirement are built into the system by means of programmed procedures.
- On receipt of an electronic invoice, a programmed procedure matches the invoice data with the order data, automatically produces a customer bill, and makes a posting to the accounts payable ledger and the accounts receivable ledger. Note that the flow of goods follows a direct path from vendor to customer, as a result of which a matching of vendor invoice and a receiving report cannot be made. Instead, reliance is placed on a customer complaints system which should be based on clear agreements about applicable terms. In order to receive early customer feedback, confirmation is sent to the customer indicating that a specific shipment has been made. This confirmation may be accompanied by the bill. If a customer did not receive that specific shipment, he will notify the vendor, when

the head of the sales department will investigate what went wrong. If there is no customer reaction within a specified term, then the vendor invoice is approved by the head of the buying department by means of an electronic signature. Subsequently, a programmed procedure initiates electronic payment by means of EFT.

As we demonstrated in Chapter 3 some typical threats to traditional trade firms are:

- Ready-to-sell products. Employees may get tempted to steal these goods. Internal control measures to be taken include supervision and periodic inventory counts.
- Shop within the shop. This may cause a loss of revenues. Internal control measures to be taken include segregation of duties between sales and purchasing roles.
- Many customers. Hence, it may be difficult to obtain detailed customer information. Internal control measures to be taken include adequate controls over customer master files.
- Creditworthiness of customers. This may lead to invalid sales. Internal control measures to be taken include procedures for checking customer creditworthiness at order acceptance.
- Capital-intensive inventories. Business continuity may be endangered. Internal control measures to be taken include setting up a system of reliable and timely information provision about ordered and received goods, sold and delivered goods, and market expectations.
- Cash transactions. Cash may be embezzled. Internal control measures to be taken include cash procedures, and segregation of duties between recording, custody, and authorization with respect to cash.

In trade firms that engage in electronic communication, some of these threats must be reconsidered:

- ready-to-sell products are no longer pickable;
- Shop within the shop may become an even bigger threat because of the potential of vendors and customers bypassing the organization;
- with many customers, detailed customer information may be recorded automatically, as is actually done in customer relationship management;
- creditworthiness of customers may become less of a problem because electronic transactions require either submission of a credit-card number and expiry date that can be checked before delivery, or cash on delivery;
- inventories get less capital-intensive because the just-in-time principle is followed when deliveries go directly from vendor to customer;

- the number of cash transactions will decrease because electronic funds transfer, credit-card payments, and electronic money will gain importance.

In addition, automation as a source of threats to achievement of internal control goals becomes even more important than it used to be. However, a change in nature of automation-related controls may also be anticipated. Segregation of duties is no longer based on division of tasks between authorization, custody, recording, controlling, and execution, but between humans and machines employing the feature that computers can force their users to go through a fixed sequence of activities. This type of segregation of duties is called the new-age segregation of duties. In the electronic environments as sketched, reconciliations and control totals are substituted by analytical review procedures, which provide less hard evidence. In this setting, the so-called soft controls will also gain importance. Importantly, soft controls are predominantly discussed in management control literature. Chapter 8 will elaborate on reciprocity between internal control and management control. Finally, procedures will be put in place that apply more to the alignment between processes than to the alignment between departments. This is in accordance with the basic principles that underlie business process re-engineering (see Chapter 6).

As a result of the absence of physical inventories, flows of goods, and flows of money, some control totals and reconciliations, as embedded in the value cycle, cannot effectively be employed any more; for example, the relationship between inventory at the beginning, purchases, sales, and inventory at the end is reduced to the relationship between purchases and sales, where no stocktaking is possible, and the risk of bypassing the organization by means of direct sales from vendor to customer is substantial. However, controllability may also improve in an electronic environment since all information flows can be automatically reconciled by means of programmed procedures; for example, purchases according to journal voucher = sales according to journal voucher = batch total from vendor orders = batch total from customer orders = cash payments according to bank statements = cash receipts according to bank statements = picking ticket for vendor = confirmation of shipment by vendor = confirmation of receipt by customer. Additionally, in order to increase controllability, a separate checking database can be put in place. A checking database aims to record the details of all incoming and outgoing electronic transactions in such a way that transactions, once recorded, cannot be manipulated any more. This approach shows much similarity to the use of control registers in traditional internal control environments, in that they also contain redundant records in the primary database. For example, a company records the following data on a sales transaction in its database: customer code, product code, and quantity. The same data is recorded in a checking database. After having done this, some electronic data processing takes place where, among other things, a vendor order and a customer bill is electronically transmitted. During this transmission, the data on this transaction in the primary database are erroneously changed and the database gets corrupted as a result. By having a programmed procedure in place that compares the primary database with the checking database, which has not been changed, the primary database can be restored.

If the goods an organization trades are not tangible but bitable such as books in PDF format, movies in DivX format, and CDs in WAV or MP3 format, then this causes some additional internal control threats analogous with threats to physical goods that are not in an organization's own warehouses. When goods cannot be physically shipped any more, then the type of firm changes from trade to service. As we discussed in Chapters 2 through 4, service firms encounter some specific threats as a result of inapplicability of most value cycle-related controls. Here, again, a checking database can be employed to make a recording of all website-related events. On the basis of acquired records, a detailed reconciliation at the article level can be made between reported revenues and recorded transactions.

BPR and Internal Control

Of the seven basic principles of BPR, as discussed in Chapter 6, three have straightforward implications for internal control and, more specifically, segregation of duties:

1 Have output users perform the process. This implies pairing of duties between authorization and custody.
2 Have those who produce information process it. This implies pairing of duties between authorization and recording.
3 Empower workers, use built-in controls, and flatten the organizational chart. This implies pairing of duties between authorization and controlling.

However, the unsatisfactory pairing of duties that may result from an ill-considered implementation is not the only threat an organization faces when embarking upon BPR. Considering the strong relationship between segregation of duties and reconciliations and control totals, the latter may lose relevance for control purposes. Consider the case of an organization consisting of the following four departments: administration, purchasing, sales, and warehouse. The head of administration periodically reconciles the *soll* position of inventory at the end of the period with the inventory report contaning information on inventory at the beginning of the period (prepared by the warehouseman), the purchased goods report (prepared by the purchasing department), and the sold goods report (prepared by the sales department). This reconciliation makes sense because it may uncover any errors made by the various departments involved. When these departments are combined into processes, then the data sources are no longer separated from each other. As a result, any unintended errors will be discovered at an early stage of data processing within the process itself. However, intended errors will be concealed because any *soll* and *ist* position can be reconciled by the providers of that information, before handing it over to the head of administration. Hence, the head of administration should put some additional controls in place. Analytical review gains importance in this setting. The head of administration will have to scrutinize the general ledger in order to find eye-catching patterns like deviations from prior periods' sales. Supervision as a control device also gains importance as a substitute for internal control measures; for

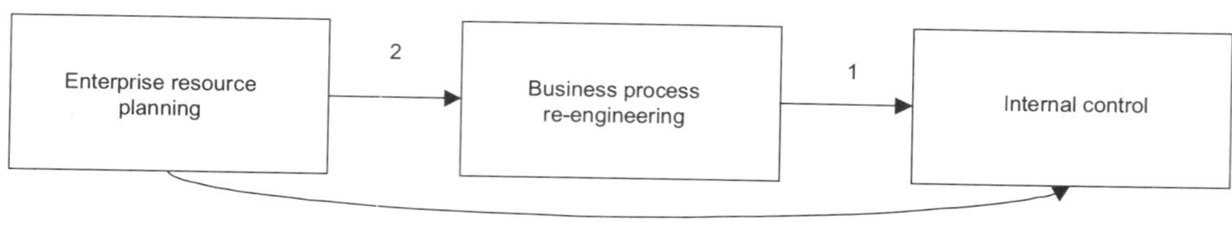

Figure 7.3 The direct and indirect relationship between ERP and internal control.

example, the process owner will supervise his people and report irregularities to a designated authority. In general, the control environment will have to be deliberately influenced toward more control consciousness in order to replace the reduced possibilities for traditional internal controls. Although the control environment is an integral component of internal control according to the COSO report, influencing it traditionally is part of management control. This issue is further discussed in Chapter 8.

ERP and Internal Control

ERP implementation has both direct and indirect effects on internal controls (see Figure 7.3). First, as we discussed in the prior section, BPR without additional measures will have a predominantly adverse effect on internal controls. Second, as we demonstrated in Chapter 6 (see Table 6.2), ERP and BPR often go hand in hand. As a result, there is an indirect effect of ERP on internal controls. Finally, ERP has positive as well as negative direct effects on internal controls, including:

- Measurement points such as the transferral of documents, physical goods, or common money from one person to another are integrated in the information system and, hence, are no longer visible. Because of this, controls based on manual inputs and outputs as done by users, often called user controls, become less applicable; for example, establishing accountability as a preventive control measure cannot be effectuated any more.
- The use of program modules that enforce application of programmed controls.
- Controls migrate from the execution stage of information system use to the implementation stage of information system development.

Chapter Cases

Case 7.1 ERP and Internal Control

Company X

Company *X* processes fluid chemicals. The purchasing department places orders based on a minimum inventory level. The chemicals are received through pipelines and stored in tanks. The company has a logistic system in which an employee of the storage department enters the received goods. The purchasing department makes payments based on bills received with each delivery of goods. Each department (among others, purchasing, sales, production, accounts receiv-able administration, storage department, controlling) has a personal computer at its disposal which is connected to a network. All financial transactions are processed in the financial system. In addition, the company uses a management information system supplying relevant managerial information. The three information systems are not integrated.

Company Y
Company *Y* processes fluid chemicals. Orders are placed automatically by the ERP system (logistics module) based on a minimum inventory level. Chemicals are delivered through pipelines and stored in tanks. The minimum inventory level is indicated by means of an automated observation system integrated in the ERP system. Subsequently, an order is placed with the supplier through EDI (Electronic Data Interchange; purchasing module). At the supplier's, the order is prepared automatically by computer and shipped automatically through the pipeline. Based on receipt through the pipeline, *Y*'s purchasing department automatically prepares a pro forma bill and sends it by means of EDI (purchasing module). Payments are made automatically through electronic money transfer.

Company *Y* takes over Company *X*. A big hurdle to take is conversion from the old-fashioned information system of *X* to the ERP system of *Y*.

Assignment

Discuss the differences between Company *X* and Company *Y* regarding the internal control measures that are to be taken. In doing so, deal with the following areas:

- input;
- documents;
- conversion;
- continuity;
- segregation of duties;
- Access security;
- information and communication technology.

Case 7.2 Lateral

A medium-sized insurance company offers three types of insurance:

- legal aid;

- vehicles;
- household effects (furniture, etc.).

Policies are sold by means of direct writings and through the mediation of agents. The following departments exist:

- acceptance and transactions;
- damage;
- administration and automation;
- cash collection;
- applications;
- procurement.

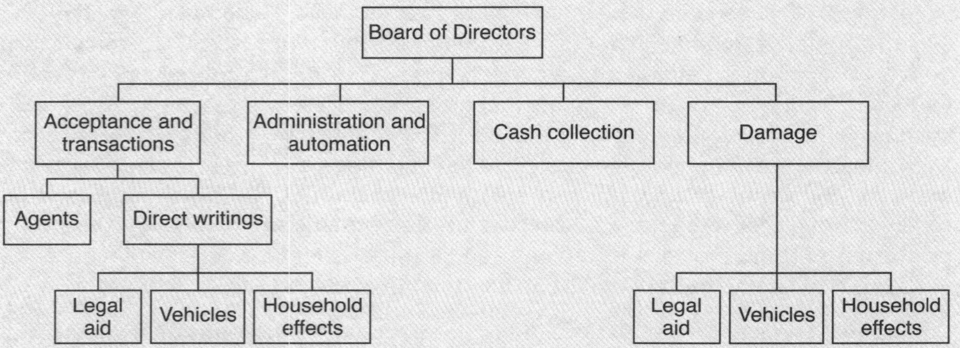

Every department has computer terminals that are interconnected in a local area network.

In recent years, the number of new policies has decreased dramatically. The number of discontinued policies has also grown. As a result, insurance turnover has been decreasing by 3% annually on average. Moreover, costs have been increasing.

The corporate controller is invited to make an analysis of the causes of these problems. He presents the following findings:

- the number of complaints from clients has been growing;
- as a result of poor communication between departments, many transactions require additional management coordination.

Most client complaints deal with:

- long delays when questions are asked by telephone about policies and loss coverage;
- frequently, no answer when trying to contact the company by telephone;
- payment of claims is often tardy;
- several departments of the firm are involved in taking out of insurances;
- answers to written correspondence are often given with a delay;

- many clients have the feeling that they do not receive the level of service that they expect;
- in cases where other insurers are involved, clients often have doubts about their interest being suitably taken care of;
- agents are often inadequately equipped to answer clients' questions.

In conclusion, the controller finds it necessary to streamline the company activities in order to become more customer-oriented and to facilitate better internal communication. Re-engineering of the business processes seems the solution.

After this radical reorganization, the company looks entirely different (see the organization chart below). A remarkable detail is that there has been no need for major lay-offs. However, a large number of the workers' occupations have been changed as a result of re-education and retraining.

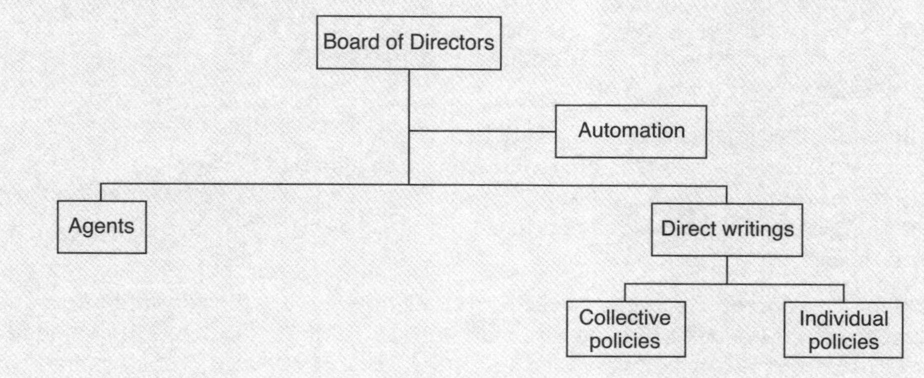

Assignments

1 Provide a normative internal control description with respect to the taking out of insurance and payments of sustained losses.

2 Make a comparison between the administrative organization before and after re-engineering efforts. Discuss the following issues at least:
- controllability in general;
- segregation of duties;
- procedures and guidelines;
- information technology;
- analytical review;
- managerial information.

Case 7.3 Internet Mechanic

Internet Mechanic is a fairly young organization. It maintains a site on the World Wide Web, where visitors can retrieve general information with respect to their own brands and makes of car. The site is also used to reserve maintenance services with affiliated garages.

Strategy
The company's strategy is focused on obtaining competitive advantages through optimal deployment of ICT and information provision. Of course, this focus manifests itself in the nature of the company's operations. Internet Mechanic would not be able to function in its present form without the current state of information technology.

Structure
Internet Mechanic consists of the following departments, which are under direct control of general management:

- automation, which maintains the website;
- commercial affairs, responsible for contacts with affiliated garages;
- planning, responsible for information provision about affiliated garages and for planning of maintenance jobs per garage.
- administration.

A visitor to Internet Mechanic's website can retrieve general information about maintenance of his or her brand and make of car. To that end, Internet Mechanic has at its disposal a database with all brands and types of cars, subclassified by year of construction, with a description of the most frequent types of maintenance service.

In addition, a visitor can decide to have an affiliated garage perform maintenance services on his or her car. To that end, the visitor records the brand, make, year of construction, mileage and type of maintenance service in the computer system. After input, the system informs the visitor about the price predetermined by the garage and the specific garage that can perform the maintenance service at the desired time. If the visitor agrees, he or she indicates this. Via the system, the order is directly reported to the garage in question. The affiliated garages themselves take care of client billing and credit management.

Internet Mechanic has already entered into contracts with a large number of garages in the Netherlands. In this context, the parties have agreed that affiliated garages may also do their own customer canvassing and maintenance.

Maintenance services that clients book with the garages directly are communicated to Internet Mechanic by the respective garages, whereupon updated planning is made available to these garages.

Internet Mechanic's revenues consist of:

- a once-only fee when garages join Internet Mechanic, and a fixed monthly fee for listing the garage on the website.
- a fixed percentage of the monthly sales that the affiliated garages generate through Internet Mechanic, as well as a (notably lower) fixed percentage of the monthly sales that the garages generate directly.

Besides the Internet site, Internet Mechanic also puts a highly modern organization model at the garages' disposal, if desired. The aim of this model is minimization of the participating garages' overhead costs. This organization model differs from the standard (at least from an AIS point of view) model in the following respects:

- The reception function has disappeared, since Internet Mechanic has completely taken over planning activities. What remains is a separate employee, charged with cash receipts (cashier). The mechanics input into the system the number of available hours per mechanic, the maintenance services that are reserved at the garage directly, and the job distribution using Internet Mechanic's software.
- The affiliated garages perform standardized services only. The mechanics keep a registration of the services performed. The shop floor consists of the following sections:
  - changing oil;
  - exhaust and shock absorbers;
  - battery and windows
- The closed stockroom has disappeared. Since Internet Mechanic has taken over planning activities, it is no longer necessary to maintain large stocks of spare parts. All jobs are totalized daily per garage. The resulting need for parts is transferred by means of EDI to a regular supplier. This supplier delivers the desired parts to the respective garage at the beginning of each working day. The parts are received by the cashier.

In the past six months, the first practical experiences with this new organization model have been acquired. It seems there are a few bottlenecks:

- Besides large levels of inventories, some garages have experienced sizeable efficiency losses.
- Contrary to expectations, there can be sizeable waiting times, in addition to unexpected undercapacity, unidentified by Internet Mechanic's software.
- After the frosty period of the past winter, water from thaw has caused some datalines to short circuit. Due to this, certain files from Internet Mechanic and the affiliated garages appeared to contain different information.
- In some cases, parts are also received by the mechanics. The absence of correct parts sometimes hinders the progress of the activities.

Assignment

1 List the threats with respect to control of the business processes within this organization. Use the following two dimensions to present your solution:
  - domains (business, information and communication, information and communication technology);
  - strategy formulation versus strategy implementation.

2 Indicate the exposure (the adverse effect) of each of these threats. For each threat, provide internal control solutions.

Case 7.4 Tempotrans

Tempotrans is a transporter of all kinds of soft drink exclusively in the European Union. The company is also involved in temporary storage of goods owned by third parties. All activities are coordinated from its headquarters, located in the Netherlands. The following departments are in place:

- planning and logistic;
- financial administration;
- workshop (includes a filling station and a car wash);
- storage and handling;
- order processing;
- ICT department.

The company is managed by a general manager and an assistant manager. The general manager is charged with commercial affairs and the assistant manager is charged with technical affairs.

The company uses a local area network (Windows NT) with one or more PCs and printers in each department. Several non-integrated applications are in use, among which are a financial standard package (multi-user) for the managerial information provision, an EDI-tool, and the industry-specific package 'Transspeed' for order processing. In recent years, Tempotrans has been experiencing substantial problems in hiring the right people for the ICT department. Once hired, it often appears that ICT persons do not think and act in accordance with the organization goals. As a result, communication with other departments does not go as smoothly as it should. Financial administration regularly indicates that it is hindered in its task execution. Although the information system seems to operate properly, financial administration is not sure whether or not the information security measures are adequate.

The company uses EDI for order processing and billing. Recently, the management of Tempotrans has reconsidered its strategy and decided to enter into e-business. This has culminated in the plan that within five years 80% of all sales transactions (including payment) will take place by means of the company's website. Simultaneously, a full integration of the companies' information systems is strived for by means of an ERP solution. An important advantage of this approach is that a sound basis is created for customer relationship management. With the implementation of these e-business applications, traditional EDI applications will be banned.

Sales are mainly generated by conducting all Benelux transports for one major soft drink producer. This producer's orders are received at order processing by EDI. This department converts the orders into standard forms which are manually put into the order processing system. The soft-drink producer initiates the billing process by sending the transport company a billing advice via EDI on a monthly basis. This billing advice indicates how much the producer expects to owe Tempotrans by reason of the transport services delivered to the producer. Tempotrans confirms this specification by means of a (hard copy) pro forma invoice.

Incidental orders from other soft-drink producers are accepted whenever capacity allows. Particularly in winter, it is important to have sufficient incidental orders to optimally utilize capacity. Order processing and billing takes place in the traditional way: orders are received by telephone or in writing and are recorded on standard order forms. Order processing bills its incidental clients on a monthly basis.

The (expensive) trucks (60 items in two weight classes) are maintained in a garage and cleaned on a weekly basis at the washing installation. Both the garage and the washing installation are located on Tempotrans' grounds and are owned by Tempotrans. This washing installation is used by third parties as well, on cash payment at a fixed rate for each wash. Also located on the grounds is a filling station, which is used (just by the company itself) as much as possible. Trucks en route may also refuel at other filling stations.

Often, goods owned by third parties are temporarily stored in one of the depositories located on the company's grounds. These goods are mainly stored in crates on pallets (sometimes the crates are empty). The company charges its storage clients using price tables in which duration of storage, volume, and weight are taken into account. Order processing bills its clients on a monthly basis.

Planning and logistics takes care of job order issuance and aims to optimize the routing of trucks by means of advanced techniques. The department uses the Transspeed package for this purpose.

Assignment

1 Provide a normative internal control description (in the form of headlines) with respect to the revenue cycle for the situation where no e-business activities are employed and systems are completely non-integrated.

2 Provide a normative internal control description (in the form of headlines) with respect to the revenue cycle for the situation where planned e-business activities have been implemented and an integrated (ERP) system is in place in accordance with the planning.

3 Tabulate the internal control differences between the situation before e-business and integration and the situation after e-business and integration. Discuss the following issues at least:

- controllability in general;
- segregation of duties;
- procedures and guidelines;
- ICT;
- analytical review;
- managerial information.

Bridging the Gap Between Internal Control and Management Control

8

... management control systems are information-based systems. Senior managers use information for various purposes: to signal the domain in which subordinates should search for opportunities, to communicate plans and goals, to monitor the achievement of plans and goals, and to keep informed and inform others of emerging developments.

Simons (1995b), p. 5

... internal control system. This system does not directly relate to strategy formation and implementation, but it is essential in any business, large or small, in order to ensure that assets are secure and management information is reliable.

Simons (1995b), p. 177

After studying this chapter, the reader should be able to:

- Identify the quality characteristics of information, organization, decision making and information systems.
- Understand how control can add value to information.
- Explain the difference between tight and loose controls.
- Explain the relationship between internal controls and management controls.
- Explain the relationship between corporate governance and control.
- Understand the differences and similarities between control classifications that have been developed in the field of management control in the last decades.
- Understand the trade-off between control and innovation.
- Systematically describe the joint role of MC and IC in controlling organizations.

Chapter Outline

Management control (MC) is aimed at implementing strategies. Unlike internal control, management control tries to influence people's behaviour within organizations directly. Hence, MC also encompasses loose controls like cultural and personnel controls, whereas internal control follows a much more technocratic approach that considers procedures and a system of checks and balances the main control instruments. This chapter investigates the relationship between MC and IC. Here, we arrive at a potential source of conflict between management and AIS professionals. Management wants to optimize organizational performance by developing products or services the market may want. AIS professionals want to record all the transactions the company engages in, to provide information that is as reliable as possible and that can be used to control the organization. However, this conflict may not be so difficult to resolve as it seems. Finding a balance between innovation and control seems to be the ultimate goal in contemporary organizations. There are several classifications of control. This chapter discusses the main developments in this field and relates them to the balancing act between innovation and control. The chapter concludes with a systematic discussion of the interrelationship between MC and IC, thereby demonstrating that a convergence of MC and IC is likely to occur.

Introduction

There are few concepts that have more notions than the concept of control. The term is usually accompanied by an adjective. As already discussed in Chapter 5, management control and internal control have many characteristics in common, yet there are differences. Historically, management control and internal control have developed independently of one another. However, the last few decades have shown a convergence which has led to much confusion among academics, standard setters, practitioners, and students. Hence, it is important to investigate where these concepts meet and how remaining differences can be resolved. This chapter argues that the gap between management control and internal control can be bridged by exploring the roots of both concepts.

Throughout this text, we have followed the efficiency and effectiveness approach to control. Obviously, we will adhere to this approach when elaborating on the relationship between management control and internal control.

Corporate Governance

In addition to the COSO report, as discussed in Chapter 2, a number of internal control and related documents have been issued in the last decade. These include the

Table 8.1 Main characteristics of the Cadbury report, the CoCo report, the SAC report, the COBIT report, SAS 55/78, and KonTraG

Criterion	*Cadbury*	*COSO*	*CoCo*	*SAC*	*COBIT*	*SAS 55/78*	*KonTraG*
Viewpoint	Financial accounting	Financial accounting	Financial accounting and management accounting	Information and communication technology	Information and communication technology	Financial accounting	Financial accounting
Primary audience	Top managers	Management	Financial managers	Internal auditors	Information managers	Financial auditors	Top managers and financial auditors
Goals	Creation of a framework for improved control Increasing reliance on financial accounting and the financial audit	Definition of internal control Guidance for improved control	Definition of internal control Guidance for improved control	Definition of internal control, control goals, and the role of the internal auditor Guidance for the employment of information and communication technology	Creation of a framework for generally applicable ICT controls	Definition of internal control Guidance for assessing the influence of internal controls on the financial audit	Better understanding of the position of non-executive directors, shareholders, and financial auditors Increasing transparency Guidance for the quality and content of the financial audit
Orientation	Conceptual	Conceptual	Conceptual	Conceptual	Conceptual	Conceptual	Implementation

Cadbury report, the CoCo report, the SAC report, the COBIT report, SAS 55/78, and KonTraG (Kontrole und Transparenz Gesetz) (see Table 8.1). The latter is an interesting case since it is not a report issued by a private body but a law issued by the German government. Although these reports and laws rely heavily on each other's findings – note that they may change over time and, hence, evoke a chain reaction – they look at internal control from the different viewpoints of different audiences and aim at different goals. COSO, CoCo, SAC, and SAS primarily want to provide a definition of internal control. Cadbury, KonTraG, and COBIT do not explicitly mention this goal, but they use a definition that closely resembles the COSO definition. All these reports give guidance to the development of more effective internal control systems within organizations. Furthermore, all these reports contribute to better corporate governance of organizations. KonTraG provides a further refinement, aimed at the implementation of recommendations of previous reports.

The overwhelming interest in internal control issues related to corporate governance came to the fore in the last decade. In brief, corporate governance deals with: (1) control; (2) decision-making power; (3) responsibility; (4) oversight; (5) integrity; and (6) accountability. Corporate governance is aimed at securing the continuity

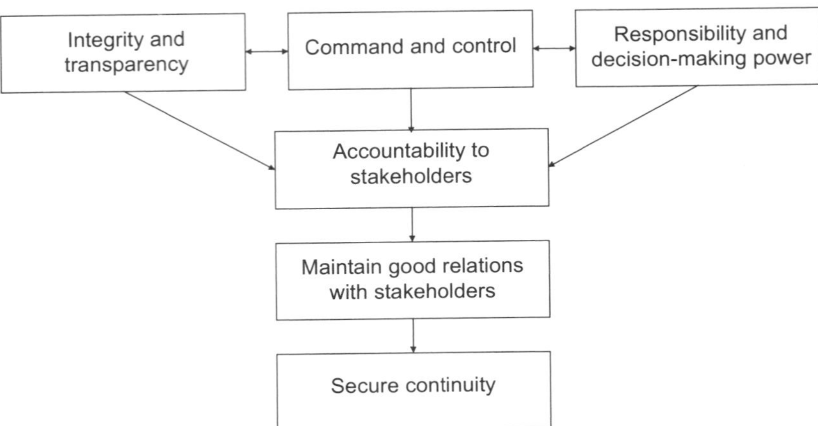

Figure 8.1 Elements of corporate governance.

of organizations by maintaining good relations with stakeholders. Therefore, organizations are held accountable for their activities, and, hence, they should undertake the right activities in the right way, thereby explicitly showing that they do so. So, organizations – by way of their management – enable stakeholders to form an opinion with respect to the quality of the control systems that are in place, decision-making power, responsibilities, oversight by independent parties, and management's integrity (Figure 8.1).

In Chapter 2, we introduced the governance paradigm as one of the cornerstones of AIS. This paradigm puts forward the role of information in governing and controlling organizations. From the comprehensive contingency framework, we learn that information cannot be decoupled from decision making in the business domain and information systems in the ICT domain. The basic tenet that runs throughout this book is that information is crucial to controlling organizations, whether it be for management control purposes or internal control purposes. We will therefore first discuss the issue of quality in relation to information, decision making, and information systems. But before we do so, it is important to get a grasp of the general concept of quality. There are several definitions of quality. An operational definition is: all the attributes and characteristics of a product or service that are important to meet explicit or self-evident needs. Quality is a user concept. The user assesses whether or not a product or service complies with her quality requirements. This implies that every generic quality characteristic is subjective by nature and, hence, may differ between persons. In addition, every generic quality characteristic is implicitly assigned a specific user-dependent weight. These weights differ between persons and are dependent on a wide range of variables, such as the complexity of the decision, personality, cognitive style, risk-seeking propensity, strategic conditions, and (organizational or national) culture.

Quality of Decision Making, Information, and Information Systems

In an attempt to make an objective assessment of the quality of decision making, some authors argue that a list can be developed containing a limited set of quality characteristics of decision making. The line of reasoning is that the higher the quality of decision making, the better the resulting decisions. The variables that may explain the quality of decision making include the number of aspects involved in decision making, the time horizon, the use of retrospective information, and the system used for decision making. In general, it is assumed that using more aspects, considering a longer time horizon, effective use of ex-post information, and applying fixed patterns lead to superior decisions. However, seen in the light of our remarks on the concept of quality and, indeed, following a contingency approach, we believe that this assumption is oversimplified.

Because the quality of a decision is dependent on the quality of information, information requirements must be determined as accurately as possible and information provision must be tailored to these requirements. Therefore, some factors that play a role in determination of information requirements must be discussed. When discussing internal controls, reliability of information provision is important, but so is reliability of the information system as well. Hence, reliability of the information system must also be discussed.

Information can be defined as processed data that is organized, meaningful, and of value to the person who utilizes it. Hence, information must posess several quality characteristics. Here again, attempts have been made to provide lists of objective quality characteristics. The quality spectrum of information is an example of such a list, but so are the quality characteristics of information systems.

Quality Spectrum of Information

When assessing the quality of information, the focus is on the degree to which information can be utilized in decision making. Figure 8.2 represents the quality spectrum of information. Information is said to be reliable if it is is valid and complete. Information is said to be relevant if it has the desired level of accuracy, is provided on time, and is understandable by the user. Together, reliability and relevance contribute to the effectiveness of information. Besides effectiveness, economy is the other main characteristic of information quality.

Validity

Information is valid if it is in accordance with the represented part of reality, in the sense that what is reported is not too high; for example, expense must have been

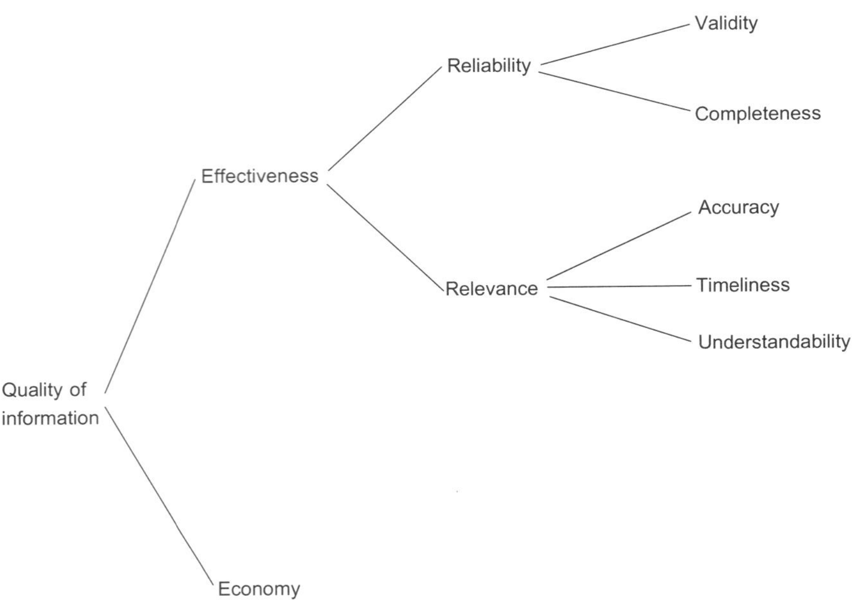

Figure 8.2 Quality spectrum of information.

incurred for the purpose of attaining organizational goals. Records of these transactions may contain expenses that are not attributable to the business or to the specific cost accounts used for the postings. As a result, the records may be partially invalid.

Completeness

Information is complete if it accords with the represented part of reality, in the sense that what has been reported is not too low. For example, the accounts receivable list of company *Q* shows a balance of €100,000, consisting of three debtors: *X*, *Y*, and *Z*. Debtor *X* has a debt of €25,000, *Y* has a debt of €70,000, and *Z* has a debt of €5,000. There are two completeness issues that can emerge. First, each of these three debtors may have a larger debt than recorded in the records of company *Q*. Second, there may be a fourth debtor who is not in the accounts receivable list of company *Q*.

Accuracy

Information is accurate if it is has the required degree of precision; for example, the higher the hierarchical level of decision making, the less precise information needs to be. The alleged bean-counter mentality of accountants is typical of providing extremely precise information to two decimal places. Obviously, the AIS can provide this precise information. However, it is not necessary, or even dysfunctional, to do so in every decision-making situation, regardless of contingent factors like the hierarchical level.

Timeliness

Information is timely if it is provided on time to affect the decision-making process. For example, suppose a client calls to place an order. The order processing clerk enters the client code (or his name), the product code, and the ordered quantity into the order-processing module of the information system. Via a programmed procedure, it is checked to see whether the client is creditworthy and, hence, allowed to be delivered to and whether the required goods are in stock. The decision to be made here is whether or not to deliver the required goods to a specific client. If the credit rating system provides delayed information, this can lead to delivering to a client who is in financial trouble. If the perpetual inventory records provide delayed information, the ordered goods may be out of stock without the system informing the order processing clerk.

Understandability

Information is understandable if it is presented in a format that is useful for and intelligible to the user of the data. Understandability concerns the unambiguous interpretability of information. In general, the more quantitative the information, the higher the understandability. For example, compare a verbal performance report with a quantitative performance report. The verbal report could read as follows: 'Business unit X performed satisfactorily. Profits increased, clients were again satisfied, the internal organization was restructured in order to meet market demand for more customized products, and some new products were developed.' The quantitative report could read as follows: 'Business unit X showed an increase in net profit of 15%. The survey-based client satisfaction index slightly dropped by 1%. The number of complaints about tardy front-office service increased by 10%, however the restructuring of the organization is expected to lead to a turnaround. Five new products were developed, two of which caused the increased profit.' Clearly, the quantitative report is much less ambiguous and, hence, better understandable. In the end, this report will lead to enhanced performance judgement of business unit X.

Economy

Information provision is economically justified if it is produced at the lowest possible cost. Here, no reference is made to the effectiveness of information because, in that case, a comparison would have to be made between the costs and benefits of information provision. This would culminate in an efficient information provision process. Because effectiveness is considered to be a separate element of the quality spectrum of information, efficiency should not be addressed within this framework.

Quality Characteristics of Information Systems

In assessing the quality of information systems, the focus is on the degree to which information systems meet the requirements of the data processing department. Figure 8.3 represents the common quality characteristics of information systems.

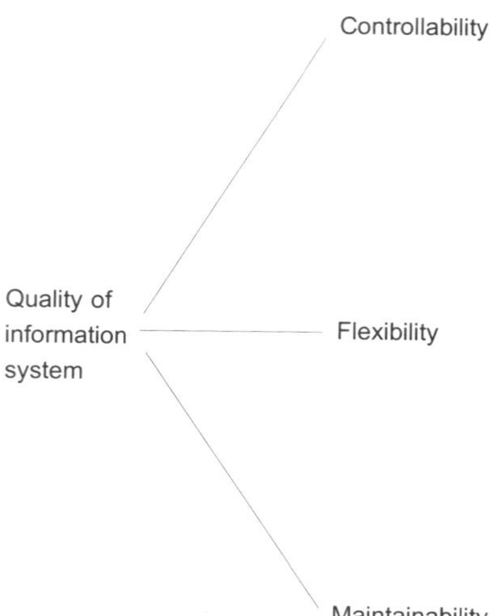

Figure 8.3 Quality characteristics of information systems.

Controllability

The aim of any information system is to provide information that meets the quality requirements as defined by the users. Controllability refers to the degree to which information systems provide information in accords with the quality requirements of the people who make use of that information system.

Flexibility

Flexibility refers to the degree to which information systems can be transferred from one environment to another. This may imply the system can easily be adjusted to changing sitiuational conditions like the state of the available ICT, or changing user requirements. In general, flexibility is a characteristic that receives more and more attention in our current dynamic environment. Flexibility, in general, has in it aspects of adaptability to changing circumstances, preparedness to change, and ability to stimulate renewal and innovation processes. Applied to information systems, flexibility then refers to the dynamic interplay between the system and its environment, the dynamic interplay within the system between its components, and the complete absence of rigidity. Flexibility in this sense may pertain to the chosen hardware platform, the operating system, and the applications, as well as to the business environment surrounding the system; for example, using a PC-based client–server architecture, instead of a customized computer system, increases flexibility because any available application for Windows can be run regardless of the PC brand or the country of origin of the software.

Maintainability

Maintainability concerns the degree to which information systems can be tested, renewed, and changed at reasonable costs. For example, a customized information system must always have a thorough technical system documentation. If this documentation is omitted, system maintenance becomes heavily dependent on the availability of the system developers who originally designed the system and wrote the software. Should these system developers no longer be available, a so-called retrofit is the only solution to regain grip on maintainability. Such a retrofit reconstructs the current system specifications.

Information Policy

Information policy is the formulation of goals, restrictions, disciplines, and guidelines regarding information provision and communication. If the availability of high-quality information is considered to be a critical success factor, information policy is a substantial element of business policy. Thus, strategic management must reconcile business policy with information policy.

An explicitly formulated information policy is not always necessary. Factors such as the nature, magnitude, and complexity of the organization, as well as the relationship between different parts of the organization, determine the required explicitness of information policy. Generally speaking, four levels exist within information policy:

- information strategy;
- information architecture;
- information projects planning;
- information projects execution.

As discussed in Chapter 5, information strategy is concerned with the choice between exploiting or mitigating information imperfections. Information architecture is concerned with designing the structure of information provision at different levels in the organization. This includes the following topics: delineation of different information systems and data records; infrastructure of data processing facilities; and organizational structure of information provision. Information projects planning is concerned with the preparation of design and change activities that culminate in a renewed information architecture. Information projects execution is concerned with the design of information systems, starting with information requirements determination and ending with implementation of the system.

Information policy is concerned with what information requirements exist among executives, as well as what data must be recorded in order to provide that information. Here, the dynamic interaction between the business domain (choosing between exploiting or mitigating information imperfections, preparation of design and change activities), the information and communication domain (organizational structure of information provision, renewed information architecture, information requirements determination), and the ICT domain (delineation of different information systems and data records, infrastructure of data processing facilities, implementation of the system) becomes most clear. The next sections will elaborate on these topics, thereby putting the information and communication domain at the heart of the organization.

Information Requirement Analysis

When analysing information needs for managerial decision making, a contingency approach is usually superior to an approach in which information requirements are determined without regard to the personal characteristics of the decision maker. However, tailoring information provision to the needs of every specific user may be very inefficient. As already indicated in Chapter 5, a fruitful solution to this dilemma is to group decision makers into homogeneous categories. These categories may then be homogeneous with respect to cognitive style, personality, leadership style, or any other personal feature influencing an individual's decision-making behaviour. As a result, information provision or control systems are not customized to specific individuals, but to groups of individuals, which makes the alignment problem considerably less complex.

The higher the decision-making level, the more a contingency approach is needed. Decisions at the strategic level are less routine, more complex, and more subjective. This implies that it is more difficult to make these types of decision, and hence to discern the right from the wrong decision. As a result, the information needed at this level is not objectively determinable. Tailoring information provision to the subjective needs of an individual or a group of individuals may resolve this issue. Hence, the choice of strategy to determine information requirements is dependent on the decision-making level where the information is needed.

In determining information needs, the following approaches may be followed (see Rockart 1979):

- The by-product approach. In this approach, not much attention is paid to actual information needs of decision makers at the tactical and strategic level. Rather, information needed for operational decision making (e.g. what and where to buy needed goods) serves as the basis for management reports.
- The null approach. This approach pays only limited attention to formal, periodical information provision. For every specific situation, information needs are determined independent of previously determined information needs.
- The key indicator system approach. This approach is based on an objective analysis of the factors that contribute to a business's financial health. Exception reports are the most important statements provided here.

- The total study process approach. This approach focuses on alignment of an organization's information systems. The approach is top–down, following an analysis of the information needs based on rigid system development methodologies.
- The critical success factor approach. By following this approach, the flaws of former approaches should be found. This approach combines organizational strategy with organizational structure to arrive at optimal information provision. Ideally, information requirements are derived from the symbiosis of organizational strategy and structure.

Table 8.2 summarizes the main characteristics of each of these approaches. Within each of these approaches, a combination of information acquisition strategies may be used. The simplest strategy is to interview decision makers and ask them what information they deem necessary. This is called the *servant strategy* (e.g. interviews, surveys, brainstorming, or administering a Delphi). The disadvantage of this technique is a possible interviewer and respondent bias, and the decision maker may not be able to express his needs until he encounters a certain situation. A strategy that mitigates the potential biases of the servant strategy is the *reference strategy*. This strategy infers information requirements from the information analyst's knowledge of similar decision-making situations. To make this strategy work, the analyst must have a set of reference models at her disposal; for example, the typology of organizations, which we use for determining threats to the accomplishment of the organization's goals, may also be used for information analysis purposes. When reference models are non-existent, a *developmental strategy* can be used. A thorough study is made of the decision-making problem and the information system needed to deal with this problem (e.g. a waterfall approach to system development like SDM [system development methodology]). Finally, an *evolutionary strategy* can be used when there is an extreme level of uncertainty due to complexity, dramatic increases in information needs, and a lack of expertise among users and developers of information systems. The information requirements are discovered by experimenting with the development of an information system as is the case when applying a prototyping approach (see Chapter 6).

Within AIS, the following questions may be asked in relation to managerial information provision: What are the CEO's information requirements and what is the frequency of this information? What data must be recorded in order to provide the required information? Strictly speaking, methods of information requirement analysis are not discussed within the field of AIS. In other words, information requirements are considered to be environmental factors. Traditionally, the fields that address problems of information requirement analysis are information management and organization studies. However, in view of ongoing ICT proliferation, every user of information systems must gain some ICT proficiency. Hence, our broader contemporary view on AIS also encompasses information requirement analysis, since this forms the basis of any information system.

Table 8.2 Main characteristics of each of the five approaches to information requirements determination (based on Rockart 1979)

Characteristics	*By-product approach*	*Null approach*	*Key indicator system approach*	*Total study process approach*	*Critical success factor approach*
Aimed at management information	No	Yes	Yes	Yes	Yes
Aimed at transaction processing	Yes	No	No	No	Yes
Adapted to specific decision making at the strategic level	No	Yes	Yes	No	Yes
Attention to management control	Yes	No	Yes	Yes	Yes
Ability to provide objective and quantifiable information	Yes	No	Yes	Yes	Yes
Leads to well-thought-out information requirements by managers	No	Yes	No	Yes	Yes
Provides an integral approach to problems	No	Yes	No	Yes	Yes
Attention to the cost aspect of information systems	Yes	No	Yes	No	Yes
Attention to the completeness aspect of information	No	No	No	Yes	Yes

Management Control and Internal Control

There are some significant differences between management control and internal control. However, these differences have been subject to change during the evolution of both disciplines. As sketched in Chapter 1, internal control has a long history in some continental European countries. In the USA, the internal control notion did not come into play until the late 1940s. Management control, on the other hand, seems to have a more Anglo-Saxon tradition. However, it is hard to deny that disciplines like internal control and management control must have originated when the first businesses were founded. It was not until certain critical complexity levels were reached (e.g. separation between ownership and leadership, strict separation between white-collar and blue-collar workers, multi-product businesses, vertical integration, diversification, and third-party finance constructions) that the disciplines became codified in textbooks and journals, taught in schools, and considered to discuss themes relevant for practice and theory.

In brief, we believe the main differences between management control and internal control are:

- Management control starts from strategy, whereas internal control starts from transactions.
- Management control usually follows a contingency approach, whereas internal control predominantly follows a cycle or a typology approach.
- Management control has a predominant behavioural orientation, whereas internal control has a more technocratic orientation.

The comprehensive contingency framework, as introduced in Chapter 5, provides guidance for positioning of management control and internal control. When we try to reproduce the origin of the fields, management control seems to have evolved from strategy implementation problems. Hence, the driver of management control is strategy. Internal control, on the other hand, seems to have evolved from the need to organize transactions within and between firms. Hence, the driver of internal control is the transaction. Thus, management control starts from the upper layer in the comprehensive contingency framework, and proceeds top–down toward strategy implementation. Internal control – on the other hand – starts from the lower layer in the framework, and proceeds bottom–up to meet management control. In the end, management control and internal control may converge, resulting in a discipline called organizational control or just control. Another distinction that may be resolved in the near future is that in management control problems a contingency approach is followed whereas in internal control problems a cycle approach is followed. Combining cycles into organizations, as demonstrated in our discussion of the typology of organizations in Chapters 2–4, is an example of a contingency approach *avant la lettre*. A third difference between the disciplines is that management control tries to influence people's behaviour within organizations directly, whereas internal control is more technocratic in nature. Again, a convergence may be expected since internal control increasingly encompasses attention to the human factor. The definition and internal control components, as discerned by the COSO report, are illustrative of this observation; for example, the control environment in the COSO report '... sets the tone of an organization, influencing the control

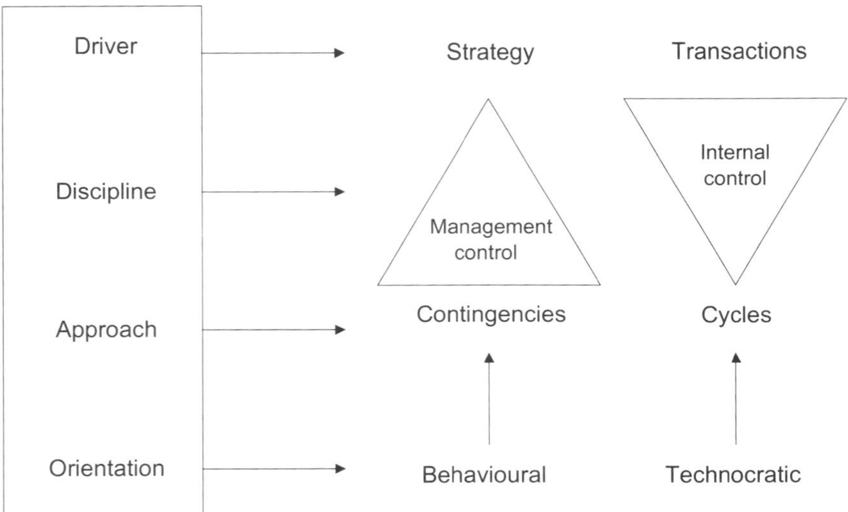

Figure 8.4 The drivers, approaches, and orientation in management control and internal control.

consciousness of its people . . .' (COSO 1994). Figure 8.4 summarizes the differences between management control and internal control.

If we want to effectively bridge the gap between internal control and management control, the feasibility of a convergence between both disciplines with respect to the former three differences must be examined. Therefore, we will discuss the main control frameworks as found in management control literature and try to relate them to the internal control notion as developed in the COSO report.

Strategic Planning, Management Control, and Task Control

In accordance with the hierarchical levels that can be distinguished within organizations, we can identify three management – or planning and control – levels. We have already made a distinction between the strategic level, the tactical level, and the operational level. Anthony, who can be considered the godfather of management control, developed a planning and control framework that also consists of three layers: strategic planning, management control, and task control (Anthony, 1965). In his view, operational (or task) control is the process of assuring that specific tasks are carried out effectively and efficiently. At the other end of the scale, we find strategic planning which is the process of deciding on the objectives of the organization, on changes in these objectives, on the resources used to attain these objec-

Table 8.3 The characteristics of information for the planning and control concepts as discerned in Anthony's framework (adapted from Gorry and Scott Morton 1971, p. 59)

Characteristics of information	*Strategic planning*	*Operational control*
Source	External	Largely internal
Scope	Very wide	Well defined, narrow
Level of aggregation	Aggregate	Detailed
Time horizon	Future	Historical
Currency	Quite old	Highly current
Required accuracy	Low	High
Frequency of use	Infrequent	Very frequent

tives, and on the policies for governing the acquisition, use, and disposition of these resources. In this framework, management control bridges the gap between strategic planning and task control. By applying management controls, managers assure that resources are obtained and used effectively and efficiently in the accomplishment of the organization's objectives. This framework has borne the test of time. However, in contemporary writings, more attention is paid to the human factor in controlling organizations.

Gorry and Scott Morton (1971) developed a view on the informational aspects of strategic planning, management control, and task control. They position information according to the following seven dimensions: source, scope, level of aggregation, time horizon, currency, required accuracy, and frequency of use. Table 8.3 summarizes the characteristics of information for the planning and control concepts as discerned in Anthony's framework. It must be noted that the boundaries between each of the concepts are not always unambiguously determinable. Rather, there is a continuum between strategic planning and operational control, where management control plays the mediating part and, hence, may be very diverse.

In addition, most information for strategic planning has a non-routine character, whereas most information for operational control is of a routine nature. This could imply that information provision for strategic use is more difficult to automate than information for operational use. However, this is only partially true. Information provision for strategic planning is more externally oriented, and, hence, requires more advanced ICT employment than information provision for operational control. So, ICT deployment for strategic planning is often more complex. This does not mean that its potential for automation is less; for example, information from a CRM database stems from various external sources which demand advanced ICT applications like data warehouses on top of ERP systems with inter-organizational interfaces, whereas information for stock replenishment originates from the inventory files within a company.

Market Control, Bureaucratic Control, and Clan Control

A central problem of organizations is that individuals or organizational units, with only partially congruent goals, must cooperate. As a matter of fact, the main managerial activity is to have people cooperate to attain the organizational goals. When a team of individuals cooperates to fulfil a specific task assignment, such as manufacturing a certain product, then it is important for the welfare of the organization that every member of the team is rewarded in a manner that he perceives as being fair. If just one member of a team is dissatisfied with his reward, then he will adjust his efforts to work as a good team member in such a way so that the reward is more in agreement with his efforts, and, as a result, the organization as a whole will be worse off. If we consider our definition of control as all those organizational activities aimed at having organization members cooperate to reach organizational goals, then we can easily see that the real problem of organizations is the control problem. This notion of control includes problems arising from performance evaluation.

The conceptual framework for the design of organizational control systems, as developed by Ouchi (1979), makes a distinction between market control, clan control, and bureaucratic control. The goal of this classification is to identify those factors that are germane to prototypes of control mechanisms within an organization. The classification relies heavily on the control of people, trying to provide the tools needed to hire qualified people, and to provide the managerial system to instruct, monitor, and evaluate (initially) non-qualified people. The framework, albeit conceptual, is efficient when designing control systems. However, the design parameters are not specific enough to serve as a checklist for developing a mature control system. Hence, it indeed serves as a *conceptual framework* that may form the basis for another, more directly applicable framework, like the objects-of-control classification scheme.

The inclusion of market control is unique in comparison with the other frameworks discussed in this chapter because market control is an informal control, whereas the other frameworks only discuss formal controls. In order to understand the functioning of the market as an enabler of control, a basic understanding of the theory of the firm is necessary.

The fundamental problem from an accounting point of view in designing an organization is how to communicate the knowledge (i.e. information) that its members use for planning, given that such knowledge does not exist in a concentrated form, but merely as a highly dispersed set of incomplete and often contradictory bits and pieces that stem from separate individuals knowledge bases. Planning involves the complex of interrelated decisions about the allocation of available resources. The communication of knowledge for planning purposes may be economized on by means of a market mechanism. This implies that participants only need to know the price to make the right decisions. However, to make a market mechanism work, there is a need for short-term contracting, the prices of which are the outcomes. The question then arises whether this is an efficient mechanism. In 1937, Coase proposed an alternative mechanism for the market that may be more efficient under certain circumstances. This mechanism, the firm, coordinates allocation of resources by an entrepreneur who hires people, making use of long-term contracts, to bring forth products and services. These long-term contracts are of a general nature, only specifying the boundaries of the behaviour of the people hired. By introducing the concept of transaction costs, the theory of the firm argues that the hierarchical relationships between the entrepreneur and the employee may be better coordination mechanisms than markets.

There have been several attempts to extend the economic theory of the firm by integrating it with the behavioural theory of the firm (Cyert and March 1963). As will be demonstrated later, contemporary control mechanisms like clan controls (Ouchi), boundary systems, interactive control systems, and belief systems (Simons), and cultural controls (Merchant) are much more rooted in the behavioural theory of the firm than in its economic counterpart. After these integrative attempts, various efforts were undertaken to develop a more specific theory of the firm. The resource-based view attempts to explain firm value from managerial involvement in combining resources and capabilities. In this view, the firm is a unique bundle of idiosyncratic resources. In Chapter 9, we will discuss the meaning of knowledge as the most important resource in contemporary organizations, which paves the way for a knowledge-based theory of the firm.

The neoclassical price theory looks at organizations as black boxes. This implies that questions about how the internal organization is set up or why a certain internal organization is chosen are not asked, let alone being answered. Relationships between an organization and the outside world only consist of purchase contracts for the acquisition of resources and sales contracts for revenue generation. In this view, the organization is nothing more than a production function. Prices to be paid for resources and to be charged for products and services sold are determined on the market by means of the market mechanism. In a perfect market, this mechanism ensures that prices contain all the information necessary for efficient decision making. A perfect market is frictionless. There are many sellers and buyers, products and services are homogeneous, there are no barriers to entry, all organizational goals can be reduced to the simple objective of profit maximization, there is no governmental interference, and production factors are completely mobile. In such a market, prices exactly represent the value of a product or service. As a result of this perfect information, decision makers need no other information than these prices. Consequently, in a frictionless market, there is no need for formal organizations to exist because entrepreneurs will continuously enter into *ad hoc* contracts with the owners of production factors. This is exactly what was proposed in the 1930s and 1940s by theorists like Coase (1937) and Hayek (1945). However, markets are not perfect. The frictions that cause market imperfections can be classified in four categories: transaction costs, social–psychological factors, taxes and endowments, and institutional impediments.

Transaction Costs

Transaction costs are those costs involved in preparing, concluding, and realizing contracts, and enforcing the obligations as agreed in these contracts; for example, the costs of collecting information on potential vendors, prices, and other terms of delivery, costs of consulting advisors, costs of a public notary, costs of internal control systems for checking compliance with contractual arrangements, and costs of lawsuits.

Social–psychological Factors

Social–psychological factors are non-economic by nature. People may have certain preferences or aversions that cannot be justified on economic grounds. Yet these preferences or aversions may have a severe impact on the functioning of the price mechanism. For example, there may be vendors or buyers who have connections with disgraced political regimes, criminal organizations, or ideological organizations; there may also be vendors' or buyers' representatives who are considered unsympathetic or unpleasant.

Taxes and Endowments

Taxes and endowments lead to product and service heterogeneity because they create price differences that are not in accordance with the underlying characteristics of the products and services. For example, because of the differences in tax systems, one country may gain competititive advantage at the cost of another country; or protectionist government subsidies are aimed at providing better competitive power to the recipients of endowments.

Institutional Impediments

Institutional impediments may take the form of governmental regulations or private contracts that limit the discretionary actions of parties in individual markets. For example, during World War II, in some European countries food was rationed to those who had so-called food vouchers; or, in modern business, insider trading regulations, limited permission to buy and sell shares of limited liability companies, and the European Union milk quota.

Frictions that cause market imperfections are not fictitious, so, when controlling businesses, market control is certainly not the only system managers should rely on. Bureaucratic control and clan control may be far more efficient or even the only feasible control systems to employ. There are two mechanisms that underlie the classification into market control, bureaucratic control, and clan control: social mechanisms and information mechanisms.

Social Mechanisms

The social mechanism in market control is limited to norms of reciprocity. A norm of reciprocity should assure that if one party in a market transaction tries to cheat another, the cheater is punished by all members of the community in which that market transaction is completed. The severity of the punishment will typically far exceed the crime; for example, if you steal something, your hand will be chopped off. The social mechanisms in bureaucratic control are norms of reciprocity and legitimate authority. Legitimate authority in combination with norms of reciprocity imply that people hand over autonomy to their superiors in exchange for pay without risk, and accept the idea that superiors have the right to take over that autonomy and engage in command and control activities. The social mechanisms in clan control are not only limited to norms of reciprocity and legitimate authority, but also include a shared set of values and beliefs. Clan control relies a great deal on agreement about what constitutes proper behaviour. For example, within the Scottish clans, there used to be widespread consensus about how to behave toward other clan members, and also about how to behave toward members of other clans. In modern organizations, there is a tendency to rely on clan control as the primary control system. However, since the social requirements to enable this are extremely high, bureaucracy is often the only possible system, especially when there is a high personnel turnover.

Informational Mechanisms

Informational mechanisms, like social mechanisms, vary greatly between control systems. Market control requires valid and complete information on prices in order to make the price mechanism function properly. For example, if a person wants to buy a specific type of PC at the lowest possible price, he will search the Internet for all the potential vendors of this type of computer and start negotiating with each of them in order to get the lowest price possible. However, there may be vendors that he could not find on the Internet who offer even lower prices than the ones he received. Here, price information may be incomplete, and hence the price mechanism where the other vendors adjust their prices or exit the market may not work properly. As already indicated, there are not so many, if any, true markets. However, the preceding example of an Internet search for the lowest prices is not a random choice. The Internet makes markets much more transparent and may pave the way for enhanced market functioning in the near future. Yet, we still face the situation where most markets are imperfect and price mechanisms do not work. In this case, bureacracy comes into play. The informational mechanism for bureaucracy is a set of explicit rules for members of the bureaucracy about what actions to take under specific circumstances. In AIS jargon, we refer to these rules as procedures and, when these procedures are authorized by management, we refer to them as management guidelines. However, rules may be difficult or simply impossible to specify in advance. In that case, the social mechanism of legitimate authority will enable the internal control system to incompletely specify the duties of an employee, and, instead, have management specify the duties as the need arises. In AIS jargon, such terms as supervision, command and control, delegation, accountability, and monitoring are used to refer to the set of managerial activities involved with *ad hoc* duty specification. The control system that requires the least advanced informational mechanism is clan control. Here, all the information is contained in the values and beliefs of the organization. In a clan, an outsider cannot, or can only at very high cost, gain access to information regarding the decision rules used. Because information is predominantly implicit in clans, the roles of the accountant and information manager are marginal.

If some persons have more or better information than others, then this is called information asymmetry. In agency relationships, a principal (e.g. a manager) and an agent (e.g. a subordinate) communicate in order to close transactions or, in general, to fulfil specific goals. Because agents are closer to the operations and the market, there is a great chance that they have more and superior information at their disposal than their principals. For example, a warehouse manager steals goods from the warehouse, and reports them as being obsolete. The manager who receives this report must put a control system in place in order to ensure the warehouse manager is not lying. In general, there are two threats that come from information asymmetry: adverse selection and moral hazard.

Adverse Selection

In new principal–agent relationships, agents who act in bad faith engage in that relationship under more favourable conditions than agents who act in good faith. They do so because they know that their information advantage allows them to make a profit at the cost of the principal. Adverse selection takes place at the closing of a contract; for example, persons who lodge fake claims with their insurance company will pay higher premiums than those who only lodge valid claims.

Moral Hazard

People run the risk of behaving unethically if the opportunity arises. Moral hazard may then take place on execution of a contract; for example, they know that insurance companies have great difficulty checking the validity of a claim, and they exploit this knowledge by lodging fake claims.

Threats stemming from information asymmetry are behavioural in nature. Since behavioural threats can be mitigated by means of typical management controls as well as typical internal controls, the following are applicable:

- Monitoring and reporting systems, including analytical review on agents' performances. Such a system may include comparisons with other agents, other years, and budgets.
- Performance-based rewards like the bonus/malus system applied by insurance companies.
- Limiting freedom of action of agents by means of boundary systems and making effective use of programmed procedures.
- Maintaining a contract register by someone who is independent. This register will provide the *soll* position for a check on realization of the contracts.

- Systematic selection and placement of agents by means of personality tests and screening.
- Establish clear procedures on who is authorized under what circumstances in what situation.

Action Controls, Results Controls, Personnel Controls, and Cultural Controls

The objects-of-control classification as developed by Merchant (1985, 1998) makes a distinction between action controls, results controls, and cultural/personnel controls. The goal of this classification is to demarcate a set of control instruments for each category. This classification may then serve as a sort of checklist that can be applied in the design of control systems at the operational level. Hence, this framework can easily be used for developing control systems that are aimed at effective and economical execution of specific tasks.

The framework is based on the assumption that control is a critical function of management. Control problems may lead to losses and even bankruptcy. If management is defined as the process of integration of resources and tasks aimed at accomplishment of an organization's goals, control is an integral part of management. Control systems may be ineffective. The causes of deficient control systems may be lack of direction, motivational problems, and personal limitations. In Chapter 2, we discussed a risk-based approach to internal control. The first step towards mitigating risks is to try to avoid control problems. By avoidance, organizations reduce their exposure to control problems. There are four ways to do so:

- activity elimination;
- automation;
- centralization;
- risk sharing.

Activity elimination means that management turns over the potential profits and risks of a certain activity to a third party. The reasons for doing so may be that management feels they do not have the required knowledge or skills to perform this activity efficiently, they expect legal problems, or that the organization does not have the needed resources; for example, information system operation is more and more outsourced because management believes that certain third-party specialists have superior task-specific knowledge and are able to employ it more efficiently. Automation is by deployment of computerized systems. Unlike humans, computers are absolutely consistent in their behaviour, never have dishonest or disloyal motivations, and are always accurate. Computers can enforce a certain sequence of activities and, hence, make systems foolproofs; for example, in order to input data in the second screen of a program module, the first screen must have been completed.

The term 'foolproof' can be taken literally when considering the impossibility of putting one's hand into a microwave oven and then switching it on. The 'fool' who is trying to do this will soon find out that this is impossible, because the door must first be closed to start the microwave oven. Centralization means that decisions are made at a central point within the organization. Usually, this is top management. The problem of trying to influence the behaviour of others is mitigated by simply not assigning authority to others. Whether exposure to control problems can really be reduced by centralization is debatable, since allocating all decision-making authority to top management may result in too large a scope of control. A scope of control that is too large may lead to information overload and suboptimal decision making. As a result, managers may fail to effectively manage their subordinates. The solution to this paradox lies in centralization of just key decisions. Thus, not all decision-making authority should be centralized. Of course, the main problem is to find the right balance between centralization and decentralization. We will further elaborate on this topic in our discussion of the levers of control. In a way, risk sharing is comparable with activity elimination. However, when sharing risks, activities are only partially eliminated. As is the case in activity elimination, there is usually a contract that exactly specifies the rights and obligations of the risk sharing parties; for example, buying insurance for business loss (in case of fire or other events that lead to a temporary discontinuance of the business), or entering into a joint venture.

For those control problems that cannot be avoided economically, preventive or detective controls must be designed. In addition to the controls discussed in Chapter 2, action controls, results controls, and personnel/cultural controls can be put in place to mitigate the risks organizations face.

Action controls can by effectuated by combining four types of measure. First, behavioural constraints should make it difficult for people to behave inappropriately; for example, locks on desks, user IDs and passwords, and also limiting the decision-making authority of a procurement officer to a certain currency amount, and segregation of duties. Second, pre-action reviews involve discussing and scrutinizing the plans of the individuals being controlled. The reviewer can then suggest modifications, give tips on how to execute the plans, or ask for a more detailed plan before final approval is given; for example, an audit partner scrutinizes the audit plan together with the audit team. Pre-action reviews may be formal and also very informal; for example, a hallway chat on the progress of a certain activity may provide just the feedback needed for controlling these activities. Third, action accountability is about holding people accountable for the actions they have undertaken and the decisions they have made. Action accountability controls are most effective if the desired actions are well communicated, the employees understand what is expected of them, and they feel confident that their actions will lead to rewards if well executed or punishment if badly executed. For example, an organization has detailed formalized procedures for almost everything that must be done. Newly hired employees get acquainted with these procedures through training programs, and the store manager gets rewarded or punished if his people do or do not comply with these directives. Fourth, redundancy involves assigning more than one person to a certain task, performing certain activities more than once, or, in general, assigning multiple resources to a certain task. For example, a person makes a calculation and recalculates for checking purposes. In AIS, this would be called a self-check. A certain activity may also be performed twice by two different persons. For example, in the pre-automation era, insurance companies used to have so-called parallel administrations. At the end of a process, the outputs of these parallel administrations were compared with each other and reconciled by an internal control function. Nowadays, insurance companies still make use of redundancy controls, having a primary information system and a back-up information system called a data-processing hot site. The back-up system can be switched to immediately if the primary system has gone down. In general, this form of redundancy is frequently applied in organizations with massive data-processing activities such as banks, insurance companies, pension funds, and also major telephone providers, Internet providers, and Internet stores which rely heavily on electronic data processing.

Results controls can be effectuated by defining performance dimensions, setting targets for these dimensions, measuring performance, and providing rewards or punishments. Results controls are indirect controls, meaning that they are not applicable to activities or processes, but rather to outcomes of activities and processes. For results controls to be effective, the controlled people must know what is expected of them, and must be able to influence the results by behaving appropriately. In addition, the results must be measurably accurate, objective, and timely, and must be understandable. The higher the hierarchical level, the more applicable are results controls as compared with action controls. For example, the foreman (operational management) of a cleaning company may try to control his workers by supervising them on the job, watching them execute their assigned tasks, and giving additional instructions if task execution is not in accordance with an implicit or explicit plan (action accountability). The top manager of that very same cleaning company will not want to scrutinize the activities of his people but will mainly be interested in the results of the cleaning activities, asking himself the question: Will the client be satisfied with the service quality in relation to the price offered? This result of the cleaning activities may be measured by means of client satisfaction surveys (exception report), or sample-based checking which determines whether the cleaned spaces are as clean as agreed. In both instances, the top manager will only be interested in exception reports. On an even more aggregate level, the top manager may want to know if the company is gaining or losing market share or how shareholder value is developing.

Personnel controls can be effectuated by selection and placement, training, and job design and provision of necessary resources. First, selection and placement means that the right people must be selected for a certain job position; for example, if an accounting clerk is needed, then the selection process may encompass verifying that he has mastered the technique of double-entry bookkeeping. In the selection process, three categories of judgement criteria can be distinguished: education, experience, and personality. Personality is especially difficult to measure. Yet, organizations devote a lot of their time trying to find out if a person has such a personality structure such that she will probably fit in with the organization and the job assignment. Experience is a somewhat ambiguous concept. It may be task-specific or general, it may or may not have led to expertise, and its interaction with personality and education is not very well understood despite massive research efforts in both accounting and cognitive psychology. Second, training ideally should lead to employees thinking and acting the same way as management would under similar circumstances. This would save scarce managerial resources for strategy formulation, instead of serving as an organization's watchdog. Many organizations use formal as well as informal training in order to improve their personnel's performance. Formal training takes place in the classroom and may be insourced or outsourced. Informal training is training on the job whereby peers, supervisors, as well as subordinates provide feedback to newly hired people to make them learn as efficiently as possible. Third, careful job design is a necessary condition to help individual employees act appropriately so that they will have a high probability of success in their job performance. Part of job design is the provision of the necessary material resources to the employee assigned to do the job; for example, if management expects a salesman to visit customers on a regular basis, he should have a car at his disposal.

Personnel controls will help organization members feel some kind of commitment to the organization, and, as a result, need no external motivators to strive for organizational goal attainment. In order to assess the right approach to control tightness, the form of commitment that accompanies each of the three control systems within the conceptual framework for the design of organizational control systems, as developed by Ouchi, must be determined. If people are hired without any form of selection, then the applicable control system is market control. Here, the assumption is that the more an organization pays for a newly hired worker (i.e. her salary or fee) the more she will strive to internalize the organization's objectives. Because of existing norms of reciprocity, there will be some kind of self-selection among potential workers. As a result, they will not need to be monitored in order to have them work toward optimizing the organization's performance. However, if this self-selection mechanism does not work and adverse selection or moral hazard occur, then training and monitoring – often even to a high degree – will be the only effective people treatments. So, if there is a selection process, even a limited one, then newly hired people must be trained and subsequently monitored, depending on the degree to which selection has taken place. Monitoring involves instructing workers, and holding them accountable for their actions taken, to follow up on these instructions. Training, on the other hand, involves making workers aware of organizational values and educate them in order to acquire the necessary skills to perform their job appropriately. The applicable control systems are bureaucratic control and clan control if the training involves identification with organizational values and beliefs. If people are thoroughly selected at the gate, then the applicable control system is clan control. By putting a lot of effort into selecting the right people for the right position, referred to as person–task alignment, there is a great chance that people will be committed and, hence, need less monitoring. Applying tight controls may, in that case, lead to employees becoming alienated from the organization and, hence, requiring even tighter controls. Exploiting shared values and beliefs and communicating implicit customs will be the most effective control instruments, in that case as well. So, internalization and identification with organizational values and beliefs are the required forms of commitment when there is thorough selection at the gate.

Cultural controls can be effectuated by creating a coherent culture within an organization. This can be accomplished by exploiting shared traditions, norms, beliefs, values, ideologies, attitudes, and behaviours. There are five complementary instruments that enable a coherent organizational culture. First, codes of conduct may appear in various formats. In a broad sense, codes of conduct take the form of codes of ethics, corporate principles, credos, mission statements, vision statements, or communications of management's philosophy. These statements have in common that they are codified and intended to shape organizational culture; for example, a code of conduct of a commercial bank contains a section on insider trading stating that it is forbidden to own shares or any other interest in one of the bank's clients. However, codes of conduct need not be formulated that negatively; for example, the mission statement of DuPont is briefly formulated as: 'The DuPont Company will conduct its business affairs with the highest ethical standards and work diligently to be a respected corporate citizen worldwide'. Second, group-based rewards should contribute to employees cooperating to attain shared goals. Group-based rewards, as opposed to individual performance-based rewards, imply that a group of employees will receive exactly the same reward if a certain task is successfully completed. Any individual trying to gain personal advantage at the expense of his team members will be rebuked by means of some kind of social mechanism. Hence, it can be reasonably expected that group-based rewards promote goal congruence and consensus on how to accomplish these goals. Third, intraorganizational transfers tend to improve socialization processes of individuals throughout the organization. This is done by regularly transferring employees from one department, job assignment, business unit, or geographical location to another. By following this policy, employees develop a helicopter view of the organization, as a result of which they will think more holistically and act more in accordance with organizational goals instead of subunit goals. For example, a major commercial bank in the Netherlands hires management trainees with a masters degree, has them participate in a long-term training programme, and transfers them every three years to another part of the organization and (most of the time) another type of function. By doing so, these management trainees develop an overview of the whole organization and learn to break down the reviled box mentality. Fourth, physical and social arrangements help shape a desirable corporate culture in that they contain hidden messages about how people communicate and dress, how offices are furnished, how the organization's buildings are set up, what cars are driven, how technology is employed, and, most importantly, what gives the organization its *droit à l'existence*. For example, a public accounting firm wants to communicate the message that they are able to take good care of their clients because they are also able to take good care of themselves. For that reason, they have an extremely luxurious office building, with art all around, and have their people drive classy cars. Fifth, tone at the top is often considered one of the most abused and misunderstood concepts in management control. It is about management setting the right example for their subordinates. By setting the proper tone at the top, management provides the most important contribution to shaping the organizational culture. Tone at the top can be defined as consistency between managers' behaviour and their statements. The more consistency between managers' behaviour and their statements, the stronger the organizational culture.

An organization can gain from a strong culture by employing it for control purposes. Hence, a relationship exists between the five cultural control instruments and the degree of control (e.g. the stronger the tone at the top, the higher the degree of control).

Diagnostic Control Systems, Interactive Control Systems, Boundary Systems, and Beliefs Systems

To develop a knowledge-based theory of the firm, it is important to note that we do not want to explain the existence of organizations as mechanisms that deal with the shortcomings of markets. Although this view is common in the theory of the firm, we want, instead, to distinguish factors that explain why a certain organization is more successful than another. Yet, there are some fundamental concerns about the general theory of the firm that are highly relevant for a knowledge-based theory of the firm. The general theory of the firm – which is also called the contractual theory – provides a basis for the development of a knowledge-based theory of the firm. Issues to be dealt with are the nature of coordination within the firm, the organizational structure, the role of management, the allocation of decision-making authority, the determinants of firm boundaries, and the way in which competitive advantage is sought by means of innovation. It is within this arena that the relationship between control and innovation must be further investigated.

The relationship between control and innovation is tense. If a manager wants his people to be creative, and hence engage in innovative actions, he must be prepared to give up control, empower his people, and cease monitoring their activities. Only then can creativity flourish. On the other hand, that manager wants positive events to occur and negative events to be avoided (i.e. he wants his organization to be in control). In order to deal with this managerial problem of balancing innovation and control, Harvard professor Robert Simons developed a classification – the levers of control – that distinguishes between interactive control systems, boundary systems, diagnostic control systems, and beliefs systems. The explicit goal of this classification is to balance innovation and control. Before entering into detailed discussion of this framework, we should note that it is only applicable to development of a raw sketch of a control system, because the concrete design parameters that may result are highly anecdotal and global. Also, there is still no empirical evidence supporting the efficiency of this framework. Moreover, the framework does not put forward any theory. It is about how to design and employ controls in a practical contemporary setting.

A special part is played by ICT. ICT deployment can contribute to codification and diffusion of information, as a result of which the functioning of the levers of control may be improved and, hence, control problems may be mitigated when innovation is at stake. Codification refers to formalization of information into fixed structures and patterns. For example, data about a sales transaction can easily be captured in a ledger. Since a ledger is based on fixed structures, the information on this transaction can be codified. On the other hand, gossip about a manager being fired is difficult to codify within a pre-formatted structure. Diffusion refers to proliferation of information throughout an organization or an organization's environment and, hence, to the degree to which information sharing is possible; for example, the income statement can easily be transmitted via the intranet of an organization and, hence, has high diffusion potential. On the other hand, classified information on new market opportunities, to be discussed by the board of directors, has low diffusion potential because it is aimed at only a small subset of the organization.

Beliefs systems define the core values of an organization. These beliefs deal with how the organization creates value, the desired performance levels, and human relations. These systems give guidance to opportunity-seeking behaviour. (e.g. mission statements, vision statements, and credos). In beliefs systems, uncodified information plays an important role. This information must be distributed via personal channels. ICT applications like groupware or e-mail enable such a personal communication. Beliefs systems are initiated by an organization's top management, so it is top management who should make effective use of ICT applications to personally communicate their and, hence, the organization's beliefs.

Boundary systems define the risks that must be avoided. They contain formal rules that must be complied with in order to avoid sanctions. A typical feature of boundary systems is that they are always defined in a negative manner (i.e. they state what is forbidden, not what should be done). Boundary systems are aimed at enhancing individual creativity without invoking undesirable behaviour (e.g. codes of conduct if negatively formulated). The information as communicated via boundary systems is unambiguous and usually rule-based. This information need not be personal, but it is of great importance that organization members are well aware of the fact that top management supports these rules and that they must be complied with. ICT enables the continuous monitoring of people's behaviour by automating compliance testing with applicable behavioural boundaries. However, this requires further codification and diffusion.

In diagnostic control systems, the communication and measurement of critical performance variables plays an important part. Diagnostic control systems are aimed at realizing the effective allocation of scarce resources, defining targets, motivating people, determining guidelines for corrective measures, and enabling performance evaluation. The ultimate goal of diagnostic control systems is that scarce managerial attention is reallocated from management to staff who prepare budgets and business performance reports. Information that is provided by means of diagnostic control systems in highly codified (e.g. automation of early warning messages, information about multidimensional performance measures, and the continuous scanning of critical performance indicators for progress checking. The degree of diffusion could also increase as a result of ICT deployment. However, here there might be some organizational conditions, such as internal control requirements or avoiding information overload, that stop certain information from being diffused on a large scale. ICT offers ample possibilities to enhance diagnostic control systems, but, on designing these systems, it should be kept in mind that they are intended to focus managerial attention on strategy formulation and exception handling rather than on continuously monitoring subordinates' actions.

Interactive control systems are aimed at strategic uncertainties, at what keeps managers awake during the night. They are defined as the formal control systems that managers use to involve themselves regularly and personally in the decision-making activities of subordinates (e.g. customer complaints are on the weekly agenda of the board of directors, a manager's visit to the shop-floor, a plant abroad is visited by management on a regular basis, or bulletin boards are read by executives). In these systems, the content of information is more important than its form. The degree of codification is moderate in the sense that these systems provide the structures for data compression and data categorization and, hence, serve as catalysts for dialogue and debate about the meaning of information and applicable action plans. For that reason, interactive control systems must be simple to use, so that people throughout the whole organization can understand them. The degree of diffusion of information in such a system is higher than in a diagnostic control system because interactive control systems should stimulate dialogue and information sharing. As such, they are important data sources for all managers within the organization. ICT deployment can improve the effectiveness of interactive control systems in at least three ways:

- computers can transform complex data into graphical representations and tables that are easy to understand;
- by means of electronic communication, relevant global market information can be acquired, planning systems that are at lower hierarchical levels within the organization can be provided with the necessary input, and information on the buying behaviour of customers and the effectiveness of promotion actions can be obtained;
- modern database technologies enable managers to easily make what-if analyses.

Internal control, and more specifically internal accounting control or information

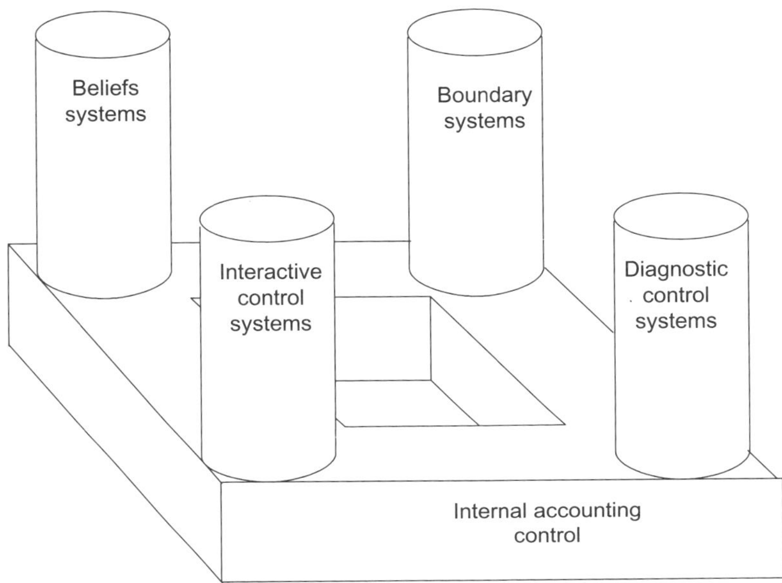

Figure 8.5 The relationship between the levers of control and internal accounting control.

control, constitutes the basis for the levers of control. The underlying reasoning is that the information used for making the levers seek a balance between control and innovation must meet certain minimum quality requirements. The aspect of information reliability is especially crucial to the proper functioning of the levers of control. Imagine the relationship between internal control and the levers of control as depicted in Figure 8.5. The four levers are bottomless cylinders that can be filled with liquid flowing into an underlying tank, the internal accounting control system. Irrespective of the cylinder chosen to fill the tank, the other cylinders will only be affected by manipulating another when the tank is filled to the rim. In other words, only when the internal accounting control system meets certain minimum requirements can the levers start communicating. Now, given that the tank is filled to the rim, every drop of liquid that is poured into one of the cylinders will start a balance-seeking process that comes to a standstill when the levels of liquid in each of the four cylinders are even.

Although conceptually appealing, visualization of the relationship between the levers of control and internal controls as a system of four cylinders and a tank does not explain how the levers work in practice. To begin with, the levers of control bridge the gap between strategy formulation and strategy implementation. Strategy has several connotations, but we believe that its meaning can be straightforward in a control settting. We don't intend to define strategy or elaborate on it, but we will mention one of its main characterisics – strategy – which is always aimed at gaining competitive advantage. In a dynamic and increasingly competitive environment, strategy must include the concept of innovation. Innovation must nowadays be pursued on a continuous basis in order to restrain the competitive forces organizations are exposed to. From a strategy implementation point of view, the question then arises whether control systems can be put in place that spawn innovation. The levers of control provide the answer to this question because this framework is aimed at controlling an organization s people and simultaneously stimulating innovation. The beliefs systems and boundary systems both provide conditions for organizational goal achievement. The beliefs systems provide positive signals for people to be creative, whereas the boundary systems serve as the brakes of the organization should people start to engage in so-called hyper-goal-oriented behaviour, disregarding applicable laws, guidelines, codes of conduct, and other implicit or explicit rules. In order to actually achieve its goals, an organization must put interactive and diagnostic control systems in place. Interactive control systems are needed for the non-cybernetic information gathering about potentially harmful or beneficial events, whereas diagnostic control systems are used for progress control on performance regarding predefined targets such as budgets, sales targets, or productivity. From another viewpoint, beliefs systems and interactive control systems are aimed at stimulating opportunity-seeking behaviour, and boundary systems and diagnostic control systems are aimed at constraining people's behaviour in order to keep the organization in control. In addition, interactive control systems can be employed on top of any of the other levers, in order to make them interactive. So, the levers of control constitute a heavily intertwined framework for reconciling the seemingly irreconcilable concepts of control and innovation.

Synthesis

This final section investigates the relationship between the management control frameworks as discussed in this chapter and the notion of internal control as put forward by the COSO report. Under the influence of the COSO report, internal control has become much broader than it used to be. Besides the COSO report, there are many other international reports on this topic and related topics such as corporate governance. As a result, management control and internal control have converged, and they will keep on converging until only one single notion of control is left. We propose to label this single notion 'organizational control' or simply 'control'.

Classroom Reservation System

A classroom reservation system at a university is badly organized. Course coordinators state their room needs at the beginning of the year by means of a form which is sent to the reservation office. Rooms are assigned on the basis of these forms. If room reservations must be cancelled because a course attracts less students than expected (which happens frequently), this is often not communicated to the reservation office. A sample test by the reservations office revealed that this causes an occupation loss of 30% (i.e. 30% of the rooms that should be occupied according to the reservation office files are not occupied). Since there is a shortage of rooms, this is a waste of valuable resources and, thus, a severe problem. To improve the course coordinators' behaviour, an incentive scheme is developed. If a room remains unoccupied although the course coordinator has reserved it, but did not cancel, a fine of €250 has to be paid. The reservation office checks occupation on a sample basis.

Exam Administration

After ongoing problems with respect to unreliable information about which students passed exams and which students failed, the exam administration of a university decides to reorganize and sharpen its procedures. The reorganization appears to be effective. One of the new procedures concerns the process of handing in exam papers, grading exams, and handing in the final grades by course coordinators. Exam administration uses special forms and formalized schedules with critical dates for communications with course coordinators and strictly follows up on procedures by performing progress checks on a continuous basis and prompting course coordinators to comply if negligent. Everybody within the university is now fully aware of the fact that exam procedures are critical to the core business of a university, and that they must be complied with at any cost. As a result, the process of handing in exam papers, grading, and handing in the final grades now goes smoothly without major exceptions.

In order to shed some light on the ongoing debate about management control and internal control, we propose the following two dimensions for analysis:

- the distinction between the business domain and the information and communication domain, again referring to the comprehensive contingency framework as introduced in Chapter 5;
- the decomposition of internal control into internal control for the control of operations and internal control for the control of information provision.

Let's consider the classroom reservation system and the exam administration cases (see Boxes) in view of the following four basic assumptions about the relationship between management control and internal control:

1 Improved management control over the people involved in information provision leads to improved information control and, hence, improved internal control over information provision (including ICT infrastructure); for example, the information sent by the course coordinators to the reservation office is more complete because there is an incentive system in place, which clearly is part of the management control system, motivating them to provide complete information (Figure 8.6(a)).

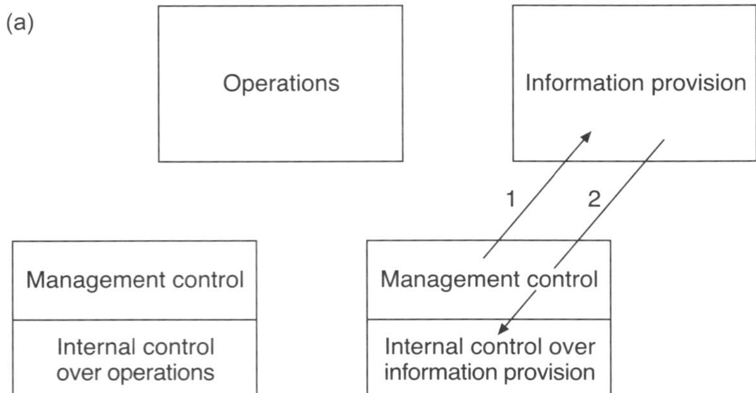

Figure 8.6(a) Improved management control over the people involved in information provision leads to improved internal control over information provision.

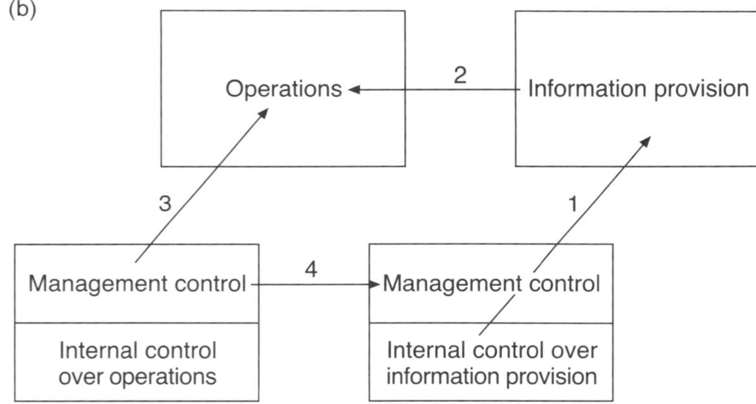

Figure 8.6(b) Improved internal control over information provision leads to improved management control over the people involved in operations and information provision.

2 Since the availability of reliable and relevant information is a necessary precondition for any control system, any measure that increases the quality of information will lead to improved management control; for example, the improved internal controls over information provision in the exam administration case lead to better information provision and, hence, better functioning of the people involved in exam administration, which supports employing management controls over these people (Figure 8.6(b)).

3 Improved management control over the people involved in operations leads to

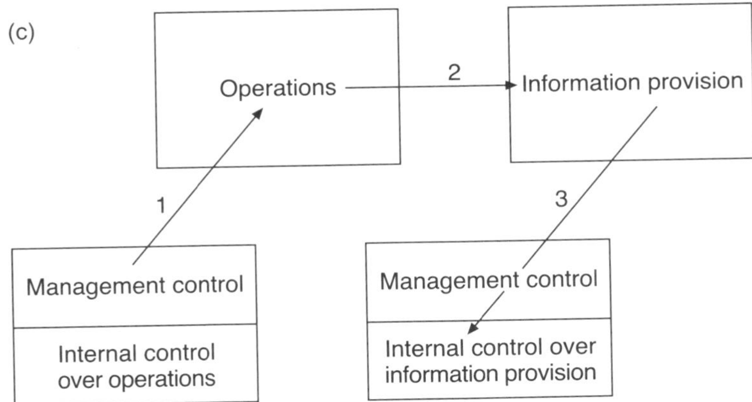

Figure 8.6(c) Improved management control over the people involved in operations leads to improved internal control over information provision.

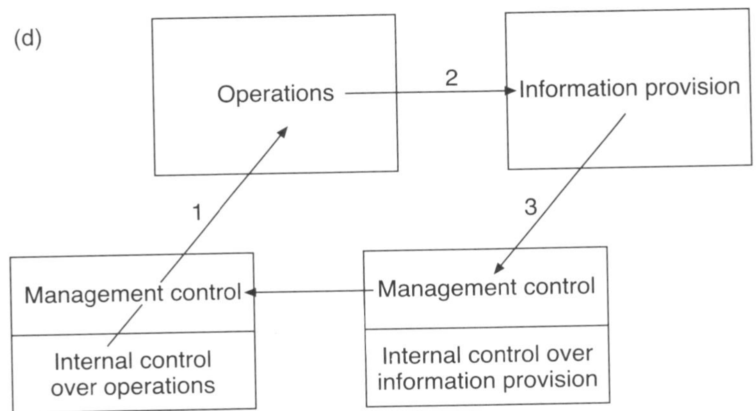

Figure 8.6(d) Improved internal control over operations leads to improved management control over the people involved in operations and information provision.

improved information provision and, hence, improved internal control over information provision; for example, the incentives given to course coordinators in the classroom reservation system lead to well-functioning operations and a control environment that is supportive of sound information provision, resulting in better internal controls over information provision (Figure 8.6(c)).

4 Improved internal control over operations enables improved information provision for or about operations because the right control environment is in place. As a result, management control over people involved in information provision and

operations improves; for example, the internal controls of exam administration lead to well-functioning operations and more reliable and timely information being sent from course coordinators to exam administration, the course coordinators are more in control, and, as a result, the people involved in teaching the courses as well as other faculty members are also more in control, both of which indicate management controls have improved (Figure 8.6(d)).

In summary, as appears from the classroom reservation system and exam administration case examples, the quality of a management control system influences the quality of an internal control system and vice versa. This reciprocal relationship begs the question whether the two notions of control should still be distinguished. We believe continuing to make a distinction is not only useless, but it is also dysfunctional because it urges users of these systems to look at organizations as the sum of completely isolated components, whereas they actually should be looked at from a holistic point of view, taking into account all emerging reciprocal relationships, interactions, and alignments.

Chaper Cases

Case 8.1 A2P

Amsterdam Planning and Production (A2P) was founded in the 1940s by five friends who were dissatisfied with their jobs at the time. After the Second World War, the time had come for a new entrepreneurial spirit that allowed a wide variety of innovative ideas to flourish. Each of the five founders had, objectively speaking, a good job and were well educated: a medical doctor, a mining engineer, a lawyer, a physicist (who had been in R&D for years), and a manager of a department store. Of course, they put a lot of thought into their wild entrepreneurial plans. To make a quick win, they got involved in manufacturing activities in the emerging computer industry. The initial product design had already been made, and a prototype would be ready within a short period of time. However, the device – an electronic calendar – appeared more difficult to develop than expected. Moreover, it did not catch on well because of its size. Potential customers found their portable paper pocket calendar much more convenient, although they liked the concept. However, the five were undaunted, especially because they had already made substantial investments in machinery and people. Thus, A2P had to clear its way to survival. Innovation was the keyword. According to the five, by continuously generating new ideas, the company could gain competitive advantage. At an early stage, the idea was adopted that actual production acitivities would have to be deployed. Apparently, the prospects for advisory services on planning and product development were much more favourable. All kinds of concept were discussed and some of them were introduced. With respect to marketing, the company cut a good figure, although the five were well aware of the fact that they needed a superior product (in this case: service) for the marketing efforts to be successful in the long run. Indeed, such a product was launched: a new technique for the manufacture of pens at low costs. This appeared to be a reasonably successful initiative, but the big breakthrough came when one of the inventors of the company began specializing in the development of presentation tools. A desktop erasable board, with a matching pen and wiper became a resounding success. However, the subsequent product idea – a thick marker that applied a transparent line of ink, to be used for accentuating texts in books and journals – woefully failed. Further research revealed that the market was not yet ready for it since destroying a book by writing in it was considered close to blasphemy at that time. With this knowledge, A2P went searching for new technologies for more efficient printing methods. Thus, some concepts were launched for products that nowadays are still in use (among others, the paperback, an automated typesetting machine, and the photocopier).

As a result of the development of a number of successful concepts, and an ever bigger number of failures, there has grown an atmosphere within A2P of experimentation and innovation: mistakes are allowed to be made, as long as there is the preparedness to learn from them. Within the company, there are still stories going around about all kinds of bold actions of the – by now deceased or aged – founders. In these stories, both successes and failures are much raunted.

A remarkable phenomenon within A2P is that all kinds of stories about early employees are brought up when another crisis threatens. One of these stories is that of Pete. Pete was chairman of a special task force established to develop ways to trump competitors. In practice, this task force was a think thank that continuously generated ideas for new products and services. Pete was an extremely capable employee who was bought from a competitor. It should be stressed that the buying of employees from competitors is an explicit policy of A2P, sometimes they even create completely new functions just to land a certain person. However, Pete started to attract the attention of his superiors because he seemed to be making more and more negative publicity about the company towards customers and vendors, including remarks on a certain technique that he thought was not viable. As a reaction to some signals from customers and vendors, his superiors engaged in monitoring Pete's behaviour for a while. All his outgoing mail was screened and his telephone calls were eavesdropped. The results were such that his superiors had to make it clear to Pete that this was unacceptable behaviour and that he could not count on any more pay rises. Pete understood this and resigned after a while, the task force being dismantled.

The company has been growing rapidly and is currently a multinational with more than 50,000 employees all over the world. There still is a policy that stimulates innovation. This is accentuated by, among other things, the fact that the current CEO – a grandson of one of the founders – is always prepared to listen to new ideas from his employees at all levels in the organization, no matter how remote this is to the core business of A2P. The employee in question is assigned half an hour to present his idea to the CEO, who may decide to allocate resources to this initiative. After three months, a formal evaluation is done and the go/no-go decision is made.

New employees, starting from a specific function category, are transferred to other positions within the company. This may include their being moved to other business units, other countries, other departments, but also to different task assignments. A2P's management believes in performance-based rewards and bases its personnel policy on this belief. However, management realizes that the implementation of such a policy may vary between countries, and even between business units. Management accepts these variations within certain boundaries, but, at the same time, stresses that a coherent organizational culture is so important that everything must be done to mitigate any differences.

Accounting systems have been specifically designed to support the innovative culture of the organization. This is apparent from the implementation of a new business performance measurement system for the assessment of percentage sales from new products. New products are defined as those that were developed the last five years. This product category must represent at least 25% of the sales of each business unit. In addition, R&D employees, marketeers, and managers are expected to regularly visit customers and potential customers to get a grasp of market and product opportunities. To have the whole enterprise gain from market and product innovations, every employee is expected to share his knowledge about the market and new technologies with his colleagues. Recently, a chief knowledge officer (CKO) has been appointed whose most important assignment is to streamline the knowledge management processes within the company. This appointment is not a coincidence. The number of successes have been meagre over the last few years, and management is anxious that competitors might take over the leading market position of A2P if new product and market ideas keep on failing to be launched. Management is even considering leaving A2P's core business to follow unpaved paths, under the assumption that strategic repositioning must be possible at any time when the prospects of gaining competitive advantage are favourable.

To turn the tide, the CKO has installed a new multidisciplinary task force with a remit to reformulate A2P's strategy. This task force contains representatives of management, the board of directors, R&D, and corporate control. This task force has extensive powers and has substantial resources at its disposal. These include its members having a so-called goldcard that allows them access to all company sites and information recorded in the information systems. In addition, all personnel are bound to follow instructions given by the members of the task force.

Assignments

1 What aspects of personnel and cultural controls can you recognize within A2P? Explain your answer.

2 Provide advice to A2P's management about the strategy to be formulated and indicate how this strategy could be implemented. Explain your answer.

Case 8.2 Baboni SRL

Introduction

An Italy-based firm with a long history, Baboni SRL has built up a good reputation over the years. Customers, suppliers, as well as its personnel believe the company is a reliable partner that always meets its obligations. The management of Baboni consists of three directors. The technical director has a degree in mechanical engineering, the financial director is a chartered accountant who used to be the financial auditor of the company, and a commercial director (an economist with a financial background). The management strongly believes in external consultants whom they see as a sounding board for periodically evaluating the company's functioning.

Purchasing

The purchasing department of the company buys about 100,000 different articles from about 3,000 different vendors. The department consists of 25 persons (including the head and her two assistants). When an order must be placed, the purchasing clerk makes a description of the article to be ordered and invites offers from four vendors. After he has received the offers, he makes a list with the prices each vendor has offered, the terms of delivery, and assessment of the reliability of each vendor on the basis of past experiences. On the basis of this list, the purchasing clerk makes the vendor choice. The head of the purchasing department requires orders above €10,000 to be approved by her. In addition, she periodically scrutinizes the lists and checks whether she would have made the same decisions as the purchasing clerks. To assess whether the clerks need help with their task assignments, the head of the purchasing department has frequent contact with them. She never forgets to remind her people not to accept gifts from any vendor under any circumstances.

Warehouse

The warehouse receives the ordered goods, keeps them until they are ordered by a customer, and takes care of delivery. This department consists of about 1,000 people, including about 150 managers and foremen. On receipt of goods, a warehouse clerk counts the goods, assesses that these goods have been ordered, and that the quality is in agreement with preset standards. When articles must be delivered to customers, the pickers take care to efficiently pick the goods from the warehouse. They prepare the goods for the packers who, in their turn, prepare each shipment for customers. The foremen see to it that this process runs efficiently. Therefore, they continuously collect information on the progress of preparing goods for shipment. Typically, a foreman will supervise his people to form for himself a picture of their functioning, but he will also scrutinize each worker's output as required by the management information system. Once in a while, he will also ask his people why they do a certain task the way they do. Sometimes, he will give them direct orders to temporarily fulfil other upcoming tasks. Once in a while, he will also carpet a worker for failing to comply with his instructions. All these control activities are guided by a set of formal and informal rules that give direction to the foreman's and his people's behaviour. The formal rules are based on management guidelines and in the hierarchical position of the foreman with respect to his people. The informal rules are based on respect for the foreman and the trust the workers have in him.

Assignment

1. Discuss the quality of the internal controls with Baboni as far as they concern purchasing and warehousing functions. Follow the classification into components of internal control as proposed by the COSO report.
2. What quality aspects of information can be identified within Baboni? Illustrate your answer with examples from the case.
3. When a distinction is made between market control, bureacratic control, and clan control, how can the control activities within Baboni be classified? Give clear examples from the case.

9 The Integrative Role of the Accounting Information System in Managing Contemporary Organizations

Information technology has had as much impact on our society as the industrial revolution. In the information age, fewer workers are making products, and a large segment of the employee population is involved in producing, analyzing, and distributing information. Information systems play a vital role in our economy and our everyday lives. An accounting information system is a special type of information system that provides information about business processes and events affecting an organization.

Moscove *et al.* (2001), p. 5

After studying this chapter, the reader should be able to:

- Understand the concept of the flexible firm as an instantiation of a contemporary organization.
- Describe the relationship between the contemporary economy, the flexible firm, and the AIS.
- Understand the role of AISs in implementing strategies.
- Understand the role of AISs in preventing, deterring, and detecting fraud in the business domain, the information and communication domain, and the ICT domain.
- Understand the role of AISs in performance evaluation.
- Understand the relationship between the AIS and some contemporary developments in the management, ICT, accounting, and internal control literature including:
  - horizontal information systems;
  - critical success factors;

- ISO standardization and certification;
- environmental accounting;
- balanced scorecard;
- just-in-time production;
- knowledge valuation;
- knowledge management.

- Identify the internal and external organizational roles that may provide assurance as a part of the internal control system.

Chapter Outline

Despite the criticism that has been launched at the tradition of over-relying on accounting performance measures, we believe the AIS – which enables such performance evaluation – is developing into a vehicle that supports managerial information provision for accountability and decision making at all levels in an organization. This chapter makes the changeover from the traditional transaction-focused discipline to the modern discipline that leaves room for information as a strategic instrument. It elaborates on the concept of horizontal information systems and contemporary control instruments. From the AIS perspective, the issues dealt with are, among others, critical success factors, performance measures, ISO certification, and knowledge management. The reader should understand that AIS is more than a discipline that just focuses on operational issues regarding reliability of information. Strategy, ICT, and relevance of information are also fully integrated into AIS. However, the point of view chosen to study these elements differs from that of adjacent disciplines, allowing AIS to maintain its own identity.

Introduction

By now, the reader must be aware that AIS is more than a discipline that just focuses on operational issues regarding reliability of information. Strategy, ICT, and the relevance of information are objects of study as well. However, pursuing a broad and, therefore, eclectic approach to a discipline always carries with it the danger that adjacent disciplines' territories are trespassed and the discipline loses its own identity. But, it should also be clear that AIS looks at organizational phenomena from an idiosyncratic perspective, namely:

- It studies strategy implementation, not strategy formulation. However, strategy formulation is an important contingent factor and must therefore be discussed briefly.

- It studies ICT from a user's point of view, not from a system developer's. Like strategy formulation, ICT is an important contingent factor.
- It studies information relevance assurance by formalizing information systems development routines, formalizing information provision, and controlling the use of information, by making nothing more than superficial analyses of the content of data records, information requirements, and management reports.
- It considers managerial involvement at all hierarchical levels in operational activities as its guiding theme.

Within this eclectic approach to the discipline of AIS, the AIS is also considered in a broad sense as playing an integrative part in the fulfilment of organizational goals in contemporary organizations.

Until now, we have left aside what we mean by a contemporary organization. However, we have discussed such phenomena as the new economy, the third wave, the information age, and the post-capitalist knowledge society. When we summarize these phenomena under the heading of the contemporary economy, we can be very brief about the relationship between the contemporary organization and the contemporary economy; namely, the contemporary organization is the organizational form that perfectly matches the contemporary economy. Going deeper into the specific characteristics of such a contemporary organization reveals some remarkable differences between this type of organization and the traditional organization (Table 9.1).

There seems to be growing consensus between managers and information specialists that new organizational forms abandon the traditional design prescriptions that praise top–down command and control, as well as fixed structures, rationality, and hierarchy as the guarantees of corporate success. In the past century, organizational thinking has been dominated by normative theories about task design, organizational design, profit maximization, and hierarchy-based authority (e.g. Taylor 1911; Fayol 1949; Weber 1946). In this view, organizations are considered mechanisms with a single goal, dedicated to transforming well-defined inputs into well-defined outputs, not being able to attain other goals or to perform other tasks other than after having consciously made adjustments to the organization. These normatieve theories are nowadays not completely obsolete since there are still extremely successful traditional organizations that apply such classical concepts as detailed work procedures and standardized products (e.g. McDonalds). In this type of organization, knowledge resides in the organization and not in the individuals working in the organization. Typical controls are rules and directives, performance evaluation, compliance-based rewards, and selection and placement. Employees are valued because of their ability to contribute to the effcient functioning of a fixed, predefined structure. This type of organization encourages people to obey orders, and to know their part in the whole instead of being interested in the intrinsic characteristics of their duties and continuously bringing this up for discussion. This type of

Table 9.1 Characteristics of traditional and contemporary organizations

Characteristic	*Traditional organization*	*Contemporary organization*
Production routine	Mass production	Flexible production
Technology imperative	Technological determinism	Technological discretion
Information systems	Legacy information systems	Multi-purpose information systems
Task demarcation	Well-defined tasks	Ambiguous tasks
Task complexity	Simple tasks	Complex tasks
Core labour force	Core of production workers	Core of highly qualified knowledge workers and a periphery of part-time workers and temporary workers
Tightness of labour relations	Lifetime employment	Employability
Degree of specialization	Differentiation	Outsourcing
Decision making	Centralized	Decentralized, workers being empowered
Controls	Tight	Loose

organization may suffice for stable tasks under stable circumstances as well as for changing tasks under predictable circumstances. However, when the circumstances become subject to change or get less predictable, employees should be able to question the rightness of their task assignments and adjust their actions in accordance with new situations. In contemporary organizations, knowledge residing in the heads of the people within the organization is a key production factor. These firms are knowledge-intensive and their core employees are knowledge workers. The new organization gives its knowledge workers discretion over their own actions and, hence, empowers them. It is self-organizing, reflective, and has an inherent ability to meaningfully revitalize itself and adjust to changing circumstances. Volberda (1996 and 1998) refers to his type of organization as the flexible firm. We will adhere to this term and use it to refer to contemporary organizations in the contemporary economy.

Flexible firms demand specific types of information systems. Obviously, these must be at least as flexible as the firm itself. Specifically, they must have a broad scope, implying that they must be able to cover all organizational activity and serve a wide variety of purposes. Enterprise-wide systems like ERP systems may meet these requirements. Considering the central role ascribed by managers (including information managers), accountants, and controllers to AISs, the continuously enhancing functionality of these systems, their ability to bridge the gap between accounting and information systems professionals, and the recent developments within the discipline of AIS with respect to more flexible ways to model organizations for the purpose of database design (e.g. REA accounting), we believe AISs are the information systems of the future. In this view, the AIS will be an integrative force in supporting the information needs of the flexible firm in the contemporary economy. However, to allow AISs to play that part, we must continuously search for ways to enhance their flexibility, simultaneously maintaining their function as watchdogs of information reliability.

Following the four main themes of this text (management, internal control, accounting, and ICT), we can conceptually decouple the AIS from internal control and model it as the pivot on which the flexible firm hinges. The following interrelationships can then be elaborated upon:

- management and internal control;
- accounting and ICT;
- management and ICT;
- ICT and internal control;
- internal control and accounting;
- accounting and management.

Figure 9.1 depicts these interrrelationships and the role of the AIS.

The Accounting Information System as a Pivot in the Flexible Firm

As can be observed in Figure 9.1, some concepts that pertain to each of the identified interrelationships have already been discussed in the previous chapters. Hence, we will not elaborate on these any more but limit our discussion to identifying the role of the AIS in supporting or enabling these concepts. In addition, some new concepts will be introduced that must be considered when looking at AISs from a managerial approach, especially in relation to the flexible firm.

Management and Internal Control

The interrelationship between managerial involvement and internal control can be characterized by whether employees should be empowered to make key decisions themselves. Within the flexible firm, empowerment is the supreme good. It is about the choice between centralization and decentralization of decision making. The levers of control, as discussed in Chapter 8, provide the tools for balancing innovation and

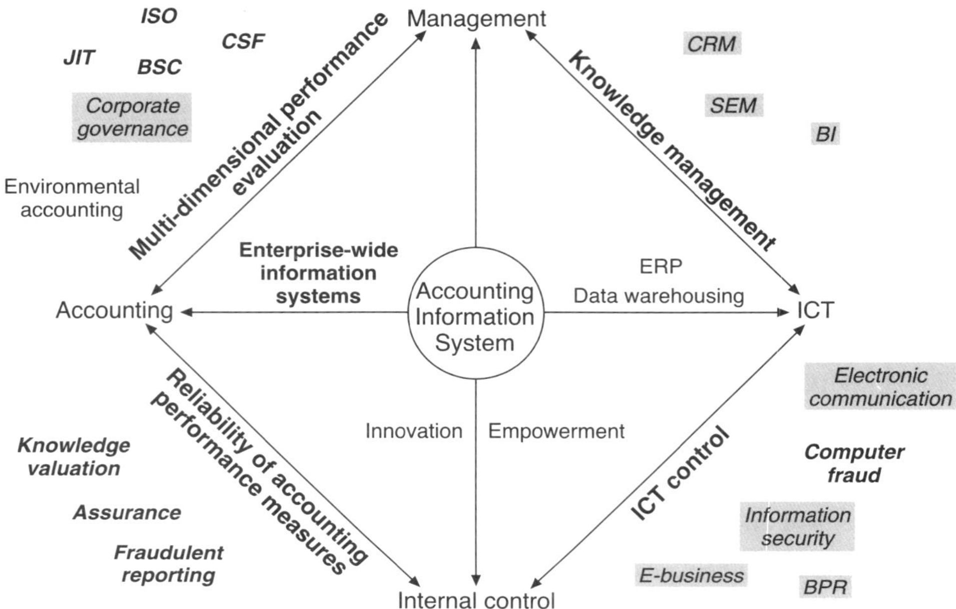

Figure 9.1 The accounting information system as a pivot in the flexible firm.

control by means of the right combination of interactive control systems, boundary systems, diagnostic control systems, and beliefs systems. As discussed, the internal accounting controls must meet some minimum requirements in order for the levers to balance properly. The controls surrrounding the AIS aimed at information reliability perform this role.

Accounting and ICT

The interrelationship between accounting and internal control can be characterized by which information systems must be employed to meet the information requirements in the flexible firm. An explicit characteristic of the flexible firm is that it has broad information systems that support a wide variety of business transactions and information needs; for example, Benetton has a unique competence to introduce new products as a result of an information system that consists of a quick response production system as well as a real-time retailer information system. Both systems are part of its ERP system, and, hence, can be considered AIS applications.

Management and ICT

The interrelationship between managerial involvement and ICT can be characterized by the way in which ICT can contribute to enhanced knowledge management. The main focus within this area is on knowledge management for enhanced customer orientation to enable the company to swiftly react to changing market conditions. Customer relationship management (CRM) thrives by the existence of information systems that enable the collection and employment of detailed customer information that shapes the relationship between the organization and its customers. Here, a detailed customer database is maintained as part of the AIS. Business intellligence (BI), on the other hand, is primarily aimed at opening up the information contained in ERP – and hence AIS – databases for managerial information provision. Strategic enterprise management (SEM) provides the link between the strategy implementation level as supported by BI and the strategy formulation level. Typical applications of SEM are executive information systems that make use of data warehouses built on top of the AIS databases of an organization's ERP system, therefore containing internal as well as external data.

ICT and Internal Control

The interrelationship between ICT and internal control can be characterized by the way in which control systems change if technology gets more complex and is being decided on at a decentralized level. When organizations enter into e-business and apply all kinds of electronic communication, specific ICT controls must be designed. As demonstrated in Chapter 7, there are two categories of ICT control: those pertaining to the ICT infrastructure and those pertaining to the operations. The AIS supports both types of control. The first, information security, by having controls in place mainly within the AIS, the second by having controls in place mainly within the organization surrounding the AIS. A special position is taken by business process re-engineering (BPR) since, on the one hand, it thrives by exploiting ICT, but, on the other hand, it negatively influences the quality of internal controls. As we have demonstrated, BPR and ERP are strongly intertwined. Since ERP is one of the most common manifestations of AISs, a contemporary AIS must be designed such that a process orientation is supported.

Internal Control and Accounting

The interrelationship between internal control and accounting can be characterized by the way in which internal controls can contribute to the reliability of accounting performance measures. A wide variety of concepts may be discussed under this heading including: knowledge valuation, assurance by independent third parties, and fraudulent reporting. Since internal controls are built in and around the AIS and are explicitly aimed at providing reasonable assurance about the reliability of accounting, the relationship between internal control and accounting is straightforward.

Accounting and Management

The interrelationship between accounting and managerial involvement can be characterized by the way in which accounting and the related management controls can contribute to enhanced decision making by applying multidimensional performance evaluation methods. For example, Asea Brown Boveri uses the accounting and communication system ABACUS to provide accurate and timely information for managerial decision making on business performance. This system provides financial as well as non-financial information.

Knowledge Valuation and Knowledge Management

Knowledge valuation is an important issue in our knowledge society. Stewart (1997) calculated that every $100 invested in IBM in 1996 bought $23 in tangible assets, and every $100 invested in Microsoft bought only $1 in tangible assets. Since the balance sheet mainly contains tangibles, representing visible business, the traditional book value of assets is an unsatisfactory measure of the true value of a firm. The explanation of this phenomenon lies in the value of intangible assets which is difficult to assess objectively, but which is considered to account for a great portion of the market-value-based balance sheet, especially in knowledge-intensive corporations like the flexible firm. Two issues emerge with respect to the relationship between the knowledge aspects of the AIS. First, the formal valuation of intellectual capital should typically take place for financial accounting purposes in order to have the financial statements regain their relevance. However, this valuation may also form the basis of managerial decision making with respect to hiring personnel or outsourcing certain tasks. Here, a measure for the return on knowledge must be developed in order to control it. Second, there is an important source of information asymmetry between management and the outside stakeholders of the firm. The less visible the capital, the more difficult it is for outside stakeholders to develop an objective value criterion. The AIS must be able to provide the true value of the firm.

Whereas the control literature has not given much attention to implementing control systems – as part of strategy implementation efforts – that explicitly consider innovation as their main goal, there is an extensive literature on knowledge management. Knowledge management has hardly been looked at from a management control or an internal control viewpoint; it is considered to be in the domain of top management when engaging in strategy formulation. The theoretical development of knowledge management draws on just a handful of concepts, of which cooperation and cross-learning are perhaps the most important ones. The production of knowledge requires a coordinated effort to balance cross-learning and cooperation between different knowledge specializations. Cross-learning involves the transfer of tacit, personal, and specialized knowledge to other members of the organization. Cross-learning is efficient if every member of the organization needs to have the same knowledge. However, only under very specific circumstances is this necessary. In general, firms exist because they are supposed to combine different functional specializations in an efficient manner. Among these specializations, only limited cross-learning is projected because this is time consuming and, hence, expensive. In addition, cooperation during the knowledge production process takes place to minimize cross-learning. In order to balance cross-learning and cooperation, coordination must take place. Coordination of cross-learning and cooperation then provides the glue that makes the organization stick. In this view, the trade-off between cross-learning and cooperation always necessitates a minimum amount of cross-learning. This may be referred to as cross-learning of meta-knowledge. This meta-knowledge is about the boundaries of each other's functional specialization: people need to know what their counterparts' specializations are.

The coordination of knowledge production is concerned with integration of different knowledge specializations in order to transform tacit into explicit knowledge (and human capital into structural capital). Opposed to the notion of knowledge specialization is that of knowledge sharing which may be represented by means of a common knowledge base. Such a knowledge base may be in a visible form such as a database, a data warehouse, or other ICT applications, or in a less visible form like the schemata and categories in the memories of the members of the organization. Because ICT only comes into play after the information dual of the business has been unfolded in the information and communication domain, our primary concern is with the less visible form of the common knowledge base (i.e. with the information dual of the business). In order to integrate different knowledge specializations, both a large common knowledge base and specialization should be fostered. Given the minimum level of cross-learning that is required to enable fruitful cooperation, the common knowledge base has an optimum size which balances cross-learning and cooperation (Figure 9.2).

The common knowledge base can be extended by means of cross-learning between different knowledge specializations (Figure 9.3). This requires coordination effort, otherwise known as the coordination of cross-learning. The larger this common knowledge base, the smaller the remaining need for cross-learning and the more discretionary the coordination effort becomes for cooperation. Cross-learning is inefficient when compared with cooperation: full cross-learning between three knowledge specializations requires each of them to acquire the knowledge of the other two. Hence, the amount of cross-learning increases progressively with the number of knowledge specializations that are active within the firm.[1]

---

[1] The number of cross-learning activities to be performed increases with the number of knowledge specializations (kns) within the organization in accordance with the following algorithm: #kns(#kns−1); for example, if there are three knowledge specializations (as in Figure 8.7), then the cross-learning activity increases: 3(3−1) = 6.

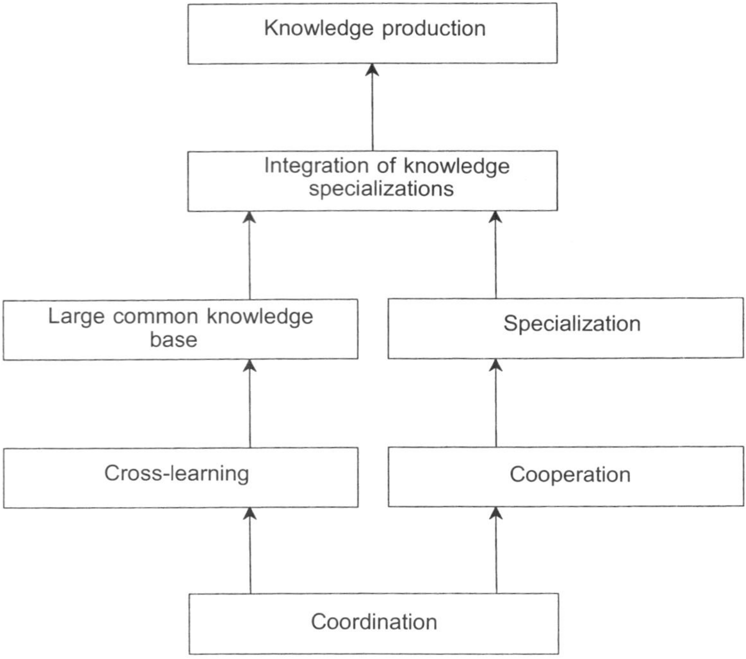

Figure 9.2 The relation between knowledge production and coordination.

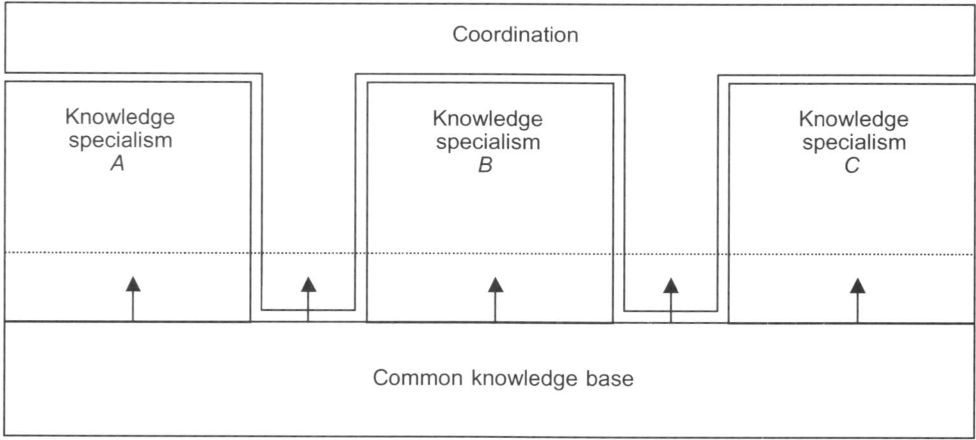

Figure 9.3 The nature of coordination between knowledge specializations and the role of a common knowledge base (adapted from Roberts 1998).

The objects-of-control framework can be used to further develop a knowledge-based theory of the firm. The knowledge-based theory of the firm, as proposed by Grant (1996b), suggests four mechanisms for integrating knowledge, which are basically control mechanisms aimed at the coordination of specialization and cross-learning efforts. These mechanisms are: rules and directives, sequencing, routines, and group problem solving and decision making. Rules and directives are vehicles for communicating personal knowledge to the organization; that is, for transforming tacit into explicit knowledge by creating a set of operating procedures about how to perform certain tasks. Rules and directives are typical instances of action controls. Sequencing refers to time-patterned sequences of activities so that each specialist's input occurs independently through being assigned a separate time slot; a subsequent activity cannot take place before the preceding activity is finished to a certain predefined degree. Just like rules and directives, sequencing is a manifestation of action controls. Merchant uses the terms 'foolproofs' and 'poka yokes' to refer to sequencing, indicating that no discretion exists with respect to the sequence of activities to be performed. Computers apply the same concept in that they force users to follow a fixed sequence of steps through a program, supported by screen layouts. Routines are relatively complex multi-person behaviours which are triggered by a relatively small number of signals or choices. As such, they constitute automated stimulus–response patterns. Teams that are used to work in a specific team setting typically make use of routines, thereby minimizing communication during the job. However, routines still require some controls to be built into the organization. Examples of such controls are pre-action reviews (action controls) and the hiring of qualified personnel (cultural/personnel controls). Group problem solving and decision making is, other than the former three, a communication-intensive control mechanism. Almost four decades ago, Galbraith (1973) had already asserted that impersonal coordination mechanisms should always be supplemented by personal and group coordination mechanisms. In terms of the objects-of-control framework, cultural and personnel controls should always perform the disciplinary role over action and results controls. Since efficiency in organizations increases with the use of impersonal coordination mechanisms that economize on cross-learning, group problem solving and decision making should be reserved to unusual, complex, and important tasks. Interestingly, in our knowledge society, more and more tasks fit this description.

In knowledge-intensive societies like the USA, Europe, parts of Asia, and Australia, value creation by means of knowledge is common. In general, a value chain indicates what processes add value to a specific intended result. Applied to knowledge, a value chain is a model that enables the efficient and effective exploitation of the production factor knowledge and may consist of the following components (adapted from Weggeman 1997):

- Strategy formulation.
- Strategy implementation can be further decomposed into:

- assessment of the required knowledge;
- inventory of the available knowledge;
- knowledge development;
- knowledge sharing;
- knowledge employment;
- knowledge evaluation.

Assessment of the required knowledge includes the activities done to determine the information, skills, experiences, and attitudes needed to implement the formulated strategy. On making an inventory of the available knowledge, interviewing techniques, surveys, and workshops can be applied to determine what knowledge is in use at a specific moment in time. The gap between the required and available knowledge indicates what knowledge should be created or acquired – by means of buying it or hiring competent people – outside the organization. The knowledge that has been developed must be shared with those who need it for the fulfilment of their tasks. During the process of knowledge employment, the knowledge worker capitalizes on her information, skills, experiences, and attitudes, in order to fulfil the assigned, acquired, or self-induced tasks. Finally, the processes of the knowledge value chain must be evaluated to enable organizational learning. Here, the processes as well as the value-adding of knowledge are subject to evaluation. Note that knowledge evaluation need not necessarily be financial (e.g. the clearing of computer files and archives or firing incompetent or unmotivated employees). The knowledge value cycle is a continuous and cyclical process. This implies that if knowledge has been evaluated and eventually valued, this may serve as input for a reconsideration of the organization strategy. Just like the alignment processes in the comprehensive contingency framework, the components of the value chain are not sequential. The processes may be executed simultaneously, before, or after one another.

The model, as depicted in Figure 9.4, sheds some light on the control factor in knowledge management. Within the business domain two control aspects related to knowledge can be distinguished: first, control of knowledge and, second, organizational control by means of knowledge. Within the information and communication domain, organizational performance can be measured aimed at knowledge evaluation. From within the ICT domain, the necessary support is acquired to enable information provision and communication. ICT can only play an indirect part in relation to knowledge management by providing the documentary support to information provision and communication.

Control of Knowledge

Following the knowledge value chain, control of knowledge refers to the control of knowledge development, the control of knowledge sharing, and the control of

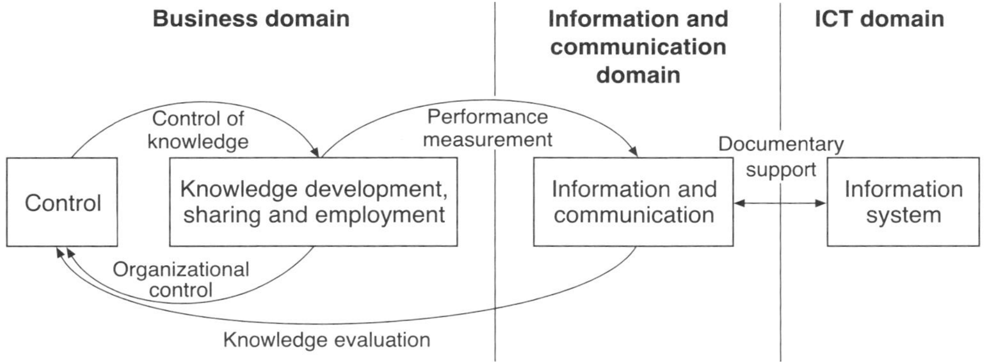

Figure 9.4 Control, information, information systems, and the elements of the knowledge value chain.

knowledge employment. Control of knowledge takes place within the business domain.

Information and communication within and between organizations leads to the sharing of ideas, thoughts, facts, and the like. When doing so, an inventory is made of the available knowledge and the required knowledge. When knowledge is developed, the gap between available and required knowledge is bridged. Internal control cannot directly facilitate the creative processes of knowledge development. Rather, the information and communication processes that lead to knowledge development will be supported by ensuring that reliable and relevant information is provided. In addition, a sound internal control system will bring calm to an organization, so that it can function like a well-oiled machine and creative processes will get going. Furthermore, management controls such as personnel and cultural controls may be applied to stimulate knowledge development; for example, assigning the right task to the right person, putting multidisciplinary teams in place, or creating master–mate–apprentice relationships will facilitate individual and organizational learning.

An Organization in Distress

Imagine an organization where people are suspicious of each other's motives and real intentions, procedures are absent or are not complied with, decision making on minor issues is heavily centralized, and bold ventures can be started independently by anybody. In this type of organization, a tremendous amount of energy has to be spent in giving detailed task assignments to people, and perform intensive progress checks on the follow-up of these task assignments. Given the scarce availability of human resources, and especially knowledge workers, there will be only limited time available to engage in creative processes, and, if the time were available (e.g. because of overcapacity), then people would not be in the mood to do so.

To control knowledge sharing within an organization, the individual competencies of the members of the organization must be recorded and reported to decision makers if considered applicable. The personnel department is the organizational unit that normally maintains the records on labour contract data such as the part-time factor and gross salary of the worker. This department will also maintain data on individuals' specific competencies. Here, data are recorded about education, experience, personality type, skills, preferences for specific tasks, performance, encountered problems, conflicts with others, and the like. By disclosing this information to authorized personnel, if necessary after aggregation, classification, or any other manipulation, tacit knowledge can be shared. The knowledge that is recorded about where to find necessary knowledge is called meta-knowledge (i.e. knowledge about knowledge). Another type of knowledge sharing deals with the content of the knowledge as present within an organization. This knowledge is not necessarily concentrated at the personnel department, but, rather, dispersed within the organization. Collecting, recording, and processing this information to provide relevant information for decision making and accountability is the main control activity here. Knowledge sharing is not just the effective and efficient use of an organization's information systems. Often, a much more important element of knowledge sharing is the creation of such an organizational culture that people automically share their knowledge with everybody else within the organization. As already seen, both beliefs systems and cultural controls, especially, provide the tools to move organizational culture in the desired direction.

The employment of knowledge often is no more than combining knowledge workers' proprietary information, skills, experiences, and attitudes with task characteristics. Personnel controls will play an important part here since they facilitate an optimal person–task alignment with respect to education, experience, personality characteristics, cognitive style, knowledge, skills, and the like.

Organizational Control by Means of Knowledge

Organizational control by means of knowledge takes place within the business domain. It is aimed at balancing control and innovation. We have already discussed the levers of control framework, as developed by Simons, which is aimed at balancing innovation and control. However, organizational control is a broad concept that may refer to each of the three planning and control concepts: strategic planning, management control, and operational control. The ultimate objective is to use a firm's knowledge as an enabler of operational excellence, effective managerial involvement, and effective strategy formulation, thereby spawning innovation. The body of literature on knowledge management mainly deals with the latter, strategy formulation aimed at innovation, and, hence, relates to control at the strategic level. For example, the CEO of a multinational software company stimulates employees from any business unit or hierarchical level to come up with ideas for new products, concepts, work processes, and the like. He will receive them and discuss their ideas. The outcome of that discusion may be that resources are allocated to a new project to work out that specific idea. However, if resources are allocated, then a diagnostic control system is put in place aimed at monitoring the progress of the project. Knowledge management may also relate to the operational level and be aimed at enhancing operational excellence. Here, the goal is less to spawn innovation than to improve work processes, and implicitly enhance internal controls. Here is a little story to illustrate the sometimes trivial nature of problems originating from inadequate work processes. A sales clerk in a department store sells a Compaq notebook and a Logitech mouse to a customer. After the customer has installed the mouse driver software, it appears that some of the original functions of the touchpad on the notebook no longer work properly. The customer returns to the store and complains. The sales clerk investigates the problem and responds that the customer should not have bought that mouse in combination with that notebook. They have an argument, but the customer realizes there is nothing for it but to go home. Of course, he is very dissatisfied. One week later, he meets a friend who also bought the same notebook and mouse, at the same store, though from another sales clerk. She encountered the same problem, returned to the store, and had the same bad experience. The knowledge management problem that arises here obviously relates to operational excellence. The first sales clerk could have easily solved this problem by making a note for his fellow sales clerks that the combination of that specific notebook with that specific mouse will cause the touchpad to malfunction. This note could have been made electronically, making use of groupware, or manually, using a register to write down customer complaints and the causes. A procedure could have been in place that would prompt the other sales clerks to scrutinize this register periodically. This type of problem is very common. It is about work processes and, hence, about insufficient attention to operational excellence. Hence, operational excellence can be defined as the concept that competitive advantage can be reached by aligning operations, information and communication, and ICT at the level of strategy implementation.

Performance Measurement

Performance measurement takes place within the information and communication domain. Currently, there is a tendency that traditional, financial performance measures are considered deficient with respect to measuring the real performance of organizations. Knowledge performance measurement is even considered a bigger problem. The imperfections in traditional performance measures have led to the emergence of innovations in the field of performance measurement, ranging from improved financial metrics to integrated financial and non-financial performance measures (e.g. the balanced scorecard of Kaplan and Norton, 1996). These innovations indeed seem able to improve the measurability of organizational performance. Furthermore, if a relation is being sought between organizational units' performance and organizational performance, then this opens perspectives for reliable performance measurement and, hence, the evaluation of knowledge; for example, measuring the increase in shareholder value may give an insight into the value-added of knowledge development, sharing, and employment.

Evaluating organizational performance is normally done by the management accounting functionary within an organization. In analogy, evaluating the performance in the field of knowledge and knowledge management can be satisfactorily done by the same functionary. By evaluating, a basis is created for adjusting which should initiate performance improvements. Here, the cybernetic approach as proposed by the management cycle is followed, indicating that knowledge management may be treated as an instance of management in general.

Fraud

Fraud can take many forms, but it always involves a deliberate action by one person to gain an unfair advantage over another person. It can be perpetrated by persons within or outside an organization. Knowledgeable insiders like employees, but also former employees, are the parties most likely to commit fraud; for example, a person who got fired, and got disgruntled at this, is a potential danger to an organization, especially when he can still get access to buildings and systems of the organization.

Fraudulent financial reporting according to the Treadway Commission is the intentional or reckless conduct, whether by act or omission, that results in materially misleading financial statements. So, fraudulent reporting in general results in misleading financial as well as non-financial statements. Fraudulent reporting may be done for several reasons, including deceiving investors or creditors in order to enhance access to the capital market (increasing shareholder value, raising cash to finance acquisitions, concealing losses, or hiding internal problems), and upholding a good reputation. Especially when the founders of an organization are still in charge, they may have less rational motives to keep a company going than when potentially less committed managers are in place. Hence, there is only an indirect gain for the perpetrator because he may secure his job, get positive evaluations, or will gain or maintain personal status. For example, the founders of the Belgian Speech technology firm Lernout and Hauspie engaged in massive fraudulent financial reporting to conceal the fact that the company was not profitable. The existence of stock option plans, the fact that executive board members owned company shares, and the availability of a revolving fund, conditional on reported earnings above a certain threshold, reinforced the incentive to misrepresent financial statements. The Treadway Commission not only recommended designing – and implementing internal controls to provide reasonable assurance that fraudulent financial reporting is prevented, they also recommended establishing an organizational environment that contributes to the integrity of the financial reporting process, identifying and understanding the factors that lead to fraudulent financial reporting, and assessing the risk of fraudulent financial reporting within the company. Considering the interpretation of these recommendations by the Committee of Sponsoring Organizations of the Treadway Commission (COSO), internal control provides the main instruments to reduce the possibility of fraudulent financial reporting. Another type of fraud is the misappropriation of assets by employees of an organization. Unlike fraudulent reporting, there is direct financial gain from misappropriation of assets for the perpetrator. In view of the objectives of internal control according to the COSO report, misappropriation of assets can also be prevented by means of internal controls.

When fraud is perpetrated – whether it is aimed at fraudulent reporting or misappropriation of assets – for which knowledge of ICT is needed, then the exposure may be much more severe. For example, by changing a few digits in a bank account number in a master file, a perpetrator may have millions of euros added to his bank account. This type of fraud is usually called computer fraud. Computer fraud includes the following:

- theft of money or goods by altering computer files;
- theft of computer time;
- unauthorized access to computer files or software for reading, copying, modification, or destruction;
- theft of computer files, software, or computer hardware;
- destruction of computer hardware;
- use or the conspiracy to use computer resources to commit a felony.

Hacking, in general, and realization of many of the threats that come from electronic communication, as discussed in Chapter 7, are instances of computer fraud. In addition, such activities as dispersing viruses and worms, superzapping, software piracy, and spamming are considered fraudulent.

Common Computer Fraud Techniques

Viruses and worms are the scourges of e-activities. Hackers find great pleasure in creating and dispersing these causes of computer illnesses. A virus is a piece of executable code that attaches itself to files or software, replicates itself, and spreads itself to other files or software on the same system or on another system; for example, a virus can be attached to an e-mail message and infect a macro in an MS Word file. Whereas viruses attach themselves to legitimate files or software, a worm is an independent piece of software. It uses the operating system to replicate itself. Often a worm exploits a bug in the operating system.

Superzapping refers to entering a system via a back door. Programmers sometimes create these back doors to maintain control over a system when in use. In addition, specific software may be used that allows unauthorized access to the system through bypassing regular systems controls.

Software piracy is the illegal copying of software without the publisher's permission. With the emergence of Internet portals which mediate between computers that contain bitable goods like texts, movies, or MP3s, software piracy also includes file piracy; for example, Napster allows the sharing of MP3 files to all computers connected to the service.

Spamming is the transmission of electronic messages to users who engage in electronic communication without having their permission to do so. With the emergence of e-business and the inevitable loss of privacy, e-mail addresses, home or work adresses, or telephone numbers of potential clients are valuable resources for direct marketing efforts. Research has revealed that the explicit choice for e-business customers to opt in (meaning that they give explicit permission to distribute their addresses to third parties) or to opt out (meaning that they have to indicate explicitly that they do not want to have their addresses distributed to third parties) is often inadequately respected by e-businesses.

Assurance Services

Assurance by independent third parties is part of the monitoring component of internal control. The financial audit has been the main assurance service provided by auditors for decades. The financial statements of an organization are designed to be a representation of the outcomes of business operations. Although these statements would ideally constitute the information dual of the business (i.e. a mirror reflection of the actual realities of business operations), they are in fact limited to measurements of income, financial position, and cash flows in accordance with generally accepted rules. The financial statement auditor assesses to what degree these statements are in accordance with the generally accepted rules of accounting for financial reporting. Here, we recognize seven features of the current financial audit:

- It is about financials, which implies that items are reduced to their impact on income, assets, liabilities, and cash flows in accordance with rules.
- It is about static representations (i.e. outcomes of business operations rather than systems or processes that produce the output).
- It is limited to assurance concerning the reliability of information and does not address other aspects of information quality.
- It is aimed at historical information, checking whether the figures are good representations of what actually happened in the period under review.
- It is solely aimed at information provision. The quality of the governance processes within organizations is not under investigation.
- It is externally oriented. The main users of the financial statements are outside the organization.
- It is aimed at strategy implementation processes within the organization.

During the last decade, a growing demand for new kinds of assurance has emerged. One driving force for new assurance services is the desire to create a flow of information to users that more closely constitutes the information dual of the business, aimed at enhancing quality of decision making in a broad sense. The information dual would then more clearly reflect not only financial items but also non-financial items, not only static information about business outcomes but also dynamic information about systems and business processes, not only the reliability dimension but also the relevance dimension, not only historical but also future events, not only information provision but also governance by means of provided information, not only external users' needs but also internal users' needs, and not only strategy implementation processes but also strategy formulation processes.

To better understand the development of assurance services, let us look at a major initiative in the USA which is related to the development of these services. Some of the impetus for assurance services originated in the work of the AICPA Special Committee on Financial Reporting, chaired by Ed Jenkins. The AICPA formed the Jenkins Committee in 1991 to address concerns about the relevance and usefulness of business reporting. In addition to recommending a broader set of business reporting information including non-financial information and information about business processes, the Jenkins Committee also suggested that auditors should play an enhanced assurance role regarding the overall quality of business reporting (AICPA 1994). As a follow-up to the Jenkins Committee recommendation and other demands for an enhanced auditor role, a round-table 'visioning' conference was held in 1993 aimed at developing a vision of future assurance services. The completed vision from that conference was presented to the AICPA board of directors, who generally embraced the vision and appointed the Special Committee on Assurance Services, chaired by Robert Elliott and briefly referred to as the Elliott Committee, to work on the development of new assurance services between 1994 and 1997 (see Elliott 1995, 1997, 1998; Elliott and Pallais, 1997).

The Elliott Committee has developed scenarios and guidelines related to three primary areas: (1) the future of current audit services, (2) extensions of current lines of audit/attest/assurance, and (3) completely new lines of assurance service. The scenarios for future audits illustrate a dramatic shift from an old paradigm in which a set of yearly financial statements is accompanied by an annual audit report to a new paradigm in which a set of real-time financial and non-financial information is accompanied by continuous assurance. The scenarios for extensions of current lines include assurance services related to comprehensive risk assessments, databases, comprehensive business performance measurements, Internet sites, and ISO 9000 (total quality management and control) or ISO 14000 (environmental impact) information. Scenarios for completely new lines include assurance services for e-commerce.

Accounting educators and researchers have become highly interested in the impact of new assurance services on future accounting education and research. For example, in the USA, the Auditing Section of the American Accounting Association appointed the Future Audit, Attest, and Assurance Services Task Force to review the work and recommendations of the Elliott Committee and to focus on the educational, research, and professional implications of future assurance services. This Task Force developed a set of responses in three areas. The first area concerns the impact that emerging assurance services will have on the accounting and auditing curriculum and educational delivery methods. The second area concerns research issues and opportunities presented by new assurance services. The third area concerns additional professional issues presented by the move to provide future assurance services. Since assurance is a major part of the monitoring component of internal control, these implications also pertain to internal control and the discipline of AIS.

A phenomenon on the increase is the operational audit. Basically, the operational audit is an internally oriented assurance service. What used to be the internal audit department within, mostly, large organizations has been transformed into the operational department, broadening its scope. However, whereas the internal audit department mainly supported the work of the financial auditor, the operational auditor is much more an assurance provider on behalf of an organization's management. This led some organizations to maintain the internal audit role, simultaneously creating an operational audit role.

The financial audit as well as the traditional internal audit can be positioned in the comprehensive contingency framework in the information and communication domain at the strategy implementation level. The Elliott Committee defines assurance services as independent professional services that improve the quality of information, or its context, for decision makers. In view of the assurance services that have emerged in the last decade, we believe the phrase '. . . or its context . . .' refers to the business domain and the ICT domain. Considering the similarities between the operational audit and assurance services in general, the operational audit as well as assurance services can be positioned in any cell of the comprehensive contingency framework.

Environmental Accounting

In Chapter 5, we discussed the notion of sustainability and triple bottom-line accounting incorporating economic, societal, and environmental performance measures. Having an environmental management system in place is an important issue in many contemporary organizations. An environmental management system is a coherent set of policies and accounting and administrative measures aimed at gaining an insight into controlling, and reducing the effects of operations on the environment. Environmental accounting, which is a component of such a system, imposes some specific requirements on an organization's AIS. The inventory of materials that may be harmful to the environment – this is mainly chemical or nuclear waste – probably has a negative value because the costs of destroying or removing it exceed its market value. Moreover, despite its negative value, it must be safeguarded carefully because, in the wrong hands, it may cause much damage to the people working within the organization, the people living in the neighbourhood of the organization, and the organization's reputation. Normally, when setting up the value cycle for an organization with a dominant flow of goods, the incoming goods lead to an outgoing flow of money and vice versa. In order to give reasonable assurance with respect to the completeness of revenues, the outgoing flow of goods is the main measurement point. When inventories have a negative value, an additional measurement point at the incoming flow of goods must be created. Whereas accountability is normally established when goods leave the warehouse, in the case of waste, accountability must also be established when goods enter the warehouse. Segregation of duties between custody, maintaining inventory records, authorization to ship goods, and shipment procedures remain the same. In addition, authorization includes the decision to take these goods in stock and the receipt procedures. When flows of waste become substantial, a so-called waste balance provides a suitable control tool. In general, a materials balance can be used to safeguard valuable assets like gold or diamonds, or to enable analytical review on reconciliations and control totals that have big upper and lower margins because of existing uncertainties (e.g. agricultural yields or the fat content of milk may vary substantially between years). A materials balance contains quantities measured in common denominators that are applicable to the material at hand. The idea is that what goes in (the left-hand side of the balance) must come out (the right hand side of the balance). The acceptable difference between input and output with respect to a waste balance will be dependent on the threat to the environment and its exposure.

Just-in-time Production

Just-in-time (JIT) production is a production planning system that tries to minimize inventories by producing as a response to customer orders or to work according to short-run production plans. Hence, it is a form of pull manufacturing. As a result, the organization can become more customer-oriented and gain efficiency. The philosophy that underlies JIT production is minimization of non-value-added activities such as waiting time, transportation, and inspection, and reduction of waste and dropout. When setting up a standard calculation, allowed costs of waste, dropout, and reprocessing must be eliminated from the standard costs. Because a JIT system continuously strives for improvements, standards must be reconsidered regularly and sharpened as improvements unfold. In view of adequate operational planning and control, differences between realizations and standards must be reported continuously. In addition, traditional business performance reports and variance analyses, eventually on an exception basis, will still have to be prepared for higher managerial levels. Organizations in a flexible production environment must develop new performance indicators such as quality of products and service, processing time, and timely delivery. An important issue in the accomplishment of shorter processing time and, hence, shorter production cycles is the reduction of machine set-up time. Hence, set-up times must be recorded and analysed to detect deviations from applicable standards in a timely fashion. Another important issue is the importance of preventive maintenance for machines and equipment. Since in a JIT system there is no slack, when a machine breaks down, the whole production process will come to a standstill. Hence, there must be measurement points for the effectiveness of maintenance; for example, the number of hours each machine has been in use and out of order because of defects. Capacity usage reports do not have priority in JIT systems because the main goal of JIT is not to maximize capacity usage, but to ensure an undisrupted production process.

ISO Certification

ISO is the acronym for International Organization for Standardization. This organization issues standards for process improvements. ISO certification is the result of ISO standardization. When an organization complies with ISO standard, it can be certifiied. Issuing an ISO certificate is an assurance service that may be performed by auditors. To acquire an ISO certificate, organizations must document their quality control system. However, documenting a quality control system does not mean that the products and services of an organization that has an ISO certificate comply with applicable quality standards, it just means that there are procedures in place that are aimed at product and service quality. In this sense, the process an organization engages in when trying to acquire an ISO certificate leads to formal procedure descriptions. This is where the relationship with AIS and internal control becomes clear: ISO certification as well as formalization of procedures leads to enhanced internal controls. Because ISO is concerned with process improvements, it also is closely related to total quality management (TQM). TQM is strongly focused on the employees in an organization and its goal is to make them collaborate in such a way that products (including services) are produced that meet the customers' demands. Quality assurance is another type of assurance service that may be offered by auditors. The auditor then assesses whether, in a given production process, measures are being taken to manufacture products that have a quality acceptable to customers. ISO has gained worldwide recognition which makes it increasingly important in our new economy; for example, the European Union requires suppliers of specific products to be ISO certified. Currently, there are two big families of standards: the 9000 and the 14000 series. ISO 9000 includes such standards as ISO 9000 : 2000 (quality management systems, fundamentals, and vocabulary), ISO 9001 : 2000 (quality management systems, requirements), ISO 19011 (guidelines on quality and/or environmental management systems auditing), ISO 10005 : 1995 (quality management, guidelines for quality plans), and ISO/TS 16949 : 1999 (quality systems for automotive suppliers, particular requirements for the application of ISO 9001 : 1994). For example, the purpose of ISO 9001 : 2000 is to establish a starting point for understanding the standards and to define the fundamental terms and definitions used in the ISO 9000 family so that misunderstandings about their use are avoided. Whereas ISO 9000 is concerned with quality management, ISO 14000 is concerned with environmental management. ISO 14000 includes such standards as ISO 14001 : 1996 (to help an organization establish a new or improve an existing environmental management system, it specifies the requirements for an environmental management system that may be objectively audited for self-declaration or third-party certification), ISO 14004 : 1996 (again to help an organization establish a new or improve an existing environmental management system, it provides guidance to help an organization do so that goes beyond the requirements of ISO 14001), and ISO/TR 14061 (to assist in the implementation of ISO 14001 and ISO 14004 by forest management organizations and the forest products industry.

The Strategic Role of Information

The value chain according to Porter (1985) is a timeless instrument for analysing company activities in view of the added value they have in satisfying customers. The value chain is primarily intended to facilitate strategic decisions about how to approach the market to control competitive forces. For example, a company may decide to follow a cost–leadership strategy, attempting to obtain competitive advantage by offering its products at low prices. The company should attempt to purchase these goods at the lowest possible prices, obtain production efficiencies of scale, pass on the low sales price to potential consumers when selling the goods, and should set up an efficient distribution system. By introducing *measurement points* in the value chain, the company gains insight into the factors that may thwart a certain strategy. Those measurement points have to generate information about the factors that are critical to realizing organizational goals. These factors are usually termed *critical success factors*. Introducing measurement points allows measuring the progress of a process and being able to adjust it. The question is: What is measured? Basically, the only thing measured is what directly influences the attainment of a company's critical success factors. These measurements are developed by defining performance measures for those processes that require information or on which information is provided. This way, information provision, built from the processes, comes into being and gives insight into the extent to which strategic business goals are met. This information can consist of financial, quantitative, and qualitative elements (Figure 9.5).

An instrument that is helpful in organizing categories of information provision is the balanced scorecard (BSC) as introduced by Kaplan and Norton (1992). In this

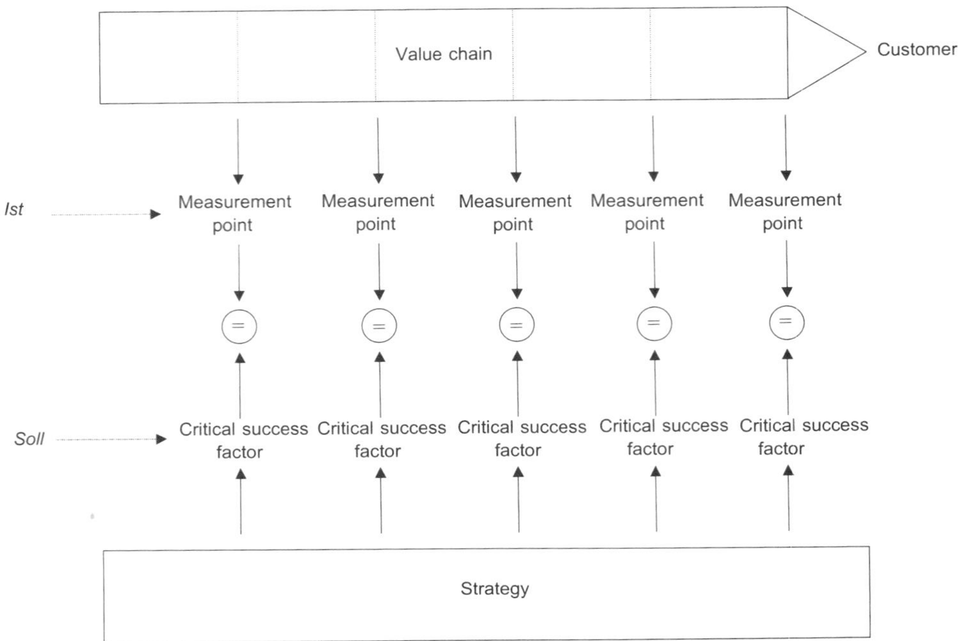

Figure 9.5 The value chain and its related AIS components.

measurement and reporting system, basically four categories of information are distinguished:

- information on financial performance;
- information on client satisfaction;
- information on value added by internal processes;
- information on the company's innovative ability and learning power.

The number of information categories may be increased; for example, reporting in a governmental institution may introduce a societal dimension. The balanced scorecard should be seen as a checklist for information provision that explicitly ties strategy to information provision. By organizing monthly reporting according to the BSC classification, a clear understanding can be gained of the extent to which a company is resisting competitive forces. It will be clear that the implementation of such a system has important consequences for the information system and the internal organization. For example, an AIS designed to contain only general ledger-based financial data for financial reporting will have to be dramatically re-organized to also incorporate non-financial data for managerial information provision. Reporting performance measures without the relevant reference values (norms) is useless. Therefore, a first aspect that needs to be embedded in any information system is the structural gathering of normative values that will be reported together with actual values. For example, when it is decided to use benchmarking, this means that information on benchmark partners is to be collected and recorded in the information system. This information serves as the norm against which the organization's realized performance is marked. The applicable checks on standards are of an entirely distinct nature. After all, how can administration or the internal control department determine that the respective reference values are reliable and relevant to the benchmarking process? For example, a critical success factor for an investment bank is risk control. The investment institution will use as its benchmark the extent of risk control directed at competing investment institutions. The performance measures defined, based on this critical success factor, are, among others, tracking errors, the value at risk, and the partial/modified duration. To use these performance measures as benchmarks, they need to be defined carefully. Also, we need to determine whether the information collected on these variables from the benchmark partners enables us to give the concepts a uniform meaning. This way, benchmarks change from control means to objects of control. In the business intelligence system that supports the benchmarking process, these types of complex control need to be taken into account when designing the system. Even when simpler norms are used (e.g. last year's figures or budgets), it is important to know that the meaning of these normative values is unambiguous and that this information is reliable. The elements of accounting and administrative organization that are important in this respect are, among others, documentation of the information system, the procedures followed when collecting, processing and providing normative values, setting up a project organization, security for data communication when collecting or transmitting data through electronic data interchange, and confidentiality of information.

As can be seen from Figure 9.5 (and Figure 1.3), information is always (directly or indirectly) important in the process of client satisfaction. The customer must be made the focal point to ward off competitive forces. When management just wants to assign tasks and hold people responsible for their performance, it may be sufficient to put a so-called vertical information system in place. However, such a system does not measure the value-added of activities with respect to customer satisfaction. Instead, a horizontal information system may be put in place that uses an index of value-adding work to distinguish between work relevant and work irrelevant to the needs of the customer. So, a vertical information system is not effective in an approach in which attention is focused on customers. To be able to actually use information as a strategic instrument, horizontal information systems need to be developed. In such systems, the value chain and the occurring measurement points are considered the basic principles, following the credo that only activities that add to client satisfaction are to be performed. This process approach leads to an entirely different AIS, in which the traditional segregation of duties disappear and relationships in the value cycle lose their meaning because they cannot be effected in an independent way. The quality criteria applicable to information and the information system also get other weights. Reliability of information will lose importance at the cost of relevance. Technocratic control measures embedded in the accounting and administrative organization will have to be replaced by control measures embedded in the more extensive management control system. Personnel control and organizational culture will gain importance, influencing information provision. Management will have to react in a fast and adequate manner to take corrective measures. Insight into the available knowledge potential of personnel is a matter of attention for organizational and accounting design activities. Managing knowledge, including implicit knowledge, will become a critical success factor for gaining competitive advantage in such a view. ICT will become more important than ever because of the need to be able to have the most effective information at our disposal quickly, to communicate fast with other parts of the organization in order to solve problems and turn negative developments on time. Activating tacit knowledge and bringing information to the surface for benchmark processes and quality assurance, in general, is made possible by effective use of ICT. Working in teams receives a new impetus, since teams do not have to meet physically to be able to make decisions. The control of such decision-making processes is of an entirely different nature since there can be many more persons involved, and autonomous circuits of collaboration may arise that can lead to a power shift. The new horizontal information systems will have to be able to deliver the information that contemporary organizations command and, at the same time, provide the instruments to keep a grip on the organization that matches the need for control of that specific organization.

In conclusion, for the AIS to be able to play the role of the information system of the contemporary organization, it must be as flexible as that contemporary organization. This implies that an important feature of any AIS is the ability to sense new developments, adapt, and provide the information needed so that the organization can act proactively in view of these new developments. Indeed, a true challenge.

Chapter Cases

Case 9.1 Envico

The Envico foundation aims to promote human environmental awareness.

Strategy
The foundation's strategy is focused on developing as broad a range of activities as possible and, thus, realizing its idealistic goal on the broadest scope.

Activities
The foundation develops the following activities to realize its strategy:

- keeping a library and information centre;
- publishing six periodicals;
- all other activities that its staff members consider important contributions to the attainment of the foundation's goal.

Within the framework of the latter activities, some more and less successful initiatives have been developed such as sponsoring scientific research, organizing symposia, broadcasting idealistic advertisements through various media (radio, television, the Internet, billboards, and the like), contributing towards the extra costs of environment-friendly production processes, carrying out environment-friendly production processes, nature-improvement programmes (such as tree planting days), soil cleaning activities, and helping to dismantle and remove environment-harming production installations. The foundation emphasizes that it does not want to employ an aggressive approach in performing these activities.

The foundation's committee consists of five members, which includes a chairman, a secretary, and a treasurer. The committee's tasks are mainly of a policy-making and controlling nature. The general manager is charged with the foundation's daily management and is in charge of the following departments: secretariat, public relations, library, information centre, and administration. In all, the foundation employs approximately 60 persons. The majority of these employees are part-timers, most of whom are volunteers and are only reimbursed for expenses.

For its information provision, the foundation uses a local area network (LAN) with PCs in all departments. Should the systems manager fall ill, his tasks are taken over by an employee from the administration department (nicknamed 'the hacker'), who is normally responsible for subscriptions and members' administration.

The foundation is subsidized by the Ministry of Economic Affairs. The subsidy is awarded annually, based on the annual budget prepared by the foundation. This budget consists of four subbudgets:

- a budget to cover general administration costs, such as reimbursement for expenses and employees' salaries and the rent of the building where the foundation is housed;
- a budget to cover the costs of the library and information centre;
- a budget to cover the costs of publishing the periodicals;
- a budget for other activities.

At the end of the year, the Ministry settles up, based on actual administration costs, the actual costs for the library and information centre and the actual costs of publishing the periodicals. The budget for other activities is not subsidized by the Ministry. To cover these costs, the general manager approaches private individuals and companies for financial support. The general manager has proved to be increasingly successful with these attempts in the past couple of years.

Private persons as well as companies can subscribe to the periodicals. The rate for private persons is several times lower than the rate for companies. However, companies do receive a discount on the subscription rate when they subscribe to two different periodicals. The subscription period is one year. Third parties can place advertisements in the periodicals at a fixed rate per (part of a) page. A mail-order company delivers the periodicals to its subscribers. The printing of the periodicals is put out to an external printer.

Members of the library (including the information centre) are allowed to borrow five books at a time, for a maximum of one month. The membership fee is a fixed annual amount. When the lending period is exceeded, a fine is charged per day that the book is overdue. After advice is obtained from the department head, a desk clerk of that department orders the books and brochures. A desk clerk also receives the order. Most of the time, the invoice is included with the delivery. The desk clerk sends these invoices to the financial administration. The library is connected to the LAN and uses standardized software for:

- receiving membership fees and fines;
- cash sale of periodicals;
- cash payment of books and brochures purchased against cash on delivery.

At the end of each working day, a desk clerk deposits the cash in a safe. The clerk is only allowed to deposit. At the end of each week, the department head retrieves the money from the safe and pays it into the bank. All desk clerks are authorized to order books, receive money, and to make payments. In the past couple of years, the number of missing books has increased. So, too, have back membership fees.

The activities of the information centre consist in supplying information both written and via telephone (such as brochures) to interested parties, organizing free exhibitions about the development of the environmental movement, and organizing presentations to groups of pupils. In addition, the centre has started providing information through the Internet, at a minimal charge. The website is developed by an external bureau.

The subscriptions are administered by means of software developed by the systems manager. This software:

- records the permanent information on subscribers and library memberships;
- prepares payment slips for subscription and membership fees;
- records receivable subscription and membership fees.

Considering current political developments and the dependence on subsidies, the foundation committee is worried about the foundation's survival. In addition, the committee repeatedly discusses the issue of liability of the managers.

The head of financial administration reports to the general manager on a monthly basis. Each quarter, the most important numbers are also reported to the committee. The committee has commissioned strive for environmental goals in a balanced manner. To measure its effects, the committee periodically receives information based on a kind of 'balanced scorecard', consisting of environmental factors, social factors, institutional factors, and economic factors.

Assignment

1 List the threats to the control of the business processes within this organization. Use the following two dimensions to present your solution:
   - domains (business, information and communication, information and communication technology);
   - strategy formulation versus strategy implementation.

2 Indicate the exposure of each of these threats.
3 For each threat, provide control solutions.

Case 9.2 Pinpoint

In a professional bureaucracy, knowledge is often the main production factor. By employing its knowledge the right way, an organization can gain competitive advantage.

Pinpoint is a professional bureaucracy. It consists of 17 business units that are occupied with various areas of management consultancy including finance, subsidies, takeovers, control, and information. The organizational structure is flat, with one general manager who is in charge of the whole organization. His main task is to control the organization's knowledge in order to control the organization itself. These are the two control aspects inherent in knowledge management.

The general manager has a specific view on the production factor knowledge. Together with some authors in the field of knowledge management, he believes that knowledge is an instance of intellectual capital and that intellectual capital can be distinguished into structural capital and human capital. An organization's human capital mainly consists of tacit knowledge and its structural capital mainly consists of explicit knowledge. In his view, human capital can be managed through the dynamic interplay between the human resource management department and the professionals, whereas structural capital can be managed using standard information system applications and control procedures. Since knowledge as a production factor is getting more and more important, he recognizes the tension between human capital and the structural capital. Too much knowledge is tacit, begging the question whether a more active approach to human capital should be pursued to restore the imbalance between intellectual and human capital.

Assignment

1 Make an inventory of threats in the field of knowledge management within Pinpoint.

2 Give an indication of the controls that may be put in place by Pinpoint.
3 How could the threats in the field of knowledge management within Pinpoint be mitigated by means of information system applications and organizational measures?
4 Give an indication of the way in which Pinpoint could implement its strategy aimed at exploiting its knowledge. Note that you don't need to formulate the right strategy but, rather, the arguments for making certain strategic choices.

Case 9.3 RGE

RGE collects and processes real estate prices from all over the world. The company has the following three revenue-generating activities:

1 Making comparative studies on behalf of clients.
2 Monthly publication of standard reports on the basis of continuing research into real estate prices.
3 Advertisement revenues from the company's website.

Sub 1
Clients pay a fee per man-hour. The number of man-hours is determined on the basis of a post-calculation. Of course, a price indication is given to the client.

Sub 2
Monthly standard reports are available on paper as well as electronically. The sales prices of these reports are fixed. However, the hard-copy version is considerably more expensive than the electronic version.

Sub 3
A fixed amount per advertisement is paid by the advertiser. In addition, a fee for every hit on the advertisement at RGE's website is charged.

RGE was founded ten years ago and has grown into a medium-sized company that employs about 75 people.

To collect real estate data, the company subscribes to several databases. For these services, RGE pays fixed monthly subscription fees along with a fee per data request. In addition, a fixed amount is paid to the cable provider who enables electronic data transmission.

Assignment

1 How can RGE be classified in the typology of organizations?
2 What threats are inherent to this type of organization?

3 What threats are specific for RGE?
4 Discuss the role of information in this organization. Illustrate your essay by means of a schematic representation of the role of information in governance processes.
5 What reconciliations and control totals will the head of administration want to perform to get a grip on the completeness of revenues in this organization?
6 How can RGE's management get reasonable assurance about the validity of costs related to obtaining real estate data?

Communications of Accounting Information Systems

10

There are situations where recordings or manuals are very important. The most evident example is the boyscout handbook of the Disney characters Huey, Dewey, and Louie. This book solves all their problems.

Adapted from Noordam *et al.* (1996), p. 8

After studying this chapter, the reader should be able to:

- Define the criteria that play a role in deciding whether or not to formally describe the control system in an AIS manual.
- Distinguish between the stages in a control communication process.
- Demarcate the goals of control descriptions.
- Make a trade-off between a verbal or a schematic control system description.
- Understand the importance of communication and related change processes in implementing controls.
- Distinguish between the potential users of the control description.
- Define the organizational conditions that must be met in order to develop a successful control description.

Chapter Outline

Every organization has a control system, usually built in and around the AIS. However, as we have seen in Chapters 3–5, there may be differences in its forms across firms. Like differences in control systems, there may be differences in the way controls are communicated toward members of the organization. An organization may want to describe its controls formally in an AIS manual. Another organization may want to rely on informal procedures that are not codified, but are merely known and almost automatically employed by its people. This chapter discusses if and how a control system should be formally described in order to optimize the system's efficiency. Hence, the communications of AISs will be the central theme. If it is deemed necessary to make a formal description, then it is of major importance that the users of that description are well defined. It is also of great importance to make an inventory of conditions in order to efficiently make such a description. Choosing the right tools to describe the AIS and related controls is key to communicating the AIS. Besides the primary decision of choosing between software packages for describing controls, this also comprises paying attention to key AIS terminology and related controls. Communications of AISs therefore include developing and employing an AIS ontology. It is important to recognize that recording and definition, as such, can never be goals in their own right. They are an integral element of operating the business. All in all, communications of AISs, whether they be formal or informal, provide the finishing touch in managerial approaches to AISs.

Introduction

By now, the reader must have a good understanding of the intertwined relationship between AISs and control. Every organization has a control system. However, the way it is set up and its quality may vary between organizations. Within our propagated contingency approach (Chapter 5), a formalization of controls in a control handbook or an AIS manual may improve control quality in some organizations, whereas it may be ineffective in others.

This chapter discusses if and how a control system should be formally described in order to optimize the system's efficiency. This question can be broken down into two subquestions with respect to communications of the AIS and embedded controls. The first pertains to communicating the need for controls: How will the rationale of a control system have to be communicated? The second pertains to description of the controls: How will the controls have to be described to optimize the system's efficiency? It should be noted that these questions are interrelated because a clear communication to users of the underlying reasons for developing a specific set of controls will increase the likelihood that the control system's efficiency improves.

We will follow a stepwise approach to the communication of controls (Figure 10.1).

The Purpose of a Control Description

Whether or not a control description must be made depends on the purpose of making such a description. If the description is a goal in itself, then the result is not so much of a surprise: a beautifully designed handbook without value-added for the attainment of organizational goals. Such a handbook may as well not be written, because often it is stored in a chest of drawers, where it remains until a new handbook is written. In general, we can identify the following potentially illegitimate reasons for formally describing an organization's controls in a handbook or another type of manual:

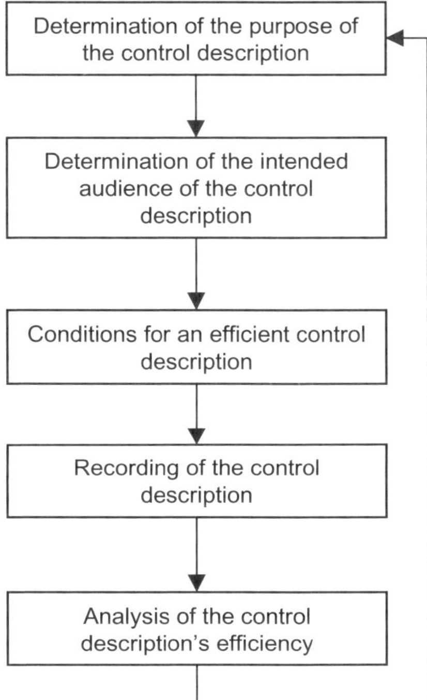

Figure 10.1 The stages in a control communication process.

- The financial auditors advise to formalizing controls. The organization formalizes the internal controls without analysing the costs of such a formalization and the benefits of incurring lower audit fees.
- Benchmarking shows that competitors, vendors, and customers also have formalized control descriptions. The organization takes over this practice without investigating whether having formalized internal controls is the critical success factor of their benchmark partners.
- The organization engages in rituals with respect to control description routines, without questioning their relevance.

Valid purposes for engaging in formal control descriptions include:

- The description serves as a communication tool to assign tasks and responsibilities to workers within the organization.
- Ensuring continuity of operations, when employees leave the organization and their knowledge may get lost for the organization. This is especially relevant in knowledge-intensive firms, where there is much tacit knowledge.

- Operations and information provision must be optimized. Hence, the control description process initiates organizational change.
- The control environment necessitates formal procedures.
- Laws and regulations require fomalized procedures.
- National culture is characterized by uncertainty avoidance.
- Workers are only to a limited extent 'selected at the gate'. Instead, they are simply controlled by means of tight procedures, receive training in applying these procedures, and undergo intensive compliance monitoring.
- If an organization's management strives for an enhanced control environment, it may be meaningful to formalize controls in a control manual, just to set the right tone at the top.

A Specialist Staff Lay-off

After a major restructuring, Philips discovered that its huge specialist staff, involved in developing and describing procedures and other tight control measures, did not add value to the organization and laid off the majority of them, transferring some others to other departments with often completely different task assignments. The lesson learned was that tight controls were not that critical to the attainment of its organizational goals.

Intended Audience

Besides determination of the purpose of a formal control description, identification of the intended audience is of major importance for its efficiency. Essentially, everybody within an organization is one way or another involved in AISs and embedded controls. This implies that any member of the organization may belong to the intended audience. However, the nature and the degree of detail of the control description will differ between the various roles and hierarchical levels that are to be considered users of the description.

Just like differential characteristics of information at different decision-making levels, there are differential characteristics of control descriptions at different decision-making levels. In general, control descriptions at the strategic level are more global than control descriptions at the tactical and operational levels. For example, a middle-manager only wants information on the internal control quality of some key processes when it crosses a minimum threshold such that customers will switch to a competitor as a result. This implies that a control description must be set up such that initially only the degree of detail is presented that matches the decision-making level. Only if a decision maker explicitly indicates that she wants a description intended for another level, will she be able to acquire it. This type of alignment

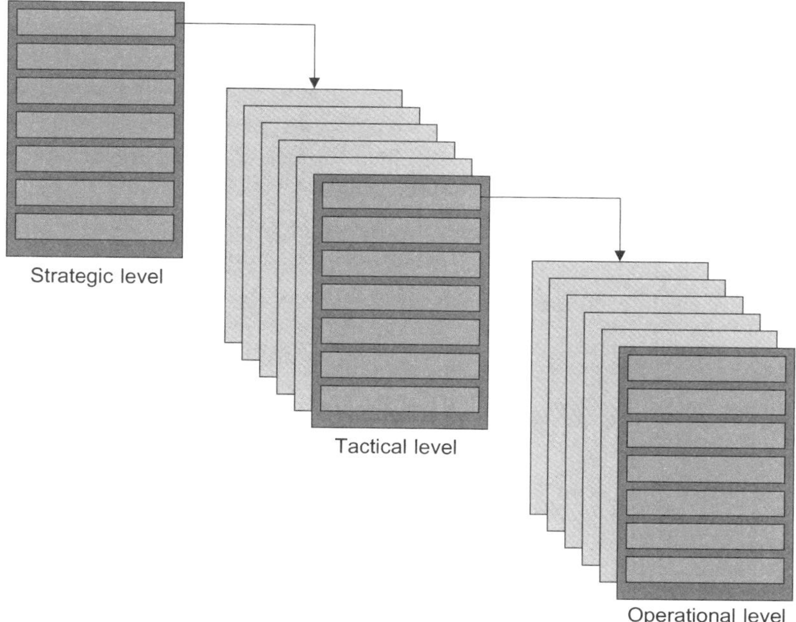

Figure 10.2 Hypertext structures applied to decision-making levels.

to people with the same characteristics (i.e. the same decision-making level) shows some resemblance to alignment of personal characteristics in the five-layer contingency framework, as presented in Chapter 5. Because of a better tailored alignment and, hence, improved understandability, the efficiency of such a control description will be enhanced.

A tool to develop and employ differential control descriptions for different decision-making levels is hypertext. With the advent of the Internet, hypertext structures have become popular. But the concept is, of course, much older that the Internet. Hypertext is a feature of most modern text processors that enables going down from a higher level document to the next lower level document. When an organization comprises three decision-making levels, then a hypertext-enabled control description consists of three levels at a maximum. Figure 10.2 depicts the concept of hypertext structures as applied to decision-making levels.

A Control Description at Three Decision-making Levels

The following partial procedure could be presented to a warehouse clerk. On receipt of goods:

1 check the bill of materials against the goods received;

2 check the goods received against the vendor order, retrievable from the system by entering the vendor code, the product codes, and the quantities;

3 establish accountability if the documents and receipt match by signing off the bill of materials;

4 if the shipment is in accordance with the bill of lading and the vendor order, then enter the 'goods received in good order' code into the system;

5 if the shipment is not in accordance with the bill of lading or the vendor order, then return the goods and enter the 'goods returned' code into the system.

The equivalent partial procedure for the head of logistics may read as follows:

1 acquire a monthly statement of the goods received in good order and the goods returned due to shipment errors by the vendor;

2 analyse this statement and adjust prognosis of logistical capacity usage for the next twelve-month period.

The equivalent partial procedure for the general manager may read as follows: acquire an analysis of the capacity usage of the factory concerning average vendor performance about shipment errors.

Conditions for an Efficient Control Description

Before the actual control description can be made, some conditions must be attended to, including:

- planning of the description process;
- existing control descriptions;
- overcoming resistance against controls;
- choosing between verbal and non-verbal descriptions.

Information about gaining an insight into the applicable controls can be acquired via three channels. First, interview those people with key roles within the organization (e.g. the head of the purchasing department in order to get an insight into buying procedures). Second, observe organizational processes while they take place. This may occur systematically or *ad hoc* (e.g. walking around the shop floor may give you a good impression of what is really going on in an organization, although this is an extremely unstructured approach). Third, read both the verbal and schematical representations of organizational processes (e.g. there may be notes, schemes, a website, and other more or less formalized documents that provide an insight into the set-up of processes and procedures).

Interviews

Interviews may be used to obtain the information needed to prepare a control description. A badly organized interview may cause the control description to be deficient. Hence, it is important that the following critical success factors are considered, when interviews are being held, as part of the control description process:

- Make it clear from the outset what the objective is and the time needed for the interview.
- Make an assessment of the information you expect to get from the interviewee.
- Avoid noise such as telephone calls, ICQs, e-mails, or colleagues entering the room that may distract the interviewee.
- Make sure that the interviewer as well as the interviewee are well introduced.
- Use open-end questions as much as possible (why, how, what, etc.) instead of closed-end questions that can only be answered with a simple 'yes' or 'no'.
- Present a summary of the key points of the interview to the interviewee so that she can make corrections if deemed necessary.
- If the nature of the investigation allows, stimulate the interviewee to come up with suggestions to improve the controls and the internal organization in general. These may be better or more creative than the interviewer might have come up with himself.
- Make clear follow-up appointments by scrutinizing the interview report and the controls description, and monitor whether these appointments are being kept.

Planning

Given the pervasive influence of control – being an integral part of management – throughout any organization, preparing a control description is not a solo action that can be casually executed. It is important that the control description process is considered a project with all its attendant features. Hence, this process includes, among other things, putting together a project team with a clear-cut demarcation of each person's responsibilities and authorities, setting up a progress control system, and formalizing the goals and the explicit agreement of each participant to aim to achieve these goals.

To select members of the project team, a choice must be made between people with internal roles and those with external roles, or a combination of the two. This choice is mainly dependent on the goal of the description, and the complexity of the organization's processes. If the goal is to make a description for internal use without any form of judgement about the effectiveness of the control system, and the organization's processes are complex, then it is generally advisable – for reasons of efficiency – to have people with internal roles dominate the project. If the goal is to have someone review the effectiveness of the control system, and the organization's processes are simple, then it is advisable – for reasons of independence – to have external parties dominate the project. In the case of a description solely intended for an organization's own use and simple organizational processes, as well as a description for review purposes and complex organizational processes, then budgetary and human resource constraints will determine what mix of internal and external role personnel there should be to participate in the control description project.

A critical success factor for a control description project is the designation of a process owner. This is a common approach for many change processes. An important factor that explains what person is to play the part of the process owner is the size of the company. If the company is big enough to have a controller, which is an internal control role, or an information manager in place, then one of them should adopt the role of process owner. If the company is limited in size, then the head of financial administration should play this part.

Like so many complex projects, the processing time of a control description project often exceeds the planned processing time, and the costs exceed budgeted costs. To prevent a control description process from becoming a runaway project, some specific measures can be taken, including:

- Formulate a clear plan containing the goals, the team, the process owner, the description technique to use, the time frame, and the budgeted costs. Have this plan go through several iterations, involving various people, in order to improve it.
- Prioritize the organizational processes to be described. Here, a trade-off must be made between the easy-to-describe processes, which can quickly provide an insight into the organization's functioning, and the more complex processes needed to solve organizational problems.
- Make appointments with interviewees at an early stage of the project. It is always important to include department heads and other middle-managers in the sample because they will ultimately be responsible for compliance with the control description. In addition, the automation department should be involved, because of the interdependency between controls and ICT proliferation throughout the organization (see Chapter 7).
- The control description should be discussed with the interviewees who provided the necessary input for the description. Thus, the description will undergo some iterations. To avoid perpetual discussions about the reliability of a description, it is important that the number of iterations be limited. This, along with deadlines for providing comments, should be unambiguously communicated to all participants.
- Regular progress reports must be provided to all participants. As in any project, measurement points and milestones must be determined in advance and be reported on in terms of progress and costs according to plans. Especially, analysis of differences between realization and plans and the consequences of

these differences for the remainder of the project are important matters of attention.

- Inform everybody within the organization about the control system to be described in an organization-wide project. By following this approach, any resistance against the project and potential organizational changes will be mitigated.

Existing Control Descriptions

If there are existing control descriptions, then the question emerges whether they can be used to facilitate the new control description. Of course, this may improve efficiency. However, it may also cause an anchoring and adjustment effect. Anchoring and adjustment is a heuristic frequently employed by people in judgement tasks when they revise their judgement toward a reference point. An existing control description may serve as such a reference point. If this control description is not an adequate representation of the actual situation (any more), then the anchoring and adjustment heuristic may cause the new description to contain misrepresentations too. Because of this effect, it is not advisable to use an existing control description as a basis for the new description. Also, if the control description is initiated to invoke organizational change, existing descriptions are often not usable. Finally, if there are existing descriptions of processes and procedures, made for a purpose other than a control description, then they cannot be used as a basis for the new control description. However, the new control description must be consistent with existing descriptions of processes and procedures if they are still valid; for example, there is a description of procedures prepared for acquiring an ISO certificate.

Overcoming Resistance against Controls

If there is resistance against controls, then there will be resistance against the control description project. As a result, people may refuse to cooperate as interviewees or even deliberately sabotage the project. Often, an analogy can be made between control and a product with unequivocal qualities but without a market. Like this product, control must be marketed to show potential customers that it is a good product. Overcoming resistance is the main marketing goal of control. The process of overcoming resistance against controls includes the following phases:

1 Identification of the sources of resistance. This is about who resists and where within the organization.
2 Assessment of the magnitude of resistance. This is about the question whether there is one isolated case or a more structural problem.
3 Prioritization of the identified sources. Here, for each source of resistance, an indication is given if something needs to be done about this.

4 Detecting the causes of resistance for each identified source. A distinction must be made between causes on the demand side and causes on the supply side; for example, demand-side causes relate to obstruction by future users, while supply-side causes relate to the quality of the proposed controls or the control description.

5 Analysis of the causes of resistance. Some of the causes may be easily reparable, whereas others may be more difficult to repair. Causes of resistance include:
  - fear of the unknown in general;
  - resistance against having to adopt new procedures;
  - the not-invented-here syndrome; people who contributed to the development of the legacy system will put effort into maintaining it;
  - fear of being transferred or fired;
  - fear of being exposed as having a backlog in knowledge and skills; for example, when future users feel they need more training and education as a result of change, they may resist it.
  - fear of new hierarchical structures.

6 Making an inventory of solutions; for example, by training and educating future users, they may become the most fanatical proponents of the changeover. Solutions can be categorized as communication, leadership, or participation. Table 10.1 gives an overview of potential solutions from a managerial point of view.

Table 10.1 Overview of potential solutions to problems of overcoming resistance

Communication	*Leadership*	*Participation*
Distinguish between audiences and try to discover who are the opponents and the proponents.	Find proponents of the changeover and employ them to promote the change process.	Have future users participate in the change process by inviting them to advise on solutions to detected problems and to read and comment on the draft control description.
Strive for a sober control description, which is focused on the intended audience and and their resistance.	Set up a project organization and appoint line as well as staff positions.	Formulate control measures on the basis of advice and not as prescriptions.
Choose communication channels and format that are aligned with the specific situation.	Try to become accepted as the change agent by making quick wins.	Informally collect information about needs, experiences, and reactions with respect to the ongoing change process.
Communicate clearly that a control system is beneficial to both the organization and the individuals within it.		

7 Choice and implementation. Here, it is important to have a clear understanding of who will be responsible for choosing between the alternative solutions to conquer resistance.

Choosing between Verbal and Non-verbal Descriptions

In view of the solutions for overcoming resistance against control change processes, it is of vital importance that these processes are well communicated. Because communication is essentially the process of sending and receiving data or information, which can be done by means of manual or computerized recordings, control descriptions enable communication of controls and control change processes. Communication always takes place between two actors. An actor can be one person or a group of persons. When a sender of a message announces part of his mental position to the receiver, then this is denoted as communication. The sender uses expression to transmit the message in a transferrable format, whereas the receiver uses interpretation to understand the message. This implies that the sender and the receiver must master the same language. However, people can master a language actively or passively. Actively mastering a language implies that actors use that language to formulate and understand messages. Passively mastering a language means that actors understand the messages received, but cannot formulate them themselves. For control descriptions, the same distinction can be made. The user (i.e. the receiver) must understand the technique (i.e. the language) used to describe the controls, but does not need to know how to make such a description herself. However, the control specialist (i.e. the sender) who prepares the description must not only understand the technique, but must also be able to apply it to describe control systems.

There are two main categories of control description techniques: verbal and schematic. The advantage of verbal techniques is that they make use of the natural language that the users master at least passively. The disadvantage is that accessibility of the resulting verbal descriptions is often low, due to the inherent inefficiencies of natural language. Especially when there are many and complex organizational processes, verbal descriptions may become too extensive. Also, the maintainability of these descriptions is suboptimal because a change in one procedure often influences many other procedures. The risk then emerges that certain interdependencies are overlooked, as a result of which the control description becomes less reliable. The main advantage of schematic techniques is that they potentially incorporate interdependencies between procedures, as a result of which consistency increases. Also, the required quantity of paper is considerably less than for verbal descriptions because the information density is generally higher for schemes than for texts. The disadvantage of schematic descriptions is that users must at least passively master the language of the technique, which requires specific training. A final aspect that is important in choosing between verbal or schematic control description techniques is the explicit preference of future users for texts or schemes. This, together with the implicit goal of having an organization-wide adoption of the developed control description, leads to the conclusion that an unambiguous choice between a verbal and a schematic description cannot be made. Therefore, a combination of verbal and schematic description techniques seems to be the most appropriate solution. However, this immediately begs the question as to how this combination should be effectuated. Hence, we must search for new modes of control communication that overcome the aforementioned disadvantages. The hypertext structure, as discussed in this chapter might, be an example of such a new communication mode.

When a schematic description technique is used, a software package that meets the specific needs of the organization must be chosen. Once chosen, to gain efficiency benefits from familiarity with the product, the organization must stick to this package for a reasonable amount of time. Hence, just as in any software selection process, considerable effort must be put into selection of the graphics package. Factors to consider include:

- The degree of goal support. As we have demonstrated, control descriptions may be developed for various purposes. Dependent on the formulated goals of the description, different software choices may be made.
- User-friendliness. There are two aspects to this factor. First, the ease with which users can get acquainted with the software to actively master it. Second, the ease with which users can read and interpret the output of the package.
- Existing knowledge and skills with respect to specific software. Training people to work with new software can be extremely costly. This may force the choice for a specific package.
- Flexibility. If an organization continuously changes, then software that is easy to adjust to these changing circumstances will provide greater benefits than software that is difficult to adjust.
- Costs of the package. Costs not only pertain to the initial acquisition of the software, but also to the labour time involved in describing controls with this package and maintenance costs.
- Personal preferences of the users of the software.

If a specific schematic technique and supporting software have been chosen, the knowledge and skills needed to work with it must be transferred to users. This transferral takes place by means of in-house or external courses and on-the-job training. Irrespective of the balance between formal courses and on-the-job training, the basic principles of a schematic technique must be taught to all people involved; for example, the symbols and their meaning, as well as how to start and find your way through the program, are usually considered basic principles. An important critical success factor for implementation of specific software like graphics packages is access to someone within the organization (or even outside) who can answer practical questions about schematic techniques and operating the software. Usually, someone at a non-specialized help desk is not fully equipped to fulfil this task.

Recording of the Control Description

The control system of an organization is traditionally described in a comprehensive control handbook or an AIS manual that is accessible to anybody within the organization, has a uniform layout, and does not distinguish between decision-making levels or any other contingent factors. Contemporary views about recording of control descriptions adopt a contingency approach to enable alignment to specific users – as in the lowest level in the five-layer contingency framework (Chapter 5) – and, hence, a priori overcoming of resistance.

Traditional Recordings of Control Descriptions

When the goal of a control description is set and there is agreement on the way in which the conditions will be met, recording of the control description can be made. The control description must answer at least the following questions:

- What actions must be described? As already indicated, a primary distinction can be made between describing controls for cycles or for types of organization. However, at the most elementary level – the action level – this distinction no longer makes any difference; for example, if vendors send bills, which is still the case in most organizations, vendor invoice handling is an activity that must be described regardless of whether the control handbook is cycle-oriented or typology-oriented.

- What information is needed to perform a certain action? This question deals with the information individuals need for decision making and accountability; for example, if a sales clerk must decide on whether or not to accept a customer order, she has to collect information about the customer's creditworthiness and the goods' availability.

- What data must be recorded to be able to provide the necessary information? This question is about the files to be used, the links between these files, and the links between these files and program modules.

- Who is authorized to perform a certain action? Here, a description must be made of the authorizations given to individuals to perform the identified actions. Because a description of control is being made, and not a description of the internal organization in general, segregation of duties is the main theme. However, if there is an existing description of the internal organization, then this may well serve as a starting point for the description of segregation of duties.

- How must each action be performed? Dependent on the choices made with respect to, among other things, tight and loose controls, action controls and results controls, centralization and decentralization, and process orientation versus functional orientation, detailed directives for the execution of tasks can be more or less elaborate.
- What controls are needed to provide reasonable assurance that each action leads to the desired results? Here, the same contingencies apply as in the detailed directives for task execution. As we have seen in Chapter 8, a wide choice of controls is available ranging from traditional management controls to traditional internal controls.

Traditional control descriptions may suffer from problems of maintainability and resulting lack of relevance for the processes described. We believe a contemporary approach to control descriptions should distinguish between the business domain, the information and communication domain, and the ICT domain within the comprehensive contingency framework used throughout this text.

Contemporary Recordings of Control Descriptions

If better maintainability of control descriptions is strived for, then those elements that are subject to change must be discerned from those that are relatively inert. Seen in relation to the current dynamism within organizations and their information provision, ICT is a factor that continuously and rapidly changes. When a control description is modularized by differentiating between the business domain, the information and communication domain, and the ICT domain, its maintainability improves because each of these domains has its own specific change dynamism. An additional effect may be that accessibility to and understandability of the control description improves. Many methods for information analysis employ this distinction in abstraction levels. The domains discerned in the comprehehensive contingency framework are based on such a distinction. An information analysis method that employs a similar distinction and is specifically developed for change processes is the dynamic essential modelling of organizations (DEMO). DEMO considers three abstraction levels: the essential level, the informational level, and the documentary level. As will be explained, these levels show much similarity to the business domain, the information and communication domain, and the ICT domain, respectively. Although not referring to the domains in our comprehensive contingency framework, and certainly not developed for making control descriptions, the underlying concept of DEMO is appealing when trying to develop improved control descriptions.

Let's consider the following excerpt from a traditional control description of a housing corporation that owns about 1,500 houses in one city in France:

The front-office clerk asks whether the person seeking housing (PSH) has some kind of tie with the city and briefly explains the city housing regulations. If the PSH has a tie with the city, he receives a registration form, the housing catalogue with all the houses available for rent, and a sheet of A5 paper, giving information about the registration; for example, that the PSH must make an appointment for the registration to take effect, and that he must take his wage slip showing deductions with him. When submitting the registration form, the PSH has to pay a €20 registration fee. The PSH is given a receipt, and a copy of the receipt is put into a designated document file along with the registration form. The front-office clerk then tells the PSH that he will receive written confirmation of registration within two days. After the PSH has received confirmation from the registration department, the registration is considered official.

The Essential Level

This level is comparable with the business domain. The organization is considered a system of actors who use conversations to negotiate about actions to undertake, their results, and the individuals involved in their execution. The actors at this level are subjects who have authorizations and responsibilities, and who mutually influence their behaviour by means of communication. The organization is reduced to its essence. The so-called performative conversations and, hence, the business transactions only take place at this level. Man is considered a social actor. Changes in operations occur at this level. Starting points for any model of the essential level are descriptions of procedures and discussion reports. DEMO extracts transactions from these descriptions and reports. In DEMO terminology, a transaction may only be denoted a transaction if it leads to new facts. Hence, the following phrases, taken from the above control description excerpt, pertain to the essential level:

- *the PSH has to pay a €20 registration fee.*
- *After the PSH has received confirmation from the registration department, the registration is considered official.*

The essential level consists of four partial models, each answering one of four questions, and each serving one of four purposes:

- Who is involved in an action? To get an insight into the individuals involved in a specific transaction, the communication model is created. The communication model consists of three elements: a transaction, the actors involved, and the transaction result (a new fact). Table 10.2 lists these elements for the above phrases.
- When will an action take place? To get an insight into the timing of a specific transaction, the process model is created. A verbal description of the process model could read as follows: *'After a PSH has paid the registration fee, and the registration department has processed all the applicable data, the PSH is registered.'*

Table 10.2 Transactions, actors, and transaction results in the communication model

Transaction		Actors		Transaction results
		Initiator	*Executor*	
T1	Cash receipt	PSH	Front-office clerk	Registration fee is received
T2	Registration	Front-office clerk	Registration department	PSH is registered

- How will the action be done? To get an insight into the way a transaction is carried out, the action model is created. A verbal description of the action model with respect to T2 could read as follows: '*A request for registration is received. This request is accepted. If registration can take place considering the applicable rules, the registration is actually effectuated.*' The action model makes a link to the informational and the documentary level. Hence, each element appearing in the action model will also appear at the information level and the documentary level.
- What information is needed to perform the action? To get an insight into the information needed to carry out a transaction, the fact model is created. A verbal description of the fact model with respect to T2 could read as follows: '*Information is provided for the registration.*'

The Informational Level

This level is comparable with the information and communication domain. The organization is considered a system of actors who exchange information, store information, or derive information from existing information. Information stands for the content of a message, not the form. The actors on this level do not have any authorizations, but are merely supporting and enabling toward the essential level. Man is considered a rational actor. Changes in information provision occur at this level. The following phrases, taken from the above control description excerpt, pertain to the informational level:

- *The front-office clerk asks whether the PSH has some kind of tie with the city and briefly explains the city housing regulations.*
- *If the PSH has a tie with the city,*
- *with all the houses available for rent,*
- *information on the registration; for example, that the PSH must make an appointment for the registration to take effect,*
- *that he will receive written confirmation of registration within two days.*

If transaction T2 from Table 10.2 is taken as an example, the verbal control description at this level could read as follows: *'The following information is needed to register a PSH: tie of the PSH with the city, salary, houses the PSH applies for, name of PSH, address, city, zipcode, telephone, e-mail, etc.'*. Clearly, this is about the content, not the form.

The Documentary Level

This level is comparable with the ICT domain. The organization is considered a system of actors who produce, file, move, and destroy documents. The document stands for the form of a message, not the content. At this level, the informational level is supported and enabled. Man is considered a physical actor. Changes in ICT occur at this level. The following phrases, taken from the above control description excerpt, pertain to the documentary level:

- *he receives a registration form, the housing catalogue*
- *and a sheet of A5 paper, giving information*
- *and that he must take his wage slip showing deductions with him.*
- *When submitting the registration form,*
- *The PSH is given a receipt, and a copy of the receipt is put into a designated document file along with the registration form,*
- *The front-office clerk then tells the PSH.*

If transaction T2 from Table 10.2 is again taken as an example, the verbal control description at this level could read as follows: *'The registration information is recorded in the registration form. The PSH must therefore bring with him: his wageslip showing deductions, an employer's reference, an excerpt from the registry office, a passport or driver's licence. The PSH receives: the housing catalogue and the guidelines for registration.'* Clearly, this is about the form, not the content.

Considering our definition of ICT as all the electronic media used to transport information between senders and receivers and to support or enable communication, ICT pertains to the documentary level. Any change in an organization's ICT initially only leads to changes at the documentary level. Suppose the housing corporation of our example decides to allow registration via the Internet, then the control description at the documentary level of transaction T2 could change as follows: *'The registration information is received via the website of the corporation. In addition, the PSH must send by separate mail: his wageslip showing deductions, an employer's reference, an excerpt from the registry office, a copy of his passport or driver's licence. The housing catalogue and the guidelines for registration are available at the website.'*

At the informational level and the essential level, no changes need to be made to the control description unless the organization enters into an ICT-enabled restructuring. As we have seen in Chapter 7 about the dynamics of internal control and ICT and also Chapter 5 about the continuous alignment between the business, information and communication, and ICT, ICT-enabled restructurings are not unlikely to take place. Although this partially reduces the efficiency gains in describing controls as sketched in this section, we believe that the basic idea behind this segmented approach is still appealing.

Analysis of the Control Description's Efficiency

As in any management cycle, performance evaluation is an integral part of our approach to control descriptions. The question we must ask ourselves is whether or not the prepared control description is economically justified and effective and, hence, efficient. Any substantial deviations from predefined standards may lead to rewriting the control description if redefining the standards cannot be justified. For this purpose, we must develop a set of performance measures for evaluation of the control description. Much of what has been written in this chapter provides input for development of such measures. Since Figure 10.1 depicts the steps to follow when a control description is prepared, we will use it as a benchmark for identification of relevant measurement points. Since there may exist a wide variety of performance measures, and much depends on the creativity of the evaluator of the description's efficiency, we will not elaborate on these measures. Rather, we will provide a brief checklist of questions to be asked to get a global insight into the efficiency of a control description, and that may trigger the evaluator's creativity in developing detailed performance measures (Table 10.3).

As can be seen in Figure 10.2, from each step in the control description process, a move backward towards one of the preceding steps might be possible. This indicates that developing a control description is an iterative process. However, this also indicates that developing a control description implies continuous interaction between the parties involved. Since controls in any form are pervasive throughout any organization, as we have demonstrated in this text, every individual in an organization is influenced by the prevailing controls. So, developing a control description is actually a continuous communication process aimed at making the control system tick.

Another element of communicating the AIS and the embedded controls is to develop a common language that every individual within and outside the organization understands. Lately, much effort has been put into the creation of AIS ontologies. We therefore conclude this chapter with some thoughts about AIS ontologies.

Toward an AIS Ontology

In Chapter 2, we concisely referred to an ontology as the directory and dictionary of a discipline or a system. A more precise definition would be a coherent set of core

Table 10.3 Checklist for assessing the efficiency of a control description

#	*Step*	*Question*
1.	Determination of the purpose of the control description	Is the control description used in accordance with its objectives?
2.	Determination of the intended audience of the control description	Is the control description used by the intended audience?
3.	Conditions for an efficient control description	Are the conditions for an efficient control description being met?
	(a) Planning of the description process	Has a customized plan been used?
	(b) Existing control descriptions	Have existing control descriptions been thoughtfully used?
	(c) Overcoming resistance against controls	Has resistance against controls and the control description been overcome?
	(d) Choosing between verbal and non-verbal descriptions	Has the right balance been accomplished between the verbal and the non-verbal control description?
4.	Recording of the control description	Is the control description sufficiently: • maintainable? • understandable? • reliable? • economical?
5.	Analysis of the control description's efficiency	Is the control description efficient?

constructs that underlie a phenomenon in the real world. We also indicated that the academic literature on AIS increasingly recognizes the need for such an ontology. AIS has done without an ontology since its inception. However, this does not mean that an ontology used to be considered expendable, it merely indicates that developing an ontology for a relatively young discipline, that is subject to continuous change and that still does not have its own paradigm, is extremely difficult. As we also indicated in Chapter 2, we do not have the pretension to develop an AIS ontology. Whereas we tried to resolve some terminological issues in that chapter, we want to provide some food for thought in this final chapter.

McCarthy (1979, 1982) is one of the AIS theorists who have put a great deal of effort into prescriptive research aimed at developing methods for enhancing the development of AIS as a discipline and AIS as a system. REA modelling – his brainchild – is getting more and more attention and recognition, and forms the basis for a steady stream of research. From that starting point, researchers are currently, among other things, trying to model organizations and their information systems on the basis of information flows. Conceptually, this is a first step toward an AIS ontology.

This theoretical approach may ultimately lead to a classification of information systems which closely resembles other systems, such as ecosystems and architectural, psychological, political, or economical systems. Even such an ambiguous system as the animal kingdom may be a role model for an AIS classification. McCarthy (ECAIS 1998) proposed thinking about information systems as having as many different but well-defined appearances as the range between the amoeba and the *Homo sapiens*. Obviously, the cornerstones of AIS as identified in Chapter 2 (albeit closer to the roots of the discipline) and our comprehensive contingency framework as employed in the second half of this text (which is further removed from the roots of AIS) serve the same function; namely, they are working toward an AIS ontology. Specifically, the relationship between internal control and ICT as discussed in Chapter 7, the relationship between internal control and management control as outlined in Chapter 8, as well as the roles of assurance providers and the developments in management science as outlined in Chapter 9, build on the comprehensive contingency framework and the cornerstones of AIS and, hence, may be considered a first step toward an AIS ontology.

From a practical viewpoint, having an AIS ontology would benefit the communications of AIS and related issues. From a theoretical point of view, such an ontology would benefit the development of a real AIS theory with its own paradigm. From an educational point of view, having an AIS ontology would enhance the efficiency of education and learning processes. All in all, these are valid reasons to work toward such an ontology.

Chapter Case

Case 10.1 Tax Consulting Firm

Introduction

A tax consulting firm makes tax returns and provides advice regarding income tax, corporation tax, sales tax, etc. for a large number of clients (about 4,000).

The annual number of returns and advice engagements is approximately 15,000. Duration of the engagements ranges from a couple of weeks to one year.

The firm is managed by ten partners. In addition, the firm employs:

- 48 consultants;
- ten secretaries;
- one administrator with five clerks;
- two telephone operators.

Various consultants specialize in areas like sales tax and company tax. Partners and employees regularly take internal and external courses.

The administrator, partners, secretaries, and consultants all have personal computers that are connected by a network. The firm uses standard software packages for hour registration, word processing, making returns, etc.

Engagements
All engagements are confirmed in writing. Multiple engagements per client are possible. All agreements with clients are recorded in the automated system.

Fixed-fee Engagements
With a number of clients a fixed fee per type of return is agreed upon (including objections and appeals).

Reimbursement Engagements
For these engagements, the firm provides the client beforehand with an estimate (expenses made by firm on behalf of the client).

Should the actual amount to be reimbursed exceed the estimate, the responsible partner notifies the client in time.

The client is usually billed based on hours worked at an hourly rate, which varies per category of personnel. In all, there are eight different hourly rates.

The firm bills its clients once every three months. Prior to billing, the amounts that are to be billed are presented to the responsible partner. He has the authority to alter the billed amount in exceptional circumstances.

Business Process Re-engineering
Recently, the company has lost some major clients. Deficient internal communication processes are identified as the main causes. To regain the desired level of quality, the firm has initiated a quality control committee. This committee is to judge all important returns and advice engagements prior to providing them to clients. However, this is not enough according to the management. A business process re-engineering project is unavoidable.

Assignment

1. You are asked to describe the control system of this company before and after re-engineering. Obviously, the information on hand is far too limited. So, you decide to start out by collecting more information on this business. What additional information do you need to be able to make an adequate control description?
2. You want to present your thoughts on how to approach the control description to several people with different roles within the organization. What roles would you like to address? Why do you want to address these specific roles? What contingent factors would you take into consideration when telling your story to these people?
3. What media would you prefer to use to optimize communication of the control system? What contingencies apply here?

FURTHER CASE STUDIES Appendix

Comprehensive Case 1

Interrelation

'Interrelation' is the first international relationship mediation agency on the Internet.

The general manager supervises the following subordinate departments (among others):

- secretary (one full-time employee);
- relationship advisory department (four full-time employees);
- bookkeeping department (one full-time employee);
- relationship advisory field organization (six full-time employees);
- system administration (one full-time and two part-time employees).

The six-part employees from the relationship advisory field organization regularly visit customers who want to communicate their wishes orally, they produce videos and they organize cultural afternoons and delightful dinners. The two part-time system administration employees maintain the home page and the supply files.

Applicants who announce themselves via the home page of 'Interrelation' receive information about the firm and the possibilities for mediation. If an applicant decides to make use of the services of the firm, then an intake interview is held, partially electronically. For this intake interview a fee of €25 is charged. This amount is paid by the customer through his credit-card number and his pin code. In most cases, immediate feedback is given to the client about the expected success rate.

If the applicant wishes to become a client of the firm, then a base fee is charged per quarter, as well as a fee for recording his/her personal data in the supply file. There are three variations in presentation style in the supply file:

- only verbal data;
- verbal data and a photo;
- verbal data, speech, and animation.

The latter presentation style may only be used by clients who have an ISDN connection. For each presentation style, a different fee is charged. Video recordings can be made by the firm. For this service, a fixed base fee as well as a fee per minute is charged. Billing for this service takes place once a month. To retrieve data from the supply file a fee per hour is charged with a minimum of half an hour. When a client is interested in someone whose record is in the supply file, then the firm announces this to the supply client. This is done by electronically transferring a code. For each such announcement, a fixed fee is charged to the (demand) client. For clients who feel that this approach is not personal enough, the firm organizes cultural activities or delightful dinners. The supply client to whom a client is attracted will be invited to that activity. The fee charged for this service varies between €100 and €400.

Assignment

1 (a) What criteria are used in the typology of organizations?
(b) What is the function of this typology of organizations when describing a normative internal control system?
(c) How can 'Interrelation' be classified in this typology of organizations?

2 Provide a normative internal control description of 'Interrelation'. Pay special attention to the segregation of duties and the tasks that are performed by each employee.

3 (a) What internal control measures must be taken with respect to the integrity of the EDP system?
(b) What additional internal control measures must be taken in order to compensate for the limited possibilities for segregation of duties?

4 (a) What is meant by the term ICT?
(b) Name five applications of ICT.

5 (a) What are accounting controls, administrative controls, detective controls, and preventive controls? Give an example of each.
(b) What is meant by internal control according to the COSO definition?

Comprehensive Case 2

Beverages Transport

A company engages in transport of beverages within the Benelux countries, as well as in the temporary storage of goods for third parties. A central office in the Netherlands coordinates all activities.

The company consists of the following departments:

- planning and logistics;
- financial administration;
- workshop (includes a filling station and a car wash);
- storage and handling;
- order processing.

The company is managed by a general manager and an assistant manager. The general manager is charged with commercial affairs and the assistant manager with technical affairs.

The company uses a PC network with one or more terminals and printers in each department. An integrated standard financial software package is in use (multi-user application) to facilitate management information provision within the company. In addition, the company uses EDI for order processing and billing. To that end, the company has specific software at its disposal.

Sales are mainly generated by conducting all Benelux transports for one major soft-drink producer. This producer's orders are received at Order processing by EDI. This department converts the orders to standard forms. This conversion is an integrated process. Besides this external integration, internal integration is also striven for in the shape of linking order processing to planning and logistics. The soft-drink producer initiates the billing process by sending the transport company a billing advice via EDI on a monthly basis. This billing advice indicates how much the producer expects to owe the transport company by reason of the transport services delivered to the producer. The transport company confirms this specification by means of a (hard copy) pro forma invoice.

Incidental orders from other beverage producers are accepted whenever capacity allows it. Particularly in winter, it is important to have sufficient incidental orders to optimally utilize capacity. Order processing and billing takes place in the traditional way: orders are received by telephone or in writing, and are recorded on standard order forms. Order processing bills its incidental clients on a monthly basis.

The (expensive) trucks (60 items in two weight classes) are maintained in a garage owned by Tempotrans. The trucks are cleaned on a weekly basis in a washing installation located in the company's grounds. This washing installation is used by third parties as well, on cash payment at a fixed rate for each wash. Also located in the grounds is a filling station, which is used (just by the company itself) as much as possible. Trucks en route may also refuel at other filling stations.

Often, goods owned by third parties are temporarily stored in one of the depositories located in the company's grounds. These goods are mainly stored in crates (full or empty) on pallets. The company charges its storage clients using price tables in which duration of storage, volume, and weight are taken into account. Order processing bills its clients on a monthly basis.

Planning and logistics takes care of job order issuance and tries to optimize the routing of trucks by employing advanced techniques. The department uses specific software to do so.

Assignment

1 (a) Characterize this organization in the typology of organizations.
  (b) Which inherent threats are associated with this type of organization?
  (c) Which specific threats are distinguishable in this organization?

2 (a) Describe the administrative and organizational conditions with respect to the various budgets.
  (b) Describe the administrative and organizational conditions with respect to the use of automation in this organization. Besides standard and specific software, also consider the use of EDI.

3 Which procedures need to be supported by management guidelines? Explain your answer.

4 What information does management need to control the company? Indicate the required frequency of each piece of information.

5 What segregation of duties needs to be implemented in this organization to achieve sufficient internal control? Indicate the employee and/or department, task, and the corresponding duty in terms of segregation of duties.

6 What reconciliations and control totals will financial administration make to achieve sufficient assurance about the completeness of revenues from transportation activities, storage activities, and the washing installation? Provide your answers in formula form as much as possible, along with an explanation and sources of the components of the formulas.

Comprehensive Case 3

MarioToys

Introduction

As a trade organization in the 1920s and 1930s, MarioToys concentrated on toy import and sale. After the Second World War, the company started producing its own brand of puzzles. Since 1985, MarioToys has focused on the development of party games and the development, production, and sale of computer games and puzzles. The party games are produced and sold under licence, not on the company's own account.

The company, which started with only a few employees, has grown fast, especially during the last ten years. Currently, the company has 200 employees. Two branches at different locations in the same city have been added to the original branch. Revenues have increased to €100 million on an annual basis.

Management consists of pragmatic and hard workers, who have succeeded in obtaining leading positions within the company. Since communication is mainly by word of mouth or by telephone, a formal information system is limited.

Strategy

MarioToys' strategy focuses on obtaining competitive advantage in current markets by innovating as much as possible. However, possibilities for accessing new markets are held open at all times.

Structure

The general manager manages three branches located at *A*, *B* and *C*.

The branch at location *A* consists of two production departments one for puzzles and the other for boxes for computer games (85 employees), the production planning department (5 employees), a warehouse for raw materials and finished products (5 employees), and an automation department (3 employees).

Location *B* consists of the following departments: sales (15 employees), general purchase (3 employees), personnel, main administration, payroll, and factory accounting (together 10 employees), as well as the warehouse for finished products and shipping (6 employees).

The branch at location C has a computer games production line (20 employees), a warehouse for raw materials and finished products (3 employees), an administration department with a receptionist/telephone operator (5 employees), and the research and development department (40 employees).

General

The general manager directly manages all the departments mentioned above. In the 'old' days, when a major part of production and sales was concentrated at one location, there were frequent informal contacts and most decisions were made by a limited group of people, mostly based on information provided by the heads of department. According to the general manager, this has always been one of MarioToys' strong points. New products were constantly put on the market and appeared to be successful too. In the past couple of years, communication has diminished. Many new employees have been recruited, and only a small core of people still know each other. The general manager foresees large problems in case internal communication does not improve. However, since he does not know how to solve the problem, he decides to hire a consultant.

The consultant tells him the organization is facing a problem concerning knowledge management. Because the general manager is a fairly down-to-earth person, he has trouble understanding the recent knowledge management hype. But after an explanation by the consultant, he starts to see the advantage of the suggested approach. However, he sticks to his opinion that the company should remain level-headed. He wants to look for solutions that are mainly at the operational level, and wants to make optimal use of ICT, information provision, and the possibilities offered by the organization.

Budgeting

For five years, a budgeting system is used because this is stressed by the company's auditor. The general manager sees the practical advantages offered by the system, but it does entail a lot of hassle. The head of administration prepares the budget on an annual basis. Because the head of production at location A has the best overview due to his past experience, he supplies the administrator with the necessary budgeting information. By making a few calls, he collects the most relevant information from his colleagues and passes this on to the administrator. The administrator estimates the remainder of the information based on data from the past. The sales department does not provide any budgeting information. The head of administration reports to the general manager twice a month, mostly one month after the conclusion of the relevant period.

Administration

Administration is responsible for bookkeeping, payroll, and the complete accounts payable administration. Each year, the auditor relates these accounts to factory accounts. Requests for information have increasingly kept the head of administration from his work. He has made a complaint about this to the general manager.

Special cases, such as an overview of tangible fixed assets, are kept on memorandum accounts (i.e. not integrated in the accounting system).

Automation

The head of the automation department is a very service-minded person. He has a good record for predicting users' demands. Therefore, he is the person to decide on the priority of automation projects. Users' requests for changes in software are given to the programmer. Unfortunately, implementing changes takes a long time. Changes in software necessitated by program failures are mostly made directly by the operator.

Every month, the head of the automation department distributes the password changes to the key officers. Because there has been a recent fire in the computing centre, a number of files have been lost. The solution consisted of inputting 20,000 invoices again and one program had to be written anew.

Warehouse

The warehouse managers make their purchases based on the level of inventory. At the auditor's request, the warehouse managers take stock once a year at year end. The inventory accounts are kept by the warehouse managers. There is a considerable backlog. A lot of purchases concern amounts up to €1,000 and are paid in cash by the warehouse managers because of the discount for cash payment.

Production

The production planning department plans production and controls its progress. On a daily basis and per production order, the production managers report on the actual usage of raw and auxiliary materials, man and machine hours, as well as the quantities produced.

The head of factory accounts analyses production results in consultation with the production planning department and the responsible production managers. On a weekly basis, he informs the general manager about his analysis of capacity and efficiency variance for each department.

Sales

The sales department keeps the accounts receivable, since it has to be able to quickly judge buyers' solvency. Production and sales blame each other for inventories that are sold out. Exports have increased somewhat. Most of the time, exports are given priority over other orders. Partly due to this phenomenon, the number of orders that are late is increasing.

Research and Development

This department is concerned with the research and development of new computer games, party games, and puzzles.

On an annual basis, a number of new computer games are marketed. Considering technological developments, the duration of computer games is limited and prices erode fast.

The production and sales rights of the party games are under licence to national and foreign games producers. For this licensing, MarioToys receives a once-only compensation for a number of games. For the other party games, the company receives an amount per game that is sold.

Other

The general manager has been increasingly hard to get hold of lately, because he is in frequent contact with the unions and the workers' council. This is a problem since all financial decisions regarding transactions exceeding €1,000 need to be taken by him. Fortunately, the department managers have acknowledged the practical problem of the general manager's absence. Therefore, they sign the decisions themselves. The accounts payable administration is responsible for processing all transactions in the accounts payable file. The administrator produces a payment disk and sends it to the bank. The company has had a big dispute with its bank when the liquidity deficit amounted to €3,000,000 last August. The matter was taken care of by increasing the interest rate by 1% in favour of the bank.

Assignment

1. List the threats to the control of the business processes within this organization. Use the following two dimensions to present your solution in the comprehensive contingency framework:
   - domains (business, information and communication, information and communication technology);
   - strategy formulation versus strategy implementation.
2. Indicate the exposure to each of these threats.
3. For each threat, provide control solutions.

Comprehensive Case 4

Easy Living

Easy Living is a housing corporation that owns about 15,000 houses for rental purposes. Daily maintenance (predominantly repairs as a result of customer complaints) is done at the corporation's own expense. Major maintenance is outsourced under the condition that the maintenance plans, the improvement plans, and the plans for building new houses are drawn up by the corporation itself.

The board of the corporation primarily engages in oversight activities. The executive committee is chaired by the chief executive officer and further consists of the chief technical officer and the chief financial officer. Besides the executive committee, the following departments exist:

- technical department;
- administration and automation;
- projects (for planning and control of maintenance, improvement, and new housing);
- rental;
- facilities (including the post room, reception desk, copy service, and canteen);
- personnel department.

The technical department consists of about 50 employees who are occupied with the daily maintenance of the houses. For the purpose of these activities, this department has a number of trucks at its disposal. These trucks contain the necessary tools and materials. The administration and automation department consists of about 10 employees who are responsible for accounts receivable (including the rents), accounts payable, inventory records (including the houses), general ledger, project records, and the payroll records. There is a local area network which is functionally managed by the administration and automation department. The projects department consists of three project managers who are responsible for major repairs, improvements, and building of new houses. The project managers are supported by about 15 assistants. The rental department consists of about 5 employees. The facilities department consists of about 10 employees.

The corporation receives an annual government subsidy as a contribution to the operational costs of the houses. For that purpose, there are specific requirements for reporting to national and local authorities. The maintenance and service costs are allocated to tenants on the basis of a specific formula. Most tenants receive a rent subsidy. The corporation mediates in subsidy applications and bills tenants who make use of this service for a fixed annual amount. Rent subsidies are directly paid to the corporation so that tenants only have to pay the monthly rent less the monthly subsidy. Since tenants frequently damage the houses, the corporation decided to insure all its houses a couple of years ago. The annual insurance premiums as well as the damage claims are substantial.

There are two types of building contract: fixed-fee contracts and actual-cost contracts. On executing fixed-fee projects, often additional or subtractive work is agreed. Actual-cost contracts are settled on the basis of post-calculation.

The company has an ERP system. This ERP system contains a module for project management. The corporation's policy is to integrate data processing as much as possible.

Assignment

Provide a general normative description of the internal controls.

Comprehensive Case 5

Oldeman

Introduction

Oldeman was founded in 1905 (by Mr G.J. Oldeman) as a supplier to the building industry in Belgium. Since its inception, the company has evolved from a trade firm into production and mining of river sand and gravel, transportation, and production of mortar and concrete products. The company has a strong position in all sectors of the building industry. It employs about 1,500 people, working in about 70 subsidiaries. The annual turnover of the group is about €400 million, with a balance sheet total of about €200 million.

Strategy

Oldeman continuously searches for expansion opportunities by means of external growth. It thereby focuses not only at Belgium, but also at neighbouring countries. In the company's current market, acquisition and investments are made aimed at increasing economies of scale. Competition in the building industry is severe, but there are differences between the sectors where Oldeman is active. Ten years ago, Oldeman established four strategic business units (SBUs) in order to gain competitive advantage:

- production and mining;
- trade and transport;
- mortar;
- concrete products.

Each subsidiary is embedded in one of these SBUs.

Culture

The organizational culture can best be characterized as conservative, commercial, and technique-oriented.

Organization

Oldeman has a management team consisting of the directors of two business units (one of which is the great-grandson of the founder), the company lawyer (secretary), and the chairman (a grandson of the founder). There is a board of outside directors chaired by another grandson of the founder. This board takes its responsibilities seriously and often questions policies and decisions made.

Production and Mining

This SBU mines sand, gravel, chippings, and limestone in Belgium and neighbouring countries. Production facilities embed the most recent technologies. Lately, it has become more and more clear that competitors are trying to enter this sector of the market. Oldeman's management knows that the acquisition of a permit to mine these raw materials may take between 10 and 15 years and, hence, is not really worried about the increasing competition. Also, management is not occupied with increasing pressures from society to apply concepts from sustainable management. However, it realizes that in the near future substitute raw materials must be found. Alternatives in this respect are concrete waste (strictly separate collection and storage is necessary), limestone pits in Germany (however, most of these pits are owned by the cement industry), sea gravel, and excavation of Norwegian and German mountains (however, strictly speaking, this is nothing more than applying traditional methods to other geographical locations).

Trade and Transport

Oldeman's tradition as a trade firm goes way back. Transportation activities used to be considered an integral element of operating the business. The basic principle has always been that the complete logistical process between production and customer must be controlled. To realize this, Oldeman has concluded long-term contracts with inland carrying traders and has made some major investments in trucks and vans. In order to make more efficient use of these vehicles, the company's management team considered offering transportation services to third parties as well. After having started preparations for these new activites, it appeared that things did not get off the ground as intended as a result of an inadequate internal organization and information provision. On the one hand, the management team recognized that internal organization and information must change in order to make the new strategy successful, but, on the other hand, they hesitated to provide the necessary financial resources for improvements. In addition, the transportation sector was faced with increasing regulations and expenses as a result of longer travel times, higher fuel prices, and various environmental charges.

Mortar

The company owns an interest in more than 30 mortar businesses in Belgium. This is about 40% of the whole market. Customer wishes are satisfied as much as possible by producing and transporting mortar. For that purpose, the fleet of trucks and vans is equipped such that mortar can even be delivered to places that are very difficult to reach. Innovations such as high-power concrete and auto-condensing concrete – frequently enter the market. In spite of the fact that Oldeman covers a great deal of the market, competition has been fierce. Oldeman has tried to get a grip on prices by systematically outsourcing certain activities and specializing in certain parts of the concrete market. Of course, this has consequences for its participation in mortar businesses and use of its trucks and vans.

Concrete Products

This series of products is wide-ranging, consisting of, among other things, precast concrete, piles, drains, tiles, kerbstones, ornamental paving and infrastructure for building and industrial projects. As a result of the great diversity of products within this SBU, Oldeman has moved itself into a position where competing is extremely difficult. In order to maintain its position in this market, the company has become involved in various small but specialized businesses. Many of the people who founded these businesses continue to manage them and are heavily involved in centralized decision making. One of the indicators of this skewed power concentration is the fact that many of these businesses use their own sales and delivery people. Oldeman should take over these activities.

Automation

The company still does not have an integrated information system. However, some of the companies Oldeman are involved in use their own ERP packages. For the consolidated annual report, data are provided as hard copy and manually input by head-office clerks.

Oldeman's management team recognizes that the Internet will have a major influence on business operations and that developments in this area will give the company a completely new position with respect to its competitors. In the near future, several business processes will make use of the internet and other forms of electronic data interchange (EDI), giving the company the incentive to reformulate its ICT strategy.

Assignment

1. List the threats to control of the business processes within this organization. Use the following two dimensions to present your solution in the comprehensive contingency framework:
   - domains (business, information and communication, information and communication technology);
   - strategy formulation versus strategy implementation.
2. Indicate the exposure to each of these threats.
3. For each threat, provide control solutions.

Use one comprehensive table to present your solution.

Comprehensive Case 6

Multistore

Introduction

Multistore is a wholesaler with a wide range of products including office supplies, consumer electronics, food, and household utensils. The company has 15 distribution centres all over Europe.

Marketing

The company has three main customer groups: chain retail stores, homes for the elderly, and small wholesalers. For each customer group, different prices apply. These prices change frequently. Periodically, the company has special discount programmes. During designated periods, prices are reduced by 5–15%.

Logistics

Customers place their order at the distribution centres. Dependent on specific arrangements with customers, delivery takes place daily, weekly or every two weeks.

Billing and Cash Collection

Transactions of regular customers are billed once a week. Transactions of incidental customers must be paid on delivery. All invoices are prepared at the head office. Invoices for chain retail stores and homes for the elderly are printed and mailed at the head office. Invoices for small retailers are printed and mailed at the distribution centres. Cash in payment of credit sales is received via the bank of Multistore's head office. Payment terms are eight days. On overrunning this term, interest is charged. Cash on delivery is paid to the truck drivers. Each month, the head office sends to all its customers a statement of accounts receivable as at the beginning of the month, received cash, and the new accounts receivable including the interest due.

Automation

Each of the distribution centres has its own minicomputer which is connected to the mainframe at the head office by means of a wide area network. Data storage is centralized in a database located at the head office.

Assignment

1. Name the most important computer files that are used in the minicomputer of the distribution centres. Give an indication of how records are laid out in these files and nominate the functionary who is authorized to update each element of these records. Note that updates made by a programmed procedure must also be taken into account.

2 What are the main characteristics of a central database like the one Multistore uses? Mention two advantages and two disadvantages of using central databases.

3 What risks can you identify with respect to storing and updating data at Multistore? Make a distinction between risks at the head office and risks at the distribution centres. What computer security controls must be applied to mitigate these risks?

4 Give a normative description of the procedures for processing cash receipts from debtors.

5 Give a normative description of the procedures for processing cash receipts by drivers.

Comprehensive Case 7

Mobitel

Mobitel is a provider of mobile telephone services in the Netherlands. The company has just been founded and is busy installing sites (transceivers) all over the Netherlands. Currently, coverage is about 50%. Due to substantial investment in new sites, there will soon be full coverage. However, in view of its deficient coverage in the first year, Mobitel aims to limit its activities in the consumer market. In this market, the company is striving for 50,000 subscriptions.

Products

Mobitel offers four different mobile subscription types. Dependent on the call frequency and the time of day, users can choose the most favourable subscription type.

In addition to mobile telephone services, Mobitel offers the following products:

- voicemail and short message services;
- call divert services (automatic connection to regular telephones);
- information services (travel and traffic, restaurants, weather, etc.);
- switch option (switching to a second call or starting a new call without ending the first call);
- telephone operator service (request the operator to dial a number).

International Roaming

Calling and being called abroad is referred to as international roaming. Mobitel has entered into contracts with a number of foreign providers of mobile telephone services for international roaming.

Distribution

Mobitel has made agreements with a variety of retailers for the resale of subscriptions and cellular telephones. These retailers place their order with Mobitel by means of e-mail or fax. Typically, orders consist of telephones, accessories, and SIM cards (Subscriber Identity Module). A subscriber can only make or receive a call when the SIM-card is inserted in the telephone. Ordered goods are delivered within one day together with the invoice. SIM cards have a value of €50 each. When a retailer has brought in a subscriber, Mobitel refunds this amount. In order to simplify administration of the cards, Mobitel considers giving them in consignment.

Retailers receive a fixed commission for each new subscriber they bring in. For each subscription type, a different amount of commission is paid. Subscribers are obliged to use the telephone they bought from Mobitel (by way of a retailer). For this purpose, a unique number (IMEI number) is assigned to each telephone and SIM card in order to check that the telephone has been bought from Mobitel.

Sometimes, all-in packages are sold. In this case, a so-called subsidy (a discount on the selling price) is granted provided the telephone is connected to the network within two months. The fixed commission for the retailer is lower for these all-in packages. If the telephone is not connected to the network within two months, the difference between the regular selling price and the discounted selling price is billed to the retailer.

Rates

There are three types of rate:

- a fixed entrance fee is charged to cover the cost of making the actual connection to the network; this fee does not differ between the various subscription types;
- a rate per call minute – a high rate for calls made between 8.00 a.m. and 8.00 p.m. and a low rate for calls made between 8.00 p.m. and 8.00 a.m;
- a monthly subscription rate that differs between each of the four subscription types.

The higher the monthly subscription rate, the lower the rate per call minute.

For each additional product, a specific set of rates is in place. For voicemail and short message services, regular rates per call minute are charged when voicemails are retrieved or text messages are sent. For call divert services, a special rate is charged. For information services, regular rates per call minute are charged as well as a fixed surplus for the payment of the fee of the information provider. For the switch option, regular rates per call minute are charged. For the telephone operator service, a fixed amount per request is charged. When a connection is made, the regular rates per call minute are charged.

When a user makes a phone call abroad, the rates of the local network operator are charged to the user by way of Mobitel. Mobitel receives a fixed provision percentage for these international roaming phone calls. When a user is called abroad, the rates of the local network operator are charged to him, whereas the caller is charged only for regular Dutch rates per call minute to a mobile telephone.

Because Mobitel's network does not have complete coverage, discount programmes are set up on a regular basis. The nature of these discount programs varies per period. Among the possibilities are discount on the entrance fee, discount on the subscription rate, discount on the rates per call minute, or a combination of these.

Organization

The following departments are in place:

- sales;
- administration and ICT;
- products (including the telephone help desk);
- billing;
- buying;
- technical maintenance department;
- logistics;
- customer services.

Mobitel has one central office in the Netherlands as well as a number of local maintenance stations.

Mobitel employs about 150 people. In the short run, the company will grow to about 400 employees. Most will be provided by means of temp agencies. If employees perform satisfactorily, they will obtain a permanent appointment after three months and they will then receive a fixed salary. Sales persons work in their own district. They receive a bonus for the net number of connections made by retailers in their district. The net number of connections is the number of new subscriptions minus the number of subscriptions cancelled in the last six months.

Assignment

Provide a general normative internal control description.

Comprehensive Case 8

Jean le Crocque

Introduction

Jean le Crocque (JLC) is an internationally renowned designer of household utensils. He is the founder of the company that carries his name. The companies' clients are manufacturers who do not have design expertise. They have JLC make designs for them which they then take into production.

Strategy

JLC strives for continuous renewal of the designs of its existing products. The design of completely new products is considered to be the core business of the company. Sometimes this is order-based, but occasionally designs are made at the the company's own risk. JLC has never performed any production activities itself.

Organization

Jean is the managing director of the company. Due to the fact that he founded the company and his charismatic leadership, decision making is heavily centralized. However, Jean's main interest lies in the commercial side of doing business. Under his supervision, the following departments are in place:

- controlling (one full-time controller);
- marketing (one full-time marketeer);
- design department (20 designers and a head designer).

The head designer has been with the company since its inception. He plans all activities and assigns tasks to the designers.

Orders

Orders are received for a single design or a small series of household utensils. For each order, a contract is written. There are two types of contract:

- For small orders, a fixed price is agreed. The manager does not make a formal precalculation, but makes an estimate based on his experience. He commits himself to the client for this price. From the offers the manager has made in the past, it can be seen that his estimates are almost always sufficient to cover the actual costs and the projected profit margin.
- Bigger orders are based on actual costs. JLC makes a rough estimate of the costs to be incurred per phase of the design process, and commits itself to account for the expenses at the completion of each phase. Per phase, a concept invoice is made. The manager reviews all the concept invoices and often makes substantial adjustments.

Two big clients have agreed a blanket order that guarantees a minimum annual turnover of design hours at reduced rates. The reduction typically is about 20% of the regular rates. These reduced rates will also hold for surpluses above the minimum annual turnover. The rates are adjusted annually. For all orders, it has been contractually agreed that a design is considered completed when the managers as well as the client have formally approved it.

New Strategic Developments

Jean has recently decided to start a new business initiative. He wants to develop new products, and have them produced and marketed for the account and risk of JLC. Because the company does not have the necessary experience to undertake actual manufacturing activities, the technical and financial risks of this initiative are considered high. In order to reduce these risks, JLC wants to outsource the production of these goods to a limited number of manufacturers. A second initiative is the insourcing of buying activities so that the quality of the materials bought for supply to the manufacturers can be tightly controlled. For this purpose, a warehouse has been rented from one of the main manufacturers which can be used for the storage of the materials. This warehouse is located in the centre of the Netherlands. It is operated by the manufacturer's warehouseman. It is agreed that the warehouseman maintains inventory records and is accountable to JLC for the inventory.

Implementation of the New Strategic Initiatives

A number of representatives are hired by JLC. They will visit potential clients for acquisition of new orders. For that purpose, they are given a catalogue with products that JLC has developed for its own account and risk.

For alignment of sales and production activities, a production coordinator has been hired. He invites offers from various manufacturers and chooses the manufacturer on the basis of time of delivery, price, and quality of the goods. The production coordinator draws up a contract for each production order. All the manufacturers in JLC's portfolio can supply all the required goods. In order to cut costs or reduce the time of delivery, the production coordinator does not always follow regular procedure. Instead, he tries to play off manufacturers against each other. He also monitors inventory at the warehouse.

Manufacturers, invoices are sent to the production coordinator. He checks them by dividing the total amount by the number of ordered articles. On checking, it regularly appears that manufacturers have combined two or more production orders on one invoice, whereas the production coordinator has allocated the total amount to just one order. Also, deliveries often exceed ordered amounts and the warehouseman has failed to inform the production coordinator about this.

Management in Distress

Jean is becoming a star. He makes appearances on TV commercials and talk shows and his private life is a regular item in the tabloids. As a result of his outside activities, he is less visible in the company. So far, nothing has gone wrong, but some employees are starting to worry about the negligence of their manager. They argue that this might become a problem since Jean has never delegated any of his managerial tasks.

Assignment

1. List the threats to control of the business processes in this organization. Use the following two dimensions to present your solution in the comprehensive contingency framework:
   - domains (business, information and communication, information and communication technology);
   - strategy formulation versus strategy implementation.
2. Indicate the exposure to each of these threats.
3. For each threat, provide control solutions.

Comprehensive Case 9

Flashy New Sites

Flashy New Sites (FNS) is an Internet service provider. Subcribers can access the Internet via FNS with their dial-up account using a computer, a modem, and canned software. FNS offers several pages with a broad scope of information, such as weather reports, exchange rates, games, and advertisements. In addition, FNS provides links to other websites and e-mail services. FNS employs about 50 people.

FNS has a customer department that canvasses for new subscribers and maintains a help desk for the technical problems of clients. The help desk consists of a number of technically educated employees, who can answer clients' questions by telephone. The telephone number of FNS is a commercial number. The client is charged a fee per minute by way of the telephone bill. FNS receives a fixed percentage of these revenues.

Canvassing is done by means of a free telephone number that is advertised in computer magazines and journals. Additionally, FNS provides complimentary CD-ROMS to computer retailers as add-ons to the computers they sell.

There are two rates: a low fixed subscription rate with a high rate per minute access time, and a high fixed subscription rate with unlimited free access time. The subscription rate is billed in advance at the beginning of each month. The access time is billed at the beginning of the subsequent month. If a client fails to pay in on time, his user ID is blocked, as a result of which logging on is impossible. After having received the payment, the client is connected again at no charge. However, in that case, there will be no refund of forgone access time.

Competition among Internet service providers is severe. Therefore, FNS gives discounts to current clients for bringing in new clients. FNS has a commercial department that deals with advertisements to be placed on FNS's website. The rates per advertisement are mainly based on the number of site visitors. This is a relatively important source of revenue. Advertisers pay a fixed amount per advertisement per period.

There is an IS infrastructure department that maintains the computers for the dial-up facilities. Furthermore, this department has arranged with a national telephone provider that subscribers can always log on via a local telephone number. For that purpose, a large virtual stock of call minutes is bought from this national telephone provider. FNS has the required hardware and software in place to measure the usage of call minutes. Connection to the World Wide Web is obtained via another central Internet service provider, for which purpose a fixed capacity line is hired. This line is rented at a fixed annual amount which is independent of the intensity of data traffic.

The development department monitors the rapid technological developments concerning the Internet. Only a small part of the department's capacity consists of employees with a fixed labour contract. The remaining personnel needs are covered by temporary employees.

Clients demand the latest technology with respect to modems, software, etc. Threats such as viruses and hackers urge FNS to take information security measures. The development department determines what technologies FNS should apply.

An important condition for success is the speed and availability of the Internet connection. The speed is predominantly determined by the backbone of the Internet service provider. The capacity of this backbone is fixed annually. The availability of the connection is dependent on the number of outside lines that FNS has at its disposal. These lines require substantial investment in hardware. This hardware has a limited economic life of about one year.

The financial system is integrated with the other systems. An external vendor has provided this package on a turnkey basis. This vendor also does maintenance. An external auditor has certified the package.

Assignment

Provide a general normative internal control description.

Comprehensive Case 10

Metropolis

Metropolis is a medium-sized city that uses Internet applications to improve services for its inhabitants. The following Internet-related activities are employed:

- information provision and public relations;
- electronic services;
- local democracy (especially polls).

Furthermore, use is made of intranet applications for communication between several local and national authorities for internal work processes.

Information Policy

The city has a clear policy with respect to its information provision and information systems. The basic goal of this information policy is to strive for ICT proliferation at all levels within the municipality. The basic condition in trying to accomplish this goal is that the technical specifications of security and logistics of Internet and intranet application must be standardized. Also, Metropolis strives for as much transparency as possible for its inhabitants and other stakeholders. ICT can enable this transparency.

Operational Problems

The managerial information provision and administrative organization of Metropolis have their specific difficulties in implementing the Internet and intranet applications as intended. An important factor is compliance with laws and regulations that have not yet been adjusted for contemporary ICT developments. An example of the latter is the non-recognition of an electronic signature by the legislature. Another example is the recording of reaction times. There are still no management guidelines on this issue. However, uncodified Internet rules prescribe that an acknowledgement must be sent within one day after receipt of an electronic message. Of course, the official critical terms of general municipality law are applicable. Furthermore, the policy of ICT-proliferation is often difficult to implement.

Information and Public Relations

Metropolis is not the only city that has an Internet site for information and public relations. Many cities, some of them very small, have an Internet site that contains information about that city. Often, it is possible to ask questions or make suggestions to a civil servant. Some cities, Metropolis included, publish public information via the website. This concerns by-laws, memo's from the city council, minutes of council meetings, and reports of advisory committees. The periods over which this information may be retrieved varies between six months and five years. Furthermore, all manner of brochures about Metropolis and affilliated cities may be ordered via the website.

E-business

All standardized municipal services may be requested and sometimes delivered via the website. The following services, especially are facilitated by the Internet:

- retrieval of data from the civil administration and the register of real property;
- registration for municipal duties;
- application for building permits, travel documents, and the like;
- reservation of marriage dates, including the option to broadcast the ceremony via the Internet;
- objections against municipal duties and ongoing plans;
- reporting changes of address;
- retrieval of information about job openings and the possibility to apply for jobs;
- registration for public tenders;
- giving orders to collect garbage;
- reporting deficiencies in public sites and lodging complaints;
- notifying the police of small crimes (stolen bikes, vandalism, etc.);
- retrieval of housing information.

Sometimes, transactions resulting from these Internet activities require a real signature. The Internet form is then printed by the citizen, filled out, undersigned, and sent by regular mail. If there are financial consequences to an Internet transaction, they are handled by a hard-copy invoice and payment by bank transfer, cheque, or cash. Payment may be done before or after delivery of the service. This is dependent on the creditworthiness of the citizen and the maximum acceptable credit risk for the transaction. If the credit risk is too high, then an alternative procedure is followed and execution of an order will only take place after the required payment has been received. Partly because of this, there are fixed rates for transactions and/or fixed advance payments or bails.

Local Democracy

The local authorities are aware of the fact that one of the most interesting challenges of the Internet in relation to municipal matters is enhancement of local democracy. Currently, relevant political decisions are available on Metropolis's website. However, this is unsatisfactory because published decisions invoke reactions from citizens. If decisions have already been made, increased transparency is illusory because adjustments are no longer possible. The city council considers a proactive approach to decision making a matter of great importance. Therefore, citizens' opinions must be collected in advance of the city council making decisions. A simple example of this is to take note of the contents of the website (citizens' opinions, needed information, irrelevant information, etc.). The local authorities also want to put questionnaires on the website in addition to regular paper and pencil questionnaires for citizens who do not have an Internet connection. Local democracy may also be enhanced by opening a discussion board for public discussions on municipal matters between citizens, the city council, and the mayor and aldermen. Themes that may be discussed include new plans and projects, local drugs policy, and long-term visions. Furthermore, a weekly publication about working documents in progress for polling purposes is strived for. Of course, there are several problems with such an interactive approach to municipal decision making (e.g. impossibility of reconciling all opposed interests, financial and regulatory conditions, the fact that political primacy will remain in the hands of the official authorities). Ultimately, voting for the usual national and local elections and opinion polls will take place via the Internet. However, the city council considers this a distant goal because there are still many regulatory issues to be resolved.

Assignment

1. List the threats to control of the business processes in this organization. Use the following two dimensions to present your solution in the comprehensive contingency framework:
   - domains (business, information and communication, information and communication technology);
   - strategy formulation versus strategy implementation.
2. Indicate the exposure to each of these threats.
3. For each threat, provide control solutions.

Use one comprehensive table to present your solution.

Comprehensive Case 11

Paint It Black

Paint It Black (PIB) develops and produces all kinds of paint. PIB is a family-owned company, founded by the grandfather of the current director/owner. The company sells paint in cans of different sizes. Customers are painters and specialized paint retailers. In addition, PIB is getting into the market of large do-it-yourself stores. PIB has negotiated blanket contracts with these do-it-yourself stores for guaranteed purchases and quick deliveries. PIB's turnover amounts to €25,000,000 annually. Its annual profit is about €500,000.

The following departments are in place under the management of director/owner Art Biggs:

- management secretariat (1 person);
- laboratory (6 persons);
- purchasing department (6 persons);
- factory, consisting of the production planning department and the production department (25 persons);
- warehouse, consisting of the raw materials warehouse and the finished products warehouse (6 persons);
- sales, consisting of an internal service department and external service department (15 persons);
- financial administration (10 persons).

The tasks of these departments are as follows:

Management Secretariat
The task of the secretariat is to support the director/owner. The secretary is a well-educated person who has been with the company since Art Biggs took over.

Laboratory
The laboratory develops new types of paint. To keep track of new trends and colours, the laboratory frequently meets with the sales department. When developing new paints, the company has to comply more and more with rigid environmental laws and regulations. Furthermore, the laboratory determines the operations list (including the bill of materials) together with the factory.

Purchasing
Raw materials are purchased from different vendors. All potential vendors and their products are recorded in a vendor file.

Factory
Every week, the production planning department prepares the production schedule for the next week. Lately, the sales department has been receiving more and more rush orders from large do-it-yourself stores.

There are four production lines within the production department. The production process mainly entails the mixing of raw materials (e.g. colours, acrylic, etc.) in accordance with the operations list. Finally, the finished products are canned. Production lines are almost completely automated.

Assignment

1 Within PIB, there are three decision levels: decision making for strategic planning, decision making for management control, and decision making for operational control. Describe the differences between these levels and give an example of a decision that has to be made within PIB at each of these levels.
2 A number of threats can be identified with respect to the production process of PIB. Mention three of these threats and indicate briefly how these threats can be mitigated by means of control measures.

The production process within PIB is governed by an automated planning and control system. An important disadvantage of this system is that there is no integration with the procurement system and the warehouse system. As a result, the production department often runs out of raw materials. Director Art Biggs has read some papers on ERP systems (enterprise resource planning). According to his advisor from consulting firm Megalomania, the implementation of such a system will lead to better alignment between the production process and the ordering system, and hence to uninterrupted production.

Assignment

3 Give a global indication of how the selection and implementation of an ERP system at PIB should take place.
4 Mention four advantages that PIB could achieve by implementing an ERP system.

Art decided to implement the ERP system and, after a while, it appeared to work properly. As a result of the implementation, the traditional functional orientation of the internal organization has been abandoned. This structure seemed rather archaic and inefficient. It was necessary to adopt a more market-based approach, one that takes more account of the specific requirements of customers. PIB distinguishes three customer groups: traditional specialized paint stores, large do-it-yourself stores, and industrial businesses (automobiles and the like). The three customer groups are profit centres in the sense that they are accountable for their turnover and financial results. Art Biggs decided to take more of a back seat in the new arrangement and restricted his function to policy making and management by coaching. Although appealing, this did not work out the way he wanted. He feels that he is withheld relevant information and that the three customer groups do not cooperate in the company's interest.

Assignment

5 PIB is considering applying data warehousing on top of the ERP system. The functionality of data mining especially seems interesting. What are the advantages for PIB of data warehousing, and data mining in particular?

Almost every individual within PIB makes use of the ERP system. The R&D people (formerly the laboratory) form an exception. They do not use the system because they find the provided information irrelevant. For the development and testing of new paints, the laboratory increasingly cooperates with large customers, providers of raw materials, and other paint manufacturers. The R&D people believe that groupware could be supportive of their tasks.

Assignment

6 Indicate and motivate what functionality of groupware could be of use to the R&D people of PIB.

7 Explain why most groupware applications cannot be developed by means of a traditional, linear system development methodology.

Comprehensive Case 12

Confection Business

Introduction

A Dutch clothing manufacturer solely produces ladies' coats which are supplied to a few wholesalers and to a large number of independent clothing stores in the Benelux countries. Seen in the light of the seasonal nature of sales, it is customary for buyers to place their orders (so-called pre-orders) on the basis of presented lines. Expectations regarding fashion trends play an important role in compilation of carried lines. There are two lines: spring collection and autumn collection. Each line consists of about 20 items, each of which is available in a few designs and a large number of sizes (stock-keeping units).

Organization

The organization employs about 250 people and is managed by the commercial director and the financial director. The following departments exist:

- production, including the production planning department (200 employees);
- buying and styling (6 employees);
- sales (20 employees);
- warehouse and shipping (6 employees);
- administration (5 employees);
- automation (3 employees).

Buying and Styling

This department is responsible for the design of carried lines as well as for the buying of drapery. Buying takes place in the Netherlands as well as abroad. Delivery of drapery takes four to ten weeks. Lining and accessories are only bought in the Netherlands and have very short delivery times. The design drawings are recorded in the computer system. These drawings are used by the production department to manufacture the coats.

Sales

This department takes care of advertising and publicity, order processing, and billing. The lines for a certain season are settled in due time before the season starts and are made public by means of fashion shows and catalogues. After these presentations, orders are placed by buyers within three months. These orders account for about two-thirds of annual sales. In case of disappointing sales, certain items or designs may be taken out of the collection. In that case, running orders for these items or designs are cancelled by the clothing business. For orders that are placed after three months (sequel orders), the prices of the coats are considerably higher.

Production
The production cycle starts after the orders have been received. For sequel orders, production takes place on the basis of stock available. The production process starts with the cutting of the drapery on the basis of the design drawings. This is done by means of fully automated cutting machines in the cutting department. Subsequently, the cut drapery is sewed and the lining attached in a large production hall. The coat is then completed by making buttonholes and pockets, pressing and attaching buttons, etc. Many activities are done by machines that require manual throughput of drapery. At the end of the production process, the coats are examined in a quality control department. If deemed necessary, modifications are made.

Deliveries
Deliveries are concentrated in a two-month period for each season. For the spring season, this period ends on 31 March and, for the autumn season, this period ends on 30 September. Delivery of sequel orders takes place six weeks after these dates. Billing to customers takes place on delivery. Domestic customers must pay within 14 days after delivery, foreign customers within 30 days. Transportation is outsourced.

Financing
The financing needs of the company fluctuate in accordance with the seasonal movements of sales. For that purpose, the bank has granted a flexible short-term credit facility that is linked to the trend in sales, inventories, accounts receivable, and accounts payable. The financial director is responsible for maintaining contact with the banker and supplies a quarterly financial report on financial results and expectations with respect to the cash position.

Recent Developments
As a result of the ongoing increase in personnel costs, favourable wage developments in southern Europe, and enhanced transportation opportunities, the management has been considering moving part of the production process (excluding cutting) to Portugal. Management is considering hiring local personnel, training them, and deploying them in the production process under Dutch supervision. The shipment of raw materials and semi-manufactured products will be done by a specialist shipping agent.

Assignment

1 Provide a normative internal control description with respect to the production activities within this business.

2 Provide an analysis of the information requirements of the financial director for monitoring the cash position of the business.

3 Give an indication of the changes in the information requirements of the Dutch management as a result of moving some production activities to Portugal.

Comprehensive Case 13

Company in Agrarian Products

Introduction

A large company dealing in agrarian products such as grain, oilseed, and oil engages in trade as well as transport by sea and transfer by train.

Trade

Products of different qualities are traded. The company purchases mainly from large agrarian producers (annual blanket-order contracts, at fixed prices). Additionally, the company purchases on international exchanges, at current market prices. These market prices follow a highly fluctuating course. A number of products are traded on futures markets. All prices are quoted in US dollars. Purchase prices do not include transport expenses.

Goods are sold to domestic processing companies, at sales prices quoted in Dutch guilders, carriage paid. Annual blanket-order contracts as well as once-only contracts at current market prices are used.

Transport and Transfer

For transport, storage, and transfer the company owns 15 seagoing vessels, approximately 100 silos in large international seaports, and about 100 train wagons and trucks for container transport.

In addition, the company has entered into contracts with a number of shipowners and carriers to guarantee annual purchase of transport and storage capacity at fixed, predetermined rates. Possible shortages or surpluses of transport and storage capacity are resolved by renting or letting on a daily basis, for transport on the so-called freights market. Prices may differ considerably from regular internal rates. These rates are revised every three months.

Automation

The company is highly computerized. Most transactions take place by means of electronic data communication. The policy of management is aimed at stimulating deployment of interorganizational information systems in order to be as competitive as possible.

Assignment

1 Provide a normative internal control description (by means of headlines) for:
   (a) the trade process; and
   (b) the transport and transfer process.

2 Provide an analysis of the information requirements for this business at different managerial levels. Base your analysis on identification of critical success factors. Indicate what data must be recorded in what files for this information provision.

Comprehensive Case 14

Insurance Company

Introduction
An insurance company insures privately owned cars. The following departments exist:

- acquisition and agent contracts;
- client administration;
- damage;
- automation;
- financial administration and controlling.

New Insurances
Third-party insurance is the basis for any car insurance policy. This insurance covers the sustained losses caused by the client's car to properties of third parties. The premium for this type of insurance is dependent on the weight of the car. It is possible to extend coverage of third-party insurance with the following insurances:

- Bodywork insurance that covers the risks of damage to the client's car. The premium is dependent on the value of buying a new car.
- Passenger insurance that covers the risk of injury to passengers. The premium is a fixed amount per policy.

A discount may be given on the total amount of the insurance premiums as a result of a no-claims bonus. The exact level of the discount is dependent on the number of years that the insured has been driving his car without claiming damages. New insurance may start on any day and is valid for a period of one year.

The selling of insurance is done by agents. They receive a bonus for each newly underwritten policy. This bonus is a fixed percentage of the premium.

Application for insurance is done by the applicant by means of filling out and signing a standard proposal form. This form is submitted via the agent to the insurance company. One of the questions on this form concerns permission to directly debit the premium automatically from the client's bank account. About 60% of the insured are willing to give this permission. The remaining insured pay by means of a bank transfer form.

The process of underwriting and policy processing is highly automated. During the night, the new policies and the new documentation are printed. The following print-outs are also done:

- premium receipts by means of bank transfer forms;

- orders for direct debit via the central clearing institute.

Insurance documents are sent to the insured immediately after acceptance. The policy conditions contain a section that states that insurance is only valid after the insurance premium has been paid.

Damage

Damage is integrally handled by the insurance company. This process is highly automated.

When an insured vehicle is damaged, the insurance company is notified by means of a standard form. This form contains a description of how the accident happened. The form is signed by all parties who were involved in the accident. In addition, the insured is required to report on the nature of the (visible) damage as well as on the presumed guilty party. He also has to report on the involvement of the police after the accident took place. Damage is only covered when a completed form is received by the insurance company.

Every received form is recorded in an electronic damage file. This damage file contains all the information with respect to the damage notification. Guilt establishment is further evaluated by the insurance company on the basis of the form and, if present, the police report.

There are two kinds of damage: personal injuries and car damage.

Personal injury is suffered by a person who has been involved in an accident and may lead to compensation of the costs of medical care and material and psychological injury. To assess the extent of the injury, and the relationship between the claimed injury and the accident, a medical expert is hired. Payment for medical expenses is generally paid to the insurer of the person who suffered damage. In that case, that insurer bills the insurance company for this amount. Compensation for material and psychological injury is directly paid to the person who suffered the injury. Personal injury is covered on the basis of third-party insurance or on the basis of the passenger insurance dependent both on where the passenger was sitting during the accident and on the specific circumstances under which the accident took place.

Car damage is defined as damage to any vehicle involved in the accident. This may be the insured's vehicle, but also another vehicle if the insured is found guilty of the accident. Before payments for sustained losses are made, a loss adjuster is hired who assesses the extent of the damage. Repairs may not take place before the loss adjuster has assessed the extent of the damage. Losses to the insured's vehicle are only paid when bodywork insurance has been taken out. These damages may be paid either to the owner of the vehicle or to the repair company. Losses to another vehicle are paid on the basis of third-party insurance. This damage may (when the insured is found guilty of the accident) be paid to another insurance company (as long as bodywork insurance has been taken out) or to a third party (repair company or owner of the other vehicle). If the damage is paid to another insurance company, then the loss adjuster will not be hired by the insurance company. Instead an invoice will be sent by the other insurance company to compensate them for hiring the loss adjuster.

Assignment

1 Provide a normative internal control description with respect to both new insurance and the integrity of the insured clients' file.
2 Provide a normative internal control description with respect to the handling of damages regarding:
   - car damage;
   - personal injury in so far as this concerns medical costs.

No attention should be paid to:

- problems of adjustments to current policies, own risks, and additional costs like the ones made for towing the vehicle away;
- the reimbursement of automatic cash withdrawals.

BIBLIOGRAPHY

Accounting Education Change Committee (1990). *AECC Statement* (No 1).

AICPA (1994). *Improving Business Reporting – Customer Focus* (Report of the Special Committee on Financial Reporting [Jenkins Report]). Jersey City, NJ: AICPA.

AICPA (1998). Top five competencies. Paper presented at *CPA Vision 2000*. Jersey City, NJ: AICPA.

AICPA (1998). Inside AICPA: WebTrust rolls on. *Journal of Accountancy*. February, 98.

AICPA (1997). *Report of the Special Committee on Assurance Services*. Jersey City, NJ: AICPA.

American Accounting Association (1986). The future structure, content, and scope of accounting education. Preparing for the expanding profession. *Issues in Accounting Education*, Spring. Sarasota, FL: AAA.

Anthony, R.N. (1965). *Planning and Control Systems. A Framework for Analysis*. Boston: Harvard Graduate School of Business.

Baker, C.R. (1998). A discussion of theoretical approaches to management information and control systems. Paper presented at *Proceedings of ECAIS*. Maastricht: Datawyse.

Bell, T.B., F.O. Marrs, I. Solomon, and H. Thomas (1997). *Auditing Organizations Through a Strategic-Systems Lens*. KPMG Peat Marwick.

Benbasat, I. and A. Dexter (1979). Value and events approaches to accounting: An experimental evaluation. *The Accounting Review*, October.

Blocher, E.J., R. Roussey, and B.H. Ward (1988). The subject matter of auditing. In A.R. Abdel-khalik and I. Solomon (eds), *Research Opportunities in Auditing: The Second Decade* (pp. 133–153). Sarasota, FL: American Accounting Association.

Boisot, M.H. (1986). Markets and hierarchies in a cultural perspective. *Organization Studies*, 7.

Boisot, M.H. (1995). *Information Space. A Framework for Learning in Organizations, Institutions and Culture*. London: Routledge.

Boisot, M.H. (1998). *Knowledge Assets. Securing Competitive Advantage in the Information Economy*. Oxford: Oxford University Press.

Brackney, K.S. and G.L. Helms (1996). A survey of attestation practices. *Auditing: A Journal of Practice and Theory*, **15**(2), 85–98.

Brecht, H.D. and M.P. Martin (1996). Accounting information systems: The challenge of extending their scope to business and information strategy. *Accounting Horizons*, **10**(4), 16–22.

Breed, N.F., D.J. Out, and O. Tettero (1994). *Informatiebeveiliging* (Onderzoeksprogramma telematica gidsprojecten). Alphen aan den Rijn/Diegem, Netherlands: Samsom Bedrijfsinformatie.

Carcello, J.V., W.F. Messier, and D.N. Ricchiute (1998). *Research Opportunities in Assurance Services* (Working paper).

Certified General Accountants Association (1996). *Professional Practice, Analysis and Evolution* (A report to the CGA Canada Education Committee), October.

Choo, C.W. (1997). *The Knowing Organization. How Organizations Use Information to Construct Meaning, Create Knowledge, and Make Decisions*. Oxford: Oxford University Press.

Chow, C.W., Y. Kato, and K.A. Merchant (1996). The use of organizational controls and their effects on data manipulation and management myopia: A Japan vs U.S. comparison. *Accounting, Organizations and Society*, **21**(2/3).

Ciborra, C.U. (1993). *Teams, Markets and Systems. Business Innovation and Information Technology*. Cambridge: Cambridge University Press.

Clegg, S.R. (1990). *Modern Organizations – Organization Studies in the Postmodern World*. London: Sage Publications.

Coase, R.H. (1937). The Nature of the Firm. *Economica*, **4**.

COSO (1994). *Internal Control – Integrated Framework* (report of the Committee of Sponsoring Organizations of the Treadway Commission. Executive Summary).

CPA Journal (1996). The CPA Journal symposium on the future of assurance services. *The CPA Journal*, May, 14–28.

Craig, Jr, J.L. (1994). Robert Elliott: Leading the profession. *The CPA Journal*, October, 18–24.

Craig, Jr, J.L. (1994). Serving the profession's assurance function: An interview with AICPA vice-president Dan Guy. *The CPA Journal*, January, 36–40.

Craig, Jr, J.L. (1998). Survival of the fittest. *The CPA Journal*, January, 16–23.

Cullinan, C.P. (1998). Evidence of non-Big 6 market specialization and pricing power in a niche assurance service market. Paper presented at the *Waterloo Assurance Services Research Symposium, March 1998*.

Cyert, R.M. and J.G. March (1963). *A Behavioral Theory of the Firm*. Englewood Cliffs, NJ: Prentice-Hall.

Davenport, T.H. and L. Prusak (1998). *Working Knowledge. How Organizations Manage What They Know*. Boston: Harvard Business School Press.

Dunn, C.L. and W.E. McCarthy (1997). The REA accounting model: Intellectual heritage and prospects for progress. *Journal of Information Systems*, Spring.

Drucker, P.F. (1988). The coming of the new organization. *Harvard Business Review* (January–February).

Drucker, P.F. (1992). The new society of organizations. *Harvard Business Review* (September–October).

Drucker, P.F. (1993). *Post-Capitalist Society*. Oxford: Butterworth Heinemann.

Earl, M.J. (1996). *Knowledge as Strategy. The Potential Power of Data and the Human Factor in Data Management*. London Business School.

ECAIS (1998). *Proceedings of the First European Conference on Accounting Information Systems, Antwerp, Belgium*. Maastricht: Datawyse.

Edvinsson, L. and M.S. Malone (1997). *Intellectual Capital. Realizing your Company's True Value by Finding its Hidden Brainpower*. New York: Harper Business.

Elfring, T. and H.W. Volberda (1999). *New Directions in Strategy*. London: Sage Publications.

Elliott, R.K. (1994a). Confronting the future: Choices for the attest function. *Accounting Horizons*, **8**(3), 106–124.

Elliott, R.K. (1994b). The future of audits: The power of information technology is threatening the audit function. *Journal of Accountancy*, September, 74–82.

Elliott, R.K. (1995). The future of assurance services: Implications for academia. *Accounting Horizons*. **9**(4), 118–127.

Elliott, R.K. (1997). Assurance service opportunities: Implications for academia. *Accounting Horizons*, **11**(4), 61–74.

Elliott, R.K. (1998). Assurance services and the audit heritage. Paper presented at the *Waterloo Assurance Services Research Symposium, March*. Waterloo: University of Waterloo.

Elliott, R.K. and D.M. Pallais (1997). Are you ready for new assurance services? *Journal of Accountancy*, June, 47–51.

Elliott, R.K. and D.M. Pallais (1997). Build on your firm's strengths. *Journal of Accountancy*, August, 53–58.

Elliott, R.K. and D.M. Pallais, D.M. (1997). First: Know your market. *Journal of Accountancy*, July, 56–63.

Elliott, R.K. and D.M. Pallais (1997). To market, to market we go. *Journal of Accountancy*, September, 81–86.

Fargher, N.L. and A.A. Gramling (1996). A new market for attestation services: The performance presentation standards of the Association for Investment Management and Research. *Auditing: A Journal of Practice and Theory*, **15**(Suppl.), 72–91.

Fargher, N.L., L.R. Gorman, and M.S. Wilkins (1998). Timely industry information as an assurance service – evidence on the information content of the book-to-bill ratio. Paper presented at the *Waterloo Assurance Services Research Symposium, March*.

Fayol, H. (1949). *General and Industrial Management*. London: Pitman.

Fisher, J. (1995). Contingency-based research on management control systems: Categorization by levels of complexity. *Journal of Accounting Literature*, **14**, 24–53.

Galbraith, J. (1973). *Designing Complex Organizations*. Reading, MA: Addison-Wesley.

Gelinas, U.J., S.G. Sutton, and A.E. Oram (1999). *Accounting Information Systems* (4th edn). Cincinnati, OH: South-Western College Publishing.

Glover, S.M., D.F. Prawitt, and M.B. Romney (1999). Implementing ERP. *Internal Auditor*, February.

Goold, M. (1991). Strategic control in the decentralized firm. *Sloan Management Review*, **32**(2).

Gorry, G.A. and M.S. Scott Morton (1971). A framework for management information systems. *Sloan Management Review*, Fall, 55–70.

Grant, R.M. (1996a). Prospering in dynamically-competitive environments: Organizational capability as knowledge integration. *Organization Science*, **4** (July–August).

Grant, R.M. (1996b). Toward a knowledge-based theory of the firm. *Strategic Management Journal*, **17** (Winter Special Issue).

Grant. R.M. (1997). The knowledge-based view of the firm: Implications for management practice. *Long Range Planning*, **3** (June).

Grant, R.M. (1998). *Contemporary Strategy Analysis. Concepts, Techniques, Applications* (3rd edn). Malden: Blackwell.

Gray, G. and R. Debreceny (1998). *Electronic Commerce Assurance Services and Accounting Information Systems: A Review of Research Opportunities* (Working paper). Singapore: NTU.

Greenstein, M. and T. Feinman (1999). *Electronic Commerce: Security, Risk Management and Control*. Boston: Irwin McGraw-Hill.

Hamel, G. and C.K. Prahalad (1994). *Competing for the Future*. Boston: Harvard Business School Press.

Havelka, H. D., Sutton, S.G., and Arnold, V. (1998). A methodology for developing measurement criteria for assurance services: An application in information systems assurance. *Auditing A Journal of Practice and Theory*. **17**(Suppl.), 73–92

Hayek, F.A. (1945). The use of knowledge in society. *The American Economic Review*, **4** (September).

Helms, G.L. and K.S. Brackney (1998). Attestation services: Opportunity for practice growth. *The CPA Journal*, February, 50–53.

Henderson, J.C. and N. Venkatraman (1993). Strategic alignment: Leveraging information technology for transforming organizations. *IBM Systems Journal*, **32**(1), 4–16.

Hofstede, G.H. (1980). *Culture's Consequences: International Differences in Work-Related Values*. London. Sage Publications.

Holder, W. and K. Pincus (1997). *The Impact of Future Assurance Services on Accounting and Auditing Education* (working paper prepared for the AAA Auditing Section Task Force on Future Audit, Attest, and Assurance Services). Sarasota, FL: AAA.

Hollander, A., E.L. Denna, and J.O. Cherrington (1996). *Accounting, Information Technology, and Business Solutions*. Chicago: Irwin.

Holstrum, G. (1997). *Future Audit, Attestation, and Assurance Services: Overview of the Challenges for Accounting Education, Research and Practice* (working paper prepared for the AAA Auditing Section Task Force on Future Audit, Attest, and Assurance Services). Sarasota, FL: AAA.

Holstrum, G.L. and Hunton, J.E. (1997). New forms of assurance services for new forms of information: The global challenge for accounting educators. Paper presented at the *Eighth World Congress of Accounting Educators, Paris, October*. Tampa, FL: USF.

Hope, J. and T. Hope (1997). *Competing in the Third Wave. The Ten Key Management Issues of the Information Age*. Boston: Harvard Business School Press.

Hope, T. and J. Hope (1996). *Transforming the Bottom Line. Managing Performance with the Real Numbers*. London: Nicholas Brealey.

Horovitz, J.H. (1979). Strategic control: A new task for top management. *Long Range Planning*, **12**, June.

Hunton, J.E. and G.L. Holstrum (1998). The role of information systems auditors in WebTrust Assurance. *IS Audit & Control Journal*, **3**, 39–43.

IFAC, Education Committee (1998). *Information Technology in the Accounting Curriculum* (International Education Guideline #11 [IEG #11]). New York: IFAC.

IFAC, Education Committee (1998). *Competence-Based Approaches to the Professional Preparation of Accountants* (International Education Discussion Paper). New York: IFAC.

Inmon, W.H. (1996). *Building the Data Warehouse* (2nd edn). New York: Wiley.

Itami, H. (1987). *Mobilizing Invisible Assets*. Cambridge, MA: Harvard University Press.

Jaenicke, H.R. and Whittington, R. (1997). *Expansion of Assurance Services – Implications for the Profession* (working paper prepared for the AAA Auditing Section Task Force on Future Audit, Attest, and Assurance Services). Sarasota, FL: AAA.

Jenkins, B.P., P. Cooke, and P. Quest (1995). *An Audit Approach to Computers*. London: Institute of Chartered Accountants in England & Wales. Coopers & Lybrand.

Kaplan, R.S. and D.P. Norton (1992). The balanced scorecard, measures that drive performance. *Harvard Business Review*, **70**(1), January–February, 71–79.

Kaplan, R.S. and D.P. Norton (1996). *The Balanced Scorecard, Translating Strategy into Action*. Boston: Harvard Business School Press.

Keen, P.G.K. and G.L. Bronsema (1981). *Cognitive Style Research: A Perspective for Integration* (working paper). Sloan School of Management. Boston: MIT.

King, R.R. and R. Schwartz (1998). Planning Assurance Services. *Auditing: A Journal of Practice & Theory*, **17**(Suppl.), 9–36.

Kinney, W.R. (2000). *Information Quality Assurance and Internal Control for Management Decision Making*. Boston: Irwin/McGraw-Hill.

Koreto, R.J. (1997). In CPAs we trust. *Journal of Accountancy*, December, 62–64.

Langfield-Smith, K. (1997). Management control systems and strategy: A critical review. *Accounting, Organizations and Society*, **22**(2).

Laudon, K.C. and J.P. Laudon (2000). *Management Information Systems. Organization and Technology in the Networked Enterprise* (6th edn). Upper Saddle River, NJ. Prentice-Hall International Editors.

Learned, E.P., C.R. Christensen, K.R. Andrews, and W. Guth (1969). *Business Policy: Text and Cases*. Homewood, IL: Irwin.

Leenaars, J.J.A. (1995). Functiescheidingen in historisch en toekomstig perspectief. *MAB*, Maart.

Leonard-Barton, D. (1992). Core capabilities and core rigidities: A paradox in managing new product development. *Strategic Management Journal*, **13**, Special Issue, 111–125.

Levinthal, D.A. and J.G. March (1993). The myopia of learning. *Strategic Management Journal*, **14**, Special Issue, 95–112.

Libby, R. and J. Luft. (1993). Determinants of judgment performance in accounting settings: Ability, knowledge, motivation, and environment. *Accounting Organizations and Society*, **18**(5).

Lowe, E.A. (1971). On the idea of a management control system: Integrating accounting and management control. *The Journal of Management Studies*, **8**.

Lusk, E.J. (1979). A test of differential performance peaking for a disembedding task. *Journal of Accounting Research*, Spring.

MacDonald, A.P. (1970). Revised scale for ambiguity tolerance: Reliability and validity. *Psychological Reports*, **26**.

Maes, R. (1998). Short outline of a generic framework for information management. *Proceedings of ECAIS*. Maastricht: Datawyse.

March, J.G. (1991). Exploration and exploitation in organizational learning. *Organization Science*, **2**, 71–87.

McCarthy, W.E. (1979). An entity-relationship view of accounting models. *The Accounting Review*, October.

McCarthy, W.E. (1982). The REA Accounting Model: A generalized framework for accounting systems in a shared data environment. *The Accounting Review*, July.

Merchant, K.A. (1982). The control function of management. *Sloan Management Review*, Summer, 43–55.

Merchant, K.A. (1985). *Control in Business Organizations*. Boston: Pitman.

Merchant, K.A. (1998). *Modern Management Control Systems: Text and Cases*. Englewood Cliffs, NJ: Prentice-Hall.

Miller, D. and M. Chen (1994). Sources and consequences of competitive inertia: A study of the U.S. airline industry. *Administrative Science Quarterly*, **39**, 1–23.

Mintzberg, H. (1983). *Structure in Fives. Designing Effective Organizations*. Prentice-Hall International Editions.

Moscove, S.A., M.G. Simkin, and N.A. Bagranoff (2001). *Core Concepts of Accounting Information Systems* (7th edn). New York: Wiley.

Myers, P.S. (1996). *Knowledge Management and Organizational Design*. Oxford: Butterworth-Heinemann.

Nelson, R.R. and S.G. Winter (1982). *An Evolutionary Theory of Economic Change*. Cambridge, MA: Harvard University Press.

Newell, A., and H. Simon (1972). *Human Problem Solving*. Englewood Cliffs, NJ: Prentice-Hall.

Nimwegen, J. van, and E.O.J. Jans (1978). *Grondslagen van de Administratieve Organisatie*. Alphen aan den Rijn, Netherlands: Samsom Bedrijfsinformatie.

Nonaka, I. (1991). The knowledge-creating company. *Harvard Business Review* (November–December).

Nonaka, I. and H. Takeuchi (1995). *The Knowledge-Creating Company. How Japanese Companies Create the Dynamics of Innovation*. New York: Oxford University Press.

Noordam, P.G., J.B.B. van den Oever, and M.C. Kamermans (1996). *Handen en voeten aan de Administratieve Organisatie, Vastleggen gericht op analyse, ontwerp en beheersing*. Alphen aan den Rijn: Samsom Bedrijfsinformatie.

Ouchi, W.G. (1979). A conceptual framework for the design of organizational control mechanisms. *Management Science* (September).

Overbeek, P.L. and W.H.M. Sipman (1999). *Informatiebeveiliging* (2nd edn). 's-Hertogenbosch, The Netherlands: Uitgeverij Tutein Nolthenius.

Pallais, D.M. (1995). Positioning the audit function for growth. *Journal of Accountancy*, July, 14–15.

Penrose, E.T. (1959). *The Theory of Growth of the Firm*. New York: Wiley.

Peters, T.J. (1992). *Liberation Management*. London: Macmillan.

Peters, T.J. and R.H. Waterman (1982). *In Search of Excellence*. New York: Harper & Row.

Pfeffer, J. (1998). *The Human Equation. Building Profits by Putting People First*. Boston: Harvard Business School Press.

Polak, N.J. (1922). *Is een algemene Inrichtingsleer bestaanbaar?* Inleiding voor de veertiende Accountantsdag van het Nederlandsch Instituut van Accountants, September. Amsterdam: NIVA.

Porter, M.E. (1980). *Competitive Strategy: Techniques for Analyzing Industries and Competitors*. New York: Free Press.

Porter, M.E. (1985). *Competitive Advantage: Creating and Sustaining Superior Performance*. New York: Free Press.

Preble, J.F. (1992). Towards a Comprehensive System of Strategic Control. *Journal of Management Studies*, **29**(4).

Prusak, L. (1996). The Knowledge Advantage. *Strategy & Leadership*, March/April.

Quinn, J.B. (1992). *Intelligent Enterprise: A Knowledge and Service Based Paradigm for Industry*. New York: The Free Press.

Read, W.J. and Tomczyk, S. (1992). An examination of changes in the scope of services performed by CPA firms. *Accounting Horizons*, **6**(3), 42–51.

Ridgway, V.F. (1956). Dysfunctional consequences of performance measurements. *Administrative Science Quarterly*, December.

Roberts, H.J.E. (1998). Management accounting and control systems in the knowledge-intensive firm. Paper presented at the *21st Annual Congress of the European Accounting Association, Antwerp, Belgium, 6–8 April 1999*, Norway: Sand Viha.

Rockart, J.F. (1979). Chief executives define their own data needs. *Harvard Business Review*, **57**(2).

Romney, M.B. and P.J. Steinbart (2000). *Accounting Information Systems* (8th edn). Reading, MA: Addison-Wesley.

Roos, J., G. Roos, L. Edvinsson, and N.C. Dragonetti (1997). *Intellectual Capital. Navigating in the New Business Landscape*. Macmillan Business.

Saint-Onge, H. (1996). Tacit knowledge. The key to the strategic alignment of intellectual capital. *Strategy & Leadership*, March/April.

Sanchez, R. and A. Heene (1997). *Strategic Learning and Knowledge Management*. Chichester: Wiley.

Scheyögg, G., H. Steinmann. (1987). Strategic control: A new perspective. *Academy of Management Review*, **12**(1).

See, C., and Mock, T.J. (1999). The market for assurance services in Singapore. *Accounting and Business Review*, **6**(2), July.

Senge, P. (1990). The leader's new work: Building learning organizations. *Sloan Management Review*, Fall, 7–23.

Simons, R. (1994). How top managers use control systems as levers of strategic renewal. *Strategic Management Journal*, **15**.

Simons, R. (1995a). Control in an age of empowerment. *Harvard Business Review*, March–April, 80–88.

Simons, R. (1995b). *Levers of Control. How Managers Use Innovative Control Systems to Drive Strategic Renewal*. Boston: Harvard Business School Press.

Simons, R.H. (1999). *Performance Measurement and Control Systems for Implementing Strategy*, (1st edn). Englewood Cliffs, NJ: Prentice-Hall.

Sorter, G.H. (1969). An events approach to basic accounting theory. *The Accounting Review*, January.

Spencer, L.M. and S.M. Spencer (1993). *Competence at Work: Models for Superior Performance*. Chichester: Wiley.

Srivastava, R.P. and T.J. Mock (1998). A decision theoretic approach to webTrust Assurance Services. Paper presented at the *International Symposium on Audit Research, Sydney, June 1998*.

Starreveld, R.W., B. de Mare, and E. Joëls (1994). *Bestuurlijke Informatieverzorging* (4th edn, Deel 1). Alphen aan den Rijn: Samsom.

Starreveld, R.W., B. de Mare, and E. Joëls (1998). *Bestuurlijke Informatieverzorging* (4th edn, Deel 2a). Alphen aan den Rijn: Samsom.

Starreveld, R.W., B. de Mare, and E. Joëls (1998). *Bestuurlijke Informatieverzorging* (4th edn, Deel 2b). Alphen aan den Rijn: Samsom.

Sternheim, A. (1928). Administratieve inrichtingsleer en kostprijsberekening. Unpublished paper.

Stevenson, H.H. and D.E. Gumpert (1985). The heart of entrepreneurship. *Harvard Business Review*, **64**, March–April, 85–94.

Stewart, T.A. (1997). *Intellectual Capital. The New Wealth of Organizations*. London: Nicholas Brealey.

Sveiby, K.E. (1997). *The New Organizational Wealth. Managing and Measuring Knowledge-Based Assets*. San Francisco: Berrett-Koehler.

Taylor, F.W. (1911). *The Principles of Scientific Management*. New York: Harper & Row.

Teece, D.J., G. Pisano, and A. Shuen (1997). Dynamic capabilities and strategic management. *Strategic Management Journal*, **18**, 509–533.

Toffler, A. (1980). *Powershift: Knowledge, Wealth, and Violence at the Edge of the 21st Century*. New York: Bantam Books.

Ulrich, D. (1998). Intellectual capital = Competence × Commitment. *Sloan Management Review* (Winter).

Utterback, J.M. and W.J. Abernathy (1975). A dynamic model of process and product innovation. *Omega*, **3**(6), 639–656.

Uzumeri, M.V. and Tabor, R.H. (1997). Emerging management metastandards: Opportunities for expanded attest services. *Accounting Horizons*, **11**(1), 54–66.

Vecchio, R.P. (1991). *Organizational Behavior* (2nd edn). Fort Worth, TX: The Dryden Press/Harcourt Brace Jovanovich.

Volberda, H.W. (1996). Toward the flexible form: How to remain vital in hypercompetitive environments. *Organization Science*, **7**(4), 359–374.

Volberda, H.W. (1998). *Building The Flexible Firm: How to Remain Competitive*. Oxford: Oxford University Press.

Waller, W.S. and W.L. Felix (1984). The auditor and learning from experience: Some conjectures. *Accounting Organizations and Society*, **9**(3/4).

Wand, Y. and R. Weber (1990). An ontological model of an information system. *IEEE Transactions on Software Engineering*, November.

Weber, M. (1946). *From Max Weber: Essays in Sociology* (edited by H.H. Gerth and C. Wright Mills). New York: Oxford University Press.

Weber, R. (1999). *Information Systems Control and Audit*. Englewood Cliffs, NJ: Prentice-Hall.

Weggeman, M.C.D.P. (1997). *Inrichting en besturing van kennisintensieve organisaties*. Schiedam, Netherlands: Scriptum Management.

Wernerfelt, B. (1984). A resource-based view of the firm. *Strategic Management Journal*, **5**, 171–180.

Wijk, R.A. van and F.A.J. van den Bosch (1998). Knowledge characteristics of internal network-based forms of organizing. In S. Havlovic (ed.), Academy of Management Best Paper Proceedings.

Williamson, O.E. (1975). *Markets and Hierarchies*. Englewood Cliffs, NJ: Prentice-Hall.

GLOSSARY

Access control matrix: A computerized table containing the allowed combinations of users, actions, software modules, and data.

Access control: All those measures aimed at preventing logical access to an information system.

Accounting and administrative organization (AAO): The system of organizational measures with respect to data processing aimed at information provision for management, entity functionality, and accounting purposes.

Accounting control: *See* Information control.

Accounting information system (contemporary view): The information system that processes all data relevant to an organization to provide users with information they need to operate their organizations.

Accounting information system (traditional view): The information system that processes financial, transactional data to provide users with information they need to operate their organizations.

Accounting: The activity aimed at collecting, classifying, summarizing, and analysing data in order to provide information for decision making and accountability within organizations and between organizations and their stakeholders.

Accuracy: The quality aspect of information referring to information having the required degree of precision.

Action controls: Controls on processes that are based on monitoring the activities performed to work toward certain results.

Adjusting entries: The journal entries made at the end of the period, after the trial balance has been prepared and before the balance sheet and the income statement are prepared.

Administrative control: *See* Operational control.

Adverse selection: In new principal–agent relationships, agents who act in bad faith will be inclined to engage in that relationship under less favourable conditions than agents who act in good faith.

AIS: The discipline that studies the structuring and operation of planning and control processes which are aimed at: providing information for decision making and accountability to internal and external stakeholders that complies with specified quality criteria; providing the right conditions for sound decision making; and ensuring that no assets illegitimately exit the organization.

Application service provider (ASP): A company that offers a website containing software that can be used from a distant location and that need not be downloaded in order to be able to use it.

Artificial intelligence (Al): The overall category of software that covers neural networks and expert systems.

Assurance services (Elliott committee): The independent professional services that improve the quality of information, or its context, for decision makers.

Attributes: The elements of a record belonging to a primary key.

Authenticity: One of the threats to information quality evolving from ICT proliferation, referring to the sender and receiver of a message being who they claim to be.

Availability: One of the threats to information quality evolving from ICT proliferation, referring to information being at the intended user's disposal, on time, and at the right place.

Batch total: The sum of a range of figures calculated for control purposes.

Beliefs systems: All those systems that define the core values of an organization, and that deal with how the organization creates value, the desired performance levels, and human relations.

Beliefs systems: The explicit set of beliefs that define basic values, purpose, and direction, including how value is created, level of desired performance, and human relationships.

Benchmarking: The process of identification, familiarizing, and adopting superior practices as observed in one's own or other organizations, aimed at improving one's own performance.

BIDE formulas: A set of formulas that relates a position's value at the beginning of a period (*B*), its increase during the period (*I*), its decrease during the period (*D*), and its value at the end of the period (*E*) for control purposes.

Bill of lading: The document containing the details of a shipment, including the responsible party, the party who is going to pay, the contents of the shipment, destination, source, and special instructions. It usually has the status of a legal contract.

Bill of materials: The document containing the components and raw materials used in one unit of a finished product.

Bit: A binary digit that may only take the values of 0 or 1.

Boundary systems: All those formal rules that must be complied with in order to avoid sanctions. The formally stated rules, limits, and proscriptions tied to defined sanctions and credible threat of punishment.

Bureaucratic control: The idea that control can be realized by imposing hierarchy, legitimizing authority, and rules onto people.

Business intellligence (BI): The category of applications that are primarily aimed at opening up the information contained in ERP databases for managerial information provision.

Business process re-engineering (BPR): The thorough analysis and complete redesign of business processes and information systems to achieve dramatic performance improvements, making optimal use of the possibilities of ICT.

Byte: A group of eight bits forming one character like a digit in the decimal system or a letter of the alphabet.

Check digit: A redundant digit added to a number transported via electronic communication, for control purposes.

Clan control: The idea that control can be realized by developing shared values and beliefs, and relying on the moderating role of traditions.

Clearing account: A general ledger account established for control purposes which must equal zero at the end of the period under report.

Communication: The process of sending and receiving data or information.

Completeness: The quality aspect of information referring to information being in accordance with the represented part of reality, in the sense that what is reported is not too low.

Confidentiality: One of the threats to information quality evolving from ICT proliferation, referring to only allowing authorized persons to have access to specific parts of information.

Contingency: A situational factor that, individually and collectively, affects the efficiency of an organizational design parameter.

Control activities: All those activities aimed at ensuring that management directives are carried out.

Control environment: The norms and values of the organization with respect to control consciousness.

Control: All those organizational activities aimed at having organization members cooperate to reach the organizational goals.

Controllability (of information systems): The degree to which information systems provide information that is in accordance with the quality requirements of the people who make use of that information system.

Corporate governance: All those managerial activities aimed at securing the continuity of organizations by maintaining good relations with stakeholders.

Critical success factor: The limited number of factors critical to realizing an organization's goals.

Cultural controls: Controls on creating and maintaining the desired organizational beliefs and values.

Customer relationship management: The process of collecting, recording, and retrieving customer-specific knowledge.

Cycle counting: Making up an inventory by periodically counting a subset of the total inventory, such that at the end of the period under reporting each inventory item has at least been counted once.

Data administrator (DA): The organizational role supporting the functioning of a database from a user's perspective. The DA must have administrative skills to handle managerial and policy issues, and to interact efficiently with database users.

Database administrator (DBA): The organizational role supporting the functioning of a database from a systems department perspective. The DBA must have technical skills to handle the detailed database design work and to tune it for efficient use.

Database management system (DBMS): A specialized computer program that handles all the data traffic to and from the database. It is the main software to operate a database.

Database: A set of interrelated data aimed at avoiding data redundancy and following a multiple logical view of data.

Data dictionary: A representation of all the information about the data elements contained in a database.

Data directory: A representation of the contents of a database aimed at locating a certain data element in the database.

Data manipulation language (DML): A language used for maintaining a database which includes such operations as altering, adding, and deleting portions of it.

Data mining: The process of reducing large data sets to manageable proportions for further analysis like OLAP.

Data processing cold site: An infrastructure identical infrastructure of the primary system which allows a copy of the primary system to be built within a relatively short period of time, when it breaks down.

Data processing hot site: A redundant, completely identical system to the primary system, to be used when the primary system breaks down.

Data query language (DQL): A language used to retrieve data from the database for further processing like sorting, categorizing, summarizing, calculating, and presenting that information in a format that is understandable to the end-user.

Data recovery: The activity of restoring data that were erroneously destroyed or modified.

Data warehouse: A large database covering all the data needed for decision making and accountability which is subiect-oriented, integrated, time variant, and non-volatile.

Data: The most elementary representation of applicable parts of reality, which does not have meaning until it is processed.

Data-modelling: The process of defining a database in such a manner that it represents the most important parts of an organization and its environment.

Date and time stamping: Adding the date and the time to a message for giving the receiver reasonable assurance that the message has not been delayed, that it isn't a message that has been sent earlier, and that it has been sent in the right order relative to other received messages.

Decision support system (DSS): A computerized information system aimed at the improvement of human decision making.

Diagnostic control systems: Controls on outcomes that are aimed at realizing an effective allocation of scarce resources, defining targets, motivating people, determining guidelines for corrective measures, and enabling performance evaluation.

Diagnostic control systems: The formal information systems that managers use to monitor organizational outcomes and correct deviations from preset standards of performance.

Economy (of information): The quality aspect of information referring to information being produced at the lowest possible costs.

Electronic commerce: All the sales-related activities that make use of electronic communication by means of the Internet.

Electronic data interchange (EDI): The standardized business-to-business transferral of electronic messages.

Electronic funds transfer (EFT): Effectuation of payments by using electronic communication devices.

Encryption: Transformation of information by means of a specific algorithm into a format that is not understandable by those who receive it but don't know the algorithm to transform it back to the original format.

Enterprise resource planning (ERP): An integrated, process-oriented, organization-wide ICT solution designed to facilitate the achievement of an organization's goals and objectives.

Environmental management system: A coherent set of policies, and accounting and administrative measures aimed at gaining an insight into, controlling, and reducing the effects of operations on the environment.

Event logging: Keeping a logfile to record critical security incidents.

Executive information system (EIS): Software that allows end-users at the tactical and strategic managerial level to produce the information they find necessary themselves.

Expert system (ES): A computerized information system aimed at partially or entirely replacing human decision making by presenting proposed decisions to its users.

Extended business reporting language (XBRL): An XML-based taxonomy aimed at financial accounting in a standardized format, containing tags attached to variables and their meaning.

Extended markup language (XML): A platform-independent, expandable, and self-describing language specifically designed to create webpages and links between webpages and that eliminates the need for software for translating documents that are in different formats into one uniform format.

Extranet: A network that uses the Internet protocol for making selected organizational data and information available to third parties.

Firewall: A combination of software and hardware that concentrates all the electronic communication between an internal network (usually within one organization) and the outside world (the networks of other organizations) at one point for the purpose of keeping unwanted messages out of the organization, and securing wanted information.

Fixed administrative rate: The monetary value used to record all inventory items of a specific category. The FAR is based on estimated average purchase prices. At the end of the period under reporting, the price-differences between the FAR and actual prices are analysed to adjust the new FAR, and to prepare the financial statements.

Flexibility (of information systems): The degree to which information systems can be transferred from one environment to another.

Flexible firm: A stereotype of the contemporary organization in the new economy, which has knowledge as its main production factor and is able to adjust swiftly to changing market conditions.

Foreign key: An attribute that contains a reference to primary keys of other files.

Fraud: The deliberate action of one person gaining an unfair advantage over another person.

Fraudulent (financial) reporting: The intentional or reckless conduct, whether by act or omission, that results in materially misleading (financial) statements.

Fraudulent financial reporting (Treadway Commission): The intentional or reckless conduct, whether by act or omission, that results in materially misleading financial statements.

General journal: The journal voucher used to record infrequent or non-routine financial facts, including adjusting entries.

General ledger: The internal statement containing summary data for every asset, equity, liability, revenue, and cost account of an organization.

Groupware: The software that enables more efficient communication within organizations, and between organizations, or, more specifically, within any group that works towards a certain deliverable.

Hacking: The activity of purposely trying to make one or more threats to information quality (confidentiality, integrity, availability, and authenticity), as a consequence of ICT proliferation become a reality.

Hypertext mark-up language (HTML): A language specifically designed to create web pages and links between web pages and that eliminates the need for software for translating documents that are in different formats into one uniform format.

ICT control: All those activities employed by or on behalf of an organization's management to ensure the proper functioning of an organization's information systems.

Incremental system development approach: A system development method that abandons the strictly stepwise approach, as in the SDLC, in favour of a heuristic approach that makes small steps one at a time and that favours trial and error.

Information and communication technology (ICT): All the electronic media used to transport information between senders and receivers and to support or enable communication.

Information architecture: The design of the structure of information provision at different levels in an organization.

Information control: Information control can be defined as all those activities employed by or on behalf of an organization's management to ensure the reliability and relevance of information provision for internal or external use and the proper functioning of underlying information systems. Also denoted as Accounting control or Internal accounting control.

Information management: The discipline that deals with the production of information which nowadays always makes use of ICT. Traditionally, this discipline is also denoted as an Information system.

Information policy: The formulation of goals, restrictions, disciplines, and guidelines regarding information provision and communication.

Information strategy: Deliberately choosing between exploiting or mitigating information imperfections.

Information system: A set of interrelated components working together to collect, retrieve, process, store, and disseminate information for the purpose of facilitating planning, control, coordination, and decision making in businesses and other organizations.

Information: All the processed data that contribute to the recipient's understanding of applicable parts of reality.

Integrity: One of the threats to information quality stemming ICT proliferation, referring to protecting information from becoming valid or incomplete.

Interactive control systems: The formal control systems managers use to involve themselves regularly and personally in the decision activities of subordinates.

Intermediate billing: A billing system where the customer invoice is prepared on the basis of the customer order and, at the same time, the ordered goods are picked by the warehouse based on a copy of the customer order.

Internal accounting control: *See* Information control.

Internal control: Control of judgements and activities of others in so far that control is conducted for the management of an organization by or on behalf of that management. A more detailed definition is given by the COSO report: 'Internal control is a process, effected by an entity's board of directors, management and other personnel, designed to provide reasonable assurance regarding the achievement of objectives in the following categories: effectiveness and efficiency of operations, reliability of financial reporting, compliance with applicable laws and regulations, and safeguarding of assets'.

Internet: The international network of independent computers that communicate electronically.

Internet portal: A website that is a major starting point for users when they want to find information or conclude a transaction on the internet.

Internet protocol (IP): The method by which data is sent from one computer to another on the Internet.

Internet protocol secure (IPsec): A secure variant of the Internet protocol which makes Internet connections as secure as private networks. IPsec is frequently used to create virtual private networks.

Internet service provider (ISP): company that has an infrastructure in place to provide individuals and organizations with a connection to the Internet.

Intranet: A network that uses the Internet protocol for communication within organizations via a LAN or a WAN.

ISO: International Organization for Standardization.

Job order costing: Determination of the costs for each customer order or production order.

Job time: The time a worker spends on an assigned task.

Job time ticket: A document containing the time a worker has spent on each task assigned to him.

Journal voucher: A chronological statement of the financial facts that have occurred in an organization during a certain period of time.

Just-in-time (JIT) production: A production planning system that tries to minimize inventories by producing in response to customer orders or to work according to short-run production plans.

Knowledge management: The process of assessment of the knowledge an organization needs to gain competitive advantage and making an inventory of the available knowledge, and, on the basis of the gap between necessary and available knowledge, developing, sharing, employing, and evaluating knowledge for organizational learning.

Lapping: Accounting early for expenditures or accounting late for receipts aimed at temporarily withdrawing money from the organization.

Local area network (LAN): A computer network that does not go beyond a certain geographical location.

Maintainability (of information systems): The degree to which information systems can be tested, renewed, and changed at reasonable costs.

Management (institution): The individuals or groups of individuals who engage in business administration (management as an institution). The process of integration of resources and tasks aimed at accomplishment of an organization's goals (management as an activity).

Management accounting: The discipline that is concerned with the use of information for the purpose of making decisions and ultimately controlling organizations.

Management control: All those activities management employs to have its people think and act in accordance with the organization's goals.

Managerial information provision (MIP): The systematic gathering, recording, and processing of data aimed at provision of information for management decisions (choosing among alternative applications) for entity functionality and entity control, including accountability.

Manufacturing resource planning (MRP II): An integrated, computerized planning and control system for production operations. It is an enhancement of MRP and the predecessor of ERP.

Market control: The idea that control can be realized by relying on the price mechanism and norms of reciprocity.

Master file: A file containing data that do not change frequently or that may only change as a result of transactions recorded in a transaction file that has a reference to the primary key in the master file.

Materials requirements planning (MRP): A computerized inventory management system aimed at reducing inventories, starting from sales forecasts rather than from expected requests by internal departments.

Megabytes (MB): A measure for storage capacity on electronic media. One MB contains 2^{20} bytes. Compare with KB (2^{10} bytes) and GB (2^{30} bytes).

Message authentication code (MAC): An extra data element attached to a message as a check on the correct transferral of that message.

Microprocessor: An integrated circuit that consists of millions of electronic switches that can be switched on or off.

Monitoring: A process that assesses the quality of a system over time.

Moral hazard: The risk that any person will behave unethically if the opportunity is there.

Move ticket: The document that identifies the location to which components and raw materials are transferred and the time of transfer.

Near money: Goods, typically of low intrinsic but high nominal value, that serve as proof of cash receipts in payment of services.

Neural network: A computerized system aimed at partially or entirely replacing human decision making, and that contains learning mechanisms for fine-tuning embedded knowledge, just like humans do when encountering new cases.

Online analytical processing (OLAP): The concept of enabling users of information systems to easily and selectively extract and view data from different points of view.

Ontology: A coherent set of core constructs that underlie a phenomenon in the real world. An ontology provides a directory and dictionary. Such phenomena include disciplines or systems to be modelled. In essence, an ontology is the starting point of a theory.

Operational control: Operational control is the process of ensuring that specific tasks are carried out effectively and economically.

Operational excellence: The concept that competitive advantage can be reached by aligning operations, information and communication, and ICT at the level of strategy implementation.

Operations list: The document that identifies the components and raw materials used for a certain order, the man and machine hours spent on the order, and other order details needed for billing and checking purposes.

Packing slip: *See* Packing ticket.

Packing ticket: The document containing the items to ship to each customer. The packing ticket is usually attached to the shipment to indicate its contents.

Periodic inventory accounting system: Accounting for the value of inventory in such a way that results can only be determined after having made an inventory count.

Period-to-date figures: Cumulative figures for a specific period, to be compared with the same cumulative figures in a previous period.

Perpetual inventory accounting system (*Permanence de l'inventaire et des profits et des pertes*): Accounting for the value of inventory in such a way that results can be determined at any moment in time, without making an inventory count.

Personnel controls: Controls on the hiring and functioning of workers within an organization.

Physical security: All those actions aimed at prohibiting access to hardware, data, and programs for unauthorized persons by means of physical measures.

Picking ticket: The document containing the items to collect from the warehouse by the warehouse personnel. The picking ticket authorizes the warehouse to release the goods to the shipping department or the carrier.

Planning: The complex of interrelated decisions about allocation of available resources.

Point-of-sale (POS) systems: Systems that make use of an optical scanner to read a bar code containing product data that refers to a certain inventory item and triggers further processing in the inventory files and the cash or accounts receivable files.

Post-billing: A billing system where the invoice is prepared on the basis of the packing ticket and the goods are packed on the basis of customer orders.

Pre-billing: A billing system where the invoice is prepared on the basis of the customer order, and the goods are packed on the basis of the invoice.

Pre-emption (in electronic communication): The deletion of certain messages when the electronic communication network gets overloaded.

Pretty good privacy (PGP): The software for encrypting and decrypting e-mails, files, and digital signatures that are sent over the Internet, making use of a PKI (public key infrastructure).

Primary key: A unique identifier of a record.

Principles of accounting system design (PASD): The discipline that studies the principles of the systematic recording of sequential and interrelated actions in a firm which culminate in accounts that reflect the conduct of business.

Priority (in electronic communication): processing of prioritized messages before any others, when the electronic communication network gets overloaded.

Process costing: Determination of costs for each cost centre such as a department or a process.

Prototyping: An approach to systems development in which a simplified working model of an information system or a part of an information system is developed in order to enable user testing.

Public key infrastructure (PKI): The encryption method that enables users to securely and privately exchange data through the use of a public and a private key pair that is obtained and shared through a trusted third party.

Quasi-goods: *See* Near money.

Receiving report: The statement containing notification by the warehouse of the receipt of goods.

Record: A collection of data values that describe specific attributes of an entity.

Results controls: Controls on outcomes that are based on confronting the results of activities with a preset standard with respect to these activities.

Risk asssessment: The identification and analysis of relevant risks to the achievement of objectives.

Routing control: Predetermining the path a message must follow to be sent securely.

Routing sheet: *See* Operations list.

Secondary key: An identifier of a record that need not be unique because it may refer to a group of records.

Secure electronic transaction (SET): A system for ensuring the security of payment information on the Internet by means of a PKI.

Shop time: The time a worker is present at the site where he is supposed to perform his duties.

Smart card: A plastic card that contains a chip, which is a microprocessor combined with a memory chip.

Software piracy: The illegal copying of software and files without the publisher's permission.

Source data automation: The use of automated input devices to represent data in machine-readable form.

Spamming: The transmission of electronic messages to users who engage in electronic communication without having their permission to do so.

Strategic control: The processes aimed at formulating the right strategy, given the specific circumstances of an organization.

Strategic enterprise management (SEM): The category of applications that are aimed at information provision for strategic decision making, thus enabling managers to link strategy formulation to strategy implementation, drive product and customer profitability, and increase shareholder value.

Strategic planning: The process of deciding the objectives of the organization, changes in these objectives, the resources used to attain these objectives, and the policies for governing the acquisition, use, and disposition of these resources.

Subsidiary ledger: A ledger used to record all the financial facts pertaining to one specific subaccount of the general ledger.

Substantive tests: Controls, generally performed by the financial auditor, aimed at directly establishing the reliability of the financial statements.

Superzapping: Entering a computer system via a back door, bypassing regular systems controls, created by programmers to maintain control over the system after implementation.

Systems development life cycle (SDLC): A strictly linear process for the development of information systems consisting of a number of stages that must be gone through in a prescribed sequence.

Task control: *See* Operational control.

Teleprocessing monitor (TPM): A piece of software aimed at controlling access to specific parts of the database.

Theoretical collection register: The normative position of the entries to an account receivable ledger, which is used for control purposes when the entries are fixed periodical amounts.

Theoretical disbursement register: The normative position of the entries to an account payable ledger, which is used for control purposes when the entries are fixed periodical amounts.

Timeliness: The quality aspect of information referring to information being on time to affect the decision-making process.

Total quality management (TQM): A philosophy focused on the employees in an organization aimed at making them think and collaborate in such a way that products (including services) are produced that meet the customers' demands.

Transaction file: A file containing data that changes on the basis of transactions.

Trial balance: A trial balance is the copy of all general ledger account balances into one list.

Understandability: The quality aspect of information referring to information being presented in a format that is both useful and intelligible to the user of the data.

Validity: The quality aspect of information referring to information being in accordance with the represented part of reality, in the sense that what is reported is not too high.

Value chain: A model that represents business processes as value-adding activities toward a specific intended result.

Value cycle: A schematic representation of events in businesses that lead to changes in inventory, accounts receivable, accounts payable, and cash.

Value-added network (VAN): A public network that tries to enhance the functioning of data processing and information provision by interfacing the different hardware and software components used by participants in the network.

Virtual private network (VPN): A relatively secure communication infrastructure within an extranet.

Virus: A piece of executable code that attaches itself to files or software, replicates itself, and spreads itself to other files or software on the same system or on another system.

Voucher: An internal document that contains data on a purchase transaction for checking, recording, and authorization purposes.

Voucher package: The set of documents related to a purchase transaction, consisting of the purchase order, the vendor invoice, and the receiving report.

Wide area network (WAN): A computer network that goes beyond a certain geographical location.

Worm: A worm is an independent piece of software that uses a computer's operating system to replicate itself.

Zero balance check: A check on a general ledger clearing account that assesses whether its balance equals zero.

INDEX

Access control 161
Accounting and administrative organization (AAO) 4–5
  relationship with IC and MIP 30
Accounting and ICT 226
Accounting and internal control 227
Accounting and management 228
Accounts receivable 74–75
Action controls 203–208
Administrative and organizational conditions 60–62
Administrative organization (AO) 3, 5
Adverse selection 202
Agency theory 13–14
Agrarian age 155
AIS, role of 225–226
AIS theory 12–13
  agency theory 13–14
  transaction–cost theory 13–14
Application service provider (ASP) 136–137
Assurance services 238–240
ATM cards 130
Authentication 164–165

Banks 99–100
Barings bank 20–22
Beliefs systems 208–212
BIDE formula 37–38, 70–71
Billable man-hours 40
Billing system 72–73
Boundary systems 208–212
Budgets 81–83
Bureaucratic control 198–199
Business intelligence (BI) 150
Business processing re-engineering (BPR) 147–148
  relationship with internal control 173–174

Central processing unit 131–132
Clan control 198–199
Codes on information security 165–168
Committee of Sponsoring Organizations of the Treadway Commission 20, 116
Communication devices 133–137
Competency control 49
Comprehensive contingency framework 113–115
Confirmations 164
Contemporary organizations 223–246
  characteristics of 224
Contingency factors 106–107
Contingency framework 107–108
  alignment with global characteristics 109
  alignment with industry characteristics 110
  alignment with national characteristics 109–110
  alignment with organization characteristics 110–111
  alignment with personal characteristics 111–112
Control activities 23
Control concepts 116–118, 121–123
Control description 254–256
  conditions for efficiency 258–265
  efficiency analysis 270
  intended audience 256–258
  recording of 265–270
  verbal and non-verbal 263–265

Control systems, effectiveness within the economy 113
Controllers 7–8
Corporate governance 184–186
COSO-report 20, 212, 237
Cost–benefit analysis 35
Cost price calculation 82
Credit limits 74–75
Credit policy 74–75
Critical success factors 243
Cultural controls 203–208
Custody control 50
Customer relationship management (CRM) 148–150
Customer-oriented trading 75

Database management systems (DBMS) 141
  data dictionary and directory system (DDDS) 141
  data manipulation language (DML) 142
  data query languages (DQLs) 142
  teleprocessing monitor (TPM) 141
Databases 140–143
Data recovery 163–164
Data warehouses 140–143
Date and time stamps 164
Decision support systems (DSS) 143–144
Demilitarized zone (DMZ) 162
Description of the internal controls 62
Detailed checks 45
Detective controls 117
Diagnostic control systems 208–212
Digital signature 165
Direct checks 46
Double-entry bookkeeping 32
Dynamic essential modelling of organization (DEMO) 266

E-activities 155–156
E-business 146–147
  relationship with internal control 168–173
Economic evaluation 155
Efficiency control 49
Electronic data interchange (EDI) 40
Electronic funds transfer (EFT) 137
Encryption 159–161
Enterprise resource planning (ERP) 139–140
  relationship with internal control 174–175
Environmental accounting 240–241
Errors 63–64
Evaluation of weaknesses in internal controls 59
Event logging 161
Execution control 49
Executive information systems (EIS) 145
Extended mark-up language (XML) 136
Expectations control 48

Feedback systems 163
Financial auditor 7–8
Firm flexibility 224–228
Formal checks 47
Fraud 236–238

General normative internal control description 59–60
Governance paradigm 25–27
Government institutions 100–101
Groupware 144–145

Hackers 157–158
High-performance computing and networking (HPCN) 128
History of AIS 4–5, 10–11
Human factors 10
Hypertext mark-up language (HTML) 136

Indirect checks 46
Industrial age 155
Information 11–13
  quality spectrum of information 187
    accuracy 188
    completeness 188
    economy 189
    timeliness 189
    understandibility 189
    validity 187–188
  strategy 119–120, 243–246

Information age 155–156
Information and communication 23
Information and communication technology (ICT) 7–8, 125–150
  applications 138–145
  -enabled innovations 145–150
    relationship with internal control 168–174
  and internal control 153–179, 227
  managerial uses 126–127
Information manager 7–8
Information policy 191–192
Information provision 31–34
information requirements 56–58
  analysis 192–194
Information systems (IS) 3, 127–137
  components of 127–128
  development 137–138
  quality characteristics 189
    controllability 190
    flexibility 190
    maintainability 191
Informational mechanisms 201–202
Input devices 128–130
Institutional impediments 200
Insurance companies 98–99
Interactive control systems 208–212
Internal accounting controls 116
Internal control (IC) 3, 6, 19–24
  activities 23
  description 62–63
  differences 59
  information and communication 23
  monitoring 23–24
  risk assessment 21–22
  weaknesses 59
International Organization for Standardization (ISO) 242–243
Internet portals 146
Internet protocol (IP) 161
Internet protocol secure (IPsec) 161

Just-in-time (JIT) production 241–242

Knowledge and organizational control 234–235
Knowledge, control of 232–234
Knowledge valuation 228–232
Knowledge management 228–230

Labour, division of 35–38, 70
Lapping 76
Linear approach to systems development 137–138
Local area network (LAN) 133–136

Management and ICT 226–227
Management and internal control 225–226
Management control (MC) 184, 196–197
  and information control 183–216
Management cycle 27–30
  see also Governance paradigm
Management information system (MIS) 11
Managerial information 63
Managerial information provision (MIP) 3, 5–6
  relationship with AAO and IC 30
Manufacturing resource planning (MRP II) 139
Market control 198–199
  adverse selection 202
  informational mechanisms 201–202
  institutional impediments 200
  moral hazard 202–203
  social mechanisms 200–201
  social–psychological factors 200
  taxes and endowments 200
  transaction costs 200
Mass-production organizations 77
Material checks 47
Materials requirements planning (MRP) 139
Measurement points 243
Message authentication codes 165
Monitoring 23–24
Moral hazard 202–203
Myers–Briggs type indicator (MBTI) 113

Near-money 96
Negative checks 46
Normative internal control descriptions 58–59

OLAP database 150
Ontology 270–272
Operational controls 116
Operationalizing national culture 110
Operationalizing organizational culture 111
Operationalizing personal characteristics 112–113
Organization types 41–43, 60
see also Contemporary organizations, Production organizations, Service organizations, Trade organizations
Organizational strategy 119–120
Organizations offering knowledge and skill 97–100
Organizations offering space and time 93–97
Output devices 133

Payroll clearing account 39
People management 10
Performance measurement 235–236
Period matching 72
Period-to-date figures 44–45
Personnel controls 203–208
Physical security 162–163
Piece-production organizations 77, 84–85
PIN cards/numbers 130
Point-of-sale systems 129
Policy control 47–48
Positive checks 46
Post-billing 73
Pre-billing 73
Preventive controls 117
Price policies 71–72
Principles of accounting system design (PASD) 4–5
Priority and pre-emption 164
Problems and solutions 54–63
  contemporary approaches 54–56
  determination of control concepts 121–123
  determination of organization type 60
  determination of position in the contingency framework 119–120
  see also Threats
Production organizations 76–80
  budgets and variance analysis 81–83
  mass production 77, 83–84
  piece production 77, 84–85
  production planning 81
Progress control 50
Prototyping 138–139
Public key infrastructure (PKI) 161

Quasi-goods 94–96

Rapid application development (RAD) 28
REA accounting 33–34
Reconciliations and control totals (RCTs) 37–41
Redundant data 40
Related disciplines 8–10
Results controls 203–208
Risk assessment 21–22
Routing control 161–162

Secure electronic transaction (SET) 161
Security *see* Codes on information security, Physical security
Segregation of duties *see* Labour, division of
Self-checking 50
Service organizations 91–93
Social mechanisms 200–201
Social–psychological factors 200
Standards control 48–49
Stocktaking 66, 70
Storage devices 130–131
Strategic enterprise management (SEM) 150
Strategic planning 196–197, 243–246
Sustainability 109
Systems development life cycle (SDLC) 137–138

Task control 196–197
Taxes and endowments 200
Telebanking 99
Terminology *see* Internal control (IC)
Threats 67–69, 121–122
  from ICT proliferation 157–165
  in production organization 78–80
  in service organization 92

Total checks 45
Total quality management (TQM) 242
Trade organizations 66–76
  threats to trade firms 171–173
Transaction costs 200
Transaction–cost theory 13–14
Trial balance 39
Triple-entry bookkeeping 32–33
Twinning programmes 108

Universal product code (UPC) 129

Value cycle 34–43, 170
  for a trade firm 170
Variance analysis 81–82
Virtual private networks (VPN) 136

Waterfall approach to systems development 137–138
Wide area network (WAN) 134–136